PELICAN BOOKS

A594

MYSTICISM IN WORLD RELIGION

SIDNEY SPENCER

MYSTICISM
IN WORLD RELIGION

SIDNEY SPENCER

GLOUCESTER, MASS.

PETER SMITH

1971

TO MY WIFE

IN GRATITUDE FOR HER

INVALUABLE HELP

AND

ENCOURAGEMENT

Contents

CONTENTS

Preface

A GREAT deal has been written in recent years about mysticism, but (apart from a short work published in the U.S.A. entitled *An Introduction to Comparative Mysticism* by J. de Marquette) no attempt has hitherto been made in English to present an account of the various types of mystical religion in a single volume. It is to fill that gap that the present work has been written. As a student of mysticism for many years, I have been impressed by the need of a careful and comprehensive survey of the whole field. Generalizations about mysticism are often misleading because they rest on an insufficient factual basis. Before we can fruitfully generalize, we must know something of the different forms which mysticism has assumed through the ages. I have endeavoured in this volume to deal with these different forms. In doing that, I have taken into account the chief work which has been done by specialists. As far as possible in a book of this size, moreover, I have allowed the mystics to speak for themselves by including numerous quotations from their writings.

It is my conviction that mysticism is of the utmost importance to religion and so to the future of mankind. At a time when religion is met, as never before on a similar scale, with the challenge of materialist philosophy, and when the growth of scientific knowledge of the forces of Nature and the power which this brings with it are a constant temptation to men to neglect the things of the spirit, it is all the more necessary that the inner life should be quickened and renewed. But if the life of religion is to be renewed, there must be a renewal of vision and of understanding; and nothing can be of so much value from this standpoint as the study of the experience and teaching of the mystics.

My indebtedness to students of mystical religion is evident on every page. I have given at the end a list of the chief works which I have consulted, and to which I would refer readers for further study. I would like to express the very great gratitude which I feel to the Spalding Trustees in Oxford for the generous help which they have given me. I am also indebted to the Librarians of Dr Williams's Library, of Manchester College, Oxford, and of the Buddhist and Theosophical Libraries for their kind assistance.

SIDNEY SPENCER

CHAPTER 1

Mysticism in Primitive Religion

WHAT is characteristic of the mystics is the claim which they make to an immediate contact with the Transcendent. Such contact typically assumes the form of knowledge, often described in terms of vision, and of union. Experience of this kind belongs in its developed expression to the higher forms of religion, but in the lower culture also traces of it may be found. An illustration of the occurrence of supernormal states of consciousness among primitive peoples is the experience known to the Eskimo as the 'angakoq' or illumination. This illumination is said to come to the novice in the course of his training for the office of 'shaman' (or prophet). After long hours of waiting, during which the spirits are invoked, he suddenly feels within him a luminous fire, which gives him powers of perception unknown to others. His range of vision is said to be extended beyond the house where he is, and beyond the mountains. He perceives future events, and sees souls in distant regions and in the land of the dead.[1] A more specifically mystical experience is related in the autobiography of an American Indian, 'Crashing Thunder', a member of the Winnebago tribe. On one occasion, 'Crashing Thunder' tells, he became aware, as he prayed to Earthmaker (a North American deity), sitting among his fellow-tribesmen, of the presence of Earthmaker and of his own soul in its unity with him and with the souls of his fellows.

I prayed to Earthmaker. And as I prayed, I was aware of something above me, and there he was. That which is called the soul ... that is what one calls Earthmaker. This is what I felt and saw. All of us sitting together, we had all together one spirit or soul. I did not speak to them and get an answer to know what had been their thoughts.[2]

In primitive religion a place of outstanding importance is held by men who act as intermediaries between their fellows and

1. Eliade, *Le Chamanisme*, pp. 69f.
2. Radin, *Primitive Religion*, p. 278.

the unseen or transcendent order. Such men are of different types.

(*a*) Among primitive peoples generally there are to be found diviners and sorcerers. The diviner is held to possess secret knowledge concerning the past or the future derived from the observation of external signs and omens, like the flight of birds, or from the spirits of the dead, who are believed to give this knowledge to men in a state of trance. Sorcerers are practitioners of magic, who seek to utilize the occult power inherent in the unseen order for the benefit of men or for their harm.

(*b*) Alongside the diviners and sorcerers there are sometimes priests, who offer sacrifice, and seek to win the blessing and favour of the divine powers for their fellows. Many primitive peoples, like the Australian aborigines, have no priests, but where priesthood exists the priest is the representative of the community in its relation to the Transcendent. The office is usually hereditary, but it may also arise from personal experience of 'possession' by gods or spirits. That is the case, for example, in West Africa, where the experience often occurs in the first instance at a public religious ceremony. In this case the priest is not merely the representative of the community, but the organ of the Transcendent.

(*c*) Where the priest acts in this capacity, he is in fact assuming the character of a prophet or 'shaman'. It is the distinguishing mark of the prophet that he serves as a mouthpiece of unseen powers. Among the Nuer in the Sudan the prophet is held to be permanently possessed by a spirit, which lives in him and speaks through him. The experience of possession comes in a trance, which may be induced by prolonged fasting, practised in solitude. It carries with it powers of healing, of prediction, and of insight enabling the prophet to offer spiritual guidance to those who seek it. The prophet endeavours to identify himself completely with the spirit. 'A prophet seeks so complete a union with the spirit that he is no longer himself but the spirit.'[1] That is a significant indication of the mystical quality of the prophet's experience. The 'spirit' concerned is here, not a departed human soul, but the divine Spirit worshipped by the Nuer, acting not directly, but

1. Evans-Pritchard, *Nuer Religion*, p. 318.

through an individual 'spirit of the air', conceived as a particular manifestation of the divine (see p. 14 below).

Among primitive peoples the greatest significance is attached to the experience of ecstasy and trance as a means of contact with the unseen. The utterance of a man in trance is commonly held to emanate from the spirits of the dead. 'The primitive seer or prophet stands midway between the mystic and the medium'.[1] The phase of religion which centres in the work of the inspired prophet or seer is known as 'Shamanism' – from the word 'shaman' used among the Tunguses of Central and Eastern Siberia. (The same type of religion is found among the Eskimo, the Australians, and many tribes of North and South America.) The shaman has to undergo a lengthy training; he prepares himself for his work by fasting and solitude. He receives instruction from an old shaman, who teaches him the lore of spirits. He is often a man of psychic abnormality, but it is significant that his trouble is cured by the exercise of his arts. He acts as healer, rain-maker, diviner, and exorcist, purifying a house where death has occurred by driving away the ghost. He is not a mere medium: he sees the spirits, and enters into communication with them, but he is not their passive instrument. Rather is he their master; he controls the powers through which he works. Yet he is not, typically, proud or overbearing. Among the Yakuts of Siberia it is said that, while the shaman must be possessed of inner strength, he must not be presumptuous. In his study of Shamanism, Eliade has shown that its characteristic feature is ecstasy, and that in this experience the belief in spirit-possession is in reality secondary and derivative, and not primary. From ancient times, he says, the religion of Central Asia was marked by the worship of a supreme Sky-God, but in course of time this belief became progressively less significant; it was replaced by the cult of ancestral spirits and other beings. As a result the belief in spirit-possession was introduced. The primary and fundamental aspect of ecstasy is the ascent of the soul of the shaman to Heaven, where it enters into communion with the divine. Even when the notion of spirit-possession was introduced, it did not entirely displace the earlier symbolism; the ascent to Heaven remained.

1. Dawson, *Religion and Culture*, p. 71.

A similar ecstatic experience plays a part in the initiation of Australian medicine-men. Among the Wiradjuri the novice goes into a tomb and receives magical stones (it is said) from the dead. He is then led into the camp of Baiame (a High God), who sits on a crystal throne. In North and South America also, as among the Eskimo, the shaman's initiation is linked with an ascent to Heaven. This is particularly noteworthy, since it was believed that in ancient days there was no barrier between Heaven and earth; men could mount to Heaven in their bodies and converse with the gods. In the ecstatic ascent of the soul the bliss of primeval times is thus restored. In ecstasy the shaman passes into another realm of being, where he transcends the limitations of his normal state as a man; he dies to this normal state and is reborn into a higher condition. The experience of spiritual death and rebirth is represented symbolically by the behaviour of the shaman, who imitates the cries and actions of animals and wears their skin. That is to say, he transforms himself into an animal-spirit. In early times animals were often worshipped, being regarded as stronger and wiser than men, and so as more directly related than they to the transcendent order. The animal with which the shaman identifies himself is, moreover, a mythical or ancestral animal. The identification thus represents the attainment of the higher mode of being into which men enter in their ascent to the heavenly regions. We shall see in a later chapter that the experience of ascent to Heaven was the central feature of Jewish mysticism in its earliest phase. (See pp. 176–8 below.) There can be little doubt that in the religion of primitive peoples likewise it had a mystical significance; it was a means whereby expression was given to the sense of contact with the divine.

It is clear from what has been said that experience of a mystical order occurs in primitive religion among prophets or shamans. It is evident, further, from the study of primitive religion that in the very nature of the religious consciousness there is an inherent tendency to mysticism. Primitive religion presents itself to us in a great variety of different forms – in the worship of ancestors, of Nature-spirits, of animal-spirits, in the belief in totems and High Gods. Attempts have been made to show that one or other of these types of religion was original, and that all others have developed from it. No such attempt has been successful, and today students have in general abandoned the quest of origins in that sense. But if it is not possible to discover in what particular form religion had its beginnings, it is possible to see the common spiritual root from which the various types of religion have sprung. The great mistake which was formerly made by anthropologists was to look upon religion from an unduly intellectual point of view – to suppose that it had its beginning in the desire for explanation or understanding. Tylor, for example, in *Primitive Culture* identified religion with Animism, conceived as 'the belief in spiritual beings'. Animism is certainly of the utmost importance as a phase of religious thought. Yet to define religion in such terms is to miss its essential feature. As Otto has shown in *The Idea of the Holy*, the fundamental factor in religion is not belief or thought; it is rather intuition or feeling – the sense of the 'numinous', the awe-inspiring, the Transcendent. In the words of E. O. James:

> Religion may be defined as the recognition of, and the desire to establish and maintain beneficial relations with, the supra-mundane sacred order manifesting itself in the universe.[1]

It is in the sense of, and the response to, the Transcendent that we have the unifying factor in the different forms of primitive religion. Evans-Pritchard's work on *Nuer Religion* is particularly illuminating in this connexion. For the Nuer the object of religion is Kwoth or Spirit. As they conceive it, Spirit is both one and many. The supreme Spirit (or God) is invisible, ubiquitous, like wind and air, and yet somehow localized in the sky. The High Gods so widely worshipped, or at least acknowledged, among primitive peoples, as recent research has emphasized, are in general Gods associated especially with the sky. As Eliade has said: 'The simple contemplation of the vault of the sky produces a religious experience in primitive consciousness.'[2] The contemplation of its mystery and its boundless greatness gives rise to the sense of a transcendent Being dwelling in it, and so manifesting itself especially in celestial phenomena like rain and thunder, yet

1. *Prehistoric Religion*, p. 231.
2. *Traité de l'histoire des religions*, p. 47.

at the same time endowed with measureless wisdom and power. It is a significant indication of the mystical quality of the primitive religious attitude that the concepts in which it finds expression are often lacking in the exclusiveness and rigidity characteristic of the conceptions typical of certain forms of historical religion. Thus among the Nuer it is believed that rain and lightning not only come from God, but themselves are God (in one aspect). So, also it is said among the Bantu in time of rain, not 'rain is falling', but 'Leza [the High God] is falling'. That is to say, the High God is at once exalted over all things and identified with the phenomena which reveal his activity. We have here a foreshadowing of the attitude of developed mysticism in some of its forms, which tend (as we shall see), while affirming the divine transcendence, at the same time to identify God with the world in which He dwells. Spirit is in itself for the Nuer a supreme mystery resting on 'intuitive apprehension.'[1] But Spirit is revealed in particular spirits, notably in the 'spirits of the air', which are both separate beings associated with natural phenomena or wild animals and at the same time identified with God Himself. In praying and offering sacrifice to the spirits, men are praying and offering sacrifice to God in a particular manifestation.

> The spirits of the air are many, but also one. God is manifested in, and in a sense is, each of them. ... What is distributed in a number of beings, though different, is yet the same, and though divided, yet a whole.[2]

Here again we have an anticipation of the outlook characteristic of developed mysticism, with its recognition both of the undivided unity of the infinite Spirit and of the multiplicity of the individuals in whom the Spirit lives.

In Nuer religion the 'numinous' assumes many different forms. One of the spirits of the air is Col, the spirit of lightning. But Col is not merely an individual; he embraces in his own being a multitude of other spirits (known as colwic spirits), who are human beings struck by lightning and by that very fact exalted above their human condition and made divine. In one aspect they remain individuals, so that, like the spirits of the air,

1. Evans-Pritchard, op. cit., p. 321.
2. ibid., pp. 51f.

they may enter into men and possess them temporarily or permanently. Yet they are also merged in Col, and through Col in God. For the Nuer, as for the mystics of all religions, human individuality as we know it is not final; men may be deified, and united in the divine. It is, however, typical of the gulf which lies between nascent and developed mysticism that for the Nuer deification occurs by an accident, and not by an inner process of development; the accident, moreover, is not welcomed, but regarded as a misfortune which men seek to ward off by the offering of sacrifice.

Among the Nuer the 'numinous' takes other forms – 'spirits of the earth', totems, 'Nature-sprites', fetishes. The totems are chiefly animals or birds which for some reason evoke the idea of Spirit, and which come to be regarded as sacred to a certain group of kinsmen. The spirit of the animal chosen is the tutelary spirit of this group, and is the object of prayer and sacrifice on the part of its members. 'Nature-sprites' are spirits associated with meteorites or with certain fishes, trees, or grasses, and belong to individuals whom they protect and help, if sufficient offerings are made to them. Fetishes are also owned by individuals, who use them for their own advantage. They are magical objects (pieces of wood) possessed by spirits and known as 'medicines'. They are the lowest and most material form of Spirit known to the Nuer.

Nuer religion thus recognizes many different objects of reverence and worship - 'different ways of thinking of the numinous at different levels of experience'.[1] Behind and within them all lies the mystery of Spirit, the apprehension of which is the fundamental fact of the religious life and the unifying element in all its diverse modes of expression. What is true of Nuer religion is true in substance of primitive religion as a whole. What gives Nuer religion its distinctiveness is the central place of Spirit as the unifying factor. In general there is among primitive peoples no conscious expression of a common factor. Where there is a High God, regarded as supreme, the belief has elsewhere no organic relation to the cults found alongside of it. Whatever may have been the case in earlier times, it is the cults of lesser powers

1. ibid., p. 316

which have been predominant traditionally. Where he is acknowledged, the High God himself is rarely worshipped or prayed to; and if he is worshipped, he is worshipped directly, and not also (as among the Nuer) through the medium of other powers. There are, however, certain exceptional instances of unifying vision. Among the Yaos of Nyasaland there is found a belief in Mulungu, 'the Old One' or 'the Great One', who made the world and is the great agency in human affairs. Yet Mulungu is not merely an individual being. The name is used to cover the ancestral spirits as objects of worship, and to indicate the spirit-world as a whole, the aggregate of the spirits of the dead. But it has a still wider meaning. When Yaos see anything which strikes them as peculiarly mysterious, like a rainbow, they say: 'It is Mulungu.' Among the Nilotic peoples we find a similar attitude. The Shilluk, for example, worship Juok as the Creator of the world; but anything which baffles their understanding is also described as Juok. In certain North American tribes there is a similar indication of the unity which is felt to underlie the diverse manifestations of the Transcendent. Among the Sioux the term Wakan (or Wakanda) is used to denote all that is mysterious or divine. The gods are the embodiment or medium of Wakan, but the same quality or power which they possess supremely is felt to be present in all that is sacred. Thus a shaman is Wakan; the totems are particular forms of Wakan – the powers which they possess arise from its presence in them. Among the Tlingit the word Yok is used in much the same sense – to denote the supernatural power which is felt to reside in all that arouses the consciousness of divine mystery. All the gods and spirits which men worship are Yok: the sky-spirit is Yok as manifested in the sky, the bear-spirit is Yok as manifested in the bear, the rock-spirit is Yok as manifested in the rock. In Melanesia the term Mana is used likewise to indicate the sense of supernatural power which is felt to be present in all spirits, and is believed to be transmitted from the spirits to whatever is striking or mysterious in human life or in the objects and forces of Nature.

Terms like these are exceptional. It is their main significance that they mark a certain recognition of the common element in the objects of religious reverence and worship. In any case the common element is there. Everywhere beneath the forms of religious ceremony or observance, whether it be the cult of ancestors, of animals, of Nature-spirits, of the Sky-God or the Earth-God (or Goddess), there lies the awareness of the Transcendent, which moves men's hearts with awe. In the very nature of the religious consciousness, therefore, we have the seed of mysticism. It has been said that mysticism is 'a heightened noesis (knowledge) of the numinous'.[1] The dawning of religion is itself the awakening, however dimly, of that knowledge. It is when men pass from dim awareness to the certainty which comes from immediate contact that mysticism arises.

1. Urban, *Humanity and Deity*, p. 438, n. 1.

CHAPTER 2

Hindu Mysticism

IT is fitting to begin our study of mysticism in the historical religions by considering the mystical aspects of the religion of India. For in Indian religion mystical experience holds a central place.

More than other religions [Sir Charles Eliot has said in the Introduction to his great work, *Hinduism and Buddhism*] Hinduism appeals to the soul's immediate knowledge and experience of God ... The possibility and truth of this experience is hardly questioned in India, and the task of religion is to bring it about.

In our own time significant testimony was borne to the mystical emphasis characteristic of Indian religion by C. F. Andrews, whose religious outlook was revolutionized by his contact with it.

When I went deep into the heart of India [he said] I found the whole emphasis to be laid on the realization of God within the soul.[1]

That 'realization' is the keynote of Hindu piety.

I. THE UPANISHADS

So far as it is known to us historically, Indian mysticism had its beginnings in the experience of the seers whose teaching is recorded in the Upanishads. The word 'Upanishad' means 'secret' or 'esoteric teaching'. The books so named have been described as 'practical manuals of mystic teaching'. They had their origin in the instruction given by certain teachers to groups of disciples. They represent a remarkable combination of fantastic speculation of a mystical character and profound intuitive insight. Indian religion in the earliest form known to us with any certainty was a polytheistic Nature-worship with an elaborate ritual of prayer and sacrifice.[2] The hymns of the Rig Veda (com-

1. *What I Owe to Christ*, p. 155.
2. Little is definitely known of the religion of the Indus Valley civilization.

posed about 1500–1000 B.C.) were intended to accompany sacrifice. In the course of its development this religion gave rise to certain conceptions of a divine and all-embracing Unity, which find expression in some of the later hymns. It is the vision of this divine principle of unity which forms the starting-point, the fundamental presupposition, of the Upanishads, the earliest of which probably belong to the eighth century B.C. The quest for a deeper and more ultimate Reality than the Vedic gods found its fulfilment among the Upanishadic seers, who claimed to know by direct intuitive insight the supreme and universal principle of being. The sages, it would seem, withdrew from the life of the world, and devoted themselves to meditation in the forests, gathering round themselves groups of learners to whom they imparted the secret they had won. The records of their teaching were at first transmitted orally among their followers. The records constitute the early Upanishads. The Upanishads commonly assume the form of a dialogue in which a teacher who possesses the higher knowledge sets out to explain it to an inquirer. In some instances we find the same material preserved in different Upanishads. Favourite passages were evidently passed from one group to another; they were used for meditation in more than one locality. The Upanishads do not present us with a developed philosophy; they contain trends of thought differing among themselves in some respects. Yet everywhere they teach the same essential truths.

The religion of the Upanishads is pre-eminently inward and spiritual. It represents therefore a strikingly different tendency from the preoccupation with the rites of sacrifice which was characteristic of Vedic religion. In the Mundaka Upanishad there is a direct attack on ritual. Sacrificial forms are described as 'unsafe boats'; those who rely upon them are 'deluded, like blind men led by one who is blind' (1:2:7–8). Elsewhere sacrifice is interpreted allegorically, while its common form is ignored. In some of the later Upanishads it is suggested that sacrifice may have a rightful, although subordinate, place. This points to the compromise which was eventually adopted, whereby Upanishadic teaching, instead of being allowed to develop in rivalry to the established cultus, was incorporated in the official system. This was done by means of the fourfold scheme of life prescribed for members of the Brahmin or priestly caste. According to this a man, after living the life, first of a student who learns the Vedas from a teacher, then of a householder who fulfils his ritual obligations, becomes on the approach of old age a hermit, meditating on the inner meaning of the ritual, and finally an ascetic (a sannyasi), devoting himself purely and simply to the quest of mystical knowledge.

What is the nature of mystical knowledge as the Upanishads understand it? In the Chandogya Upanishad we are told (in Book VI) that a certain man named Uddalaka sent his son Shvetaketu to a school for the study of the Vedas. (Such schools were attended by members of the priestly families.) After twelve years the young man returned 'very proud of his learning'. Uddalaka then inquired of him: 'Have you asked for that knowledge which makes a man hear what is not heard, perceive what is not perceived, know what is not known?' Shvetaketu was unaware of the possibility of such knowledge. Uddalaka proceeded to instruct him by means of certain analogies. He told him, for example, to take a piece of salt and put it in water, and to come to him again the next morning. In the morning he bade him bring the salt. Shvetaketu looked into the water, but could not find the salt. His father told him to taste the water. The son said it was salt. 'Look for the salt again,' his father said. 'I cannot see the salt,' he replied, 'I can only see water.' 'In the same way, my son,' said Uddalaka, 'you cannot see the Atman [the Spirit]. But in truth He is here. An invisible and subtle essence is the Spirit of the whole universe. That is reality; that is truth; that art thou.'

In these words of Uddalaka there is conveyed to us the essential secret of the Upanishads - the inner knowledge of divine Reality, with which man himself in his deeper being is one; the supra-conscious experience which is characteristic of all developed mysticism, in which the distinction between knower and known is transcended, and man is thus lifted into union with the Infinite. As the Chandogya Upanishad puts it elsewhere: 'This is my Self within the heart, greater than the earth ... greater than the sky, greater than all worlds ... This is Brahman' (III: 14:3–4).

'Atman' and 'Brahman' are the keywords of the Upanishads. Brahman was originally the mysterious power of prayer or spell, but in the Upanishads it signifies the ultimate Reality, which we call 'God' – the Power manifested in the whole universe. Atman meant in the first place 'vital breath', but it came to mean 'spirit', 'self', the ultimate essence in man. It is the essential teaching of the seers that Brahman and Atman are one. Ultimate Reality, that is to say, is Spirit – the cosmic or universal Self. In the Upanishads the two terms are used interchangeably.

It is sometimes said that the Upanishads characteristically teach a doctrine of Pantheism, while side by side with this there is in certain passages another or theistic current of thought radically inconsistent with it. But Pantheism in the proper sense is the doctrine that God is purely and simply identical with the universe in space and time. It is therefore wholly incompatible with divine transcendence.[1] Yet for the Upanishads God is essentially transcendent. He is 'eternal, without beginning or end, greater than the great, changeless' (Katha Upanishad, I: 3: 15). It is for this reason that He is ineffable. No words or thoughts are adequate to express the supreme mystery of His being. 'Words and thoughts turn back from Him, and find Him not' (Taittiriya Upanishad, II: 4: 1); 'the Atman is not this, not this. He is inconceivable, for He cannot be conceived, unchangeable, for He is not changed' (Brihadaranyaka, IV: 2: 4). He is described as both being (sat) and non-being (a-sat), since His nature transcends all forms of being known to us in our experience of things in space and time, yet He is the one Reality which underlies all things.

The statement is often made that ultimate Reality is typically conceived in the Upanishads as impersonal. It is true that 'Brahman', like our own term 'Reality' or 'the Absolute', is neuter. But 'ultimate Reality' or 'the Absolute' is not for us necessarily impersonal. In the Upanishads, as has already been pointed out, 'Brahman' is used interchangeably with 'Atman' or 'Spirit', and while Spirit for the Upanishads is free from the limitations of finite personality, it is certainly not impersonal in the sense of being on a lower level of existence than a human person, like a

1. For another interpretation of Pantheism see W. T. Stace, *Mysticism and Philosophy*.

mere unconscious force of Nature. Atman is described as 'intelligence', as 'consciousness' (and in that sense as 'light'), as 'bliss'. The supreme Spirit (says the Brihadaranyaka) is an ocean of pure consciousness, boundless and infinite' (II: 4: 12). 'He is all-knowing and all-wise', says the Mundaka. 'The wise perceive clearly by the knowledge (of Brahman) the blissful Immortal which shines forth;' 'He is the light of lights;' 'His radiance illumines all this world' (II: 2: 7, 8, 10, 11). In the words of the Chandogya, He is 'the Infinite which alone is joy' (VII: 23). In some Upanishads the supreme Reality is spoken of in directly personal terms. In the Isha He is Isha or Ishvara, 'the Lord', and this conception is elaborated in the Shvetashvatara. 'Him who is the supreme mighty Lord of lords, the highest Divinity of divinities, the supreme Ruler of rulers, paramount, Him let us know as the adorable God, the Lord of the world' (VI: 7). He is the Maker of all, and the cause both of transmigration and of deliverance.

Along with the thought of the divine transcendence, there is in the Upanishads an equal stress on the divine indwelling, and it is characteristic of their teaching that the two aspects are constantly brought together. 'Concealed in the heart of things,' says the Katha, 'lies the Atman, smaller than the smallest atom, greater than the greatest spaces' (I: 2: 20) – transcending spatial dimensions. 'The Light which shines there beyond the heaven, behind all things, behind each, in the highest worlds ... that is assuredly this Light which is here within, in men' (Chandogya, III: 13: 7). Divine immanence became through the influence of Upanishadic teaching 'an axiom for the religious thought of India'. And that immanence is by its very nature the immanence of the Transcendent. 'The one God is hidden in all beings. He is the all-pervading, all-filling inner Self of all beings, the Overseer of all activities' (Shvetashvatara, VI: 11). When Uddalaka reveals to Shvetaketu the supreme secret, 'That art thou', it is this transcendent mystery that he has in mind: the essence of our being, the inmost reality of our life – of all being and of all life – is the Spirit which is greater than all worlds. 'All this universe is in truth Brahman; He is the beginning and end and life of all' (Chandogya, III: 14: 1). The affirmation of identity is not the affirmation of a bare identity excluding difference, such as Pantheism implies; it is the affirmation of an identity known only to the higher, mystic consciousness, in which man rises beyond his finitude into oneness with the Eternal. Most significant in this connexion is a passage in the Brihadaranyaka, where the seer, in affirming unity and identity, affirms at the same time otherness and distinction of being. 'He who dwelling in the earth, is other than the earth, whom the earth knows not, whose body the earth is, who inwardly rules the earth, is thy Self, the inward Ruler, the Deathless' (III: 7: 3). The speaker proceeds to make the same assertion of the whole range of phenomenal being, up to the body and mind of man: 'He who, dwelling in all beings, is other than all beings, whom all beings know not, whose body all beings are, who inwardly rules all beings, is thy Self, the inward Ruler, the Deathless.' Brahman dwells in all things, so that all things are His body – the medium through which He manifests Himself. Yet He is other than all things, ruling or controlling them from within. And it is He – the inner Ruler of all things – who is the inmost Self of man. It is significant that in the Shvetashvatara, where the divine transcendence assumes a directly personal form, as 'the supreme mighty Lord of lords', He is also said to be all-pervading, the inner Soul of all. Because He is the inner Soul of all things, He identifies Himself with all. In the very Upanishad where the divine transcendence is expressed most unmistakably, we find the most apparently Pantheistic statements. 'Man art Thou and woman, boy and maiden, the aged tottering on a staff; Thou comest again to birth and gazest here and there' (IV: 3). God is infinitely exalted over all phenomenal being, yet He takes the form of phenomena and is their very heart.

The Upanishads do not present us with a systematic or wholly consistent philosophy. Their essential purpose is a practical one – to promote God-realization. It was in later times that attempts were made to systematize and harmonize their teaching. As has already been indicated, their approaches are to some extent divergent, but what is mainly significant is the common ground between them. However their vision may be expressed, they are agreed in regarding the universe as a partial manifestation of divine Reality. The Atman is the principle of unity holding all things together. 'As all the spokes are held together in the hub and felly of a wheel, just so in this Soul all things, all gods, all worlds, all breathing things are held together' (Brihadaranyaka, II: 5: 15). The Chandogya draws a material analogy. 'Just as by knowing a lump of clay, all that is clay can be known, since any differences are only words and the reality is clay,' all things made of clay being only modifications of one original substance, known by different names – so (it is implied) by knowing Brahman, we know the Reality of which all things are superficially different expressions (VI: 1: 4). Brahman is the Reality – the sat – of the universe.

It is sometimes said that in the Upanishads the world is conceived, according to one trend of thought, as an illusion (maya). This was the doctrine developed by Shankara in later times, as will be shown below, on the basis of Upanishadic teaching; but it does not appear in the Upanishads themselves. In the Shvetash-vatara, it is true, we are told that Nature is maya, and that 'the mighty Lord' is mayin (IV: 10). But the word maya meant originally magical power, and here it may signify the product of such power, the Lord being the artificer. Certainly it is taught in the Upanishads that the world does not stand on the same level of reality as Brahman. Relatively to His changeless and eternal Being (sat), enduring amid the flux of finite things, the changing and perishable world is sometimes described as a-sat or non-being.[1] Yet it is not suggested that the world is a pure illusion. The typical outlook and aspiration of the Upanishads are expressed in the prayer of the Brihadaranyaka: 'From the a-sat [the world of change] lead me to the sat [the Real, that which 'is'], from darkness lead me to light, from death lead me to immortality' (Brihadaranyaka, I: 3: 28). 'Darkness' and 'death' are the realm of a-sat, and it is only through the knowledge which comes of mystical realization that man can overcome his subjection to it.

The relative reality of the world is implied in the conception of divine indwelling. It is implied also in the occasional references

1. The usage of the Upanishads varies as regards the term sat. Commonly it indicates Brahman as the supreme Reality, but sometimes it stands for the existence of the world of change.

to creation. In the Chandogya, creation is described as a process of transformation resting on desire. 'In the beginning there was One without a second ... That Being thought *Would that I were many; I will create!*' (VI: 2: 1–3). The emergence of the universe is thus conceived as emanation from the Absolute. In the Mundaka we have a number of analogies. 'Even as a spider sends forth its thread, even as plants arise from the earth and hairs from the body of a man, even so the whole creation arises from the Eternal' (I: 1: 7); 'as from a fire aflame thousands of sparks come forth, even so from the Creator an infinity of beings have life and to Him return again' (II: 1: 1). In creating the world, it is said, the Spirit enters into it; He becomes the many of the visible universe. Yet though He is manifested in the universe, He remains transcendent. 'The one Inner Self of all beings shapes itself to form after form, and is also outside them. As the sun, the eye of the whole world, is not defiled by the external faults seen by the eye, even so the One Inner Self of all beings is not tainted by the sorrow of the world, being external to it' (Katha, II: 2: 10–11).

It is the fundamental thought of the Upanishads that Brahman is the supreme Reality, transcending all things, yet immanent in all. And it is the purpose of the seers to lead men to the immediate apprehension of His presence. The motive which inspires their work is the conviction that only in that mystical knowledge can men find deliverance from the woes of life: 'all else is fraught with sorrow.' 'Our heart is restless', they say in effect with St Augustine, 'until it finds rest in Thee.' Man cannot find enduring satisfaction in the things of time and space, they tell us, since in his own deepest being he transcends them. The inmost Self of man is eternal and all-pervasive, but in our present phase of being we are finite creatures, separate from one another and from God, subject to all the chances and changes of mortality. We are led therefore to seek the knowledge which will set us free from the bondage of finitude and mortality. It is this dissatisfaction with the finite, this consciousness that man's true home is in Eternity, that underlies the common accusation that the outlook of the Upanishads is 'life-denying' or pessimistic.

For the Upanishads this quest is the quest of release from the round of rebirth (the samsara). They take it for granted that man is born not once, but many times on earth. In the Vedic hymns there is no trace of this conception. At death, they teach, the soul either takes up its abode in the heaven of light with Yama, the ruler of the realm of the dead, or else, in the case of evil-doers, it is hurled into 'unfathomable darkness, whence none shall return'. In the Upanishads, if the soul passes into heaven or hell at death, it is only as a temporary dwelling-place prior to its return to earth. Associated with the doctrine of transmigration is the belief in karma – the law of the deed. 'According as a man acts and behaves, so is he born; he who does good is born as a good man, he who does evil is born as a bad man' (Brihadaranyaka, iv: 4: 5). It is taught in some passages that a man may be reborn in the form of an animal. The Chandogya declares that 'those whose conduct here has been evil will quickly attain an evil birth, the birth of a dog, the birth of a swine or the birth of an out-caste' (v: 10: 7). In any case, whatever the quality of their conduct, the souls of men are involved in the samsara, and it is from the necessity of rebirth that the Upanishads show the way of release.

The way of release is the way of God-realization, and this involves a stringent moral training. It is sometimes alleged, as a criticism of the Upanishads, that their emphasis is insufficiently ethical. The criticism rests upon a singular misunderstanding. The preoccupation of the Upanishads is the attainment of mystical insight, but (as Professor Mahadevan has pointed out) 'they assume on the part of the aspirant a high grade of ethical culture'.[1] As the Katha puts it: 'He who has not ceased from evil-doing, he who is not tranquil, he who is not composed, whose heart has not gained peace, cannot reach this Self even by right knowledge' (i: 2: 24). Stress is laid on the necessity of achieving such qualities as uprightness, charity, liberality, mercy, non-injury to life (ahimsa). Above all, a man's desire must be set on Brahman. 'A man whose mind wanders among desires, and is longing for objects of desire, goes again to life and death according to his desires' (Mundaka, iii: 2: 2). Evil has its roots in the ignorance –

1. *History of Philosophy, Eastern and Western*, i: 70. See also Hiriyanna's chapter on 'The Ethics of the Upanishads' in *The Quest after Perfection*.

the avidya or lack of spiritual knowledge – whereby we identify ourselves with our immediate ego in its narrowness and separateness, and it is this ignorance which must be overcome. 'Who knows Him dwelling in the secret place of the heart cuts asunder the bonds of ignorance even in this human life' (Mundaka, II: 1: 10).

The knowledge which brings deliverance is the mystical knowledge of Brahman whereby men are united with Him. 'He cannot be seen by the eye, and words cannot reveal Him. . . . By the grace of wisdom and purity of mind, He can be seen indivisible in the silence of meditation' (Mundaka, III: 1: 8). The Spirit is known by His own self-revelation to the seeking soul; the vision is attained only by the man whom the Spirit chooses (III: 2: 3). When the vision comes, it brings the fullness of joy. Brahman Himself by His essential nature is bliss, and the man who knows Him, and is united with Him, shares His eternal joy. 'To the wise who perceive Him as abiding in the soul, to them is eternal bliss – and to no others' (Katha, II: 2: 12). 'All else is fraught with sorrow.'

Union with the Spirit is in one aspect a present possession. Here and now the seer enters upon that liberation (mukti) from the fetters of the narrow self which lifts him beyond the necessity of rebirth. 'Beyond the darkness I know Him, the great Spirit, shining as the sun. Knowing Him is immortality; that only is the path by which men escape death' (Shvetashvatara, III: 8). Immortality for the Upanishads is identification with the infinite and eternal life of the Spirit. 'Being Brahman [i.e., in the essence of his being], he attains Brahman' (Brihadaranyaka, IV: 4: 6). Here and now 'he becomes established in the supreme undecaying Atman' (Prashna, IV: 9).

The consciousness of unity with the Spirit is for the seer a present fact, so that, while he retains his individuality, he transcends it. Consequently it is evident that individual existence is of itself no barrier to the realization of infinitude. Yet the question has still to be answered, does individuality persist after death? 'Into Brahman,' says the Chandogya, 'when I go hence, I shall enter' (III: 14: 4). What does that 'entrance' involve when bodily life has ceased? Certainly the inmost life of the soul is indestructible. As the Katha puts it in a well-known passage: 'If the slayer thinks to slay Him [the Atman], if the slain thinks of Him as slain, both these understand not; He slays not, nor is He slain' (I: 2: 19). The sage here affirms the deathlessness of the supreme Spirit, 'hidden in the inmost heart of the creature here.' Immortality is oneness with that Spirit. In the Katha we are told that 'in the case of the man who has gone forth some say that he is, while some say that he is not'. Nachiketas asks Yama who are right, but no explicit answer is given. The seer, it is said, 'gains that goal from which he returns not to rebirth'; he 'reaches the end of the journey, the highest place of Vishnu' – i.e. the condition of divinity which is the consummation of man's quest (I: 3: 8f.). The author employs an analogy sometimes used by Christian mystics to indicate the nature of the divine union. 'As pure water poured into pure water becomes one with it, thus verily is the self of the seer, who has attained to wisdom' (II: 1: 15). A similar analogy is drawn in the Mundaka. 'Just as the flowing rivers disappear in the ocean, casting off name and form, even so the knower, freed from name and form, attains to the divine Person, higher than the high' (III: 2: 8). This must not be taken to imply the mere cessation of individual being. 'The souls (as Radhakrishnan says in his commentary) attain universality of spirit.' As the seer adds, they are identified with Brahman Himself, and in that identification – in that fusion of being with the Infinite – they find immortality. In his freedom from the limitations of finitude the liberated soul, on departing from this world (it is said in the Taittiriya), 'goes up and down these worlds assuming the form he desires' (III: 10: 5).

In the Brihidaranyaka it is stated, in the course of a dialogue between the sage Yajnavalkya and his wife Maitreyi, that 'after death there is no consciousness' (IV: 5: 13). Maitreyi is bewildered by the assertion. But Yajnavalkya makes it clear that he is using the term 'consciousness' in a limited sense, as applied to our ordinary experience, with its duality of subject and external object. 'As long as there is duality, one sees the other, one hears the other, one thinks of the other, one knows the other.' But it is the very essence of the higher state that such duality is transcended. In the present experience of the mystic, and so in the final consummation beyond death, the soul is one with Brahman in a union excluding all duality. Thus the prayer of the same Upanishad is answered, and the soul is led 'from the unreal to the Real, from darkness to light, from death to immortality'.

II. THE BHAGAVAD GITA

Second only to the Upanishads in its importance as a source of mystical religion in India is the Bhagavad Gita (the Song of the Lord). Of all Indian religious writings the Gita is, indeed, the most widely known and loved. Its influence in stimulating the life of personal devotion may be compared with that of *The Imitation of Christ*. Yet in one way it differs markedly from the *Imitation*: it is not only a guide to religious living; it is also a compendium of mystical philosophy. That is not to say that we shall find in the Gita, any more than in the Upanishads, a fully elaborated or wholly unified system of thought. How far the teaching of the Gita is really consistent with itself is a subject of controversy. Some European commentators have not only detected differing trends of thought; they have on this basis propounded the view that the Gita is of composite origin. Indian exponents, by contrast, have in general upheld its substantial unity of origin. The most common view of its date has been that it belongs to the last century or two B.C., though some students have put it later. Dasgupta, indeed, in his *History of Indian Philosophy*, regards it as earlier than the time of Buddha.

The most distinctive conception of the Gita, in comparison with the Upanishads, is that of the avatar or incarnate Deity. Its teaching is given by Krishna, the charioteer of Arjuna, on the eve of a battle, in which the latter is about to be involved against a host of his kinsmen. Arjuna is troubled by doubts concerning his duty. Krishna, who is God incarnate, removes those doubts, and proclaims the truths of religion. Now, this conception of Krishna as an avatar introduces a distinctive note into the religion of the Gita. The infinite and eternal Spirit of the Upanishads is embodied in a human person, and so there is imported into religion a spirit of personal devotion (bhakti), which comes, as we shall see, to form its centre. This principle was of the utmost importance for the whole development of mystical religion in India.

Yet the outlook of the Gita is in essentials substantially the same as that which is characteristic of the Upanishads. God, as the poet sees Him, is Brahman, 'the Imperishable, the Supreme,' 'the Light of all lights and luminous beyond all the darkness of our ignorance,' eternally transcending the created world of which He is the source and the goal – 'the Father of this universe, the Mother, the Ordainer, the imperishable seed of all and their eternal resting-place' (IX: 17 f.). 'Thou art the supreme Immutable [Arjuna cries] whom we have to know; Thou art the high foundation and abode of the universe; Thou art the Guardian of the eternal laws; Thou art the everlasting Soul' (XI: 18). Just as in the Upanishads, equal stress is laid on the immanence as on the transcendence of God. 'He is seated in the hearts of all, unperishing within the perishing' (XIII: 18, 28). In a striking passage in the Eleventh Book, Krishna reveals himself to Arjuna in his supreme form, as God. Arjuna's eyes were opened, and he saw 'the whole world multitudinously divided, and yet unified in the body of the God of gods' (XI: 13). He was overwhelmed by the glory of the vision. 'Such is the light of this body of God as if a thousand suns had risen at once in heaven.' He saw the splendour and majesty of God revealed in all things. 'Homage to Thee on all sides,' said Arjuna. 'For thou art each and all that is. Infinite in might and immeasurable in strength of action, Thou pervadest all, and art every one' (XI: 40).

God is for the Gita 'Vasudeva' – the God in whom all things dwell, and who dwells in all things. 'He who sees Me everywhere, and sees everything in Me, of him will I never lose hold, and he will never lose hold of Me' (VI: 30). Like the Upanishads, the Gita is very far from being a text-book of abstract philosophy. Running through it is the practical purpose of promoting the devotional and mystical life. The vision of God as the all-pervading Life of the universe, yet in the height and depth of His Being immeasurably beyond it, is the goal of endeavour and the guiding star of life. All the analogies we can employ are insufficient to express the ineffable mystery of God's Being and His relation to the world. 'He is within and without born beings, unmoving and moving, far away and yet near; He is indivisible, but seems to divide Himself in born beings' (XIII: 15f.). Like the Upanishads,

the Gita uses language which appears superficially to suggest a
sheer Pantheistic identification of God with the world. 'I am
taste in the waters, I am the light of the sun and the moon ...
I am the pure odour of the moistened earth and the fire's red
heat; the life in all beings am I and the austerity in the austere'
(VII: 8f.). In the words of Arjuna, quoted above: 'Thou art each
and all that is; Thou pervadest all, and art every one.' In one
aspect, it is clear, God is conceived as identifying Himself with all
that the universe contains. But, as in the Upanishads, such identification is far from involving a pure and simple unity; it is far
from implying a mere equation of the being of God with that of
finite things. All that is said of the divine transcendence and the
divine glory is incompatible with that. It is Krishna, in whom the
divine Perfection is incarnate, who can yet identify himself with
all things; it is God in the fulness of His glory who is 'each and
all that is'. In the Eighth Book Krishna is described as Adhiyajna,
'the Lord of Sacrifice' or 'the Sacrifice from above'. God Himself, that is to say, enters by a supreme self-offering into the life
of all things; He takes to Himself the limitation of the finite; He
creates out of His eternal Life a world of beings divided from
Him, yet one in essence with Him.

But what is the particular relation to God of the human soul?
What is the nature of human destiny? What is the attitude towards God and the world to which the Gita calls us? In the
Second Book the poet speaks in a well-known passage (quoted in
part from the Katha Upanishad, see p. 28 above) of the necessity
which is laid upon us, if we are to achieve a right understanding,
to distinguish between the outer and the inner life of man. The
life of the body is subject to birth and change and death, but in
the body there is that which is immune to all change and decay –
that which is 'illimitable, eternal, indestructible'. 'This is not
born, nor does it die ... It is unborn, ancient, everlasting; it is
not slain when the body is slain.' After death it comes again to
earth: 'It casts away old, and takes up new, bodies as a man
changes worn-out raiment for new.' The writer here is plainly
speaking not of the soul as we commonly conceive it, but of
something greater – of what Christian mystics have called 'the
spark of the soul' – which is indestructible because it lies beyond

time and space. In the Katha Upanishad the reference is to the Atman – the universal spirit – immanent in the individual, 'hidden in the inmost heart of the creature here'. The Gita also refers to the Atman, but with a difference; it refers to the Atman as in some sense individualized. 'It is an eternal portion of Me (Krishna says) – an eternal phase of the divine Life – which becomes the jiva (the soul) in the world of living beings' (xv: 7). The Gita offers a new and distinctive conception. It teaches, as Aurobindo says in his commentary, that 'each manifesting spirit is an eternal individual, an eternal unborn, undying power of the one Reality'.[1] In this respect, as on some other issues, the doctrine of the Gita represents a fusion of Upanishadic teaching with the philosophy of the Sankhya – a system of thought which was originally altogether independent of the Upanishads, and represented a radically different outlook. The Sankhya taught an unresolved pluralism – an infinite number of eternal individuals (purushas). The system may have been at first theistic, but in any case the purushas are essentially separate from one another. The Gita took over the conception of an infinite number of eternal individuals and combined it with the Upanishadic vision of the Atman as the one eternal Reality, so that for the Gita the purusha is a phase of the life of God.

In accordance with this outlook, there is no real ambiguity concerning the nature of our ultimate goal. 'Never at any time was I not,' says Krishna to Arjuna, 'nor thou nor these lords of men, nor shall any of us ever cease to be hereafter' (ii: 12). The goal of our being is not to lose our individuality, but to find it in the eternal life of God. Concerning the goal, the Gita uses such phrases as 'coming' to Krishna, to Brahman, to the supreme Person (the Purushottama), 'entering' His Being, 'becoming' Brahman. Mukti (release) is called perfection, the supreme goal, the blissful state, the eternal indestructible abode. 'He who is happy within,' we read, 'who rejoices within, who also has light within, becomes Brahman, and attains to the Nirvana of Brahman' (v: 24). He enters into the full realization of union with the divine, 'he attains the eternal changeless abode' (xviii: 56).

Krishna is himself in one aspect the embodiment of the goal.

1. *The Message of the Gita*, p. 200.

For Indian thought the Incarnation has not the uniqueness and exclusiveness characteristic of the Christian doctrine. Every soul is divine in its deepest being; but in Krishna the soul is consciously divine. The personality of Krishna is not conceived as unique in human history. 'Whenever there is a decay of right-eousness and a rising of unrighteousness, then I loose myself forth into birth. In order to save the good and to destroy evildoers, I am born from age to age' (IV: 7f.). The avatar is born for a particular purpose. But by the very nature of the case he is born as a mani-festation of that which all men have it in them to become. 'The avatar', says Aurobindo, 'is a direct manifestation in humanity by Krishna, the divine Soul, of that divine condition of being to which Arjuna, the human soul, is called by the Teacher to arise[1].'

What, then, is the way which leads men to the goal? The Gita offers a synthesis. It speaks of three paths – the path of know-ledge (jnanamarga), the path of work (karmamarga), and the path of love and devotion (bhaktimarga). Stress is laid now on one, now on another, of these paths, for they are conceived as comple-mentary and not exclusive. In one aspect, the way of life is the way of knowledge – the knowledge of truth and reality, the knowledge of the self in its oneness with God. Such knowledge comes initially as instruction from a teacher, as Arjuna learns from Krishna. Beyond that is the immediate vision of divine Reality. As a means to this attainment the Gita recommends the practice of yoga – a method of mental training described in Book Six. The method is one of self-mastery and concentration of the mind on God. 'Motionless like the light of a lamp in a windless place is the controlled consciousness of the yogin who practises union with the Self ... When the mind is thoroughly quieted, then there comes upon the yogin, in whom passion is appeased, the bliss of the soul that has become Brahman. Thus freed from the stain of passion, and putting himself constantly into yoga, the yogin easily and happily enjoys the touch of Brahman, which is an exceeding bliss' (VI:19, 27f.)

The Gita also stresses the necessity of action. Krishna bids Arjuna put away his doubts and fulfil his caste-duty by taking his

1. op. cit., p. 68.

part in battle. It rejects the view which had come to prevail in India that the highest state is that of the sannyasi, who has renounced all activity. Those who attain Nirvana in Brahman 'are occupied in doing good to all creatures' (vi: 25). It was commonly held that action binds us to rebirth: what really binds us, the poet teaches, is not action, but the desire for its fruits. The true sannyasi is he who neither hates nor desires. The right way of life lies in the spirit of detachment and disinterestedness, and in the surrender of ourselves and all our actions to God.

Such surrender is the outcome of devotion (bhakti). The way of bhakti is the way most distinctive of the Gita, and it is the stress on this principle which constitutes its supreme importance for the development of religion in India. Arjuna offers his love and devotion to Krishna as the visible manifestation of God – the embodiment in human form of the divine grace and love. He symbolizes the response of the human spirit in utter devotion and self-giving to the divine Presence. Bhakti may exist on different levels, but wherever it exists, it purifies the soul, and prepares the way for union. 'He who offers to Me with devotion a leaf, a flower, a fruit, a cup of water, that offering of love from the striving soul is acceptable to Me ... If even a man of very evil conduct worships Me with undivided worship ... swiftly he becomes righteous of soul, and comes to eternal peace. Be assured that none who loves Me shall perish' (ix: 26, 30f.). In its fuller development bhakti has been described as 'the unitive stage', the climax of the mystical life. 'Of all yogins he who, with all his inner self given up to Me, for Me has love and faith, him I hold to be the most united with me in yoga' – the way of union (vi: 47). The whole act of living is to be turned into a continuous union – a continuous offering of the self to God. He who follows the way of bhakti abandons all self-seeking, all pride and wrath, all disquiet, all attachment to earthly things; his heart is filled with divine grace, and goes out in selfless compassion and longsuffering to all; he practises constant 'recollection', taking refuge in God in the midst of his activities. He thus enters into a conscious realization of the divine indwelling presence. 'Those who turn to Me with love and devotion, they are in Me, and I in them' (ix: 29); they dwell in God by the whole endeavour of their lives, and God dwells in them as the ruling power of all their actions.

III. THE VEDANTA

The Upanishads, as we have seen, do not present us with a systematized philosophy. They contain trends of thought to some extent divergent, the implications of which are not fully developed. It was natural therefore that on the basis of their teaching different philosophies should arise in course of time. These philosophies, taken together, are known as the Vedanta – literally 'the end of the Vedas', i.e. the doctrines set forth in the closing portions of the Vedas (the Upanishads). It is sometimes assumed among Western exponents of Indian thought that the Vedanta forms a single unified system. What that means in effect is that its teaching is identified with a particular interpretation. For in reality it comprises a number of schools of thought differing radically from one another on certain issues. It is important to understand these differences, since they entered deeply into the religious attitude of their exponents, and coloured the later forms of Indian mysticism. We shall consider here the three leading types of philosophy comprised in the Vedanta.

(a) The Philosophy of Shankara

The mode of thought which has been dominant in Indian mystical philosophy finds its fountain-head in the work of Shankara, who lived in the eighth and ninth centuries of our era (probably from A.D. 788 to 820). Shankara was not only a philosopher of amazing grasp and subtlety; he was a mystic, a practical religious reformer, and the founder of a religious order (the Smarta), which still enjoys the greatest prestige. His writings are penetrated by the light of vision and inspired by the ardent desire to lead men to the saving truth. His teaching rests upon a twofold basis: it is an exposition of the principles of the Upanishads and an interpretation of mystical experience.

The philosophy of Shankara is known as Advaita (non-dualism). He did not himself originate this philosophy, for its main principles were expounded before his time by Gaudapada; but he gave the type of thought in question its classical expression.

In one sense Shankara was, like Spinoza, a 'God-intoxicated' philosopher. For him the one Reality is Brahman, and it is in the knowledge of that Reality alone that men can find true freedom and abiding joy. As the Upanishads teach, Brahman lies beyond the reach of intellectual consciousness. He is in Himself 'without qualities'. His nature 'no man can define'. But He is the fullness of being and knowledge and bliss – 'a self-shining Light that illumines all that is'.[1] 'Reality belongs to the [hidden Self, whose form is consciousness, whose body is bliss, whose glory is unspeakable.'[2]

Shankara maintains that the nature of the Absolute is directly experienced in the state of dreamless sleep. It is commonly assumed by Indian teachers that dreamless sleep is not a merely negative condition, but a state of restful joy; it is thus a revelation of ultimate Reality. What, however, is of far greater significance for ourselves is the stress which Shankara lays on anubhava or the direct perception of Reality, which is described as 'perfect knowledge' or 'perfect intuition'. In this condition the soul knows itself as one with the universal Spirit. Here, in the words of a modern writer, speaking of his own experience, 'all self-consciousness is lost in the all-pervading consciousness of the unnameable One'.[3]

It is characteristic of the Advaita that the relation between Brahman and the soul is conceived as one of pure and simple identity. The mystic vision in which God alone is known is taken as the essential clue to the nature of Reality. All else, it is inferred, is illusory – of the nature of maya. The mystic, Shankara declares, possesses the 'certainty that the Eternal is real, the fleeting world is unreal'.[4] And 'the fleeting world' includes the whole realm of finite experience – all that is subject to time and change and multiplicity. 'The whole empirical reality with its names and forms ... rests upon avidya.'[5] Shankara's attitude to the world is not altogether clear or consistent, although its

1. *Vivekachudamani* (*The Crest-Jewel of Wisdom*) in C. Johnston's translation, p. 41.
2. ibid., p. 51.
3. Quoted by Winslow Hall in *Recorded Illuminates*, p. 56.
4. *The Crest-Jewel of Wisdom*, p. 11.
5. Radhakrishnan, *Indian Philosophy*, 2nd edition, II: 579.

general tenor is plain enough. He sometimes suggests that the world is an illusion due simply to the blindness or ignorance (avidya) of finite beings. At other times he suggests that the world-appearance, illusory as it is, springs from the power (shakti) of Brahman. The clue to the significance of maya lies in the Indian notion of magic, and particularly the magical power which enables a man or a god to create a phantom of himself – a form which bears his image, but has no substantial existence, which serves to manifest his being, although the manifestation is illusory. Brahman is thus, as Shankara suggests, the great Magician (Mayin), who creates the world as a phantom of Himself. Since he is the one Reality, when our eyes are opened by mystical insight, we shall see His presence beneath the veil of maya. Shankara illustrates the false appearance of the world in time and space by an experience familiar enough in India - the mistaking of a snake for a rope. He uses other analogies. Thus he says: 'As the darkness that is its opposite is melted away in the radiance of the sun, so all things visible are melted away in the Eternal.'[1] When we become one with the Eternal, the world-mirage disappears. Shankara follows out the logic of his position to the utmost extreme. The whole process of life and death and rebirth, with its struggle and suffering, its good and evil, its bondage and deliverance, is an illusion. 'The binding and the getting rid of bondage are both mirages ... There is no limiting or letting go, no binding or gaining of success; there is neither the seeker of freedom nor the free [i.e., as a finite individual]; this verily is the ultimate truth.'[2] All limitation and all individuality belong to the sphere of maya. The sage who has attained the hidden knowledge has learnt to distinguish his true being from that of the personal self which 'sees, hears, speaks, acts and enjoys' – which is possessed of individuality and ethical qualities. 'How should righteousness or sin belong to me, who am above form and change, who experience ever partless bliss?'[3]

For Shankara the keynote of true wisdom is in the words of the Chandogya Upanishad: 'That art thou' (see p. 20 above).

1. *The Crest-Jewel of Wisdom*, p. 88.
2. ibid., pp. 88f.   3. ibid., p. 78.

He interprets this saying as a simple and direct affirmation of identity without difference – an affirmation which therefore relegates individuality and finitude, growth and striving and attainment to the realm of maya. The whole stress for him is on the 'That'. His view is at the opposite pole to that of the pantheist who says: 'I and all things in their finitude are God.' 'I am not this separate life,' he says, 'but the supreme Eternal.'[1] That is for him the meaning of the seer's words. If we are divine, he assumes, we cannot also in reality be human; if we are infinite, we cannot also in reality be finite; if we are in eternity, we cannot also in reality be in time. He is anxious above all things to safeguard the eternal perfection of Brahman, with which in mystical experience man knows himself as one; and in his judgement that necessarily rules out as illusory all that is contrary to it.

Shankara drew with relentless logic the conclusions which seemed to him to be entailed in the perception of mystic unity. Normal experience was a mirage. That, however, did not imply that men could afford to ignore its necessities.

> Dreams are true while they last:
> And do we not live in dreams?

Shankara was not responsible for the extravagances of a modern Vedantist like Vivekananda who declared that 'all men are saints' and that 'it is a calumny to say that any human being can be guilty of sin'.[2] Because in my true being as the eternal Spirit, I am incapable of sin, it by no means follows that in the sphere of maya the thought of sin can be dispensed with. In that sphere the round of rebirth is a fact, the law of karma, which binds us to it, is a fact; the suffering which springs from it is a fact. By the logic of fact we are led sooner or later to seek for freedom. And the winning of freedom involves a rigorous process of self-conquest.

Shankara holds that from the empirical standpoint it is possible to attain deliverance in the present life. The liberated soul (jivanmukta) 'looks on this world as a land beheld in dream'; 'even while this body lasts he regards it as a shadow'; 'he has no

1. *The Crest-Jewel of Wisdom*, p. 47.
2. Quoted by Farquhar in *Modern Religious Movements in India*, p. 203.

sense of personality or possessions'.[1] He is free from the binding force of action, yet he acts out of pure generosity and benevolence. In the final stage of his growth he no longer recognizes even the relative truth of the finite; he looks only to the unbroken unity of the Infinite. When his physical being comes to an end, the limiting conditions of his individuality are dissolved; nothing of his personal selfhood remains to stain 'the white radiance of Eternity'.

The sage lives increasingly in the sphere of the higher knowledge, which brings him the truth of being. Side by side with that, Shankara recognizes the necessity of knowledge of a lower order – the knowledge of things as they appear. To this type of knowledge belongs the conception of a personal God – Ishvara (the Lord) or the saguna Brahman (the Brahman with attributes), as distinguished from the nirguna Brahman (Brahman in His absolute reality, to whom no attributes can be assigned). The love and worship of Ishvara is necessary to the man who is not yet free from the fetters of maya. Shankara himself wrote hymns in honour of Shiva, Vishnu, and other deities – forms of Ishvara. For him Ishvara is Brahman seen through the veil of maya. Brahman is reflected in maya as an infinite divine Person, whose being is related essentially to the world of which He is the Lord. Ishvara certainly exists in His infinite personality in the same sense that we exist in our finite personalities. But just as our being is in the last resort dissolved in the eternal reality of Brahman, so it is with the being of Ishvara.

Shankara has a good deal to say in a positive sense about the Lord, just as he has a good deal to say in a positive sense about the constitution of the individual self and the spatio-temporal world. Just as he is keenly aware of the immediate facts of the world, illusory as they ultimately are, so he looks beyond those facts to the creative Power in which they are rooted – even though that Power itself has no final reality. Ishvara is at once immanent and transcendent. He is the omniscient and omnipotent cause of the universe, and its animating breath. He transforms Himself into the universe, yet He is raised immeasurably above it. He has no incompleteness, no sense of need, and therefore Shankara

1. *The Crest-Jewel*, p. 68.

holds that He has no conscious motive or purpose in creation. He regards the activity of the Lord in creation as sport (lila), 'proceeding from His own nature without reference to any purpose'. Creation is, in other words, the spontaneous outflow of His life and joy. From another point of view creation is necessary in each of the successive world-systems to which it gives rise, in order that the unrequited deeds of the souls in former systems may reap their due harvest of good and evil.

The soul of man is for Shankara both identical with and subordinate to Ishvara. The Lord Himself enters into creation in the form of the individual self, which is at the same time dependent upon Him. To illustrate His relation to the soul, he uses certain analogies, while recognizing their inadequacy. The soul is part of the Lord, as a spark is part of the fire. The sparks are the fire itself divided up. If they are separated from their source, they will perish. So with the soul and Ishvara – though it is separated only in appearance, through its ignorance, and it cannot perish. The soul, again, may be considered as a reflection of the Lord, like an image of the sun in water. In its finite individuality it is not directly identical with Him, any more than the image is just the same as the sun; yet it is not anything else. This analogy points to another important truth. A particular image of the sun in water does not necessarily tremble because another trembles. So the souls, while one with Ishvara, are independent of one another. There is no confusion of acts and fruits among them.

An objection raised to Shankara's conception of the relation of the Lord to the soul has a particular interest from the Christian point of view, since it has to do with the problem of divine impassibility. Just as a man suffers from an injury affecting his hands or his feet, so it was suggested that on the basis of Shankara's view Ishvara must Himself experience the suffering endured by the souls which are part of His being. Shankara cannot admit any such possibility. Suffering, he holds, arises in man because he wrongly identifies himself with the body. Such an error is impossible to the omniscience of Ishvara. It is worthy of note that Shankara regards as illusory, not only a man's identification of himself with his body, but equally his identification of himself by the ties of affection and sympathy with his fellows. We must identify ourselves only with God. This, however, does not involve an attitude of indifference to others. Ishvara Himself, while He does not enter into the pains of His creatures, is yet compassionate towards them. And it is the spirit of 'impassible compassion' which is characteristic of the Advaitin. It is perhaps significant in this connexion that the highest form of goodness in India is ahimsa (non-violence) rather than love.

(b) The Philosophy of Ramanuja

From early times there has been at work in India a type of piety characterized above all by bhakti, which plays so great a part in the teaching of the Bhagavad Gita. An account will be given of the main features of this movement at a later point (see pp. 47ff.). What concerns us here is the philosophy to which it gave rise. The great exponent of this philosophy was Ramanuja, who lived two or three centuries after Shankara. (His dates are commonly given as A.D. 1017–1137.) Like Shankara, he was a mystic and an active worker for practical religion. He was in fact himself the supreme pontiff of his own branch of Hinduism (Vaishnavism). As a boy he was trained by a teacher belonging to the Advaita school, but he soon rebelled against its distinctive tenets, and this revolt became the starting-point of a long polemic.

Although the difference between Ramanuja's teaching and that of Shankara was in one aspect of fundamental importance, there was a great deal of common ground between them. Ramanuja's philosophy is known as a variety of Advaita. But, in contradistinction to Shankara's system of pure and simple nondualism, it is described as Vishishtadvaita (qualified non-dualism). It is a system of identity in difference. Whereas Shankara regards unity as excluding differentiation or diversity, for Ramanuja this is involved in the very nature of the Absolute. So far from being an illusion, the manifoldness of the universe springs from a tendency inherent in the nature of divine Reality. God is eternally one, yet in that oneness there exists from all eternity the potentiality of the infinite variety of created things.

Ramanuja was concerned above all to vindicate the reality of God as infinite Personality – immune from the limitations of personality as we know it in human beings, yet endowed with its essential attributes, the Creator and Lord of the universe, the inmost Self of all beings, yet everlastingly distinct (though not separate) from them. He therefore rejected the doctrine of maya as Shankara understood it. For him maya is the marvellous power of God, manifested in the whole order of creation. For Ramanuja, as for Shankara, creation is lila or sport – the spontaneous outflow of the divine generosity. Maya is revealed especially in that which transcends the reach of our understanding. Thus it is through this marvellous power that God can at once dwell in the world and remain free from its limitations and defects. In human experience the divine power is manifested particularly in the interaction of body and soul, thanks to which action produces its necessary fruits in the operation of the law of karma.

God, as Ramanuja conceives Him, is above all a God of goodness – 'a great boundless Ocean [as he says in the introduction to his commentary on the Gita] of compassion, benevolence, parental tenderness, generosity'. He dwells in all beings as their inmost life, yet is at the same time (in the words of the Brihadaranyaka Upanishad) 'other than all beings' (III: 7; see p. 23 above). As the Brihadaranyaka has it in the same passage, He is the 'inner Ruler' of all beings, which form His 'body'. The physical world and the soul are also described as His shakti – the expression of His energy. As His body they are dependent on Him, yet one with Him. Ramanuja fully accepts the teaching of the Upanishad; 'That art thou'. But the words are not for him, as they are for Shankara, the affirmation of an identity which excludes all real difference. Just as the soul is the inmost being and life of the body, so also God is 'the supporting, controlling, all-permeating subject of the soul'.[1] Ramanuja might have said with Augustine and the Christian mystics that God is the 'Soul of the soul'. God dwells in the secret places of the heart, so that there is a mysterious union of His life with ours. Yet He stands everlastingly beyond us, and His deepest relation to us is a personal, though not an external, relation.

Ramanuja admits the validity of a relationship with God which

1. Otto, *India's Religion of Grace and Christianity*, p. 39.

is purely impersonal. Brahman, for him, is both a personal God, who showers His love and grace upon us, and the impersonal substance of all things. The spirit of man is, in one aspect, an attribute or mode of the universal substance. It is possible for men to attain, by mystical intuition, the knowledge of their oneness with Brahman in this sense – to know Him, with an immediate knowledge, as the essence of their souls. Such knowledge will deliver them from the round of re-birth; it will bring them the bliss which belongs to their essential being. Yet this form of salvation and bliss is on a lower level than that which comes from the personal knowledge and love of God. Ramanuja reverses the estimate of Shankara. For the latter, piety of a personal type, the worship of Ishvara, is provisional; on the higher plane of spiritual insight it disappears together with the Lord who is its object. For Ramanuja it is the impersonal knowledge which is imperfect. The height of vision and blessedness can only be reached by the kindling of the fire of love.

Ramanuja tells a fable which illustrates his view of the nature and destiny of the soul. A young prince once strayed from his royal home. He was taken care of by a brahmin who knew nothing of his identity, and instructed in the teaching of the Vedas. When he was twenty-six, a man whose word he could not doubt informed him that he was the son of the ruler of the country, who was eager to see him again. When he heard this, the young man was overcome with joy. His father also, hearing that his son was alive, rejoiced greatly, and ordered him to be brought back home; and so at last the two were reunited. The story symbolizes the divine nature of the soul, its alienation from God in earthly life, its discovery of the truth, the joy of its return to God, the grace of God which brought about that return, and its final union with Him. The real self of man – the spiritual ego, as distinguished from the empirical consciousness – is immutable, eternal, blissful. It is an attribute or mode of Brahman. In our normal being we are blind to our real nature; we fall into sin, and consequently we are involved in suffering. But by the grace of God our eyes may be opened to the truth, and we may surrender ourselves to Him, and share His love and His joy.

A follower of Ramanuja, Vishnu-Narayana, gave vivid

expression, in poetic form, to the experience of alienation and redemption which is fundamental to his thought.

> Because I had forsaken unity with Thee,
> Because I, fool, had made my body me,
> Because I did not know Thee, who didst dwell in me,
> Therefore I wandered through raging hells and all other births.
> To serve Thee – that indeed my very being is, which I disdained.
> Because I threw away my very self, I therefore was in chains.
> But now, through grace, I have put off the natural man,
> And have regained my true supernal self . . .
> But when was heard by God this purpose of the soul,
> Of this surrendering, longing, fleeing soul,
> Joy shone on His countenance –
> Infinite saving joy, the goal of goals, the highest of all goods,
> For this is sure – no higher good exists
> Than this, the joy upon the countenance of God.[1]

The divine joy, for Ramanuja, is not simply, as it is for Shankara, an eternal bliss, unaffected by events in time: it is also the joy of God, as the Lover of the soul, at its redemption. He does not explain how it is that the soul is involved in the toil and suffering of its separated life; he assumes that the cycle of birth and death has had no beginning. Yet the toil and suffering of the samsara is justified: the law of karma is a means of salvation, ordained by the redemptive goodness of God. Wrong-doing is the outcome of ignorance (avidya); the soul, which is one with God in its deepest being, is unaware, as in the fable, of its own identity. But avidya is not at all the same thing as the maya which reduces the whole world and the whole process of human seeking and striving to unreality. Ramanuja stresses the reality of sin as an offence against God who dwells in the soul, as its intimate Friend and Companion, and by whose grace we may come to be united with Him.

God is for Ramanuja a God of grace who seeks to unite man with Himself. His activity in the region of the finite is typified by the female figure of Shri (Beauty) or Lakshmi (Fortune) – originally the wife of Vishnu, and so 'the imaginative symbol of the creative energy of God', a power united eternally with Him.

1. Quoted by Otto in *India's Religion of Grace and Christianity*, pp. 49f.

Among the followers of Ramanuja differences arose in later times concerning her. Some held that she was indistinguishable from the Lord, others that she was a divine but finite mediator between God and men. The grace of God finds expression also in the conception of avataras (incarnations; see p. 29 above). 'As He is a great boundless Ocean of compassion,' Ramanuja says, in the passage from the introduction to his commentary on the Gita already cited (p. 42), 'He assumed various forms without putting away His own essential godlike nature, and time after time incarnated Himself in the several worlds, descending not only with the purpose of relieving the burden of earth, but also to be accessible to men even such as we are.'

The doctrine of divine grace naturally raises the question of human freedom. Ramanuja assumed that man is free, but he did not work out the implications of his conception. In later centuries his followers became sharply divided on the problem of the relation of divine grace and human effort – a problem which has loomed so large in Christian theology. One section (the Vadgalai) held that man must actively cooperate with the grace of God, as a baby monkey clings to its mother when she carries it to a place of safety. The other section (the Tengelai) said that no self-effort is needed; God's grace will suffice to save us – man is like a helpless kitten, which its mother takes in her mouth to save it from danger.

That was a later development. Ramanuja himself was content to postulate the saving power of bhakti as a response to the divine grace. For him bhakti is not merely faith or devotion; it is the knowledge and love of God – participation in the life of God by the love which is itself a form of knowledge. It can only become effective through the practice of meditation on the divine Personality. Bhakti is 'a loving, intuitive, experimental knowledge' of God as the Soul of our souls, as closely united to us as our body is united to our soul. It is only those who follow this path who can reach the highest goal – who can attain the bliss of living in and for God Himself. Ramanuja stresses the need of constant activity in this life. He rejects the possibility of any final deliverance for the soul while it remains subject to the limitations of the physical world. In the state of ultimate liberation (mukti) the soul is lifted up, by the divine grace, not to an identity of being with God, but to a participation in His qualities. It is absorbed in the bliss of eternal union with God. In that union the soul preserves its individual distinctness of being, but the sense of separateness is done away.

(c) The Philosophy of Madhva

Among the worshippers of Vishnu, opposition to the teaching of Shankara gave rise in the thirteenth century to a system which has been traditionally known as Dvaita (dualism). It is said that Madhva, the founder of this system, looked upon Shankara as the incarnation of a demon who was sent to deceive mankind. He travelled throughout the country, making war on Shankara's doctrines. A recent writer has contended that Madhva's philosophy is actually 'the highest form of Monism'.[1] In any case, however, the contrast with the Advaita remains. Madhva's position is monistic only in the sense that he regards Brahman as the one independent Reality, from whom all things are derived, and who is the operating cause of all events. There is no real agent save Brahman (who as the doer of all things is called Vishnu). Man's great error is to regard himself as a real agent. All things are the manifestation of Vishnu's creative activity, and in that sense it may be said that they are Vishnu. The individual is entirely dependent on Vishnu, and his salvation comes from the recognition of this fact. Madhva stresses the possibility of the direct intuitive realization of God, by divine grace, through the practice of meditation. The realization of God brings a continual outflow of love to Him, and this leads to the conquest of sin. In the state of salvation there is no inner identification of the soul with Brahman, but fellowship with Him and oneness with His Will.

Madhva's theology is unique in two respects. He maintains that while some souls are destined to be saved, through their response to the divine grace, others are destined to remain for ever in the samsara, while some are doomed to final perdition in Hell. Madhva, moreover, postulates a Mediator between man and God – Vayu (originally the wind-god), whom he describes as 'the

1. H. N. Raghavendrachar. See *History of Philosophy, Eastern and Western*, I: 322-37.

dearest image' and the 'son of God'. He is the instrument of divine grace, helping men to obtain deliverance. These conceptions naturally suggest Christian influence, but there is no direct evidence to support that view.

IV. BHAKTI MYSTICISM

(a) Vaishnavism and Shaivism

Reference has been made to the place which is held by the principle of bhakti (devotion) in the religion of the Gita and of Ramanuja. This principle is of central importance in the 'sectarian' movements – Vaishnavism and Shaivism – which have received the allegiance of the great majority of Hindus. These movements have at certain times produced a very real flowering of mystical religion.

The origins of both Vaishnavism and Shaivism lay outside the system of official piety based on the Vedas, but at a comparatively early date both were brought within it, while they themselves profoundly modified its character. They were responsible, for example, for the introduction of temple-worship. Vishnu and Shiva were perhaps originally the chief gods of certain tribes standing outside the main circle of Brahmanical influence. (It is often held that Shiva was in the first instance a pre-Aryan deity worshipped in the Indus Valley.) Each came to be regarded by his worshippers as the one supreme Deity, and each became the object of an ardent devotion. With Vishnu, bhakti commonly, though not exclusively, centres in one or other of the avatars – the beings, most notable among whom are Krishna and Rama, in whom He is incarnate. Both Vishnu and Shiva are identified with Brahman as He is conceived in the Upanishads. Both religions have taken over the main features of Upanishadic teaching – the doctrines of transmigration and karma, and the aspiration for deliverance from the round of rebirth and for union with Brahman. Each cult presents us both with an elaborate mythology (God in each case has His consort, interpreted philosophically as His Shakti or energy)[1] and with a core of mystical aspiration and mystical experience.

1. This conception gave rise to a distinct type of religion known as Shaktism.

The history of Vaishnavism and of Shaivism affords in some respects a strikingly parallel development. Thus in both movements an active part was played from about the seventh century of our era by a succession of poet saints in South India, who wrote in the vernacular (Tamil). These were the Alvars and the Nayanmars respectively. The 'Alvar' is 'one who has gone deep into the knowledge of God, who is immersed in the contemplation of Him'.[1] The songs of the Alvars were collected in the tenth century, and came to be used side by side with the Vedas. Similarly with the Shaivas the devotional poems of the Nayanmars are regarded as equivalent in authority to the Vedas.

Apart from these hymns, the sectarian religions have their own body of Scriptures in the Puranas and the Agamas. Of the Puranas the most important are the Vishnu Purana and the Bhagavata Purana; the latter is concerned with the story of the early life of Krishna, which came to hold so prominent a place in Vaishnavite devotion.

The greatest and most influential of the philosophers of Vaishnavism was Ramanuja, whose work has already been dealt with. Ramanuja gave intellectual expression to the outlook of the Alvars. Closely similar to his teaching is the Shaiva Siddhanta, which originated in the thirteenth century. Some centuries earlier came the rise in Kashmir of a type of philosophy nearer to Shankara's Advaita. An important development in Shaivism was the growth of the Lingayat religion (Virashaivism) under Basava in the twelfth century, which (like Kashmir Shaivism) rejected the authority of the Vedas.

Among the leaders of mystical religion from the thirteenth century were the Maratha Saints, most notably Namadeva and Tukaram; Chaitanya, who initiated in Bengal a movement of a highly emotional type of bhakti; and Ramananda, with his disciples, Tulsi Das and Kabir. The last-named belongs to the bhakti tradition, but stands, properly speaking, outside the scope of Hinduism, since he rejected the authority of the Vedas, and made his appeal to Muslim and Hindu alike. His followers, the Kabirpanthis, have rejoined the Hindu fold. Kabir is one among a number of mystical reformers who, under the impact of Islam,

1. J. S. M. Hooper, *The Hymns of the Alvars*, p. 11.

sought after a form of faith free from the limitations of Hindu ceremonial and mythology as well as from caste restrictions. The best-known of these reformers is Nanak, founder of the Sikh religion. The most influential of all modern mystics is Rama-krishna, who, while adhering to Hindu forms of worship, regard-ed all religions as paths leading to the ultimate union of the soul with God.

(b) The Nature of Bhakti

The term bhakti is derived from the root bhaj, which means 'to adore'. Bhakti is thus adoration of God, loving devotion to Him. It involves prapatti, or complete self-surrender. All action must be performed for God's sake. Such devotion leads to the realiza-tion of God, the union of the soul with Him. The chief quality both of Vishnu and of Shiva is His boundless grace. Our em-bodied life in this world, with all its ills, is the means which He has appointed for our union with Himself; therefore we owe Him a limitless devotion. 'One should worship in supreme love,' says a Shaiva saint, 'Him who does kindness to the soul.'[1] The grace of Vishnu is revealed above all in the avatars, and especially in Krishna, who became for the Vaishnavites the object of an intense, and often passionate, bhakti.

Nine forms of bhakti are enumerated in the Bhagavata Purana. It is said that each of these will lead men to the goal, if it is followed with sufficient fervour. Among them are such practices as shravana – listening to the praise of God and reading the sacred writings – kirtana or singing the praise of God, smarana or remembering God's name. Great stress is laid on smarana. God's name should be repeated in all circumstances, regularly and con-tinuously. All difficulties are destroyed by this practice if it is accompanied by love. The remembrance of God's name is said to be Brahman; it leads to the loss of self in rapture. According to the Vishnu Purana, the repetition of the divine name brings deliverance from all sins, which 'fly like wolves frightened by a lion' (VI:8).

Chaitanya laid the greatest emphasis on kirtana, which alone in his view leads to the highest goal. The distinctive feature of his

1. Quoted by L. D. Barnett in *The Heart of India*, p. 80.

movement was the organization of sankirtana – the singing of God's name in chorus. This was associated with an extremely emotional type of bhakti. It is said that in the sankirtana men would roll on the ground and embrace one another, bursting now into laughter and now into tears, through the intensity of their feeling. Chaitanya himself lived in a condition of religious intoxication. In the joy of union with Krishna, he fell again and again in the last years of his life into a state of trance. Emotional fervour was a feature of bhakti long before the age of Chaitanya (the early sixteenth century). It was characteristic of the Alvars. According to Nammalvar, a man should allow his emotional exaltation to penetrate his being, and should not be deterred from the expression of his feelings by the fear that he will be taken for a madman. He should 'run, jump, cry, laugh and sing'.[1] A similarly emotional type of bhakti is characteristic of the Bhagavata Purana, and through its influence became widely prevalent. In the Vishnu Purana there is not the same stress on emotion, although when Prahlada asks Vishnu to grant him an enduring faith and devotion, he prays that his heart may be animated by 'passion, as fixed as that which the worldly-minded feel for sensual pleasures' (I : 20). In the first phase of his life the experience of Ramakrishna, in the nineteenth century, resembled that of Chaitanya. He was possessed by an ardent longing for the vision of Kali, the Mother Goddess, and the joy of the vision, when it came, was an overwhelming emotional experience. Devotion to Kali was throughout his life one of the mainsprings of his religion.

A prominent aspect of the bhakti movement is devotion to the guru (teacher or spiritual director). The devotee chose a guru for himself to give him instruction and to guide him in his endeavours. The guru was one who had attained the goal of God-realization. Being himself one with God, he was worshipped as God, and such worship was regarded as a means of union. Images of the chief gurus were erected in the great temples. Devotion to the guru was placed on an equal footing with devotion to God. The guru was sometimes looked on as a partial incarnation of Vishnu. Among the Shaivas, who until recent

1. Quoted by Dasgupta in *Hindu Mysticism*, p. 150.

centuries had no doctrine of incarnation, the guru was worshipped as a manifestation of Shiva, who was held to look lovingly on the disciple through his eyes. (This conception may have been the means of introducing the conception of incarnation into Shaivism.)

An interesting development occurred among the Sikhs in connexion with the relation of the guru to his disciples. It was common ground among all bhaktas that a permanent spiritual relation was established between guru and devotee. The relation was sometimes felt as an actual union. Nanak, the founder of the religion of the Sikhs (i.e. 'disciples'), was succeeded by nine other gurus, each of whom exercised supreme authority over his followers. (With the tenth guru the office ceased, the sacred writings known as the Granth Sahib henceforth replacing the authority of the guru.) It was held that all the gurus were identical with Nanak. The whole body of the disciples was also identified with them. The Sikh, it was believed, incorporated the guru in himself; he filled the being of the disciple with his own. The Sikhs were organized into sangats or holy assemblies, and it was believed that the spirit of the guru lived in the sangat. The whole company of the Sikhs was the Panth, and this, again, was conceived as an embodiment of the guru. 'The guru [it is said in the Granth] lives within his Sikhs'; 'the Sikh who practises the guru's word is at one with the guru.'[1]

(c) Conceptions of God and the Soul

In bhakti mysticism there is a considerable variety of outlook, but the typical philosophy of the movement is the 'qualified nondualism' of Ramanuja, which is closely paralleled by the Shaiva Siddhanta. Ramanuja's teaching is a formulation of the principles contained in the hymns of the Alvars. For the Alvars, as for Ramanuja, the soul (like the world as a whole) is a mode of the Supreme, yet possessing its own distinctness from Him. In its true being it is all-pervading and eternal, but it is wholly dependent on Him. Vishnu is, above all, a God of grace, the embodiment of His grace being His consort, Lakshmi.

In the Vishnu Purana emphasis is laid equally on the two

1. Quoted in *The Cultural Heritage of India*, IV: 325, note 6.

aspects of the Supreme : God is the all-embracing One, with whom man in his deepest being is identical, and the Lord of all, to be loved and worshipped as such. The nature of Vishnu is described as 'wisdom' or 'knowledge', though His reality is beyond all words. Through His infinite knowledge, He is all things. As we see them in their separateness, 'mountains, oceans and all the diversities of earth are the illusions of the apprehension' (ii: 12). 'The nature of the great Spirit is single, though its forms are manifold' (ii:14). And if we are to see the truth, we must rise to the realization of our unity with the Spirit and so with all things. 'The knowledge that this Spirit, which is essentially one, is in one's own and in all other bodies is the great end or true wisdom of one who knows the unity and true principles of things' (ibid.). The attainment of this knowledge is ascribed to Prahlada, through the practice of bhakti in the form of contemplative adoration. 'Glory to that Being to whom all returns, from whom all proceeds, who is all, and in whom all things are, to Him whom I also am ... Thus meditating upon Vishnu as identical with his own spirit, Prahlada became as one with Him ... He forgot entirely his own individuality, and was conscious of nothing else than his being the inexhaustible, eternal, supreme Soul' (i:19f.).

We have here the same experience of oneness with the Spirit as underlies the Advaita of Shankara. But whereas with Shankara that experience leads to the rejection of the concept of Ishvara – distinct from the soul, though one with it – as a passing phase of truth, belonging to the 'lower knowledge', for the Vishnu Purana that concept remains. Vishnu is both nirguna, beyond all attributes in His infinite transcendence, and saguna, endowed with all perfections. 'He is one with all good qualities ... Glory, might, dominion, wisdom, energy and all other attributes are collected in Him' (vi:5). Vishnu is 'the supreme Lord, who is all things, and from whom all things proceed' (i: 17). Thus for the Purana bhakti is at once a means of mystical attainment, in its aspect of adoring contemplation, and a permanent attitude of soul as a continuous spirit of devotion and self-surrender.

The attitude of the Vishnu Purana is, with varying emphasis, typical of Vaishnavite saints. We find in all of them an intense devotion to Vishnu, in Himself or in His incarnations, which finds its climax in the experience of union with Him. The aspiration after union with God is accompanied sometimes by a profound consciousness of sin, and the delay in its fulfilment is apt to plunge men's souls into the depths of despair. Such experiences were typical of many of the Maratha saints, who were the leaders of a great spiritual awakening which began in Western India in the thirteenth century. The Maratha saints expressed their strivings and their attainments in short poems, which became widely popular. Tukaram, the best-known of these saints, cries passionately for deliverance from sin: 'Sinful I am, and very weak, and yet Thy power, O Saviour-God, can save from blackest depths of sin and shame.'[1] He was conscious of the 'lofty mountains of desire and anger' that separated him from God, and in his despair of the possibility of God-realization, he cried out against God, accusing Him of miserliness and cruelty. He was driven to the verge of suicide, but finally the divine vision came.

Among the poet-saints of Shaivism, the Nayanmars, we find similar attitudes and experiences. In their poems, and especially in the poems of Manikka-Vacchagar, the greatest of them, there is a note of humility and adoration which (as Dr Macnicol has observed) brings them 'very near to the spirit of Christian saints'. Manikka-Vacchagar speaks with passionate love of the divine grace which has brought him the consciousness of union with God:

> When it seemed I ne'er could be with Thee made one – when nought of Thine was mine,
> And nought of mine was Thine – me to Thy feet Thy love
> In mystic union joined, Lord of the heavenly land – 'tis height of blessedness.[2]

Regarding the nature of God, the position of the poet-saints is in general that of the Vishnu Purana. God transcends all description and discursive knowledge. The bhakta stresses the divine personality; but the personal God is also the supra-personal Absolute. In the words of Tulsi Das: 'He who is un-qualified [the nirguna Brahman] takes form through the love of His devotees. How is the unqualified the qualified [the saguna

1. In Gandhi's *Songs from Prison*, p. 140.
2. Macnicol, *Indian Theism*, p. 174.

Brahman] also? As water is identical with ice and hailstones.[1] Kabir likewise speaks of God as 'without qualities', but characterizes Him as merciful, bountiful, happy, perfect, the Saviour, the Father. The Sikhs relate the distinction to the creation of the world. Apart from creation, God was 'the formless One': He became manifest, and assumed personal qualities, when He made the world, and entered into relation with it. Ramakrishna adopted substantially the same view. 'When I think of the supreme Being as inactive, neither creating nor preserving nor destroying, I call Him Brahman or Purusha, the impersonal God. When I think of Him as active, creating, preserving, destroying, I call Him Shakti or Maya or Prakriti, the personal God. But the distinction between them does not mean a difference. The personal and the impersonal are the same Being, like milk and its whiteness, or the diamond and its lustre. It is impossible to conceive of one without the other. The divine Mother and Brahman are one.'[2]

Ramakrishna sought to reconcile the philosophy of the Advaita with the continued worship of God in His personal aspect. In his experience 'ecstatic devotion to the divine Mother and her play [i.e. her creative activity] alternated with complete absorption in the serene ocean of absolute Oneness'[3]. He therefore regarded both as equally valid. What Rabindranath Tagore described as 'the play of the many' was for him just as divine as the undifferentiated unity of the absolute One. Such a view is actually quite incompatible with the Advaita. To equate the divine Mother with Brahman was unthinkable to Shankara.

It has already been mentioned that the philosophy characteristic of Shaivism – the Shaiva Siddhanta - is closely similar to the 'qualified non-dualism' of Ramanuja. Shiva is the Soul of which Nature and man are the body. Shiva works in the universe through the female principle of shakti (conscious energy), which is related to Him as light is related to the sun. Shiva is the first cause of the universe, maya or matter (not 'illusion') is its material cause, shakti is its instrumental cause. In their real nature individual souls are eternal and omnipresent; they suppose themselves to be

---

1. *The Cultural Heritage of India*, IV: 399.
2. ibid., p. 672.   3. ibid., p. 677.

finite through their ignorance (avidya). By the grace of Shiva the soul is enlightened, and attains union with Him.

The Shaivite movement gave rise in the ninth century to another type of philosophy, known as the Trika, in Kashmir. According to its teaching, the universe is the self-limitation of Shiva, the only reality, who is infinite consciousness. It is also described as His sleep or descent. It is an experience of Shiva, appearing to Him as if it were distinct from Him, like an object seen in a mirror. The individual soul is thus Shiva Himself in His self-limitation, and it is the power of Shiva alone descending upon it which can bring deliverance, the recognition of its own identity. This notion of the self-limitation of God in the universe belongs also to the teaching of the Virashaivas or Lingayats. Shiva forgets His real nature, and appears in the form of the purusha or finite soul. It is a distinctive mark of this sect that its members, when they are initiated into the cult and so enter upon the path of liberation, are invested with a linga or phallic emblem, which (as among all Shaivites) represents Shiva Himself, and is thus taken as a pledge to live in contact with Him.

In the Vaishnavite movement a distinctive type of thought is found among the followers of Chaitanya in Bengal, whose religion centres in the worship of Krishna. In the Bhagavad Gita, as we have seen, Krishna is the charioteer of Arjuna, and is regarded as an avatar, who proclaims the truths of religion. At a later time a whole cycle of myths grew up round him. The myths (related at length in the Puranas, and particularly in the Bhagavata Purana) are concerned especially with his exploits as a youth. Krishna (it is said) was brought up by a herdsman, and he spent his youth in the forest, fighting dragons and demons, and making love to the milkmaids (gopis). The story of his love affairs with the gopis, and especially with his favourite, Radha, forms the most prominent feature of the developed mythology. Since the divine activity in creation is conceived as lila or 'sport', when an avatar appears, his actions (as it came to be supposed) are not subject to the moral law which should govern the lives of men.

For Chaitanya and his followers the mutual love of Krishna and the gopis is an allegory of the love which binds together God and the soul. Chaitanya stresses, above all, intimacy and affection as the keynote of the true relation between God and man. The same relation holds between God and His shaktis or eternal energies. Krishna is the name which Chaitanya gives to Brahman Himself in His eternal being. Brahman has a human form, which is infinite and all-pervading. His substance is absolute bliss (ananda); being and intelligence (sat and chit) are His attributes. The divine abode is Vrindavana – originally the scene of Krishna's youthful activities – which is also infinite and all-pervading. The gopis are His energies; the relation between God and His energies is one of boundless love. The shaktis are infinite in number. Among them is maya-shakti, which appears as the material substance of the universe, and jiva-shakti, whereby the Lord appears in the form of finite spirits. In the earthly Vrindavana Krishna had his associates, whether servants, comrades, parents, or lovers: so in its true nature the soul is an eternal associate of Krishna. In its earthly life the soul forgets its real character, and assumes a material body, but it is only the love of Krishna which can satisfy its cravings; it is destined for union with Him. It is indeed in one aspect identical with the Lord Himself. The philosophy of Chaitanya and his movement is based on the principle of bhedabheda or difference-in-non-difference, taught in the twelfth century by Nimbarka, who also identified the supreme Spirit with Krishna. This principle is manifested in the relation between Krishna and His shaktis, and in particular in the relation between Krishna and the jivas. The soul is one with the Lord, since it participates in His spiritual nature (bliss, being, and intelligence); it is other than the Lord by virtue of its finitude. The soul is thus described as the 'separated part' (vibhinnamsa) of Krishna, as distinct from his 'own part' (soamsa). Since the soul is a fraction of His being, it is by nature a bhakta or devoted servant of Him. Through the practice of bhakti the flame of its love is re-kindled. It learns to identify itself with the servants or lovers of Krishna, as Chaitanya identified himself with Radha both in her pangs of separation from the Lord and in her joy of union with Him.

(d) The Way of Life

In its beginnings, as has already been pointed out, the bhakti movement was independent of the official system of Vedic religion. It was a movement of reform parallel to Jainism and Buddhism. It was opposed to caste restrictions and to the sacrificial cultus, and especially to animal sacrifice. In its later developments, after it had been brahminized, it continued to exercise a liberalizing influence, and from time to time it gave birth to movements of radical reform. Unlike the way of knowledge, involving the study of the Vedas (from which women and the lowest caste were excluded), and the way of sacrificial observances, the way of devotion was open to all. Among the Alvars was a saint of the depressed classes – Tirupanar, a pariah. 'Among the devotees of God,' said Narada, a medieval exponent of bhakti, 'there is no distinction of birth, learning, family, wealth, religious observances, and the like, since they all belong to Him.'[1] 'All persons, even down to the lowest born,' said Shandilya, 'have equal rights to follow the path of devotion; this has been taught by generations of authorities.'[2] Ramanuja himself preached equality in worship, declaring that bhakti wholly transcends distinctions of caste, though he also said that final deliverance could be secured only by members of the three upper castes, while for others it must be postponed until a later birth. Ramananda, who in the fourteenth century succeeded to the headship of the order of Ramanujas (followers of Ramanuja), was opposed to all caste distinctions. 'Let no man ask a man's caste or sect,' he said; 'whoever adores God is God's own.'[3] One of his disciples was Kabir, who also rejected caste. The attitude of Nanak was the same. Among Shaivas, the Lingayats were at first strongly opposed to caste, although in the course of time they came to conform to the established system. Their original attitude was shared by many of the leaders of Shaivism.

The rejection of caste distinctions within the bhakti movement and the critical attitude of reformers towards caste as an institution are expressions of the stress on inwardness for which it essentially stands. That emphasis naturally led men to recognize the insufficiency of the external forms of religion, and sometimes to regard those forms as irrelevant or even as a hindrance to the

1. *The Cultural Heritage of India*, II: 159.   2. ibid.
3. Quoted by Radhakrishnan in *Indian Philosophy*, 2nd edition, II: 709.

life of the spirit. What is essential is the love of God, which finds
its natural outcome in the love of our fellow-creatures. Yet it
cannot be said that bhakti has in fact always led to a strongly
ethical emphasis. One writer has remarked that 'there is no
necessary connexion between bhakti and character'.[1] He instances the case of Tirumangai, one of the Alvars, who was 'at
least as unscrupulous after his conversion as before it'. Tirumangai was by birth a member of the thief caste who became a devotee
of Vishnu, and who resorted to brigandage in order to raise the
funds for the building of a temple, and drowned the workmen
when they demanded payment. Such an instance is, indeed, an
extreme example of the divorce, only too common in the history
of all religions, between religious devotion and moral principles.
But unethical conduct such as that of Tirumangai was the outcome of blindness to the nature of the moral ideal which bhakti
involves, itself the result of his peculiar social background, rather
than of any intrinsic separation between devotion and character.
(We are reminded of the barbarities wrought in the name of
Yahweh by ancient Hebrew leaders like Samson or Jael.) The
motive of his evil deeds was not the desire for personal gain or
power. Bhakti involves prapatti – the surrender of self to God –
and so of necessity carries with it a certain purification of motive.
Whether actions done for the glory of God also make for the good
of man depends on the nature of the God who is worshipped. The
writer already quoted says that Vishnu 'is not essentially and
centrally righteous'. Yet in an earlier passage he points out that
'his chief quality is his condescending grace'[2] – in other words,
his boundless goodness to men. For Ramanuja, who was the heir
to the tradition of the Alvars, God was (in words already cited)
'a great boundless Ocean of compassion, benevolence, parental
tenderness, generosity' (see p. 42 above). It is true, as we have
seen, that the deeds of the avatar are not restricted by normal
moral considerations (see p. 55 above), but it is specifically stated
in the Bhagavata Purana that 'those who are not gods should
not commit such deeds, even in thought' (x: 33). Devotion to

1. J. S. M. Hooper in his Introduction to *The Hymns of the Alvars*,
p. 29.
2. ibid.

Krishna does not imply an attempt to imitate his conduct. Moreover, as we have also seen, the love-sports of Krishna are apt to be allegorized – although the endeavour to participate in them has with certain sects given rise to erotic practices. Such practices have played a certain part in the Tantric movement which has affected all varieties of Hinduism and is related especially to the worship of Shakti, the female principle or divine Energy associated with Shiva. 'Tantra' means a system or method or discipline; the word is also employed for the texts in which instructions are given for the use of the particular methods prescribed by a guru for the benefit of his disciples. Tantric religion represents in one aspect a revival of the worship of the Mother Goddess characteristic of aboriginal India. It lays the greatest emphasis on the importance of bodily development as an aid to meditation and as a means of realizing truth. The body is regarded as a microcosm: it contains secret stores of energy which correspond to the secret forces inherent in the universe. The Tantrist seeks to liberate this energy by means particularly of breath-control and the use of mantras or secret words given him by his guru. Divine powers may be projected into the body by a ritual of touch or by the visualization of a divine image. Such methods may be utilized for material ends – the cure of disease, success in love, victory over rivals, the taming of animals, or the making of rain. They may also be employed for spiritual purposes. The body itself, it was sometimes taught, may be transformed and etherealized, and finally may become immutable and divine. Through Tantric techniques men sought to identify themselves with the divine Power which they worshipped, and ultimately with Brahman, manifested as Shakti, the all-Energy of the universe.

The sexual aspect of Tantrism is a single feature of a many-sided movement. What it mainly represents is the religious significance attached to the fact of sex. It does not in general sanction promiscuity; it prescribes, under carefully guarded conditions, the union of a yogin with a yogini, normally his wife, as a symbolical expression of the union of Shiva and Shakti conceived as the source of the bliss which is the very nature of the Absolute, and as affording in itself a means of spiritual growth. The man identifies himself with Shiva and the woman identifies herself with Shakti. It is said that they 'embody a "divine condition" in the sense that they not only experience bliss, but are able to contemplate the ultimate Reality directly'.[1]

The ethical principles of bhakti mysticism are summed up by Tulsi Das. The devotees of Rama, he says, 'desire only devotion to God as the fruit of all their good deeds'; they 'have neither desire nor anger nor pride nor conceit nor delusion'; they 'neither covet nor lament, and are without attachment or aversion'; they 'have neither hypocrisy, arrogance nor deceit'; they 'are loved by all, and are well-wishers of all'; they 'are the same in sorrow and happiness, praise and blame'; they 'speak sweet words of truth'; they 'rejoice to see the prosperity of others, and grieve greatly in their adversity'.[2]

In the Vishnu Purana stress is laid on universal love as the necessary fruit of God-realization. Since God is the supreme Reality underlying all beings, to see our unity with God is to see our unity with all. So it is said that Nidagha 'beheld all beings as the same as himself' (ii: 16). Prahlada states the implications of this identification: 'He who meditates not of wrong to others, but considers them as himself is free from the effects of sin . . . I wish no evil to any, and do speak no offence, for I behold God in all beings, as in my own soul . . . Love for all creatures will be assiduously cherished by all those who are wise, in the knowledge that Hari [Vishnu] is all things' (i: 19).

In the nineteenth century the ethic of identification was the keynote of the teaching of Ramakrishna in its practical aspect. It is said of the saint himself that his sense of unity with others was so intense that a blow given to a man in the street by an enemy left a physical mark on his flesh. 'His nephew saw his back red and inflamed at the sight of a man who was scored with the whip.'[3] Ramakrishna, looking upon all beings as a manifestation of God – as 'God Himself in a particular garb of name and form' – taught that men should cherish towards their fellow-creatures

1. Eliade, *Yoga*, p. 267. See pp. 93-6 below on Tantric Buddhism, and compare the similar element in Taoism (pp. 106, 109ff. below).
2. *The Cultural Heritage of India*, iv: 404f.
3. Romain Rolland, *Prophets of the New India*, pp. 142f.

the devotion and reverence which they cherish towards God. It is this attitude which in recent years has inspired the philanthropic and reforming work of the Ramakrishna Mission. The Mission claims to have introduced into the world 'the novel method of divine worship through the service of suffering humanity as a veritable manifestation of God'.[1]

The attitude of bhakti saints to the external forms of religion has varied considerably. In general they have accepted prevailing forms, while insisting on the supreme necessity of the spirit of faith and love; but sometimes they have rebelled against them. Thus image-worship was commonly approved of as a means of devotion; it owed its place, indeed, to the sectarian religions. The image was worshipped by Vaishnavas as one of the modes of the existence of Vishnu. Yet among both Vaishnavas and Shaivas there were some who were led to protest against the practice. The Maratha saint, Namadeva, denounces 'those who adore a god made of stone ... and who say that a god of stone speaks to his devotees'.[2] We find an equally strong denunciation of idolatry in Shaiva saints like Pillai and Vemana.[3] But it is in Kabir and Nanak that the revolt against the external forms of piety receives its fullest and most thoroughgoing expression. The work of both these reformers arose out of the contact between Hinduism and Islam. Kabir was the son of a Mohammedan, but he became a disciple of Ramananda, who himself, while remaining within the Hindu fold, proclaimed the universal brotherhood of man. An early account of Kabir tells us that 'he held that religion without bhakti was no religion at all, and that asceticism, fasting and almsgiving had no value, if unaccompanied by worship ... He imparted religious instruction to Hindus and Muslims alike. He had no preference for either religion, but gave teaching that was appreciated by the followers of both.'[4] Kabir rejected the externals of both religions, including Hindu mythology and image-worship, the authority of the Vedas and Puranas, and the

1. *The Cultural Heritage of India*, iv: 681.
2. Dasgupta, *Hindu Mysticism*, p. 152.
3. See L. D. Barnett, *The Heart of India*, Chs. 19 and 22.
4. From the *Bhakta Mala* (*Garland of Saints*) by Nabha Das, *c.* A.D. 1600 (Keay, *Kabir and his Followers*, p. 50).

doctrine of avataras. Nanak, who came under his influence, adopted a similar attitude. Like Kabir, he sought to harmonize Hinduism and Islam by dismissing their externals and stressing the principle of bhakti as the one essential. Love and faith, he taught, are the one way to God-realization. In ethical matters one significant point of difference divides the Kabirpanthis (followers of Kabir) from the Sikhs. Kabir laid great emphasis on the principle of ahimsa or non-injury. In the summary of doctrine which forms an authoritative exposition of the teaching of his followers they are bidden to 'consider all creatures as one's own body and life' and to 'regard pain to any living thing as equal to pain given to God'.[1] On the other hand, the Sikhs repudiate the 'non-destruction of life' equally (in the words of Gobind Singh, the tenth guru) with 'pilgrimages, penances and austerities'.[2] It is significant in this connexion that under the stress of persecution Gobind Singh re-shaped the religious community founded by Nanak into an armed nation.

(e) The Goal

It is the essence of bhakti that it is pursued for its own sake, and not for any ulterior motive. The boundless grace of God wins from man a response in adoring and self-giving love. But such devotion has its necessary fruit in the purification of the soul, in its deliverance from the necessity of rebirth. It is universally assumed in India that ignorance and selfish desire alone are responsible for the soul's implication in this necessity. Hindu saints of every creed cry out for salvation from the chains of the samsara – the round of transmigration. They do not in general look upon the world as sheer illusion – as maya in Shankara's sense – although this conception sometimes appears in their songs (notably in the poems of Tulsi Das). But the world, in any case, has for them no abiding or essential reality. 'How can reality be affirmed [asks the Vishnu Purana] of that which is subject to change?' (ii: 12). The one reality is God, and the vision of God, which unites us with Him, is the object of their quest. Bhakti at its highest point is mukti (release). The fire of devotion (as

1. Keay, op. cit., pp. 146, 149.
2. *The Cultural Heritage of India*, iv: 326.

Shandilya says) burns up the sense of 'me' and 'mine', purges the soul of egoism, and brings about release.[1] So in the Vishnu Purana Vishnu tells Prahlada: 'Since thy heart is filled immoveably with trust in Me, thou shalt through my blessing attain deliverance' (i: 20). What does mukti imply? The saints are mystics, who have in present experience enjoyed a foretaste of the final destiny of the soul. Mystical experience is, then, the clue to the nature of the goal. The divergences which exist between them in this matter spring from their differing interpretations of that experience. For some, union with God implies a certain duality; for others it involves identification or absorption. It must be observed that there is no absolute or hard-and-fast distinction between these contrasted conceptions of the goal, since where there is union separateness is in a certain sense overcome, and identification or merging does not necessarily involve a pure undifferentiated unity; within the divine Life there may well be (as in the Bhagavad Gita, see p. 32 above) an eternal distinction of being.

For Ramanuja, as we have seen, mukti is not identity with Brahman, but participation in His qualities. In its union with God the soul preserves its individual distinctness (see p. 46 above). In Tukaram, the most widely popular of the Maratha saints, we have a definite assertion of duality – although it cannot be said that he adheres consistently to this position. 'He who worships God must stand distinct from Him; so only shall he know the joyful love of God. For if he says that God and he are one [i.e. with a pure and simple oneness such as Shankara proclaimed], that joy, that love shall vanish instantly away ... Mother and child are two; if not, where were love? Pray, then, no more for utter oneness with God.'[2] Tukaram goes so far as to ask, almost alone among the saints of India, that he may be born again and again on earth, rather than lose the distinctness of his being, so that he may engage in 'the service of Thy feet, setting us twain, lover and Lord, apart'. Yet this aspiration represents only one phase of the poet's inner life, for (like other Maratha saints) he

1. *The Cultural Heritage of India*, iv: 157.
2. J. S. Hoyland, *An Indian Peasant Mystic*, pp. 19f., quoted by E. C. Dewick in *The Indwelling God*, pp. 49f.

also experienced the identity of the self with God. For other Maratha saints, such as Jnanadeva, it is that sense of identity with God which is the clue to its final destiny; those who are united with God in this life become God after death. For Chaitanya and his followers the twofold character of the saint's experience finds expression in the 'dual-non-dual' nature of the soul (see p. 56 above). Salvation consists in the eternal experience of love. Through love the soul becomes filled with Krishna and absorbed in His being, yet even in this absorption its personal identity remains, since otherwise love could have no reality.

Among Shaiva, just as among Vaishnava saints, there are divergent interpretations of man's final destiny. In his standard exposition of the Shaiva Siddhanta, Meykander uses an analogy familiar from the Upanishads. When impurities cease to affect it, 'the soul, like the union of salt with water, will become united with Shiva as His servant and exist at His feet as one with Him'.[1] Here we have, clearly implied, the doctrine of unity-in-duality. The soul becomes one with Shiva; it is filled, as Shaivas teach, with His glory through His grace descending upon it. In the state of mukti, which may be attained in this life (contrary to the teaching of Ramanuja), the soul attains Shivatva – it is divinized. It preserves its individual identity, but its sense of separateness is done away. It enjoys eternal bliss in union with Shiva and in His service. So Umapati says: 'In supreme felicity thou shalt be one with the Lord ... The soul is not merged in the Supreme, for if they become one (one, that is, without distinction), both disappear; if they remain two, there is no fruition. Therefore there is union and non-union'.[2]

In Kashmir Shaivism, on the other hand, stress is laid on the very metaphor of 'merging' which Umapati repudiates; 'duality' is rejected without qualification. 'When the imagining of duality has vanished, the individual ... is merged in Brahman as water in water, or milk in milk.'[3] In mukti the soul is one with Brahman; but that is not to say that it has no continuing identity within

1. Radhakrishnan, op. cit., II: 730.
2. Macnicol, *Indian Theism*, pp. 169f.
3. Abhinavagupta, quoted in Radhakrishnan, op. cit., II: 734.

His being. Among the later saints of Shaivism we find the same emphasis on non-duality. Speaking of his own mystical experience, Tayumanavar (a saint of the eighteenth century) says: 'He folded me unto Himself, and blended me. . . . He made me Himself . . . Think not in thy heart of Me as other than thee; be thou without second.'[1] The inference is sometimes drawn from such experiences of identification with God that in the ultimate goal the individual being will disappear – as in the Advaita. Thus another Shaiva saint (Tiruvunthiar) says: 'Where the soul stood before, Shiva stands there in all His glory, the soul's individuality being destroyed.'[2] A modern exponent of Shaivism, however, who also speaks of the goal as identification with God, or merging in His infinite Love, draws a different conclusion. 'At the goal, the soul is filled with and enveloped in the love of God. It is then indistinguishable from God, just as a crystal pillar in the rays of the noon-day sun cannot be distinguished from the light . . . It enjoys the inexpressible bliss which knows no change, and in which all thought of lover, love and the beloved is absent . . . The seer, the seen, and the sight become one with Him who makes the seer see.'[3]

For Kabir likewise the goal is absorption in God. 'When the body dies, to what abode shall the pious man's soul go? It shall unite with Him who is beyond expression and indestructible. . . . When the idea of birth and death departs from man's mind, he shall for ever be absorbed in God.'[4] For Kabir also the goal is the reflection of present experience. 'Since my attention is fixed on God, I no longer suspect that I shall suffer transmigration; even in life I am absorbed in the Infinite.'[5] His present experience is that of absorption and the loss of self in God: 'When a stream is lost in the Ganges, it becomes as the Ganges itself; Kabir is similarly lost in God by invoking Him; I have become as the True One, and need not go elsewhere . . . Now Thou and I have become one.'[6] The seer does not say explicitly whether or not the

1. L. D. Barnett, op. cit., pp. 86f.
2. Macnicol, op. cit., p. 179.
3. Shivapadasundaram, *The Shaiva School of Hinduism*, pp. 53f., 132.
4. Keay, op. cit., pp. 88f.   5. ibid., p. 89.   6. ibid., p. 80.

soul retains its personal identity in its final destiny. But he makes it clear from his own words that the 'loss of self' of which he speaks is a loss, not of his essential being, but of the limitations which enchain him. 'They who give up pride of race and attachment ... renouncing the shoot and seed of all desire, these men become freed from body and from space.' For Kabir, as for all the greatest saints, the union and absorption into which he has entered represent, not a mere passing phase of mystical ecstasy, but a true 'spiritual marriage'. 'All my sins have been blotted out, and my soul is absorbed in the Life of the world.'[1] And it is a natural inference that the soul which has, by the grace of God, won such an experience is itself one with Him in an imperishable union.

1. ibid., p. 82.

CHAPTER 3

Buddhist Mysticism

I. THE HINAYANA AND THE MAHAYANA

BUDDHISM arose in India as a heretical movement which rejected the authority of the Vedas. In course of time it came to assume widely differing forms. The main line of division is between what are commonly known as Hinayana and Mahayana Buddhism. The Mahayana grew up in India some centuries after the death of Gotama the Buddha (Shakyamuni) in 483 B.C. It spread to China before the beginning of the Christian era, and at a later time to Japan, Tibet, and Mongolia. 'Mahayana' ('great vehicle' or 'great path') is the name adopted by its adherents in contradistinction to 'Hinayana' ('small vehicle' or 'inferior path'), by which they characterize the religion of other Buddhists. The Hinayana is known by its followers as the 'Theravada' or 'Doctrine of the Elders'.[1] It is the type of Buddhism predominant in India in early centuries, though later supplanted by the Mahayana. Buddhism virtually disappeared from the land of its birth by the tenth century, partly owing to the Muslim conquests. The Hinayana has prevailed traditionally in Burma, Ceylon, Thailand, and Cambodia. Its teaching is represented by the Pali version of the Scriptures, which claims to be the teaching of the founder, as well as by the writings of the exponents of the various Hinayana schools. The Canon of Scripture was not finally fixed until the reign of Ashoka, more than 200 years after the death of Gotama, and it is clear that it embodies the teaching of the predominant party in the Buddhist Order, which cannot be equated with the outlook of the founder himself. Attempts have been made, notably by Mrs Rhys Davids, to reconstruct the actual teaching of the founder, but these are necessarily speculative, and no such endeavour is made here.

There is no hard-and-fast distinction between the Hinayana

1. The Theravada is, strictly, one school of the Hinayana, but the term is also used to cover the whole.

and the Mahayana. In the former there were many different schools, and tendencies fully developed in the Mahayana are found in some of them. Adherents of the two lived together in the same monasteries in India. Mahayanists accept the Pali Scriptures, but maintain that they need to be supplemented by their own Sutras (reputed sayings of the Buddha). Both schools are agreed in accepting the notion, common to all types of developed Indian religion, that man is involved in the round of rebirth, and that his essential need is the 'enlightenment' (bodhi) which brings deliverance (nirvana). The main division between them devolves on the nature and significance of Buddhahood. For the Hinayana the Buddha ('the Enlightened One') is a historical person who attains enlightenment and proclaims the way of salvation to his fellows. As the Buddha he is invested with superhuman qualities, and holds a rank higher than the gods, who are conceived as finite beings subject to the necessity of rebirth. He has gained his stature through countless ages of striving, having been from the first one destined to Buddhahood (a Bodhisattva). In former ages there have been other Buddhas, and in the next age a new Buddha (Maitreya) will arise; each age has one Buddha only. The teaching of the Mahayana stands in striking contrast to this view. The Buddha is in his real essence not a historical person; he is the infinite and eternal Reality which underlies, but immeasurably transcends, the universe. The historical person, Shakyamuni, is the eternal Buddha manifesting Himself to the world, seeking in His boundless wisdom and compassion to lead all beings to the goal. All beings have the Buddha-nature implanted deep within themselves, and all are destined to the attainment of Buddhahood.

II. MYSTICISM IN THE HINAYANA

The Mahayana is a religion of a definitely mystical type. Concerning the Hinayana widely differing views have been held. Bouquet has said that it 'exists mainly as a technique for absorption in the Absolute'.[1] On the other hand, Radhakrishnan declares that its failure to hold its ground in India was due to 'its neglect of the

1. *Comparative Religion*, 1st edition, p. 131.

mystical side of man's nature'.[1] What is the truth of the matter?

(a) Negative Aspect of Hinayana Teaching

Whatever place mystical experience may hold in Hinayana Buddhism, the primary purpose of its teaching is the practical one of bringing salvation from the round of rebirth. 'Just this have I taught,' the Buddha says, 'and this do I teach, ill and the ending of ill' (*Majjhima Nikaya*, I: 140). Individual life is everywhere fraught with suffering, and it is our highest good to recognize the fact and to seek deliverance. The Buddhist of this school is convinced, in the words of Conze, that 'this world is completely and utterly worthless'.[2] That being so, the great object of believers is to secure release. It is the negative aspect of Nirvana with which the Hinayana is primarily concerned. The Buddha is said to have frowned upon speculative discussions with no bearing on deliverance.

Among the questions which Gotama refused to answer on this ground is the problem of the existence of the saint (arahat), who has reached the goal, after death. It would appear to be the logical outcome of Hinayana principles that Nirvana involves the total extinction of our being. It has sometimes been supposed that such extinction is implied in the very use of the term; but it is recognized today that that is a mistake. 'Nirvana' ('Nibbana' in Pali) is 'blowing out': what is blown out is the flame of passion or craving which binds us to life in the samsara (the round of rebirth). When Gotama's disciple Sariputra was asked what Nirvana is, he replied: 'Whatever is the extinction of passion, of aversion, of confusion, this is called Nirvana' (*Samyutta Nikaya*, IV: 251). It is possible, thus, to attain Nirvana in the present life, as the Master himself attained it when he gained supreme enlightenment under the Bo-tree. Such a possibility leaves untouched the question of our final destiny.

(b) The Problem of the Self

According to the Hinayana human personality is a compound of

1. *Indian Philosophy*, 2nd edition, I: 608.
2. *Buddhism, its Essence and Development*, p. 113.

five skandhas – the body, self-consciousness, feeling, perception, mental dispositions or impulses. In the *Questions of King Milinda* (commonly regarded as a Hinayana work of the first century A.D.) man is compared with a chariot, which is made up of wheels, axle, poles, etc. The chariot is all these things put together. So man is an aggregate consisting of the skandhas. This aggregate is always changing. The whole world, including man, is in a state of flux. Things and persons are only a succession of events. Everything is a flux of ephemeral particles or states of consciousness (dharmas). In its application to man this is the doctrine of anatta (non-self) so prominent in Hinayana teaching: there is no self in the sense of an entity (a soul) transcending the different phases of experience and enduring through them. We must 'eradicate the thought, "I am"'; we must 'crush the great "I am" conceit' (*Samyutta Nikaya*, III: 83). Belief in permanent individuality is said to be the first of the 'fetters' which chain us to the round of rebirth (*Digha Nikaya*, III: 234). There is continuity in experience, but no permanent identity.

It is true that this doctrine is not always stated unambiguously, nor is it consistently adhered to. In one passage, indeed, the Buddha declares that he has never heard the view that there is no 'self-agency' – no self in men to actuate their deeds – although elsewhere he says explicitly that we should rid ourselves of the thought 'I am the doer' (*Anguttara Nikaya*, III: 337f., *Samyutta*, II: 252). In one case he explains the difficulty of dealing with the matter unambiguously. He was asked, as he tells Ananda, in so many words, 'Is there a self?' He refused to answer, because if, on the one hand, he had said there is a self, that would have ranked him with the 'Eternalists' – believers, presumably, in the self as an eternal, unchanging reality; if, on the other hand, he had said there is not a self, he would have been regarded as an 'Annihilationist'; his questioner would have taken him to mean that formerly he had a self, but he has none now (*Samyutta*, IV: 400f.). In other passages, as we have seen, he takes a more definitely negative view. 'Neither self nor aught belonging to self [he says] can be accepted.' Consequently the view which declares, 'I shall continue to be in the future, permanent, immutable, eternal, of a nature that knows no change' must be recognized as 'simply and entirely a doctrine of fools' (*Majjhima*, I: 138). Buddhism rejects the notion of self as a persisting individual entity. The way of life for Buddhists is the way of 'self-naughting'; and 'self-naughting' is taken to imply the non-existence of self in the metaphysical sense. Two disciples are recorded as saying to the Master: 'He who has reached enlightenment has utterly destroyed the fetters of becoming. To him who is, by perfect wisdom, emancipated there does not occur the thought that "anyone is better than I or equal to me or less than I".' 'Even so,' the Buddha replied: 'men of the true stamp ... tell what they have gained, but do not speak of "I"' (*Anguttara*, III: 359). In the teaching of the Hinayana the greatest stress is laid on the ethical aspect of 'self-naughting'. It is the aim of Buddhist discipline to conquer self so completely that the thirst or craving (tanha) which leads to rebirth – the will-to-be – shall be rooted out. In spite of the claim of the founder to follow a 'middle path', his teaching is essentially ascetic, while avoiding the extremer types of austerity. In its positive aspect the distinctive feature of Buddhist ethics is the emphasis which is laid on gentleness and sympathy and the love which 'sets free the soul and comprises all good works', and 'gives light and radiance to men' (*Itivuttaka*, III: 7).

The saint does not speak of self; he has renounced the idea of self as a separate principle. Yet the Scriptures affirm in the strongest possible way the fact of personal continuity and responsibility. It is difficult, if not impossible, to justify this emphasis in the light of the analytical view of human personality adopted by Gotama. But, as Poussin says: 'From the beginning Buddhism waged an obstinate war against materialists or unbelievers, the Nastikas, who deny the reward of good actions and the punishment of bad ones in a future life.'[1] To deny survival is a wicked heresy. The sinner is confronted with his individual responsibility. Yama, the judge of the dead, says to the sinner in Hell:[2] 'Your evil deeds were not done by your mother or father or brother or sister, nor by your kinsmen and advisers ... Verily it

1. *The Way to Nirvana*, p. 45.
2. Hell is not conceived as everlasting, but its tortures are depicted in the most lurid terms.

is you alone who have done these evil deeds, and it is you who will suffer the ripening' (*Anguttara*, I: 138). We have here an emphasis on personal identity which can scarcely be reconciled with the repudiation of an enduring self. So also there is a potential continuity of memory, extending over myriads of lives, which in fact implies an actual identity of being. It is one of the distinguishing marks of a Buddha that he remembers his former lives. Buddhism asserts as a fact of experience what its theory does nothing to justify.

Now, it is sometimes said that the anatta doctrine applies only to the personal or finite self, and that the background of Buddhist teaching is in reality the vision of the Universal Self – the Atman of the Upanishads, which is one with Brahman, the ultimate Reality. Buddhist mysticism would in that event be in fact identical, in the form implicit in its teaching, with the mysticism of the Upanishads. In a number of passages Gotama denies that the constituents of personality (the skandhas) can be identified with the self. It is suggested that he is here affirming the greater Self with which man in his inmost being is one. He refers, in one instance, to a man gathering and burning grass and sticks in a grove. 'Would you say [he asks] that this man is gathering or burning us? You would not, and why?' 'Because, lord, this is not our self nor of the nature of self.' So it is, the Buddha concludes, with the factors which make up men's individual being. 'These are not yours; put them away.' They have no more to do with the inmost Self of man (as the words may appear to imply) than the grass and sticks in the wood where he happens to be.[1] In another passage he says of each of the factors of personality in turn that it is 'impermanent, painful, liable to change', and he elicits the assertion that for this very reason it is not fit to be considered as self, and must therefore be disregarded (*Vinaya*, I: 13). Again, Gotama says: 'What is impermanent is ill, what is ill is not the self. What is not self is not mine' (*Samyutta*, III: 83). Such passages would seem to carry with them the implication that there is within us a real Self, which is not to be identified with our immediate personality. In the very formula 'This is not my self', Gotama appears to postulate a Self beyond our personal being –

1. *Majjhima Nikaya*, I: 140ff.

a Self endowed with the very qualities of eternity and changeless bliss which are so plainly absent from the factors of our normal experience. He appears to imply, in other words, the Upanishadic doctrine of the eternal and super-individual Self which is the deepest life of man and which may be known by mystical insight. It is said that in his final exhortation to his followers it was this eternal Self which the Master had in mind: 'Live as those who have the Self as lamp, the Self as refuge, and no other' (*Digha Nikaya*, II: 101). And, again, it is urged that only in the light of this immanent principle can we understand such words as those of the *Dhammapada*: 'Self is the lord of self: Self is the goal of self.'

Yet this interpretation is faced with the most formidable difficulties. The general tenor of the Buddha's teaching is in line with the saying already cited: 'Neither self nor aught belonging to self can really and truly be accepted.' It was naturally impossible for him to adhere consistently to this view at the human level. He was bound to speak of the individual self, while bidding men disregard and deny it. He was stating a familiar fact of experience when he said (according to the *Dhammapada*): 'Evil is done by the self, by the self one comes to grief; evil is left undone by the self, by the self one is purified . . . No one can purify another.' And it may well have been this truth which was the purport of his final message: men must take the self as lamp and refuge, so far as it is enlightened and purified. In one place he spoke of the skandhas as a burden which the individual, the person (pudgala), bears, and which he must lay down by ceasing to grasp it – i.e., by renouncing the craving which makes for rebirth (*Samyutta*, III: 25). There is here an explicit recognition of the fact, constantly implied in his teaching, that there is in us a principle whereby we may conquer and transcend ourselves, and become 'a great self, a dweller in the Immeasurable' (*Anguttara*, I: 249). But this principle is nowhere identified with the Atman of the Upanishads. The great difficulty which stands in the way of that identification – which stands in the way of our supposing that underlying the negative attitude to the skandhas is a positive affirmation of the true self as immutable and eternal – is the absence of any such teaching in Buddhist tradition. As

E. J. Thomas has said: 'Although at Buddha's death his teaching was preserved in the minds of thousands of disciples, we find no trace of it [the Atman doctrine] even as a heresy among the Buddhists.'[1]

There is no indication in the Scriptures that Gotama was acquainted with the Upanishads or their teaching. They may not have been known during his life-time in the area of north-east India in which he lived. Some students have found evidence in the Tevijja Sutta of the *Digha Nikaya* that he pointed to the goal of union with Brahman. Here he is asked, according to one rendering, whether the different paths prescribed by the Brahmins will lead to a state of union with Brahman. He replies, in effect, that it is only the Buddhist way of renunciation and universal love which can lead to that end. 'That a man who is kind and pure in mind and master of himself – that he after death shall become united with Brahman – such a condition of things is every way possible.' If this version is correct, it must, clearly, affect our whole estimate of the Buddha's relation to the message of the Upanishads. The strange thing then would be that the passage stands entirely by itself. But, as Thomas points out, there is no good reason for supposing that the reference is to 'union with Brahman', the absolute and eternal Reality. The phrase so translated may equally mean 'companionship with Brahma' – Brahma being a particular deity, an individual member of the Hindu pantheon, to whom reference is made elsewhere in the Buddhist Scriptures.[2] As has already been mentioned, Gotama believed in the existence of the Hindu gods, but regarded them as beings involved in the samsara. He had himself attained a higher status. It was at Brahma's entreaty that the Buddha overcame his hesitation to preach the gospel, after he had attained enlightenment. 'Companionship with Brahma' is equivalent to life in the heaven of Brahma – a transient state of being, but a stage in the ascent to Nirvana. And the way to reach that heaven, Gotama says, is by the practice of his teaching. Brahman, says Thomas, 'is never mentioned by the Buddhists, nor do they ever discuss the Upanishadic doctrine of becoming identified with it'.[3] P. D. Mehta

1. *History of Buddhist Thought*, 2nd edition, p. 102.
2. ibid., p. 87.   3. ibid.

has maintained that in Canto 26 of the Dhammapada the Buddha speaks of Brahman in the sense of 'a man who has become Brahman'.[1] But it is evident from the context that the meaning here is 'brahmin', a member of the priestly caste. The Master says in effect that the true brahmin is not the man born into that caste, but the saint. 'A man becomes not a brahmin by his plaited hair or by his birth; in whom is truth and righteousness, he is blessed, he a brahmin.'

(c) Inner Training

As the passage just cited indicates, the main emphasis of Hinayana Buddhism is ethical. It aims at the transformation of personality, so that men may be delivered from the fetters which bind them to rebirth. But along with the moral training which this requires, and closely bound up with it, is the practice of a particular type of mental discipline. The essential feature of this discipline is meditation (Sanskrit, dhyana; Pali, jhana), leading to a complete concentration of mind, 'one-pointedness' or absorption (samadhi). Attention is progressively withdrawn from outer things, so that a man may become entirely unconscious of them, and may thus enter into a state of trance (also described as dhyana). It is said that the Buddha was once so absorbed while walking in the open air that he was altogether unconscious of a thunderstorm, in which two farmers were struck by lightning. In samadhi at its highest point the consciousness of self disappears along with that of the outer world. It is the culmination of the Eightfold Path which leads to Nirvana. (The Eightfold Path consists in right understanding, right resolve, right speech, right action, right livelihood, right effort, right meditation or mindfulness, right concentration.) The outcome of samadhi is a tranquillity which renders a man immune to the disturbances of sense. The saint is called 'the tranquil' (samahita). The Scriptures speak of different types of meditation and trance. These are related to the different spheres or planes of being. There are three great spheres of cosmic existence. The first and lowest is kama-loka, the world of desire or sense, which comprises not simply the physical universe, but purgatory and the realm of the lower gods.

1. *Early Indian Religious Thought*, pp. 355f.

Above this is rupa-loka, the world of form, in which there is a subtle residue of matter, so that its occupants possess the powers of sight and hearing, but not the senses of touch, taste, and smell. Beyond this is arupa-loka, the formless world, in which there is no residue of matter, although its inhabitants are still subject to the limitations of cosmic existence, and not yet free from the samsara. Kama-loka is sometimes included in rupa-loka, and we then have a twofold division.

To rise above the level of the sense-world and to enter the world of form, it is necessary to pass through four stages of meditation and trance, and to overcome what are known as the five 'hindrances' – craving, ill-will, sloth, restless brooding, doubt or perplexity. In the first stage meditation may be exercised on the impurities of the body or on love, compassion, sympathy with the joy of others. At this stage there is conscious reflection and analysis. Through the sense of detachment from desire and all that is evil the mind is filled with joy, and the disciple experiences rapture. Next verbal thinking is abandoned, while the state of joy remains. In the third jhana joy, being impermanent, is left behind, but happiness is felt. Finally the sensation of happiness disappears, and is replaced by serenity or indifference to pleasure and pain; the mind is purified and cleansed.

The Rupa Jhanas have been described as 'mystic raptures'. Yet in the account of them given in the Scriptures there is no indication of mysticism in the proper sense. The distinctive feature of mystical experience is the consciousness of the Transcendent – the immediate awareness of supreme Reality. The four trances may, indeed, lead to a higher plane of being, but their characteristic quality is subjective – a state of feeling rather than an awareness of the Beyond. The four Rupa Jhanas are succeeded by certain exceedingly subtle states of consciousness corresponding to the planes of the formless world. The adept rises successively to the perception of the infinity of space (beyond plurality and finite materiality), the perception of the infinity of consciousness, the perception of nothingness (where there is no idea or object in mind), and the stage of neither consciousness nor non-consciousness (neither presence nor absence of ideas). It is held that thus men enter into contact with the different phases of a transcendent realm of being – the formless world. Through the practice of trance they are said to attain certain supernormal faculties – the power, for instance, of creating a 'mind-formed' body, which may appear wherever they desire, the power of hearing distant sounds and of reading the minds of others, the memory of one's own past lives, the power to read the history of other beings – to see their passing away and rebirth. Such things are not stressed in the Scriptures; they are regarded as a by-product of meditation. Their significance is this: they illustrate the growth in man, through inner training, of a power and a consciousness transcending the range of normal personality.

(d) Nirvana

The four stages of formless trance do not of themselves lead to Nirvana. The formless world is not ultimate. Craving for life in that world is a fetter from which men must seek release. In the *Udana*, Nirvana is described as a plane not only beyond the level of physical experience, but beyond the plane of infinite space, of infinite consciousness, of nothingness, and of neither consciousness nor non-consciousness. But it is evident that Nirvana is itself a sphere of being which is, at least, comparable with these. For the Buddha says in one passage that if, passing beyond the formless planes, a monk 'enters into and abides in the stage of the cessation of perception and feeling – which transcends all empirical consciousness – he has now crossed over the entanglement in the world, and is one who has made Mara [the evil spirit] blind, and goes unseen by the Malign One' (*Majjhima*, 1: 160). This is evidently the final attainment. It is said that on the last night of his life the Buddha himself, having passed through the four Rupa Jhanas, and the four Arupa Jhanas, entered this plane of being. He says himself, referring, no doubt, to his own experience of enlightenment under the Bo-tree: 'I reached in experience the Nirvana which is unborn, unrivalled, secure from attachment, undecaying, and unstained. This condition is indeed reached by me which is deep, difficult to see, difficult to understand, tranquil, excellent, beyond the reach of mere logic, subtle, and to be realized only by the wise' (1: 167).

It is in the experience of Nirvana that we have the core of Buddhist mysticism. There is no sense of union with the divine, as in Hindu mysticism, but there is an immediate apprehension of supreme Reality. As Buddhaghosha says in his exposition of Hinayana teaching, Nirvana is 'attainable by means of the special cognition perfected by unfailing effort' (*Visuddhimagga*, 509). In the words of another Hinayana writing, it can be 'seen' by the perfected disciple, although like the wind it cannot be 'shown by colour or configuration' (*Questions of King Milinda*, 271). Nirvana is itself the ultimate Reality, which lies altogether beyond the sphere of compounded and perishable things. As the Buddha says in a crucial passage: 'There is an unborn, not become, not made, uncompounded; and were it not for this unborn, not become, not made, uncompounded, no escape could be shown here for what is born, has become, is made, is compounded' (*Udana*, 81). Nirvana is thus not merely a subjective state of consciousness, not merely an awareness of deliverance from the things that make for rebirth; it is the ultimate Reality beyond all worlds.[1] Since Nirvana lies beyond the sphere of finite things, its nature is utterly inconceivable; it transcends the reach of human thought. It is only through the experience of Nirvana that its nature can be known. Early Buddhism makes no attempt whatsoever to characterize the ultimate, save in negative terms. Yet the implication of these negative terms is that Nirvana is in itself a supreme positive Reality, ineffable because it transcends all that is finite.

A clear indication of the positive quality of Nirvana lies in the account given in the Scriptures of the nature of the saint who attains it. The Buddha sometimes refuses to say whether the man who enters Nirvana exists or does not exist after death. This, he says, is an unprofitable question which does not conduce to 'tranquillity, insight, enlightenment' (*Majjhima*, I: 431). Elsewhere, however, a different reason is given for his silence on this

1. This view was not universally accepted in the Hinayana. Its adherents were divided into different schools, which emphasized different aspects of the tradition. The deeper and more mystical phases of the tradition were sometimes ignored. Thus the Sautrantikas held that Nirvana was not to be regarded as a positive reality, but simply as the cessation of personal existence.

issue. In entering Nirvana a man is freed from the skandhas – the constituents of finite personality – and to such a man the conception of existence or non-existence does not apply. Just as it is futile to ask in what direction a fire has gone when it is extinguished, so it is useless to ask (as Gotama was asked) where a man who is 'freed in heart' arises (i.e., where he is reborn). It is only through the skandhas that a man is known to others, but one in whom these things are utterly done away is beyond the reach of knowledge. He is 'profound, measureless, unfathomable like the great ocean' (I: 486f.). The Buddha says, again, in a dialogue: 'As a flame blown out by the wind disappears and cannot be named, even so the recluse, when released from name and form, disappears and cannot be named.' 'He who has disappeared,' his interlocutor rejoins, 'is he non-existent, or is he free from sickness in perpetuity?' The Buddha replies: 'No measuring is there of him who has disappeared whereby one might know of him that he is not; when all qualities are removed, all modes of speech are removed also' (*Sutta Nipata*, 1073–5). To enter Nirvana is to pass beyond the categories of human thought and language – to enter the sphere of absolute and eternal Reality. What is true of the saint after death is equally true of him in the present life. Such a man 'is incomprehensible even when he is actually present' (*Samyutta*, III: 118). He is incomprehensible because he has even now passed beyond the limitations of finite being; he has transcended the skandhas by which alone his being can be defined. It cannot be said that he is distinct from the skandhas, since his body, his feelings, his personal consciousness still exist. Nor can it be said that he is comprised in the skandhas, for he is no longer limited by them. It is impossible therefore on normal assumptions to 'make out and establish the existence of the saint in the present life'. The man who has entered Nirvana 'cannot be held to be perceived as existing in truth and reality even in this life' (III: 109). By his participation in Nirvana the saint has passed into a new dimension of being which surpasses the range of human knowledge.

The mystical aspect of Buddhism is closely bound up with its ethical discipline. Nirvana involves the extinction of the sense of separate individuality and a complete detachment from the sphere of finite things. The practice of meditation and trance serves to foster this sense of detachment. But, however great the emphasis on negation and detachment, there is a positive aim in view. A recent writer, who has come in touch with all types of Buddhists, assures us that he has found that in every quarter 'Nirvana means "*summum bonum*", the highest good and the highest form of life', and that in its metaphysical aspect it 'corresponds to the mystical Satya Satyam, "the reality within reality", of the Hindus'.[1] Through meditation and trance the aspirant is brought into contact with progressively higher planes of being, and finally he attains the mystical vision of Nirvana. In that vision his being is wholly transformed. While there is no sense of union with the divine, conceived in terms of personality or super-personality, there is an immediate apprehension of the Transcendent and a participation in its nature, whereby the individual is freed from finitude and becomes 'profound, measureless, unfathomable'. His being remains, but (as Suso says of the Christian mystic) 'in another form, in another glory, in another power'. The Buddhist saint, like the Christian, is thus in effect finally transformed in union with supreme and ultimate Reality.

III. THE MYSTICISM OF THE MAHAYANA

(a) *The Philosophy of the Mahayana*

It has been pointed out in our introductory section to the present chapter that, while there is no absolute division between the two main types of Buddhism, since elements of the Mahayana are found in various Hinayana schools, the two are yet marked by a far-reaching difference of outlook. In its practical aspect this found expression in the prevalence in the Mahayana of the ideal of the Bodhisattva, who seeks to bring salvation to all beings, as opposed to that of the arahat, who finds salvation for himself alone. But the rise of the new ethical ideal did not stand by itself; it was attended by the growth of a new attitude to the universe and a new vision of reality.

In the philosophy of the Mahayana there are two main schools. It is fundamental to both that the world as it exists in time and

1. Reichelt, *Meditation and Piety in the Far East*, pp. 72f.

space is essentially illusory. Buddhism anticipates the maya doctrine of Shankara. The outlook of the Hinayana is a species of 'realism'; it does not question the reality of the world as we know it, while it emphasizes its transience. The Mahayana, on the other hand, challenges not merely the permanence, but the assumed reality, of the physical universe. This challenge is made in one of the earliest collections of Mahayana sutras (sayings attributed to the Buddha), the *Prajna Paramita* ('Perfect Wisdom'). 'All composite things are like a dream, a phantasm, a bubble and a shadow, are like a dewdrop and a flash of lightning.'[1] The sutra proclaims the doctrine of the Void (Sunya), which became the keyword of the Madhyamika philosophy, systematized by Nagarjuna in the second century A.D. (Madhyamikas are literally 'followers of the Middle Way' between existence and non-existence, affirmation and denial, realism and scepticism.) The Void has two aspects. It indicates first the unreality or emptiness of the whole range of finite experience. The world is void in the sense that it is denuded of real being. In reality there is no transmigration and no awakening, no decay or death, no obtaining of Nirvana. Real being lies beyond the sphere of time and change. It is the Void since it is empty of all assignable qualities – there is nothing that we can truly say about it; thought and language have no application to it. 'The Void of the Eastern mystic,' says Otto, 'like the Nothing of the Western mystic, is a numinous ideogram of the "wholly other". Nothing can be said of it, since it is intrinsically other than, and opposite to, everything that is and can be thought.'[2] Sunya is a new expression of the ineffable Reality described by the Buddha as Nirvana. It is indeed identified with Nirvana. In one version of the Prajna Paramita Sutra it is said to be 'the synonym of that which has no cause, that which is beyond thought or conception, that which is not produced, that which is not born, that which is beyond measure'.[3] As with Nirvana in the Hinayana, Sunya can be

1. B. L. Suzuki, *Mahayana Buddhism*, 1st edition, p. 100. The words quoted are the final verse of the *Diamond Sutra*, the most popular version of the Paramita. See E. Conze, *Buddhist Wisdom Books*.
2. *The Idea of the Holy*, 4th edition, p. 30.
3. Radhakrishnan, *Indian Philosophy*, 2nd edition, I: 663.

apprehended only by mystical intuition (prajna). 'The eye does
not see', says Nagarjuna, 'and the mind does not think [in face,
i.e., of supreme Reality]; this is the highest truth, wherein men
do not enter. The land wherein the full vision of all objects is
attained at once has by the Buddha been called the paramartha
[absolute truth], which cannot be preached in words' (*Madhyamika Sutras*, Ch. 3).[1]

The other leading school of thought in the Mahayana is the
Yogachara, which has been for many centuries the dominant
type of Mahayanist philosophy. Its teaching goes back, like that
of the Madhyamika, to certain relatively early sutras. It was
expounded and elaborated in the fifth century by two brothers,
Asanga and Vasubandhu. The Yogacharas accept the doctrine of
the Void. They describe the Absolute as Bhutatathata or Tathata
– 'Suchness', that which is such as it is, i.e., that which cannot be
compared with anything else. Like the Void, Suchness is best
described by negatives. It is above existence and non-existence
it is neither unity nor plurality as we know it. Yet in its essential
nature it is real and eternal. It is said to be 'the effulgence of great
wisdom, the illumination of the universe, the mind pure in its
nature, eternal, calm, free'.[2]

It is the distinctive tenet of the Yogacharas that the ultimate
Reality affirms itself as Mind – not mind as we know it in our
normal experience, with its separation of the knowing self and
the object which is known, but Mind as lying beyond this distinction, pure consciousness in its unbroken unity, the highest or
perfect knowledge beyond all limitations of time and space. This
Universal Mind is described as the 'Store-Consciousness' (Alaya-
vijnana). In Yogachara philosophy there is, however, a certain
inconsistency. While it identifies the Store-Consciousness with
Suchness, on the one hand, it is apt also to identify it with the
consciousness of the individual, and to explain the world of
experience from this standpoint. It thus gives rise to a variety of
subjective Idealism. 'All things [it is said] exist only in the mind' –
as they are known or perceived. The illusion of multiplicity arises
from 'our confused subjectivity'. 'If we could overcome our
confused subjectivity, the signs of individuation would disappear,

1. ibid., pp. 662f.   2. Keith, *Buddhist Philosophy*, p. 255.

and there would be no trace of a world of individual and isolated objects'.[1] It is simply our ignorance, our lack of insight or true knowledge (avidya), which causes us to imagine that there really is a world broken up into separate things and persons. To see things truly is to see them in their unbroken unity in the Absolute. The Mahayana maintains the doctrine of anatta, fundamental in the Hinayana, but it re-interprets this doctrine in a positive sense. It teaches that there is no self peculiar to individuals, but only one true Self, the Absolute. From the standpoint of the Yogacharas, however, ignorance is not a factor existing solely in finite individuals. It is something which mysteriously affects the eternal Being, existing potentially in its nature. In itself the Tathata is non-dualistic; subject and object are merged in absolute oneness in its being. This absolute oneness comes to be differentiated through the operation of the negative principle of avidya, which brings about the distinction between subject and object, knower and known, mind and Nature. The Yogachara philosophy, unlike the Madhyamika, seeks to bring the world of normal experience into some kind of relation to the realm of absolute Reality. It seeks to explain how the appearance of birth and death, time and change and multiplicity, arises out of the unbroken unity of the Eternal. 'When the Mind remains in and with itself [says Ashvaghosha], it is the great light of knowledge [prajna]. When it moves [i.e., to perceive things as external to itself], its knowledge ceases to be true, as it deviates from itself; it is then neither eternal nor blissful, nor free from defilement. On the contrary, it burns, it suffers pain, it becomes subject to decay and change.'[2]

Yet in the last resort this very 'movement' is itself unreal. We and all things 'abide in the self-sameness of the One Mind'.

(b) The Eternal Buddha

The leading conceptions of the Mahayana schools are attempts to give expression in philosophical terms to the supreme Reality, the 'eternal Buddha', the thought of which is fundamental to

1. *The Awakening of Faith in the Mahayana* (translated D. T. Suzuki), p. 56. *The Awakening of Faith* is an early Mahayana treatise by Ashvaghosha.

2. B. L. Suzuki's translation in *Mahayana Buddhism*, 1st edition, p. 34.

Mahayana religion. It was felt at an early time that the essential
characteristic of the founder of Buddhism was his enlightenment,
his knowledge, his vision of truth. In the Pali Scriptures it is
taught in some late passages that Gotama is omniscient.[1] In the
Mahayana it came to be believed that the knowledge or wisdom
(bodhi) which is the essential quality of the historical teacher
pertains to the heart of Reality itself. The Buddha-nature
(buddhata) is the supreme Reality which underlies and includes
all things. It is known as the Dharmakaya (the body of truth or
reality).[2]

In the Mahayana the Dharmakaya is both the supra-personal
Absolute, beyond the range of thought, and the supreme and
all-embracing Personality, revealed not only in the wisdom of the
historical Buddhas, but in their boundless love and compassion.
Some of the finest passages in Mahayana literature are written in
praise of this divine Reality. The Dharmakaya is at once immanent in all beings as their deepest nature, and transcendent to
them as the infinite Spirit of wisdom and compassion. It is the
Love which flows out to all beings, and leads all beings to their
goal, and at the same time identifies itself with all beings, and
includes them within itself. 'All things in the universe', says the
Surangama Sutra, 'are but the excellently bright and powerful
Heart of Bodhi ... This Heart is universally diffused, and com-
prehends all things within itself. ... Pervading all things, present
in every minutest hair, it includes the infinite worlds in its embrace.
Enthroned in the minutest particle of dust, it turns the great wheel
of the Law.'[3]

The vision of the Dharmakaya provides the clue to the true
nature of all beings. In the Dharmakaya all beings are united.
The way which leads us to the Dharmakaya thus leads to the
sense of unity with our fellow-creatures. The ethic of universal
love is an essential aspect of Mahayana mysticism. 'The tenderness that the sons of the Conquerors [the Bodhisattvas] feel for

1. See Thomas, *History of Buddhist Thought*, 2nd edition, pp. 148-50.
2. In the Hinayana, *dharma* (Pali *dhamma*) is on the one hand 'code',
'law', 'teaching', on the other hand 'thing' or 'entity'; dharmakaya is
simply 'the body of doctrine'.
3. Beal, *Catena of Buddhist Scriptures from the Chinese*, pp. 343, 352f.

all creatures,' says Asanga, 'their love, their indefatigability –
this is the marvel of all the worlds. But no! It is no marvel, since
other and self are for them identical.'[1] The thought of the identity
of all beings in the Dharmakaya, and so of their mutual interpenetration, finds particular emphasis in the Kegon and T'ien-tai
schools of Chinese Buddhism. A special feature of the T'ien-tai
school is the ceremony of initiation into the oneness of life.
The Dharmakaya is one aspect of the Trikaya (sometimes
called the Buddhist Trinity). The other aspects are the Nirmanakaya ('the Body of Manifestation or Transformation') and the
Sambhogakaya ('the Body of Bliss or Glory'). The Nirmanakaya
is the eternal Buddha in his historical manifestation. Prior to the
rise of the Mahayana it came to be held among a section of
believers – the Mahasanghikas (men of the Great Company) –
that the Buddha was a supernatural Person, of unlimited power
and knowledge, who knew all things immediately without the
aid of sense-organs. What men saw as his body was a mind-formed
image, by which he worked for their good. This Docetic view
prevailed in the Mahayana. The eternal Buddha, it was taught,
projects into the world from time to time apparitional bodies to
do His work. This doctrine is taught in one of the earliest and
most popular and influential of Mahayana writings – *The Lotus
of the Wonderful Law* (*Saddharma-Pundarika*). There Shakyamuni declares: 'I am the Father of the world, the self-born, the
Healer, the Protector of all creatures. Knowing them to be perverted, infatuated and ignorant, I teach final rest.'[2] Shakyamuni
proclaims a doctrine of continually renewed incarnation (or
appearance) which is identical with the teaching of the *Bhagavad
Gita* (see p. 33 above). The eternal Buddha appears on earth to
lead men to enlightenment, 'when men become unbelieving,
unwise, ignorant ... and from thoughtlessness run into misfortune'. The manifestation is made to the unenlightened in all
ages; Shakyamuni belongs to an infinite succession of Buddhas.
In the sutras the Buddhas are presented as preaching, not only to
men, but to great assemblies of Bodhisattvas and gods in higher

1. *Mahayana-Sutralamkara*, Lévi's translation, p. 170 (quoted by Pratt,
The Pilgrimage of Buddhism, p. 257).
2. *Sacred Books of the East*, XXI: 309f.

spheres. There they reveal themselves in the Sambhogakaya – a supernatural body emitting rays of light, the primary reflex of the Dharmakaya. 'The Body of Bliss', says Ashvaghosha, 'is infinite, boundless, limitless. ... It embraces infinite attributes of bliss and merit.'[1]

(c) *The Bodhisattvas*

The spiritual ideal of the Mahayana is rooted in its vision of reality. The Buddha-nature lies at the heart of all beings, and all are destined in the course of ages to enter into the realization of it. The true way of life is the endeavour to attain this realization. But those who are consciously aiming at Buddhahood differ enormously among themselves. The term 'Bodhisattva' is used not only of those who have entered upon the path, but also specifically of those who have advanced far towards the goal, and have thus transcended the limitations of humanity. In this sense Bodhisattvas are heavenly beings who have gained the highest degree of wisdom, power, and blessedness which is possible to those who are still finite. They have delayed their entrance into Nirvana – which lies beyond the sphere of the finite – in order to continue their work as guides and helpers of mankind. They have therefore become objects of devotion and worship, to whom men look both for spiritual and for material benefits. In this way the principle of bhakti (see pp. 44ff. above) was introduced into Buddhism. The idea of the heavenly Bodhisattvas provided the basis for the development of an elaborate mythology and an ornate ceremonial, including the offering of flowers and the burning of incense.

A Bodhisattva is literally 'a being whose essence is bodhi [enlightenment]'. Bodhi or Bodhichitta ('heart of enlightenment') is an expression of the Dharmakaya in human consciousness. It corresponds broadly to the Holy Spirit or the divine grace in Christian teaching. It is present in all beings, but it is active only in and through the Buddhas and Bodhisattvas. Like the Holy Spirit in Christian thought, it is the source of all virtues. The Buddhas and Bodhisattvas are themselves a means whereby its grace is transmitted to men. In many Mahayana writings

1. *The Awakening of Faith*, pp. 101f.

consideration is given to the question how the Bodhichitta dormant in our nature may be awakened. In his *Discourse on the Awakening of the Bodhichitta*, Vasubandhu says that we can achieve that end by thinking of the Buddhas and following their example; by observing the sufferings and infirmities of our fellow-creatures; by aspiring after the virtues of the Buddhas, their fearlessness, their compassion, their love for suffering beings.[1]

In seeking after Buddhahood men are inspired and sustained by the indwelling power of Bodhichitta. For the Mahayana the great evil is the self-love which isolates us, and blinds us to our unity with others in the Dharmakaya. Whether through our own efforts, or through the influence and help of the heavenly Saviours, it is the eternal Buddha who alone can deliver us from our narrowness and egoism. In the words of one of the greatest of the Mahayana Scriptures, the *Avatamsaka Sutra* (which has been especially influential in China): 'The Dharmakaya benefits us through its great compassionate Heart, which saves and protects all beings. It benefits us through its great loving Heart, which delivers all beings from the misery of birth and death . . . It benefits us with an aspiration whereby we are enabled to practise all that constitutes Buddhahood.'[2]

In Pure Land Buddhism, which had its beginning in India, but received its most notable development in China and Japan, we have an outstanding illustration both of the mythological aspect of the Bodhisattva doctrine and of the stress on divine grace as the necessary means of salvation. The Pure Land school is today the most vital factor in Japanese Buddhism. It finds its centre in the worship of Amitabha or Amitayus (Japanese 'Amida') – the Buddha of Infinite Light and Life. Associated with him is the Bodhisattva Avalokiteshvara ('the Regarder of the Cries of the World'), worshipped in China as Kuan-Yin (Japanese 'Kwannon'), the goddess of mercy. In a distant age Amitabha lived on earth as the monk Dharmakara, who vowed that he would devote himself wholly to the saving of others, and so would establish the Heaven or Pure Land, Sukhavati, where he now dwells with Avalokiteshvara in his body of glory. There

1. D. T. Suzuki, *Outlines of Mahayana Buddhism*, pp. 303-6.
2. ibid., p. 227.

he receives those who call upon his name in faith, and are thus united with him, participating in his infinite wisdom and love. In the Pure Land the soul is progressively purified, and by the grace of Amitabha moves on to the ultimate realization of Buddhahood, free from the hindrances of earthly life.

The invocation of the name of Amitabha plays an essential part in Pure Land Buddhism. The adherents of the doctrine emphasize the weakness and sinfulness of man. All men's works, even though they are considered morally good, are contaminated as long as they spring from self. 'Recognizing the complete impotence of our own power,' says a modern teacher, 'we must put our trust alone in the help of another's power, offered us in the original resolve of Amida. When we do so, we enter into Buddha's knowledge and are filled with his great compassion.'[1] Amida, it must be remembered, is not merely the Buddha in a particular historical manifestation or in his glorified form in the Pure Land; he is the absolute and eternal Buddha whose indwelling life saves us from ourselves. To have faith in Amida is to quicken the Buddha-nature within us. The formula Namu-Amida-Butsu ('Adoration to Amida Buddha') is not only an expression of homage and devotion to Amida, because he has made it possible for men to be born in his Pure Land; it serves also (as Suzuki has shown in a recent work, *Mysticism, Christian and Buddhist*) to symbolize the union of the devotee in all his sinfulness with the Buddha of Infinite Light and Life. 'Namu' is said to stand for the devotee as he is, so that in the act of invocation he is mystically united with Amida, and duality is done away. 'This, however, does not indicate that the devotee is lost or absorbed in Amida ... The namu has not vanished. It is there as if it were not there ... The mystery is called the incomprehensibility of Buddha-wisdom.'[2] In the Shin Buddhism of Japan, as in some forms of the bhakti mysticism of the Hindus, it is recognized that the truth lies both in union and in non-union.

In the Mahayana there is a radical re-orientation of the religious life. To enter upon the path of the Bodhisattva, a man

1. Quoted by G. F. Moore, *The History of Religions*, I: 134.
2. op. cit., p. 162.

must take certain vows. He must resolve, in particular, to save all beings, to destroy his own evil passions, to learn the truth and teach it to others, and to lead all beings towards Buddhahood. He must practise the six virtues of perfection (paramitas) – generosity or charity, moral conduct, patience and forbearance (anger is the greatest of sins), strenuous endeavour, meditation, and wisdom or intuitive knowledge. The fundamental feature of the ideal of the Bodhisattva is compassion and self-giving. 'Mahakaruna' ('the great compassionate Heart of the Buddha') becomes the actuating principle of his life. 'The fair tree of thought that knows no duality bears the flower and fruit of compassion, and its name is service of others.'[1] Through compassion and self-giving we affirm our inner unity in the Dharmakaya with all beings. The ethics of the Mahayana is the ethics of identification. 'By constant use,' says Shantideva, 'man comes to imagine that his body, which has no self-being, is a self: why then should he not conceive his self to lie in his fellows also? ... If thou lovest thyself, thou must have no love of self; if thou wouldst save thyself, thou dost not well to be saving of self.'[2]

Shantideva's work, written in India in the seventh century, is one of the classics of Mahayanist literature. It gives eloquent expression to the aspiration of the Bodhisattva: 'I would fain become a soother of all the sorrows of all creatures ... My own being and my pleasures, all my righteousness in the past, present, and future, I surrender indifferently, that all creatures may win to their end.'[3] The author bids the Bodhisattva 'Make thine own self bear the sorrow of thy fellows' and 'cast upon its head the guilt even of others' works'.[4] We are to identify ourselves with our fellows in their sufferings and in their very sins. Here is a strikingly new development in the ethics of Buddhism. In the Hinayana, while the principle of universal love is proclaimed and self is denied as a separative factor, suffering and guilt are alike conceived in terms of a strict moral individualism. Suffering is

1. From Saraha's *Treasury of Songs* in *Buddhist Texts through the Ages*, edited by E. Conze, p. 238.
2. *The Path of Light* (Barnett's translation of part of the *Bodhicharyavatara*), pp. 89f.
3. ibid., pp. 44f.   4. ibid., p. 89.

considered purely as a retributive factor – as the penalty of wrong. In the Mahayana it becomes a means of spiritual growth; it is conceived as an opportunity to cherish patience and forbearance. But above all, through the mystical insight of the Mahayana – through its vision of the all-inclusive life and the all-embracing love of the Dharmakaya – there arises the sense of the unity and solidarity of all beings in the experience both of good and of evil. 'The sickness of a Bodhisattva [it is said in the Vimala-kirti Sutra] exists in the time of ignorance, which is possessed by every being. When the sickness of every being is ended, then my sickness will also end. I am sick because beings are sick.'[1] Men share the destiny of their fellows; they suffer because of the ignorance and blindness of mankind. Goodness likewise becomes essentially vicarious or redemptive. This fact finds expression particularly in the conception of parinamana – the transference of the merit due to one's own good deeds for the benefit of others. 'All the meritorious deeds practised by the Bodhisattvas are dedicated to the emancipation of ignorant beings.'[2] As we have seen from Shantideva, the Bodhisattva consecrates the whole endeavour of his life to bring help and blessing to his fellow-creatures. We are so closely bound up with others in the unity of being that all we do and are inevitably affects them for good or ill, and the Bodhisattva is resolved to use all his powers solely for the blessing and salvation of others.

(d) Nirvana

The Mahayana brings with it a new understanding of Nirvana. In the Hinayana, as we have seen, Nirvana stands primarily for deliverance from rebirth, which is the goal of life, and so for the conquest of egoism which makes deliverance possible; it stands also for the uncompounded state of being, the ultimate Reality, which the saint apprehends and into which he enters. In the light of the new philosophy and the new ethical ideal of the Mahayana, the meaning of Nirvana and its relation to the world of birth and death are transformed. The goal of life is the attainment of enlightenment (bodhi), which is the realization of the

1. B. L. Suzuki, *Mahayana Buddhism*, 1st edition, p. 111.
2. D. T. Suzuki, *Mahayana Buddhism*, p. 285.

eternal Buddha-nature present in all beings. This is Nirvana. According to Ashvaghosha, Nirvana is 'the annihilation of the ego-conception, freedom from subjectivity, insight into the essence of Suchness, the recognition of the oneness of existence'.[1] In this aspect Nirvana has been described as 'the realization of infinite love and infinite wisdom'.[2] But this 'infinite love and infinite wisdom' which man may attain is itself the heart of reality; it is the eternal Buddha, the Dharmakaya. Nirvana is thus identified with ultimate Reality; it is the Buddha-nature, which is the essence of all things. 'All things from the beginning are in their nature Nirvana itself.'[3] Once realization comes, the illusions of time and space and separation will lose their hold upon us; we shall see that eternally we are the Buddha, eternally we are in Nirvana.

Stress on the enlightenment which brings Nirvana is specially characteristic of the Zen school of Far Eastern Buddhism. 'Zen' (Chinese 'Ch'an') is the Japanese equivalent of the Sanskrit dhyana (meditation). (See p. 75 above.) The sect so described was introduced from India into China in the sixth century, and was established in Japan at the beginning of the thirteenth century. Its influence is rivalled in the Far East only by the Pure Land school. As its name indicates, it emphasizes the practice of meditation, which culminates in a sudden flash of mystical illumination. 'Look inward,' said a Zen master, 'and in a flash you will conquer the apparent and the Void.'[4] The distinctive method of Zen is the use of a riddle (Japanese 'koan') by the teachers as a means of stimulating the mind of their disciples, and so leading them to the goal. In their concentration on such practices some branches of Zen neglect the study of the Scriptures and the accepted rules of moral discipline. It has been suggested that it was for this reason that Zen became the religion of the samurai or warrior class in Japan. Laymen sometimes retire for a period to a Zen monastery to learn the art of meditation. Owing to its stress on individual effort in the achievement of salvation

1. D. T. Suzuki, *The Awakening of Faith*, p. 87, n. 2.
2. R. Mukerjee, *The Art and Theory of Mysticism*, pp. 79f.
3. *The Awakening of Faith*, p. 121.
4. *Buddhist Texts through the Ages*, p. 296.

Zen is known as the way of 'self-power', in contradistinction to the 'other-power' of Amidism. Yet the distinction is relative, not absolute. As we have seen, the devotee in this latter school identifies himself with Amida, while in Zen 'self-power' is simply a means of bringing into manifestation the deeper reality inherent in his being. We cannot command enlightenment, for it is the uprising of the eternal Buddha within us. 'If you wish to seek the Buddha,' says a Zen teacher, 'you ought to see into your own nature, for this nature is the Buddha Himself.'[1]

What is most distinctive of the Mahayana is its reinterpretation of the relation between Nirvana and the samsara. Since Nirvana is the realm of absolute Reality, it is the Reality underlying the world of birth and death. Nirvana and samsara are not, therefore, to be regarded as two opposed spheres of being; the essence of samsara is the essence of Nirvana. This realization finds expression in what is described as 'the Nirvana that has no abode'. A man who has attained this state is said to have no abode, because through his experience of enlightenment he has risen above the samsara, yet he does not cling to Nirvana in the traditional sense – as complete and final rest. He is above samsara and above Nirvana as traditionally understood. It is his one object to bring help and blessing to his fellow-creatures. For him Nirvana is 'a realization in this life of the all-embracing love and all-knowing intelligence of the Dharmakaya'.[2] The Mahayanist teacher Devala brings the two conceptions of Nirvana into explicit contrast. 'Those who are afraid of transmigration, and seek their own benefit and happiness in final emancipation, are not at all comparable to those Bodhisattvas who rejoice when they come to assume a material existence once again, for it affords them another opportunity to benefit others. ... Nirvana, in truth, consists in rejoicing at others being made happy, and samsara is not so feeling. He who feels a universal love for his fellow-creatures will rejoice in distributing blessings among them, and will find Nirvana in so doing.'[3]

In comparison with the teaching of the Hinayana we have

1. D. T. Suzuki, *Essays in Zen Buddhism*, 1: 219f.
2. D. T. Suzuki, *Outlines of Mahayana Buddhism*, p. 349.
3. ibid., p. 364.

here a truly revolutionary change of attitude to Nirvana and to the world. We are to find Nirvana in an active love of our fellows – the realization of the infinite love of the Dharmakaya – and we are to rejoice in the opportunity of such love which material life affords. Yet the Mahayana teaches us to regard the whole world of normal experience as an unsubstantial mirage. How far are the two attitudes compatible? Reconciliation may perhaps be found, partially at least, in the thought of interpenetration rather than bare abstract unity as the distinguishing feature of the realm of real being which is Nirvana. The multiplicity which is the outcome of ignorance is the multiplicity of separate and external objects and persons. In the real universe all things are one in the all-inclusive Heart of Bodhi. So Ashvaghosha says that 'all beings are from all eternity ever abiding in Nirvana' (*The Awakening of Faith*, p. 74). In entering Nirvana we lose our separateness, but we attain an infinite expansion of being in union with the eternal Buddha. The distinctive vision of the Mahayana is the ideal of unification or interpenetrating unity. 'So long as the sages have separate being, separate ideas and separate functions, they have but finite intelligence, and they profit only a small number of creatures. But once entered into Buddhahood, they have but one being, but one infinite intelligence, but one united function, and they render service to multitudes of creatures for ever.'[1]

IV. TANTRIC BUDDHISM

A significant feature of the development of Buddhist mysticism was the rise of the Tantric school as an offshoot of the Mahayana. Reference has been made to the Tantric element in Hinduism. (See p. 59 above.) Between the fourth and the sixth centuries Tantric tendencies appear to have affected all varieties of Indian religion, including Buddhism. An early Scripture of the movement in Buddhism is the *Guhyasamaja Tantra* (the Tantra of the Secret Conclave), attributed mistakenly to Buddha. The system which this represents is known as the Vajrayana (Adamantine Vehicle), from the word Vajra, used primarily for Indra's

1. Asanga, *Mahayana-Sutralamkara*, Lévi's translation, p. 92 (quoted by Pratt, *The Pilgrimage of Buddhism*, p. 258).

thunderbolt, but here betokening Sunya (the Void), the ultimate Reality, on account of its indestructibility. It came to be held that the Vajra in this sense is embodied in five Dhyani (contemplative) Buddhas, who preside over the five cosmic skandhas or elements, and each of whom is united with a consort. It was this system of teaching which was introduced in the eighth century into Tibet, where it has provided the main features of the traditional outlook. It was introduced into China and Japan about the same time in the form of the True Word schools – Chen Yen and Shingon. A modification of the Vajrayana arose later (about the tenth century) in North India and Tibet in the form of the Kalachakra or Wheel of Time school. The centre of this system is Kala, who is regarded as the Adi-Buddha (the primeval Buddha), from whom the five Dhyani Buddhas are emanations. He is embraced by the goddess Prajna (Wisdom). There is thus in the absolute Reality a union of two principles, and it is from this union that its eternal bliss arises. But whereas in Hinduism, as we have seen, the female principle is the active principle (Shakti), in Buddhism the female principle is passive (Wisdom), and the male principle, the Lord, is the active or dynamic power, known as Karuna (Compassion) or Upaya (Skill in Means). In a Tantric work, *The Attainment of the Realization of Wisdom and Means*, it is said that 'the supreme and wondrous abode of all Buddhas, the Dharma-sphere', which abides always in all things and from which all things arise, is 'the union of limitless Compassion and of perfect Wisdom'.[1]

In its Buddhist form Tantrism is marked by the same essential characteristics as we have traced in Tantric Hinduism. The greatest stress is laid on such methods as visualization, ritual projection of divine powers into the body, and the use of sacred words or mantras. Unlimited power is ascribed to the recitation of mantras. Through them the greatest sins can be absolved; the disciple can be made safe from all danger, and he can even acquire supreme knowledge and attain Buddhahood. It was held that there was a secret correspondence of the letters and syllables comprised by the mantras to the different planes and modes of being, so that by the use of mantras men could enter into an

1. *Buddhist Texts through the Ages*, pp. 241f.

organic union with the various planes and appropriate their power. In Tibet an elaborate series of exercises, both physical and mental, was employed in order to generate 'psychic heat', which was believed to bring such power over the body that it became immune to harm and transparent. The doctrine of the psychic heat is set forth in a Tibetan treatise, *The Epitome of the Six Doctrines*, which states both the methods to be used and the results to be gained.[1] The transformation of the body was accompanied by 'great blissfulness' and the experience in every condition of conscious being of the 'ecstatic state of quiescence' (1: 2). Another doctrine expounded in this work is that of the 'Clear Light' – the mystic radiance of the Dharmakaya. The Clear Light (it was taught) was experienced constantly by the Buddhas; it was experienced at will by the adepts, and momentarily by all men at the point of death. If the dying person was able to hold fast to the Clear Light by a supreme effort of will, he remained immersed in it, and so there was no breach in the continuity of his consciousness at death; if not, as with the great majority of men, the Light of Reality faded from his consciousness. Among other powers attained by the adept was that of voluntarily relinquishing his body and taking a new form. This is known as 'the transference of consciousness'.

The sexual aspect of Tantrism is prominent in the early Scripture, the *Guhyasamaja Tantra*, which is said to have originated in secret conclaves of monks who revolted against the ascetic injunctions of Gotama. The *Guhyasamaja Tantra* certainly represents an extreme reaction against the Buddhist tradition. 'By the enjoyment of all desires, to which one devotes oneself just as one pleases, it is by such practice as this that one may speedily gain Buddhahood. ... One does not succeed by devoting oneself to harsh discipline and austerities, but by devoting oneself to the enjoyment of all desires one rapidly gains success.'[2] For the *Guhyasamaja Tantra* sexual freedom is one aspect of the antinomian principle: all social laws may be disregarded; men may kill any kind of animal, they may lie and steal and commit adultery as they please. Morality is simply a matter of human

1. See *Tibetan Yoga and Secret Doctrines* by W. Y. Evans-Wentz.
2. *Buddhist Texts through the Ages*, p. 222.

convention; its restrictions cannot bind those who see that the whole world, with all its laws and customs, is utterly illusory. This was not an inference commonly drawn from the doctrine of Sunya; and in most Tantric works a different position is adopted. Stress is laid on the ethical side of the discipline which leads to liberation. Those who aspire after Buddhahood, says Anangha-vajra in *The Attainment of the Realization of Ends and Means,* 'abandon envy and malignancy and pride and self-conceit'.[1] Saraha in his *Treasury of Songs* lays the strongest emphasis on the necessity of compassion and service of others. The one thing that can bring deliverance is the abandonment of the duality of self and others – the intuition of our unity with the supreme Reality which dwells at the heart of all beings. In the light of that vision, Saraha teaches, we may enjoy the world of sense without being defiled by it, for in its true nature the world of sense is identical with Nirvana. Sexual union is itself a symbol of the indefeasible union in the Absolute of the active and passive principles – Compassion and Wisdom – from which the bliss which is its essential nature eternally arises.

1. ibid., p. 243.

CHAPTER 4

Taoist and Confucianist Mysticism

I. TAOISM

(a) Early Taoism

ACCORDING to the traditional view, the founder of the mystical philosophy known as 'Taoism' was Lao Tse (Master Lao), an older contemporary of Confucius, said to have been born in 604 B.C. and to have written the mystical treatise, the *Tao Te Ching* (*Treatise of the Way and its Power*). Recent scholars agree that the *Tao Te Ching* (known alternatively as the *Lao Tse Book*) originated at a later time – in the fourth or third century B.C. The movement of thought which it represents must, however, go back beyond the fourth century. During the lifetime of Confucius (in the sixth century) there were hermits, who retired from the world, and lived a simple contemplative life; and it was among these men that Taoism grew up. There was a certain basis for the practice of contemplation in the traditions of ancient China. The central feature of Chinese religion was the sacrifice offered to the ancestral spirits. In the sacrifice a prominent part was played by the shih or medium, in whom, it was believed, the spirit of the ancestor to whom the sacrifice was made came temporarily to dwell. In course of time the belief arose that the spirit might be induced to remain permanently in a man. The heart must be cleansed so as to make it a fit home for the spirit; outer activities and emotions must be stilled. Thus there grew up the practice known as tso-wang, 'sitting with blank mind' (or 'in forgetfulness'), comparable to the Indian yoga or dhyana. In China, as in India, breath-control was adopted as a means of inducing this condition. In the fourth and third centuries there were many who taught and practised inner stillness, and who claimed by this means to attain knowledge of the Transcendent.[1]

The first Taoist teacher of whom we have any real knowledge

1. See Waley's Introduction to *The Way and Its Power*.

is Chuang Chou (commonly known as Chuang Tse) who lived at this time. (The date of his death is generally given as 286 B.C.) Of the book attributed to him more than half appears to have been written by his followers, but enough of his own work remains to provide us with a picture of his vivid, whimsical personality. The *Lao Te Ching* is in part, at least, older than Chuang Chou, but in view of its terseness and obscurity it may be well to commence our study of Taoism by giving an account of the latter's teaching in its main aspects. We shall then be in a better position to understand the *Lao Tse Book*. In a number of passages Chuang Chou refers explicitly to the experience of *tso-wang*. He is pre-eminently an imaginative and picturesque writer and his book is full of vivid stories illustrating his teaching. In the second chapter he speaks of a man named Ch'i who on one occasion 'leant against a low table, as he sat on the ground. He looked up to heaven, and his breath died down. Without a sound he seemed to lose his partnership of soul and body.' His disciple Yen Ch'eng said to him: 'How is it that you can make your body like a sapless tree and your mind like dead ashes? At this moment the person leaning against the table is not the person who was leaning against it before.' 'You have put it very well,' said Ch'i; 'when you saw me just now, my self was gone clean away.' Ch'i, we are to understand, had entered into the experience familiar to the mystics, in which a man is completely unconscious of outer things, and absorbed in the knowledge of the Transcendent. In another passage (in Ch. 6) Chuang Tse speaks of the progressive development of the higher consciousness in the ecstatic state. Here he refers to a Taoist teacher, Nu Chu, who says of a disciple that, after he had instructed him for three days, he was able to detach himself from the human world; after seven days he was able to detach himself from all material existence; after another nine days he was able to detach himself from his own existence. 'After that he was illumined. Being in a state of illumination, he was able to gain the vision of the One (or 'That which is unique'). Being able to see the One, he was able to transcend the distinction of past and present; having transcended the distinction of past and present, he was able to enter the realm where life and death are no more [i.e., to enter into Eternity].'

It is this state of union with the Infinite and Eternal which is the goal of endeavour for Chuang Chou. He seeks to identify himself with 'Infinity-Eternity' – to become one with 'the great Interpenetration', the supreme Reality which interpenetrates all things and makes all things one. 'The heavens and the earth and I [he says] have come into existence together, and all creation and I are one.' This supreme Reality is the Tao. The Tao holds in Taoist writings the place occupied by Brahman in the Upanishads or the Dharmakaya in the Scriptures of Mahayana Buddhism. The literal meaning of the word is 'road' or 'way'. It came to indicate among Confucianists the way of Heaven (or God) in relation to men – the moral order of the world – and so the right way of human life, the path of principle or truth. For Taoists the word sometimes means, similarly, the law operative in the universe, the way in which things work; but most distinctively it stands for the ultimate Reality which underlies the universe and finds expression in its working. The Tao is the Source of all things; it is self-existent; it transcends time and space. 'It is self-rooted [says Chuang Chou], and it existed before the heavens and the earth. ... It produced the heavens, it produced the earth. To the Tao the zenith is not high, nor the nadir low; no point in time is long ago, nor by the lapse of years has it grown old' (Ch. 6). As the ultimate Reality transcending time and space, the Tao is the supreme mystery, beyond the reach of words and discursive thought. 'What is beyond the world of space the sage holds within himself, but he does not reason about it. ... The supreme Tao cannot be talked about, and the supreme argument does not require speech' (Ch. 2). The term Tao is a symbol of That which is ineffable. As a follower of Chuang put it (in Ch. 25): 'The name "Tao" is a symbol which we use to be able to describe it at all. When we speak of it as doing something, or when we say that it is inactive, we talk as if it were a thing. How could speech possibly convey any idea of its greatness? ...Neither speech nor silence is adequate to convey a right understanding of the Tao.'

It is often said that the Tao is purely impersonal. Maspero describes it as a 'force'. Certainly it is true that the term, like 'the Absolute' or 'the Infinite', or like 'Brahman' or 'the Dharmakaya', is in itself impersonal. It is true also that the Tao transcends the limitations of finite personality. It 'has no specific action, no specific form'. Yet it is clear from what has been said that the Reality which it represents is something far beyond the level of a mere force of Nature. The very fact that man can enter into union with it in the stillness of the soul implies that it possesses a spiritual quality, a depth of being which man himself may come to share. However profound may be the mystery of the Tao, however overwhelming it may be in its greatness and supremacy, it is not wholly alien to the nature of man. It is not therefore surprising that, while Chuang does not normally use the language of personality with reference to the Tao, he does occasionally personify it as 'the Master' or 'the Lord'. Thus he cries (in Ch. 3): 'O my Master, O my Master, Thou destroyest all things, and dost not account it cruelty; Thou benefitest all things, and dost not account it kindness; Thou art older than antiquity, and dost not account it age; Thou supportest the universe, shaping the many forms therein, and dost not account it skill.'

The chief concern of Chuang Tse is to emphasize and illustrate the far-reaching change which union with the Tao brings with it. The dawning of the higher consciousness is a great awakening. When the awakening comes, we see that our present experience is a dream; we do not cling to life or shrink from death. A later writer tells us in the *Chuang Tse Book* (Ch. 18) that when his wife died, Chuang refused to mourn. 'She whom I have lost has lain down to sleep for a while,' he said, 'in the great Inner Room. To break in upon her rest with the noise of lamentation will but show that I know nothing of Nature's sovereign law.' We must accept all that comes with tranquillity of spirit, since all is involved in the order of the universe which the Tao ordains. The sage 'will neither delight in great age nor grieve over an untimely death. He will neither glory in prosperity nor be ashamed in poverty' (Ch. 12). Chuang refused to concern himself with the problems of society. In this respect his attitude was strikingly different from that of Confucius. 'Follow things as they are [he said], and do not give way to personal bias. Society will thus be ordered' (Ch. 7). So it was with the government of the wise kings in former times. 'They just made everything pleased with itself, while they maintained their poise in the Immeasurable, and wandered in the Non-existent (That which transcends finite being).' The sage benefits the world, even though he renounces it, by his union with the Tao. 'If I renounce the world, I can ride on the bird of unselfconsciousness and go out beyond space, wander in the village of Nowhere, and make my home in the open country of Emptiness. ... Be empty: that is all. The perfect man's use of his mind is like a mirror (in which Eternity is reflected). ... Thus he is able to master things and not be injured by them.' 'Emptiness' is a characteristic expression. We are reminded of the Buddhist 'Void' – that which is devoid of assignable qualities, because it is too great for such qualities to describe it (see p. 81 above). The way of the Taoist is the way of inner quiet. 'To a mind that is still the whole universe surrenders.' (Ch. 13.) Stillness is the secret of te – the power that 'could shift heaven and earth'. In later Taoism, as we shall see, the greatest emphasis came to be laid on the cultivation of magical power as a means of transcending mortality. In the *Lao Tse Book* also it is regarded as conferring immunity from danger. Chuang Chou records (in Ch. 1) a conversation concerning a 'spirit-man' who breathed in the wind and drank the dew, who mounted the clouds and made the crops ripen. 'That man [it is said] nothing can injure' – neither flood nor fire can destroy him. The same thing is said (in Ch. 2) of the perfect man. 'Neither death nor life can affect him. ... He wanders into the beyond, free of the dust and grime of the world.' It is hard to tell how far Chuang meant his readers to take his references to miraculous power literally. What he is mainly concerned to stress is, in any case, the inner power which comes to men through union with the Tao – which enables them to enter into its eternity and its omnipresence, and to meet all outer changes with undisturbed tranquillity.

The teaching of the *Tao Te Ching* is the same in essentials as that of Chuang Chou. The book is exceedingly concise and sometimes obscure, and subject therefore to varying interpretations.

Different views are held of its purpose. It has been described as a text-book for the use of disciples learning the Way from a master.[1] On the other hand, Waley regards it as a work addressed to the public at large in order to create an atmosphere favourable to Quietism.[2] He dwells upon its polemical aspect, contending that it was directed both against the Confucianists, with their emphasis on moral principle, and more especially against the Legalists or Realists, for whom the material power of the State was the essential factor in the welfare of society. Waley, in any case, recognizes that what is fundamental in the book is its mystical element.

The theme of the *Lao Tse Book* is indicated by its title: it is a *Treatise on the Tao and its Power*. The thought which dominates it is that of the Tao – eternal, unfathomable, all-pervading, inexpressible in words, the Unity beneath all multiplicity, silent and imperceptible in its working, not obtruding itself upon us, not lording it over us, not revealing itself in outer signs, yet the source of all real and enduring strength and vitality. The writer feels the supreme mystery of the Tao, its utter transcendence of all finite modes of being. It is, indeed, 'the basic mystery, the mystery of mysteries, the door into all mystery' (Ch. 1). As Otto says, Taoism 'moves wholly in the numinous'.[3] The Tao is therefore strictly 'nameless'. 'If the Tao could be comprised in words,' to quote the opening sentence, 'it would not be the unchangeable Tao.' It may even be described as 'Non-being'. 'Though all creatures under heaven are the products of being, being itself is the product of Non-being' (Ch. 40). 'Non-being' is here not nothingness, but the Reality which transcends the being of finite and temporal things (Cp. p. 21).

In the *Tao Te Ching* there is not the same clear and definite account of the experience of concentration and ecstasy as in the *Chuang Chou Book*, but it is evident in several passages that the author has that experience in mind. That is most notably the

1. E. R. Hughes, *Chinese Philosophy in Classical Times*, p. 144.
2. *The Way and its Power*, pp. 98f.
3. *The Idea of the Holy*, 4th edition, p. 206.

case in Ch. 10, where he asks (following Waley's translation):
'Can you keep the unquiet physical soul from straying, hold fast
to the Unity, and never quit it? Can you, when concentrating
your breath, make it soft like that of a little child? Can you wipe
and cleanse your vision of the Mystery till all is without blur?'
The reference here is to the practice of yoga, which was of
fundamental importance in Taoism, and to the mystic vision
which was its culmination. To 'hold fast to the Unity' is (in
Waley's words) 'to utilize the primal, "undivided" state that
underlies the normal consciousness'.[1]

The way of the mystic is conformity to, and identification with,
Tao. 'To those who have conformed themselves to the Tao, the
Tao readily bends its power' (Ch. 23). The Tao is 'the great One'
(Ch. 25). '"Great" [the writer adds] means passing on, and
passing on means going far away, and going far away means
returning.' There appears to be a reference here to the experience
of the mystic in his union with the Tao. 'By passing on and on
through successive stages of his own consciousness back to the
initial Unity, man can arrive at the Way (the Tao) which controls
the multiform apparent universe'.[2]

The condition of inner vision is cleansing from desire (Ch. 1)
and the practice of inner quiet. It is here that we find the true
secret of power. The Tao works silently and unobtrusively. 'It
clothes and feeds the myriad things, yet does not claim ascen-
dancy. . . . Similarly the wise man obtains true greatness, because
he never poses as great' (Ch. 34). One main characteristic of the
Tao is wu-wei or actionless activity. 'Tao never does (it is always
non-acting; it performs no specific or external deeds), yet
through it (as the immanent spring of life) all things are done'
(Ch. 37). Through his inner oneness with the Tao the sage also
works in the same way, and he achieves a similar result. 'Push
far enough towards the Void, hold fast to quietness, and of the
ten thousand things, none but can be worked on by you' (Ch.
16). The mystic 'finds that by being completely non-active, he can
do all things. Without striving for influence, he exercises influence
over all' (Ch. 48).

1. Waley, op. cit., p. 154.   2. ibid., p. 175.

The charge was commonly brought against Taoists, as it has so often been brought against the mystics, that they were absorbed in their own state of soul, and were indifferent to the welfare of the world. Chuang Chou sometimes uses expressions which, taken by themselves, might appear to justify the charge. The *Lao Tse Book* replies that 'the sage is all the time in the most perfect way helping men ... is all the time in the most perfect way helping creatures' (Ch. 27). The inner quiet of the Taoist sage has a dynamic potency, whereby he exerts an incalculable effect for good. In comparison with the power of the spirit (te) other types of power are impermanent and ineffective. The *Tao Te Ching* is notable for its attack on war. At the time when it was written war was endemic in China; the country was in a state of feudal chaos. Waley observes that 'the objection of the Taoist to war is not based on moral or humanitarian grounds'.[1] That is belied by the statement in Ch. 31 that 'the slaying of multitudes should be mourned with sorrow; a victory should be celebrated with the funeral rite'. The passage may, as Waley suggests,[2] embody the work of a commentator drawing on some lost pacifist writing, but he would scarcely have included it unless it was in accordance with the Taoist tradition. Yet it is true that the main emphasis in the *Tao Te Ching* is on the futility of violence relatively to the power of the spirit. 'He who by Tao purposes to help a ruler of men will oppose all conquest by force of arms. For such things are wont to rebound. ... That [violence] is against Tao, and what is against Tao will soon perish' (Ch. 30). The sage unites himself with the Tao, which is the real source of strength and victory. 'He does not boast of what he will do, therefore he succeeds. He is not proud of his work, and therefore it endures. He does not contend, and for that very reason no one under heaven can contend with him' (Ch. 22). In one or two passages the writer suggests, like Chuang Chou, that the possessor of te is immune from physical harm. 'No poisonous insects sting him, no wild beasts attack him, and no birds of prey pounce upon him' (Ch. 55). 'The horns of the wild buffalo are powerless against him; the paws of the tiger are useless against him; the

1. *Three Ways of Thought in Ancient China*, p. 95.
2. *The Way and its Power*, pp. 95f., 181f.

weapons of the soldier cannot avail against him' (Ch. 50). Whatever significance the author may have attached to such things, they are for him, in any case, altogether secondary.

The spiritual power achieved by the mystic is, for the *Tao Te Ching*, of the greatest importance to the welfare of society. 'If kings and barons would but possess themselves of it, the ten thousand creatures would flock to do them homage ... Without law or compulsion, men would dwell in harmony' (Ch. 32). Law, indeed, is futile or harmful: 'The more laws there are promulgated, the more thieves and robbers there will be' (Ch. 57). It is only through the power of the spirit that the community can be well ordered. 'The sage says: "I do nothing, and the people are reformed of themselves; I love quietude, and the people are righteous of themselves".' The emphasis of the book is throughout on simplicity and spontaneity. The sage loves kindness, sincerity, peace (Ch. 8). He requites injuries with good deeds (Ch. 63). In this last point the writer transcends the Confucian stress on justice. His general attitude to the Confucians is critical, because their teaching does not go to the root of things. He maintains, indeed, that Confucian morality and ritual have arisen only because the vision and power of the Tao are lost (Ch. 38). 'The full-grown man concentrates on the core of things, and not on the husk.'

(b) The Book of Lieh Tse

In the third century B.C. Taoism exercised a very considerable influence in China. It coloured the outlook even of Legalists and of Confucianists in spite of their radical divergence from its distinctive teaching. Among Taoist writings in this period is the *Book of Lieh Tse*. According to tradition Lieh Tse was a Taoist sage who lived in the fifth and fourth centuries B.C.[1] Chuang Chou tells us that he possessed a rare degree of power over Nature: 'He could ride upon the wind and travel whithersoever he wished' (Ch. 1). Actually he is a quite legendary figure, and the work attributed to him was probably written by Chuang's own disciples. The book is notable for two features, both of

1. The book may have been written as late as the fourth century A.D. *See* A. C. Graham's introduction to his translation.

which are important in connexion with the development of Taoism. In the first place, Confucius is treated with greater respect than in Chuang's pages, and he is often made the mouthpiece of Taoist teaching. (That sometimes happens in the *Chuang Tse Book*, but in other passages his teaching is contrasted unfavourably with that of Lao Tse). Thus Confucius is made to say (in Ch. 2): 'The man of perfect faith can extend his influence to inanimate things and disembodied spirits; he can move heaven and earth, and fly to the six cardinal points without encountering any hindrance.' This passage illustrates another feature of the *Lieh Tse Book*, which corresponds to the account of the sage given by Chuang – namely the stress which is laid on the mastery of Nature and the body as an outcome of union with the Tao.[1] The same idea, as we have seen, is found in the *Tao Te Ching* and the *Chuang Chou Book*, but here it receives greater emphasis. In another passage in the second chapter the author sets forth with particular clarity the rationale of such mastery. The secret, it is suggested, lies in the union with external things which the sage attains through his oneness with the all-pervading Tao. 'The man who achieves harmony with Tao enters into close union with external objects, and none of them has the power to harm or hinder him,' so that he can pass through metal or stone, and can walk through fire or on water. The *Book of Lieh Tse* implies that supernormal accomplishments are not merely an incidental result of inner vision; the attainment of them is an essential aspect of the mystic's purpose. Lieh Tse is recorded as saying to a disciple impatient of results, although he had not yet spent a whole season in the master's house: 'At this rate the atmosphere will never support an atom of your body, and even the earth will be unequal to the weight of your limbs.' In other words, the aim which the disciple sought, and which the master had himself achieved, was, in one aspect, the etherealization of the body. Where the disciple was lacking was in the patience to pursue the course of spiritual training necessary to this end. The end, as we shall see, was pre-eminent in later Taoism.

1. See section (*d*) below. In this aspect there is a striking resemblance between the principles and methods of Taoism and those inculcated by Hindu and Buddhist Tantrism. See pp. 59f., 93ff. above.

(c) Neo-Taoist Philosophy

In his works on Chinese philosophy[1] Fung Yu-Lan has used the term 'Neo-Taoism' to cover the movement of thought which took place in Taoist circles in the second and third centuries of our era – towards the close of the Han dynasty. Confucianism was now the official philosophy of the Empire, and Taoist teaching was accordingly toned down so as to conform with Confucian ethics. It was often held, indeed, by Taoist teachers that there was no essential distinction between the two forms of thought. Confucius was recognized as the greatest of all sages, while his attitude and teaching were re-interpreted on Taoist lines. Confucius was even regarded as superior in his spiritual attainment to the greatest of Taoist sages. Thus Kuo Hsiang in his commentary on the *Chuang Tse Book* declared that Confucius had actually entered into the mystic state – 'the state of inward silence and quietude' – of which Chuang was merely an interpreter.[2] Wang Pi, the author of a commentary on the *Tao Te Ching*, adopted a similar position. At the same time he attempted to explain why it is that the teaching of Confucius contains no reference to mystical experience. He presents the very silence of Confucius as a token of his higher knowledge. It is because Confucius identified himself with the higher sphere of reality, which is for Wang Pi the sphere of 'non-being' (wu) – as distinct from the realm of finite being (yu) – that the great sage said nothing about it. Lao Tse and Chuang Chou, on the other hand, 'constantly spoke of that in which they were themselves deficient'.[3]

In early Taoism there was a marked tendency to regard the higher life as involving not only inner detachment but an actual abandonment of the world. (We shall see in the next section the place which this principle came to hold in later Taoism.) As we should expect from their adoption of Confucianist ethics, the attitude of the Neo-Taoists was different. On this point the

1. *A History of Chinese Philosophy; A Short History of Chinese Philosophy; The Spirit of Chinese Philosophy.*
2. Fung Yu-Lan, *History of Chinese Philosophy*, II: 171f.
3. ibid., p. 170.

teaching of the *Chuang Tse Book* is not really consistent, but in the commentary already quoted it is stated that the purpose of the book is 'to teach us how to ferry over to the ordinary and encompass the existing world'.[1] We are told that the teaching of Lao Tse and Chuang Chou is commonly rejected by men of affairs because of the widespread impression 'that actionless activity is reached only by folding one's hands in silence among the mountains and forests'. The truth is that 'the sage, even when occupying the highest place at court, is mentally no different from the way he is when amidst the mountains and forests. ... The man who is perfect in perfection cannot suffer any loss [from his contact with worldly affairs]'.[2] We have here an attitude which affords a striking contrast to that of the *Lieh Tse Book*, which quotes with approval the words of a sage who declared that, owing to his inner detachment from the world, he was 'incapable of serving his sovereign, of associating with his friends and kinsmen, of directing his wife and children or of controlling his servants and retainers' (Ch. 4).

It was universally agreed among the Taoists that the man who is one with the Tao has attained a condition of tranquillity. He accepts all that comes with an even mind as the outcome of the all-inclusive order of the universe. It was sometimes held that tranquillity involved a complete absence of emotion. This view was attributed to Chuang Chou. The Neo-Taoists were divided on this issue. Kuo Hsiang observes in his commentary that Chuang's attitude in refraining from lamentation on the death of his wife 'teaches man to disperse emotion with reason'.[3] Another writer, Ho Yen, maintained, in agreement with this position, that 'the sage has neither pleasure nor anger, sorrow nor gladness'.[4] Neo-Taoists, however, often came to adopt another attitude. They sought, not to banish emotion, but to combine it with tranquillity. This view was expressed by Wang Pi. In a discussion with Ho Yen the former said:

That in which the sage is superior to ordinary people is the spirit. But what the sage has in common with ordinary people are the emo-

1. ibid., p. 236.   2. ibid., p. 235.
3. Fung Yu-Lan, *Short History of Chinese Philosophy*, p. 108.
4. ibid., p. 238.

tions. The sage has a superior spirit, and therefore he is able to be in harmony with the universe and to hold communion with Wu [Non-being, i.e., the Tao]. But the sage has ordinary emotions, and therefore cannot respond to things without joy or sorrow. He responds to things, but is not ensnared by them.[1]

The sage shares the joys and sorrows of other men, as he shares the common life of the world, but he preserves an inner freedom of spirit which makes him 'the ruler of life, not a slave'.

(d) Taoism as an Organized Religion

In early Taoism there were many different tendencies and schools of thought. Under the Ch'in dynasty, which unified the country towards the close of the third century B.C., a type of Taoism came into prominence which stands in the greatest contrast with the type familiar to us from the *Tao Te Ching* and the *Book of Chuang Chou*. Reference has been made to the supernatural efficacy attributed in these works to the power (te) which comes of union with the Tao. The main emphasis, however, is laid on that union and on the way of life to which it leads. Yet in other Taoist circles a widely different emphasis was found: the achievement of supernatural power was itself the object which men sought. In particular they strove to attain such power over the body that it might be immortalized. In the *Lieh Tse Book*, as we have seen, the etherealization of the body is regarded as a phase of the mystic's goal. This end was to be accomplished either by meditation, accompanied by breath-control and fasting, or by drugs and alchemy. It was believed that the elixir of immortality might be found in the fabled Paradise of the West or of the Eastern Sea. In quest of the secret the first Emperor of the Ch'in dynasty is said to have equipped a naval expedition, while many humbler folk went on pilgrimage.[2] An illuminating story is told concerning Huai Nan Tse, grandson of the founder of the following (Han) dynasty, and reputed author of a well-known Taoist treatise. It is said that, having found and drunk the elixir of immortal life,

1. ibid.

2. Eliade has pointed out that 'at the basis of such enterprises there was always the myth, the primordial image of a paradisal land beyond time, inhabited by the "perfected", the "Immortals", to meet whom was "to transcend the human condition"' (*Yoga*, p. 288).

he mounted on a cloud, and sailed up to heaven. By a mischance he dropped the vessel containing the elixir into his courtyard: his dogs drank the dregs and sailed up to heaven after him.

Under the Han dynasty Taoism of this order enjoyed considerable popularity. When Buddhism was introduced into China, it was regarded in popular Taoist circles as an alternative method of securing immortality – a method of a purely moral and contemplative sort. Buddhism was actually in some ways, as Maspero remarks,[1] closer to the outlook of Chuang Chou and the *Tao Te Ching* than was popular Taoism. Buddhism was, indeed, sometimes looked upon as a foreign offshoot of Taoism. It was said that the Buddha was none other than Lao Tse himself preaching his gospel in India. (The legendary life of Lao Tse does not exclude that possibility, since he is said to have disappeared in the Gobi desert.) In the second century a shrine was erected by the Emperor Houan in honour both of the Buddha and of Lao Tse and the Yellow Emperor (a mythical saint of Taoism). There was thus a certain interchange of thought among the two religions, and a frequent confusion arose between them. Buddhism won many recruits from the Taoists, and it was through the stress of its rivalry that Taoism itself came to be organized as a religious society, with its own hierarchy, its own Temple-worship, and its own monastic life. The higher officers of the Church had to know by heart the *Tao Te Ching*, which they interpreted in a manner altogether different from its original meaning. Under the Han dynasty the Taoist religion received a great deal of popular support, but it reached its greatest height of power in the Period of Disunity (from the third to the sixth century) which followed. Under the T'ang dynasty its influence waned.

As an organized religion Taoism differs strikingly from the teaching of the early mystics. The Neo-Confucianist sage, Chu Hsi, remarks that 'the disciples of Lao Tse moved further and further away from the teachings of the master in proportion to their separation from him in time'.[2] That is true in substance so far as Taoists regarded themselves as followers of Lao Tse. Yet

1. *Le Taoisme*, p. 198.
2. Reichelt, *Religion in Chinese Garment*, p. 84.

the difference was not essentially a transformation occurring in time. It has been shown above that already in the third century B.C. there was a trend in the movement very far removed from the spirituality of the sages. Moreover, the tradition of the sages was maintained and developed for some centuries by the Neo-Taoist philosophers. And it must not be forgotten that as between the sages and the leaders of the later, organized Taoist Church there was a certain measure of common ground. That is seen, not only in the recognition by the sages of the supernatural power which is brought by the Tao and the stress which they lay on the yoga technique, but also in the element of mysticism remaining in the Church.

It was the central aim of later Taoism to make man a holy and immortal person. As a guiding principle this purpose was restricted to a small minority. In course of time there came to be a sharp division between two classes of Taoists – the masses of believers and the adepts. The latter lived apart in community-houses with their wives and children. Under Buddhist influence celibacy came to prevail among them, and under the T'ang dynasty it became the general rule. The faithful in general sought longevity and a privileged position in the land of the dead. These ends were to be gained by moral conduct, and especially by acts of mercy to men and animals,[1] by participation in worship and the reading of sacred books, and by the practice of certain breathing exercises or the use of magical charms. They hoped to be delivered eventually from the land of the dead and to enter the Paradise of the Immortals, thanks to the efforts of their descendants in performing appropriate ceremonies.

It was among the adepts that the inner life of meditation and vision was cultivated. The primary aim was power over the body which should render it immune to physical danger of any kind, and should gradually transform it and make it immortal. The man who had achieved this end might appear to die, and his body to be laid in the tomb, but in fact (it was held) that was only an illusion – what was laid in the tomb was a sword or a bamboo

1. Taoism recognizes the kinship of men and other living creatures, and in its ethics there is a remarkably humanitarian emphasis.

cane bearing the form of the body. The body had been etherealized, and had entered the Sacred Island of Paradise. Immortality
was thus believed to be attained by the conservation and transformation of the living body. Physical weakness and ill-health
were regarded as a mark of sin. The sick were sent to prison to
reflect on their sins. To achieve the conservation and transformation of the body, it was necessary to practise an elaborate
technique of breath-control[1] and gymnastic exercises, and to observe dietetic restrictions, such as the avoidance of cereals.
Alchemy played a part in the process. Spiritual methods were
also held to be essential. It was supposed that the body was the
home of a great number of gods. The gods of the Taoists were
conceived as teachers and saviours, like the bodhisattvas and
Buddhas of the rival creed. The body was regarded as a microcosm, each part of it corresponding to some part of the universe.
The gods of Nature were thus also gods of the body, and each
organ of the body was believed to be occupied by a god, who
was charged with its defence against evil spirits. To keep the
gods in the body, and so to preserve it from decay, it was necessary both to enter into harmony with them by good deeds and to
establish a more direct relationship by meditation and inner
vision. The adept must concentrate his thought on the gods
within himself. By closing his eyes, he causes their light (which
is also the light of the sun and the moon) to illuminate the interior
of his body. He thus attains the experience of inner vision. In this
way the gods retain their place within him, and the forces of
decay and death are conquered.

These facts provide the background and the preliminary
stages of the later Taoist mysticism. The great majority of adepts
went no further. The mystical life in the proper sense was always
confined to a very small company of Taoists. There were, however, some who entered upon it. In the Period of Disunity there
was a renewal of the mystical tradition of the early saints. It was
recognized that the final step on the path of immortality was the
experience of contemplation and ecstasy which brought union
with the Tao. The channels of sense were cut off, and the adept

1. It was said that an adept who could hold his breath for three days
became immortal.

saw within himself the supreme Reality which underlay all things; he knew himself as one with the Tao. The union affected both body and spirit. In the words of the *Tso-wang Louen* (*Treatise on Sitting-in-Forgetfulness*), 'the Tao changes the body and the spirit. The body is penetrated by the Tao, and becomes one with the spirit; he whose body and spirit are united wholly is called a divine man ... The material body, being transformed, is identical with the spirit; the spirit, being melted, becomes subtle; it is one with the Tao'.[1] There is here an evident intermingling – as there is, doubtless, in a measure in all mystical religion – of experience and interpretation. The essential fact is the experience of union with the Tao, which interpenetrates body and spirit and overcomes all otherness and externality. It is thus the paradox of Taoist mysticism that the mystic transcends in his experience the individual immortality which is the goal of his quest. In his union with the Tao the bounds of his individual being fall away; he participates in the infinite and eternal life of the Tao, which is the ultimate reality of all things.

II. MYSTICAL ELEMENTS IN CONFUCIANISM

(a) Confucius and the Transcendent

The mystical factor in Chinese religion is represented primarily by the Taoist movement and by Chinese Buddhism, but in the official Confucianist religion there has been, thanks to Taoist and Buddhist influence, a certain element of mysticism. Confucius himself, as we have seen, was regarded in Neo-Taoist circles as the greatest of all mystics, his very silence concerning the Tao being taken as an index of intuitive knowledge. Historical study, it need scarcely be said, affords no evidence in favour of this view. It is true that we have no good ground for regarding the attitude of Confucius as Agnostic or Humanist (in the negative sense). His teaching was predominantly ethical, but the *Analects*[2] show clearly enough that he was inspired and sustained in his work by

1. Maspero, op. cit., pp. 39f.
2. The *Analects* are sayings of Confucius and his disciples, written down for the most part near his time on the basis of traditions preserved by his disciples.

the consciousness of a mission entrusted to him by 'Heaven'. He held the accepted belief in 'Heaven' (T'ien) as the supreme Being (conceived as the over-ruling Providence, the Guardian of the moral law), and he was convinced that his task as teacher and reformer was a thing which Heaven had laid upon him. Describing his own inner development, he said that at the age of fifty he was 'conscious of the decrees of Heaven', and that at sixty he was 'obedient to these decrees' (*Analects*, ii: 4). He was assured. in other words, that his work and his life were progressively in harmony with the Will of God. This conviction, impressive as it is, belongs to a different order of experience from that of the mystic's apprehension of the divine Presence. It is significant that for Confucius the 'Tao' is the way of life for man, not (as it was for the Taoists) the supreme Reality. As the way of life, it may be said that this term sums up the message of Confucius. 'Fix your mind', he said, 'on the right way, hold fast to it in your moral character, follow it up in kindness to others' (*Analects*, vii: 6).

(b) Mystical Elements in Early Confucianism

The work of Confucius was continued by a line of sages, who expounded and developed the main principles of his teaching. Among these sages one of the greatest was Mencius, a contemporary of Chuang Chou. The Book of Mencius is a record of conversations between the sage and his disciples and others; it is said to have been compiled by him in his old age with the help of a disciple. For Confucius and his successors the fundamental necessity was moral training. What is distinctive of Mencius is the mystical quality which marks the outcome of that training, and this appears to be the result of Taoist influence. Mencius claims that by the age of forty he had gained 'imperturbability of mind' – a condition of inner quiet analogous to the experience of the Taoists. Yet he apparently repudiates the technique which they pursued.

In the second section of the *Book of Mencius* there is a passage of outstanding interest. The sage was once asked 'in what way spiritual growth was achieved'. He replied: 'By skill in nourishing the vast-flowing vital energy in man' (or his 'flood-like breath-spirit'). The word translated 'vital energy' or 'breath-

spirit' is ch'i, which primarily means 'air' or 'breath'. For
Taoists of a certain school it came to represent the 'animating
principle' or 'cosmic breath' which can be utilized by means of
respiratory exercises so as to bring complete control of the body.
Mencius, no doubt, owed his employment of the term to his
knowledge of this usage. But for him the word indicates the spiritual energy of which he was conscious as a power working mightily
within him, and far transcending the range of his personal being.
When Mencius was asked what he meant by 'the vast-flowing
energy', he said: 'It is difficult to put it into words. Such is the
nature of this energy that it is immensely great and immensely
strong, and if it is nourished by uprightness, and so sustains no
injury, then it pervades the whole space between the heavens and
the earth.' The sage is here evidently struggling to express the
transcendent quality of the life of the spirit which is quickened in
him. He is aware of a life within him which breaks down the
barrier between his own being and the universe. He says elsewhere (in Section 7): 'All things belong to me.' So Chuang Chou
declared: 'I and all things in the universe are one.'

Through the intensity of his inner life Mencius appears to have
attained a mystical awareness for which the terms of his normal
thinking provided no satisfactory framework. He believed, like
Confucius, in Heaven as an overruling Providence essentially
external to man, revealing itself in 'deeds' (i.e. human deeds)
'and events'. Alternatively he thought of Heaven – as many
Confucian teachers did – as an impersonal law of righteousness.
It is in that sense that he uses the term 'Tao'. There is no
approach in his teaching to the conception of the Tao as an
immanent, yet transcendent First Principle, which was the
intellectual basis of Taoist mysticism. Mencius differed, moreover, from the Taoists in his exclusively ethical interpretation of
the way of attainment. The overflowing spiritual energy of which
he speaks is (he says) 'the product of accumulated righteousness'.
He deprecates any attempt to foster the development of the
higher consciousness by special techniques. 'The mind must not
deliberately help the growth' – any more than a peasant should
try to help the corn to grow by pulling it up and looking at it.
As with the corn, such efforts are in his view actually injurious.

By the constant exercise of the moral sense the 'flood-like spirit', which makes us one with the whole of being, will emerge spontaneously within us.

The influence of Taoist mysticism may be traced in another work which holds a leading place in Confucian tradition – *The Doctrine of the Mean*. This book has commonly been attributed to Tse Ssu, a grandson of Confucius, who lived in the fifth century B.C. Tse Ssu seems, indeed, to have been the author of the central section, but the rest of the book was probably the work of a follower of Mencius living in the third century B.C.[1] The passages of interest from the side of mysticism come from the later writer. Like Mencius, but in a different way, he dwells on the transcendent quality revealed in the being of the sage, who realizes the true capacity of human nature. It is such a man, he tells us, who alone is 'fully real' (ch'eng). The term ch'eng commonly means 'sincere', but in later, Neo-Confucianist writings it often implies 'the complete embodiment by the individual of the supreme Ultimate – the transcendent Reality – in all its perfection and goodness'.[2] In *The Doctrine of the Mean* we have an approximation to this later usage. We have seen that Chuang Chou regards the life of the world as a dream from which the mystic awakes to a truer perception of reality. The *Lieh Tse Book* likewise says: 'All that has the breath of life, all that possesses bodily form, is mere illusion' (Section 3). The position of our author is far removed from that. Yet he regards reality as something other than simple existence. It is for him a quality of being which belongs intrinsically to Heaven, and at the same time a goal to which man may attain. 'It is the characteristic of Heaven' (he says) 'to be the Real. It is the characteristic of man to be coming-to-be-real' (Section 7 in Hughes' translation). To attain reality is the way of spiritual growth. 'To be coming-to-be-real – to be on the path which leads to reality – is to choose the good and to hold fast to it.' The fullness of reality for man lies beyond the life of conscious choice and moral striving, in a state of spontaneous harmony with the law of his being. The man

1. Fung Yu-Lan, *History of Chinese Philosophy*, I: 370. E. R. Hughes takes a different view: see *The Great Learning and the Mean in Action*.
2. Fung Yu-Lan, op. cit., II : 446, note 1.

who is entirely real 'has the power to give full development to his own nature' (Section 8). But such a man does not stand apart from others. The whole world is a living unity which grows towards completeness or perfection and so towards reality (Section 10). Through love[1] and knowledge the sage breaks down the barrier between self and others, and realizes the unity of all things. He can thus, by the power within him, play a part in the universal process and 'assist the transforming and nourishing work of Heaven and Earth', and so become 'part of a trinity of power'. He is one with the Power which sustains and renews the world and leads it to its goal. (We are reminded here of Paul's vision in Romans 8 of the unity of the cosmic process, with its climax in 'the revealing of the sons of God'.) The writer feels the greatness and depth of the personality of a man who has entered into this living unity with the divine. There is a quality of being in him which far transcends the common level. 'His human-heartedness, how insistent! His depths, how unfathomable! His superhumanness, how overwhelming! Who is there who can comprehend this . . . unless he reaches out to the spiritual power of Heaven?' (Section 18). What marks out the man who has perfected his nature and so come to share the reality of the divine is precisely this – that he 'reaches out to the spiritual power of Heaven' and embodies it in himself. It is only when a man has developed the same capacity in himself that he can comprehend it in others.

(c) Neo-Confucianism

Among the followers of Confucius the influence of Taoist mysticism may be seen most notably in Mencius and the author of certain sections of *The Doctrine of the Mean*. It was not until the rise many centuries later of the Neo-Confucianist philosophy that this influence became a central factor in the outlook of Confucianism. The influence of Taoist philosophy was now reinforced by that of Buddhism, which (like popular Taoism) came to enjoy a wide measure of support during the Period of Disunity. When the unity of China was restored towards the close of the sixth century, Confucianism was re-established as the State religion. The beginnings of Neo-Confucianism may be

1. Or 'human-heartedness' (jen) – the characteristic Confucian virtue.

traced in the eighth and ninth centuries with the work of two thinkers, Han Yu and Li Ao, who revived the tradition of Mencius and *The Doctrine of the Mean*, and combined it with elements derived from Taoist and Buddhist teaching. As an organized school of thought Neo-Confucianism took its rise two centuries later with the teaching of the Ch'eng brothers (Ch'eng Hao and Ch'eng Yi). In their work we have the basis of the two distinct types of the new philosophy – the doctrine of Ideal Patterns, represented especially by Chu Hsi (twelfth century), and the doctrine of Universal Mind, the outstanding exponent of which was Wang Shou-jen (fifteenth and sixteenth centuries).

Neo-Confucianism may be regarded as a synthesis of Confucianism, Taoism, and Buddhism. The influence of Buddhist mysticism, in the form particularly of Ch'an Buddhism (see p. 91 above), was a highly important factor in its formation. Li Ao was strongly affected by the Buddhist doctrine and practice of contemplation, so that with him 'what had been a Buddhist doctrine became a Confucian doctrine as well'.[1] Both Chu Hsi and Wang Shou-jen visited Buddhist monasteries in their early years, and it is said that the former was at one time on the point of becoming a Buddhist monk. Li Ao remarked that in his day, owing to the neglect of the mystical tradition in Confucianism, the scholars 'all plunge into Taoism and Buddhism'.[2] It was the task of Neo-Confucianism to revive that tradition, and to fuse it with the new factors at work in the religious life of the country. Neo-Confucianism was itself pre-eminently a religion for scholars who sought satisfaction for their deeper religious needs. Yet it exerted an influence extending far beyond their immediate circle. The scholars themselves had much the same standing as priests in other religions. With their new interpretation of life and the universe they brought a fresh meaning into the ancient cultus, so that through the impact of their work Confucianism gained a new vitality and a new prestige.

It is common ground among Neo-Confucianists that there is in the nature of man a transcendent element, in the discovery of which lies the path of the sage. The main point of difference is in

1. Fung Yu-Lan, op. cit., II: 424.
2. Fung Yu-Lan, *Short History*, p. 267.

the interpretation given to this factor. Where Buddhist influence is predominant, it is interpreted as the Universal Mind (equivalent to the 'Buddha-nature'), with which man in his essential being is identical. With Li Ao we have a close approximation to Buddhist thought. The sage, he teaches, penetrates to his original nature, and so is able to 'radiate the infinite light of Heaven and Earth'. He reaches out beyond himself into union with all things. He practises inner quiet, which Li calls (in Taoist terminology) 'the fasting of the mind' – the absence of discursive thought – and so attains to the mystical state of ch'eng (reality) and ming (enlightenment). Under Buddhist influence, Neo-Confucianists constantly stress the breaking-down of barriers – the sense of all-embracing unity - which ch'eng and ming involve. Chang Tsai (eleventh century) speaks of the sage's transcendence of the limits of the senses, and so of the externality which sense-knowledge implies. 'The minds of ordinary men', he says in his book, *Discipline for Beginners*, 'are confined within the limits of seeing and hearing, whereas the sage, by completely developing his nature, prevents his mind from being restricted to hearing and seeing. As he views the world, there is in it no one who is not his own self'.[1] The sage 'plumbs the spiritual to its depths', and his knowledge is therefore an all-embracing knowledge and his love a universal love. 'All people are my blood-brothers, and all creatures are my companions.'[2] Ch'eng Hao's emphasis is the same. 'The man of love takes Heaven, Earth and all things as one with himself. To him there is nothing that is not himself ... He is undifferentiably one with other things.'[3] By overcoming the power of selfish desire, and by following the intuitive sensitivity which binds us to all things, we may gain the composure which brings enlightenment. The sage is composed alike in stillness and in activity. He is thus content to play his part actively in the world of affairs. As Chang Tsai remarks, he does not seek a Nirvana involving 'a departure from the universe which leads to no return'.[4] Neither does he, with the adherents of popular Taoism, cling to existence in the world. 'In life [said Chang] I shall serve unrestingly, and when death comes, I shall be at peace.'

1. Fung Yu-Lan, *History of Chinese Philosophy*, II: 491.
2. ibid., p. 493.   3. ibid., pp. 520f.   4. ibid., p. 496.

It was Wang Shou-jen who gave the most systematic exposition of the doctrine of Universal Mind. 'We know', he said, 'that in Heaven and Earth there is one spirituality or consciousness. But because of his bodily form man has separated himself from the whole ... Heaven, Earth, spirits and things are all permeated with a single force, so how can we be (in reality) separated from them?'[1] Although Wang speaks here of man's 'bodily form' as the cause of his apparent separation from the whole, he recognizes, with other Neo-Confucianists, that it is in fact egoism which isolates us. He speaks sometimes of the Universal Mind, in which all things are present, and with which all are one, as 'Heaven'. 'All of us [he declares] are this single Heaven, but because of the obscurings caused by selfishness the original state of Heaven is not made manifest.'[2] The original unity of being is expressed in the love (jen) which makes us one with all things. 'Beginning with human relationships, and reaching to mountains, rivers, spirits, and gods, all should be loved in order to extend our love ... Then we are really one with Heaven, Earth, and all things.'[3] Universal love and the intuitive knowledge of unity are the manifestation of our original or heavenly nature, which Wang describes as 'the illustrious virtue'. He dwells on the need both of the practice of love and of inner quiet. In the man who adheres to this twofold path there will come about a sudden enlightenment[4] which is also an inner transformation, described in Taoist terms as 'the conception of the holy embryo'.

Historically the main influence in Neo-Confucianism has been the school of Ideal Patterns (Li) owing to the work of Chu Hsi, whose teaching became the standard of orthodoxy in the fourteenth century. The fundamental doctrine of the school is remarkably similar to that of Plato. The Li[5] are immaterial principles or entities corresponding to the objects of experience, but independent of them. They exist in an ideal world beyond time and space, unaffected by the growth and decay of the objects of which they are the essence. Each type of thing has its own Li, which is the real object of knowledge. The Li combine with ch'i

1. ibid., p. 609.   2. Fung Yu-Lan, *Short History*, p. 315.
3. ibid., p. 311.   4. We see here the influence of Ch'an Buddhism.
5. The word is both singular and plural.

(the gaseous substance which is the material basis of the universe) to produce the world as we know it. In relation to each type of thing the Li is the chi (not to be confused with ch'i) or ultimate standard; and for the universe as a whole there is a single ultimate standard – the T'ai Chi, the 'Highest Point of Perfection' or 'supreme Ultimate'. The T'ai Chi is the all-embracing ultimate Reality, the supreme standard of perfection. It unites and includes the Li of all things, and is itself the one undivided Li of the whole. It is consequently sometimes described simply as the Li; it is also known as the Tao. It is transcendent to the universe, but immanent in it, present in its entirety in all that is, dwelling in man and constituting his deepest nature.

For this school of thought, as for the school of Universal Mind, there is thus a transcendent element in the nature of man; and it is the realization of its presence which is the goal of life. In man, as in all things, Li is combined with ch'i. In itself Li is wholly good; evil arises from man's physical endowment. Chu Hsi compares human nature to a pearl lying in muddy water, or to the rays of the sun obstructed in their shining by clouds and mists. By the conquest of selfish desire and by the practice of meditation, we may become aware of the pearl, the 'luminous something', the heavenly principle within us. 'When one has exerted oneself for a long time [Chu Hsi says] finally a morning will come when complete understanding will open before one. Thereupon there will be thorough comprehension of all the multitude of things ... and every exercise of the mind will be marked by complete enlightenment.'[1] Thus the inner discipline which Chu Hsi stresses has its culmination in an experience of sudden enlightenment, as with Wang Shou-jen.

While the school of Universal Mind obviously stands nearer to Buddhism than that of Ideal Patterns, Buddhist influence was at work in both. But in one respect there is a marked difference in their outlook from that which is characteristic of Buddhism: both repudiate strongly the monastic ideal which continued to prevail even in Mahayana Buddhism. In a significant passage Wang Shou-jen seeks to turn the tables on the Buddhists in the matter of attachment. He contends that in reality it is

1. Fung Yu-Lan, *History of Chinese Philosophy*, II: 561.

because the Buddhists are attached to human relationships that they claim to have no attachment, and seek to escape. Confucianists, on the other hand, acknowledge the ties of sovereign and subject, father and son, husband and wife, and apply to them in each case the appropriate moral principle – love (jen), righteousness or justice, mutual respect – and thus maintain an inner freedom of spirit.[1] It was, indeed, the strength of the Confucian tradition that it sanctified the duties and tasks of common life; and Neo-Confucianism, while giving new scope to the transcendent factor in human nature and human experience, fully confirmed this tradition. 'To be faithful to one's daily round,' said Ch'eng Hao, 'to be reverent to one's duties, and to be loyal to one's fellow-men – these words touch bottom in regard to things above and things below.' His brother, Ch'eng Yi, declared:

Sprinkling and sweeping of floors are in the same category as developing one's Heaven-given nature to the highest and making the very best of one's Heaven-given lot.[2]

1. ibid., II: 610f.
2. Fung Yu-Lan, *The Spirit of Chinese Philosophy*, p. 200.

CHAPTER 5

Greek and Hellenistic Mysticism

I. GREEK MYSTICISM

(a) The 'Mysteries' and Orphic Religion

THE religion of the Greeks as we see it in Homer is a highly anthropomorphic polytheism. The gods are clearly defined personalities, marked off rigidly from their worshippers, demanding prayer and sacrifice of men, and in return granting them help and favour. But alongside of this popular religion, which was the affair pre-eminently of the State, there was in classical times a religion of another type, represented by the 'Mysteries', or cults celebrated in private by groups of devotees. It was these Mystery-cults which gave rise to aspiration and experience of a distinctively mystical character. Among them there are two which are of outstanding importance – the Eleusinian and the Dionysian Mysteries.

The Eleusinian Mysteries find their centre in the enactment of the myth of Demeter, the Earth-goddess, and her daughter, Kore, the Corn-maiden, who was identified with Persephone – in her origin a pre-Hellenic mistress of the realm of the dead. The Mysteries appear to have been derived from an early agrarian festival, concerned with the promotion of fertility; but they assumed, with the introduction of Persephone, a deeper and more inward meaning. The myth tells how Persephone, while gathering flowers in the meadows, was seized by Hades, the lord of the dead, and carried off to his kingdom, and how Demeter in her sorrow wandered throughout the world in quest of her, till at last she was brought back by Hermes at the behest of Zeus. Since she has tasted the food of Hades, Persephone must spend a third of the year with him, but year by year she comes back from the underworld in the spring. The ceremonies with which the festival was celebrated were open to all Greeks, and later to men and women of all nationalities seeking initiation. They were preceded by a preliminary process of ritual purification and a lengthy period of fasting – in imitation of Demeter – intended to wash away the stains of the former life of the initiates. Eventually the initiates were led in procession from Athens to Eleusis, where they bathed in the sea and roamed along the shore with lighted torches, thus sharing the wanderings of Demeter in her search for Persephone. They entered into fellowship with the goddesses in their separation and suffering, believing that they would share their triumph over death and so attain a blessed immortality – in striking contrast to the traditional belief of the Greeks that at death men entered a land of darkness and shades. It is sometimes held that the rites were followed by a second drama characterized by a sacred marriage, in which Persephone was wedded to Zeus, and the birth of a holy child – typifying the union of the initiates with the deity and their rebirth to a new and higher life. The final stage of initiation is known as the epopteia or 'beholding'. The door of the shrine at Eleusis was opened, and the priest of the Mysteries revealed to the gaze of the initiates a sacred object in a blaze of light. According to the early Christian writer, Hippolytus, the epopteia consisted in the display of an ear of corn. If this account is authentic (it is rejected by some modern authorities), it may very well have embodied a supreme and overwhelming mystery – a divine or numinous event. The ear of wheat 'is a revelation and pledge of the goddess, who first gave this fruit to mankind through the Eleusinians. It is an epiphany of Persephone herself, her mythical first recurrence in the shape of the grain after her descent to the realm of the Dead.'[1] It is also a symbol of the initiate's rebirth.

Rohde has said that there was no mystical element in the Eleusinian Mysteries. He regards mysticism as consisting essentially in 'the ecstatic exaltation of the soul to the recognition of its own godhead';[2] and certainly there is no trace of any such experience at Eleusis. But if mysticism is viewed more broadly, if its essential element is found rather to consist in the immediate apprehension of the Divine or Transcendent, the case is altered.

1. W. F. Otto, *The Eleusinian Mysteries*, in the collective volume *The Mysteries*, p. 26.
2. *Psyche*, English translation, 2nd edition, p. 224.

It is agreed that through their fellowship with Demeter and Persephone the initiates found the assurance of a blessed immortality. Classical writers recognize, moreover, that the Mysteries brought men a certain moral elevation. Through their contact with the unseen powers presented in the myth, they gained the sense of a higher destiny in life and death. The initiate, says W. F. Otto, was 'received into the sphere of the acts and sufferings of the goddesses – into the immediate reality of their being. His vision was no mere looking on. It was a sublimation to a higher existence, a transformation of his being.'[1] The re-enactment of the myth and the culminating revelation to which it led may thus have been to some, at least, a means by which their consciousness was raised beyond things seen to the perception of divine Reality.

The mystical element in the Eleusinian Mysteries appears to have been the sense of the numinous evoked by the rites. In the Dionysian Mysteries there was a sense of actual possession by, and union with, the god. Dionysus, known also as Bacchus, was a god of vegetation and especially of the vine, and of animal life generally; he was also the lord of the souls of the dead. He was originally worshipped by the people of Thrace, to the north of Greece; the isle of Crete was another early centre of his religion. The cult spread throughout Greece and the adjoining islands. Its distinguishing feature was its orgiastic character. It was celebrated by a sacred dance, held at night by torchlight; wine was drunk as a sacrament. The dancers felt themselves to be possessed by the god, and through the ecstatic consciousness of divine possession each one was regarded as a personification of Dionysus (or Bacchus); they were called Bacchi or Bacchae. Being thus exalted to the plane of the divine, the devotees were sometimes held to attain miraculous powers – powers of prophecy, of the healing of disease, even of controlling the forces of Nature.

Dionysus was a god who died and rose again. The myth is of particular importance in connexion both with the early features of the cult and with the later development of the religion associated with it. Dionysus (known in this aspect as Zagreus) was the son of Zeus and Persephone. Zeus intended him to become the

1. op. cit., p. 30.

ruler of the world, but his plan was frustrated by the Titans, an ancient race of giants. Egged on by Hera, the wife of Zeus, the Titans tore the infant's body to pieces and devoured it. In his wrath Zeus slew them with his thunderbolt; but he caused the human race to spring from their ashes. Since man is descended from the Titans, who devoured the god, there is both an evil and a divine element in his nature. It is through initiation into the Mysteries of Dionysus that men can be purged of their evil inheritance. Dionysus rose from the dead by a miracle. The goddess Athene obtained the heart of the child, and brought it to Zeus, who swallowed it and caused Dionysus to be reborn as the son of Semele, a Phrygian Earth-goddess. The aim of the cult is union with Dionysus, who dies and is reborn. The dismemberment of the body of the god appears to be a reflection of a peculiarly savage feature of the early rites. It is said that in their frenzy the worshippers of Dionysus, as they roamed the mountains in their dance, would tear living beasts limb from limb and devour their flesh, thus partaking of a crude sacramental feast. The savage features of the cult were largely eliminated in classical times, but the eating of raw flesh long remained.

The myth of the death and rebirth of Dionysus was a prominent aspect of the Orphic movement, which exerted a considerable influence in the time of Plato. The Orphics were a band of devotees who set out to proclaim a message of salvation which appealed to all men. They were the first itinerant preachers in Europe. Their activity began in the sixth century B.C. and lasted well into the Christian era. Orpheus was, according to legend, a musician and a pioneer of civilization in Thrace; he was also a seer, who introduced the worship of Apollo. One story tells that he met his death at the hands of the female votaries of Dionysus (the Maenads), who tore him to pieces because he tried to modify their religion by the introduction of the cult of Apollo. The main fact appears to be that Orphism represents a reformed and civilized system of Dionysiac worship. In course of time a body of Orphic literature arose, comprising hymns and other poems attributed to Orpheus. Some of the hymns are quoted by Plato and later writers. They were, no doubt, collected for liturgical purposes by the Orphic brotherhoods. Orphic teaching is also known from a number of gold tablets found in tombs in South Italy and Crete, where brotherhoods were established at an early date. The tablets contain instructions to the soul concerning its conduct in the world beyond and declarations which it is to make regarding its origin and destiny, its sufferings and aspirations.

A fundamental phase of Orphic teaching was belief in transmigration. Plato refers to the belief as an ancient one (in *Phaedo*, 70). It was traditional in Thrace, as among many early peoples. The Orphics related it to their conception of the dual nature of man. According to the myth, as we have seen, man is a compound of contrasted elements. 'I am child of Earth and of starry Heaven,' the soul is made to say in one of the tablets.[1] And, again, it says: 'I have flown out of the sorrowful, weary wheel. I have paid the penalty for deeds unrighteous.'[2] For the Orphics transmigration has been moralized; it has become a cycle of purgation, in which men suffer for their sins and for the hereditary taint which lies upon them as descendants of the Titans. They seek deliverance from the round of rebirth through initiation into the Mysteries of Dionysus, and through observance of rules of ceremonial purity (like abstention from flesh-meat) and righteousness of life. The positive aim is union with the divine, not merely as an ecstatic experience through identification with Dionysus in the Mysteries, but as a permanent state of being involving liberation from the 'prison-house' of the body and the attainment of immortal blessedness. The soul in its essence is of divine origin. 'I am of your blessed race,' it says to the immortal gods, 'but fate has laid me low.' But now it has been reborn into a higher life, and it receives the assurance: 'Happy and blessed one, thou shalt be God instead of mortal.'[3]

(b) *The Mysticism of Plato and Aristotle*

The Orphic movement was the movement of a small minority of religious devotees, yet it exercised a profound influence on Greek religious thought. Little is known of the actual teaching of

1. J. E. Harrison, *Prolegomena to the Study of Greek Religion*, 1st edition, p. 574.
2. ibid., p. 586.   3. ibid.

Pythagoras, who migrated from Samos and founded a religious fraternity in Magna Graecia (South Italy), where Orphic influence was already active, towards the close of the sixth century B.C. But it is clear that he accepted the main features of the Orphic doctrine – the divinity and immortality of the soul, its imprisonment in the body, its reincarnation in successive lives, and its eventual return, through continued purgation, to the divine. It was probably the distinctive aspect of the philosophy of Pythagoras that the divine element in the soul is the power of knowledge – the power to know eternal truth, which lies in a realm transcending the senses, and is reflected in the physical world in the facts of order, proportion, harmony. At a certain time in his life, probably after the composition of his earliest dialogues, Plato came into contact with Pythagorean ideas, and it was under their influence that he developed what is most characteristic in his philosophy.

The philosophy of Plato has a definitely mystical aspect. In his greatest work, the *Republic*, he describes the training of the rulers of his ideal commonwealth: it is the essential purpose of this training to lead them to the vision of eternal Reality. In the analogy of the Cave (in Book VII) he illustrates the position of those who are unawakened to the truth – whose outlook is confined to the world of the senses. Such men are prisoners in a dark underground cavern. A fire is burning behind them, and between them and the fire is a road along which people pass. The prisoners are shackled, so that all they can see is the shadows cast by the fire on the wall of the cavern. Such, Plato says, is our situation in the physical world: the things we see are only shadows; the realm of truth and reality lies beyond. The prisoners can only see things as they are, if they emerge into the light of the sun. So, if we are to see the truth, our souls must be illuminated by the light of supreme Reality, which is the sun of the eternal world.

The ascent of the soul to the vision of divine Reality, which Plato calls 'the Good', is possible because of the essential nature of the soul. The Good is itself the highest of the Ideas or Forms – the eternal essences or ideal archetypes of things, which constitute the sphere of Reality. Plato's approach is primarily that of the logician, concerned with the problem of knowledge. But for him this approach coincides with that of the man of vision. The senses present us only with particular facts, which are in a state of perpetual flux. Knowledge by its very nature is concerned in any sphere with that which is universal and permanent. It pertains therefore to the realm of the Ideas or Forms, partially and imperfectly expressed in the particular facts of the world, but eternally transcending them. The soul belongs in its inmost nature to the world of Forms. Before its descent into the body, as Plato maintains in the *Phaedo* and the *Phaedrus*, it existed in the higher world, where it enjoyed an immediate vision of Reality. So far as knowledge is attained in our present phase of being, it is therefore recollection (anamnesis) – 'recollection of those things which in time past our soul beheld when it travelled in the company of the gods, and . . . lifted its head into the region of eternal essence. . . . For every man's soul has by the law of his birth been a seer of eternal truth.' Here we are fettered to the body 'as an oyster to his shell' – tied to its limitations and its narrow range of vision. But 'whenever men see here any resemblance of what they witnessed there, they are struck with wonder'.[1] It is especially the sight of beauty in the lower world which reminds us of the upper glories, and creates in us a force of passion or desire (eros), which finds its fulfilment in the vision of the ideal and eternal Beauty – 'the divine, the original, the supreme Beauty', in gazing on which a man is 'in contact, not with a shadow, but with Reality'.[2]

It has been said that 'Plato's religion consists in the passionate uplifting of the mind towards the realm of perfection'.[3] Normally, as we see in the analogy of the Cave, men live in a world of shadows. If they are to discover the truth, they must turn from darkness to light; they must turn the eye of the soul from the perishing world in which they live, 'until it is enabled to endure the contemplation of the real world'.[4] But the eternal world is

1. *Phaedrus*, 249f.   2. *Symposium*, 211f.
3. Adam, *The Religious Teachers of Greece*, p. 430.
4. *Republic*, 518.

not wholly divided from the world of the senses. The Forms are not only transcendent; they are immanent in the things of time and space, which participate in them. 'If a thing is beautiful, it is so for no other reason than because it partakes of the Ideal Beauty.'[1] Cornford has suggested that Plato's conception was based on mystical experience. The Forms, he contends, are 'group-souls' related to the things which participate in their nature as the deity of a mystery-cult, like Dionysus, is related to his group of worshippers. Just as the worshippers of Dionysus believed that in their orgiastic rites 'the one god entered into each and all of them', and they '"partook" of the one divine nature, which was "communicated" to them all and "present" in each,' so Plato held that the nature of the eternal Forms was communicated to, and present in, the objects which resembled them.[2] It is, in any case, the presence of the Forms in the things of time and space which, for Plato, dawns upon the soul at a certain stage of its growth, and elicits the passion for wisdom and knowledge. The lover of knowledge can be satisfied with nothing less than the vision of divine Reality. He 'strains every nerve to reach real existence', pressing on beyond the sphere of manifold phenomena, not desisting from his passion 'till he has apprehended the real nature of all things'.[3]

What is knowledge as Plato understands it? In his account of the training of the Guardians (in *Republic*, VII) he contrasts wisdom with the other virtues. The latter are 'formed in the course of time by habit and exercise'; wisdom, on the other hand, is 'a faculty residing in the soul of each person'. It is 'the eye of the soul', which is normally fixed on things below, because men are preoccupied with sensual enjoyments. They must be released from such snares, and 'turned round to look at objects that are true', if they are to know Reality. It is characteristic of Plato that he speaks of knowledge in terms of vision. 'The eye of the soul' is *nous* – the highest category of mind. A great deal of misunderstanding has arisen because *nous* has commonly been translated 'reason' or 'intelligence'. Certainly the term often has that

1. *Phaedo*, 100.
2. *From Religion to Philosophy*, 1st edition, p. 254.
3. *Republic*, 490.

meaning; but it is used also for the power of intuitive insight which brings 'a sudden flashing glimpse of the truth'.[1] In the *Timaeus*, Plato identifies *nous* with the higher part of the soul, which is divine and immortal. He describes it as 'the divinity [daimon] of each one'[2] – his guiding genius. It is through this power in the soul that it knew the Forms in its pre-existent life; and it is through the same power that it will rise again into contact with Reality. In the *Republic*, a severe intellectual discipline is imposed on the Guardians, but it is the distinctive quality of these studies that they 'tend to draw the soul from the fleeting to the Real'. The study of geometry, for example, being concerned with purely abstract and timeless relations, 'facilitates our contemplation of the essential Form of Good'. The culminating feature of the intellectual process is the study of the method of dialectical reasoning, which 'carries back its hypotheses to the very first principle of all', and leads to a strict definition of the Form of Good. But the intellectual training, necessary as it is to the education of the philosopher, is only a preparation for his ultimate experience of contemplation or immediate vision of Reality. After a prolonged period of study, followed by an extended course of practical administration, the Guardians 'must be introduced to their final task, and constrained to lift up the eye of the soul, and fix it on that which gives light to all things'.

It is characteristic of Plato's mysticism that it finds expression in terms of vision rather than of union with the divine. Union is implied in one passage in the *Republic*, where he says that the lover of knowledge, through the exercise of *nous*, 'holds intercourse with that which really exists, and begets wisdom and truth'.[3] Vision is for Plato an experience which transforms a man's soul and penetrates his life. 'It is the end and aim of all his conduct, both in private and in public.' In expounding the parable of the Cave, he speaks of the profound change of outlook which comes to those who learn to see the truth: they no longer care for the things which men commonly prize. The man who looks to eternal things has no desire to take part in men's quarrels, or to

1. Guthrie, *The Greeks and their Gods*, p. 365.
2. *Timaeus*, 90.   3. *Republic*, 490.

catch the infection of their jealousies and hates; he seeks to fashion himself in the likeness of the eternal realm, where all wrong is done away; he reproduces that order in his soul, and becomes god-like, as far as man may.[1] He devotes himself to the hard duties of public life, not because he desires it, but for his country's good.[2] The likeness to the divine which vision brings carries with it, moreover, an assurance of immortality. The soul is intrinsically immortal; in its higher nature it is akin to the Forms. But in its present fallen state the soul is subject to all manner of evils, and as long as it remains a prey to their power it is drawn again after death into the physical world, and is reborn either in animal or in human form.[3] It is only the man of vision who wins release and gains a deathless life. Such a man takes up his abode in the isles of the blessed; he becomes the friend of God and immortal; contemplating that which is true and divine, his soul goes to a kindred essence and one like itself.[4]

The object of vision is described by Plato in impersonal terms. He speaks of it sometimes as the Forms in general, more often as the Good or the Form of Good. In the *Symposium* it is the supreme Beauty. In the *Republic* (509) the Good is said to possess an inexpressible beauty, so it is evident that the supreme Beauty and the Good are one and the same. What Plato has in mind is, in any case, the unseen and eternal Reality underlying the things of time and space. That Reality may be conceived alternatively as the order of being comprising the Forms, or as the greatest of the Forms, which is the source of all the rest. The Forms are not independent realities existing side by side; they constitute an organic Whole. In the *Laws* (30–1) Plato speaks of the world of Forms as 'the original of the universe' – the model or pattern on the basis of which the physical world was made – which contains them all in itself, and which is at the same time 'a perfect living Being'. They are thus not to be regarded as mere lifeless abstractions, but as possessing a life and a perfection which earthly things can only dimly reflect. The source of the Forms is said to be the Good. Plato compares the Good to the sun: it holds the same relation to the objects of knowledge as the sun holds to the

1. ibid., 500.   2. ibid., 540.   3. *Phaedo*, 80.
4. *Republic*, 540; *Symposium*, 212; *Phaedo*, 84.

visible objects of the world. The Good, that is to say, makes it possible for us to know the Forms, and it gives them their being. It is clear that Plato does not imply that the Forms were created by any temporal process, since they are eternal. They proceed eternally, we must understand, from the ultimate Source of being.

The creation of the world in time and space is the main theme of the *Timaeus*. The Creator is the Demiurge (the 'Craftsman'), who makes the world on the model of the eternal order. It has been suggested that the Demiurge, who is also described as God, is the Good considered in its aspect as Creator (through the Forms) of the material universe. He is described as 'the best of intellectual and everlasting natures'; He 'desired that all things should be as like Himself as possible'.[1] Plato himself does not raise the question of their relationship. In fact, he nowhere attempts to coordinate the various views expressed in his dialogues on such issues. As Solmsen has shown in *Plato's Theology*, he makes different approaches to ultimate problems without seeking to unify them in a single scheme. In the *Laws*, where he deals with the proof of God and the problems of divine providence and human destiny, he thinks of God as the World-Soul – the Source of all movement and change – whereas in the *Timaeus* the World-Soul is the creation of the Demiurge.

It is impossible to attribute to Plato a completely unified scheme of theology, although the main outlines of his teaching are sufficiently consistent. It must be remembered that he uses the word 'God' in a wider sense than we commonly do. He has been described as 'a pagan polytheist', because he recognizes a plurality of divine Powers. He speaks of the souls of the heavenly bodies as 'created gods'; the world in its totality is 'a blessed god'. Yet he quite plainly affirms that one Power alone is supreme. In the *Timaeus* (41) the Demiurge is pictured as addressing the lesser gods as 'Gods, children of gods, who are my works, and of whom I am the Maker and the Father'. In the *Republic* (596f.) he refers to God as the Creator of the Forms, thus identifying Him with the Good. It has been urged that this identification cannot be intended seriously because of Plato's different approach in the *Timaeus*, and because the Form of Good stands for goodness,

1. *Timaeus*, 37, 29.

while God is a supremely good Being.[1] But, as we have shown, the Forms are not simply abstract qualities, such as 'goodness' suggests to us, but eternal realities existing in a transcendent sphere; and the Good is the ultimate Source of all being. The essential attribute of God, as Plato points out in Book II of the *Republic*, is His changeless goodness. He stresses here the crudity and inadequacy, judged from this standard, of the traditional ideas of the gods such as are taught by Homer, and the importance of avoiding these ideas in the education of children. As he says in the *Theaetetus* (176): 'The truth is that God is never in any way unrighteous; He is perfect righteousness, and he of us who is most righteous is most like Him.' This doctrine of divine goodness finds its 'philosophical fulfilment', as Adam says, in the Form of the Good.[2]

While Plato in the *Republic* identifies the Form of Good with God, he does not speak directly of God as the object of that vision which is the supreme attainment of the lover of knowledge. The vision arises, as we have seen, as the outcome of a prolonged process of intellectual discipline and inquiry, in which the philosopher is led from the appearances of the world to the Reality which underlies them. That Reality is, indeed, divine; but it is in its essential nature beyond the range of discursive thought. It is doubtless the very depth and greatness of the object of vision which is responsible for Plato's preference for impersonal language. In face of the ultimate Reality human thought and words are utterly inadequate,[3] and Plato has recourse to paradox. As he says in the *Republic*, the Good is beyond existence as we know it – it 'transcends existence in dignity and power' (509). Yet it is 'the most excellent among the things that are' (532) and 'the most blissful thing in the realm of being' (526). It 'is the limit of our inquiries, and can barely be perceived; but, when it is perceived, we cannot help concluding that it is the

---

1. Ross, *Plato's Theory of Ideas*, pp. 78f., 43.

2. op. cit., p. 443.

3. In the *Seventh Letter*, attributed to Plato, it is said that the highest in philosophy cannot be stated, but after laborious thought it arises suddenly as a fire in the soul.

Source of all that is bright and beautiful' (517). The nature of
the Good can, perhaps, be most fittingly summed up, in Armstrong's words, as 'the single transcendent Reality of absolute
perfection which is the ultimate cause and explanation of the
universe'.[1]

The philosophy of Aristotle differs widely from that of Plato,
yet it also has a mystical aspect. Aristotle began as a follower of
Plato, but in course of time he came to develop a radically divergent outlook. He came, in particular, to reject his master's
doctrine of the Forms and his conception of the soul as pre-
existent in an ideal world and as involved in a succession of
earthly lives. For Aristotle, as for Plato, knowledge pertains to
the ideal or universal essence of things; but for him that essence –
their 'form' as distinct from their 'matter' – exists, not in a
transcendent sphere, but only in the finite. In his view of the
soul, Aristotle sets aside the Orphic tradition accepted by Plato,
but at the same time he recognizes in the soul a principle which is
divine and eternal. This principle is *nous* or intuitive intelligence.
For Aristotle the soul is the principle of life common to all
animate beings, but assuming different forms according to their
nature. There is in plants a vegetative soul, in animals a sensitive
soul, in men a rational soul. But in the rational soul there are
different elements. Reason may be passive, or it may be active.
Discursive thought is passive in the sense that it receives its
content from the things about us, i.e. from the qualities (or
'forms') which they contain. Alongside this capacity there is in
us an active power (*nous*), whereby we grasp the essence of things,
and see them in their unity. *Nous* is not merely a human quality
bound up with the body and perishing at death, as with other
mental qualities. It is the essence of the life of God Himself.
'The life of God is like the highest kind of activity with us; but
while we can maintain it but for a short time, with Him it is
eternal, for it is an activity which is at the same time the joy of
attainment.' In this contemplative activity 'subject and object are
identified. . . . It has its object in itself. Contemplation is thus the
best and happiest of activities. . . . In God is life, for the activity

1. *An Introduction to Ancient Philosophy*, p. 39.

of intelligence [*nous*] is life, and He is that activity. Thus His essential activity constitutes a perfect and blessed life. We speak of God therefore as a living Being, perfect and eternal.'[1]

Nous is for Aristotle the essence of the life and activity of God. As he says in the *Nicomachean Ethics*: 'The divine life, which surpasses all others in blessedness, consists in contemplation' (x: 8: 7). But *nous* is also the true and essential being of man. 'This part of us would seem to constitute our true self, since it is the sovereign and better part. . . . It is *nous* that in the truest sense is the man.'[2] The highest aspect of the nature of man is, in other words, identical with the nature of God. A life in which the ideal of contemplation was fully realized, therefore, 'would be something more than human, for it would not be the expression of man's nature, but of some divine element in that nature'. It is the realization of this end of mystical contemplation which is the highest goal of human endeavour. 'We ought as far as possible to put off our mortality, and make every effort to live in the exercise of the highest of our faculties.'[3] Through the exercise of contemplative activity, man participates in the eternal life of God. The knowledge of God which man thus attains is the knowledge whereby God knows Himself entering into us.

II. PHILO

It is the special interest of Philo that we see in him more fully than any other writer the intermingling of Hellenistic and Jewish culture. The blending of cultures was pre-eminently characteristic of Alexandria, where he lived from about 25 B.C. to A.D. 40 or 50, and it was the seat before his time of a Judaism profoundly affected by Greek philosophy. Philo belongs to the history both of Jewish and of Hellenistic mysticism. He was an orthodox Jew, insisting on the observance of the Law, and accepting the divine authority of all that was contained in the Old Testament. His works were written mainly as commentaries on the narratives of Genesis and Exodus. Yet his thought was in fact shaped by Platonic and Stoic philosophy. By means of allegorical interpretation, he was able to read into the Bible-stories ideas derived

1. *Metaphysics*, xii: 7.
2. *Nicomachean Ethics*, x: 8: 9.   3. ibid., x: 8: 8.

from this philosophy, and so to claim that they were taught by Scripture. The method of allegorical interpretation was applied before Philo by Greek philosophers to the works of Homer, and by Jewish expositors, both in Alexandria and in Palestine, to the Old Testament. In view of his dependence on Hellenistic culture, it seems best to deal with Philo's mysticism in this connexion, especially as he exerted no direct influence on the growth of Jewish mysticism, owing to the changed conditions brought about by the Jewish revolts against Rome and the spread of Christianity.

We have in Philo, as in the Hermetic writers, a 'negative theology' which rests on the realization of the infinite glory and perfection of God. Yet, like the Hermetists, Philo recognizes the manifestation of God in the world. 'The highest art and knowledge [he says] is shown in this universe, so that it has been wrought by One of excellent and absolute perfection.'[1] God is the active Cause or Mind of the universe – 'better than the Good itself and the Beautiful itself' – who shaped matter or 'the passive substance' (the negation of true being) and changed it into 'the most perfect possible work'.[2] God is 'the Fountain of beauty'. 'The good and beautiful things in the world could never have been what they are, save that they were made in the image of the Archetype, which is truly good and beautiful.'[3] The world is God's 'only beloved Son', produced by the union of God with His knowledge.[4] For Philo, therefore, the contemplation of the world is a stage in the ascent of the soul to God, since it points us to the Source of all things. But it is only a stage. It has, indeed, a certain danger. The contemplation of the world leads men sometimes to identify the world with God, and to find in the movements of the stars the cause of all that happens on earth – as in the astral religion, derived from Babylonia, which was so widely prevalent in Philo's time. The soul's ascent is symbolized by the migration of Abraham from Ur of the Chaldees to Haran, and from Haran to the desert. We must move from the contemplation of the outer universe to the exploration of our own self and its relation to the things of sense. Thus we shall reflect that, as there

1. *The Special Laws*, 1: 34.   2. *On the Creation of the World*, 8.
3. *On the Cherubim*, 86.   4. *On Drunkenness*, 30.

is in us a mind which has the power of ruling all the phases of our being, so there is in the world a Mind which is endowed with sovereign power, exercising its providence over all things.[1] If we are to know God, we must learn to know ourselves. It is the preliminary exploration of our being in the sense-world, typified by Haran, that is the second stage in the ascent of the soul. But we must, like Abraham, migrate afar from Haran. We must not stay in the sense-world in which we are imprisoned. We must separate ourselves from what is mortal in us; we must enter deeply into ourselves. 'The friends of contemplation choose to live in solitude and darkness, so that nothing sensible may obscure the gaze of the soul.'[2]

It is the essential fact of man's nature, Philo teaches, that there is in us a capacity of self-transcendence. Man is made in the image of God by virtue of his possession of *nous*. He speaks sometimes of the divine image in man as mediated by the Logos, the 'first-born Son of God' or 'second Deity', who plays a subordinate part in his teaching, after the manner of the divine intermediaries characteristic of 'middle Platonism'. The Logos gathers up in his own being the divine Ideas in the pattern of which the world was created. It is the pre-eminence of man that he was made in the image of the universal Archetype. Philo speaks also of *nous* (the higher soul) in Stoic terms, as a warm and fiery breath, which in his conception is an immediate gift of God, 'a breath of His own Deity' sent down from above – 'a part of this great divine and blessed Soul ... a part not separated from its Source, for no part of the Divinity is truly cut off so as to exist apart; it is only an extension'.[3] Since the soul is thus in its inmost nature divine, it has the power to reach out beyond itself, to enter into contact with the whole of being in time and space. 'And when it has reached the limits of the earth and the sea, even the air and the sky ... it desires to go farther, and to apprehend, if it is possible, the Essence of God.'[4]

It is because man in his deeper being is one with God that it is possible for us to see and know Him. But the path of vision is the path of 'solitude and darkness'. While Philo speaks of God

1. *On the Migration of Abraham*, 185f.   2. ibid., 191.
3. *That the Worst is wont to attack the Better*, 90.   4. ibid., 89.

as manifested in the universe, he lays the greatest emphasis on the divine transcendence and ineffability. 'To inquire about essence or quality in God', he says roundly, 'is a folly fit for the world's childhood'; He is 'the Power that is beyond conception'.[1] It follows from the very nature of His being that He eludes the meshes of intellectual understanding, and the recognition of this truth is essential to the higher knowledge.

God is high above place and time ... He is contained by nothing, but transcends all. But though transcending what He has made, none the less He filled the universe with Himself. ... When, therefore, the God-loving soul searches into the nature of the Existent, he enters on a quest of that which is beyond matter and beyond sight. And out of this quest there accrues to him a vast boon – to comprehend that God is incomprehensible.[2]

The way which leads to the vision of God is, in one aspect, the negative way of 'self-naughting' and detachment from the world. Philo regards the 'contemplative life' as a stage which follows the fulfilment of the demands of the 'practical life'. We must fully meet the claims of men in the life of society before we can give ourselves wholly to the claims of God. 'First make yourself familiar with virtue as exercised in our dealings with men, to the end that you may be introduced to that which has to do with our relation to God.'[3] In his work *On the Contemplative Life*, he describes with great sympathy the monastic life of the Therapeutae in the neighbourhood of Alexandria. He also praised the life of the Essenes. If we are to attain the vision of God, he says, we must prepare ourselves by 'excising desires, pleasures, griefs, fears, follies, injustices'.[4] We must, by divine grace, 'leave the ranks of mortality', and 'loose the chains which the empty aims and desires of mortal life have fastened upon us'.[5] We must, indeed, renounce ourselves. 'He who has completely understood himself renounces himself completely, when he has seen the nothingness of all that is created.'[6] As Adam sought to hide himself from God among the trees of the Garden, so 'he who is

1. *On the Posterity of Cain*, 168; *On Flight and Finding*, 141.
2. *On the Posterity of Cain*, 14–16.
3. *On Flight and Finding*, 38.
4. *Questions and Answers on Exodus*, II: 51.
5. *On Drunkenness*, 145, 152.   6. *On Dreams*, I: 60.

escaping from God flees to himself'; while, conversely, 'he who escapes from his own mind flies to the Mind of the universe, confessing that all the things of the human mind are vain and unreal, and attributing everything to God'.[1] As Abraham departed from his land, his kinsfolk, his father's house, so we must leave behind in contemplation all that these things typify – the body, the senses, the use of spoken words. We must go further than that: we must in some sort leave ourselves behind. 'Be a fugitive from thyself also, and issue forth from thyself.' We must, by divine grace, enter the state of ecstasy. 'Like persons possessed and corybants, be filled with divine frenzy, even as the prophets are inspired.' If we are to enter into our true inheritance, our mind must be 'under the divine afflatus and no longer in its own keeping, stirred to its depths and maddened by heavenward yearning, drawn by the truly existent Being and pulled upwards by Him'.[2] Such a state of impassioned yearning and ecstatic contemplation can come to us only by the grace of God. 'Without divine grace it is impossible to leave the ranks of mortality.' But 'when grace fills the soul, it is possessed and inspired', and it hastens to 'that most glorious and loveliest of visions, the vision of the Uncreated'.[3]

It is characteristic of Philo, as an interpreter of Hebrew tradition, that he relates the condition of ecstasy specifically to the experience of the prophets. Modern students differ as to the relative importance in the formation of his mystical outlook of Jewish and Hellenistic influences, but in this respect the two influences actually converge. 'No pronouncement of a prophet [he says] is ever his own; he is an interpreter prompted by Another in all his utterances ... and he surrenders the citadel of his soul to a new Visitor and Tenant, the divine Spirit which plays upon the vocal organism.'[4] The prophet, he claims, is so completely possessed by the divine Spirit that while he is under the divine afflatus his personal consciousness is entirely in abeyance. 'His organs of speech, mouth, and tongue are wholly in the employ of Another.' So whenever men rise to the state of mystical ecstasy, the limited consciousness of man is replaced by

1. *Allegorical Interpretation*, III: 9.   2. *Who is the Heir?*, 69f.
3. *On Drunkenness*, 145f., 152.   4. *On the Special Laws*, IV: 49.

the infinite Consciousness of God. 'While the light of the mind is still all around us, we are self-contained, not possessed. But when it comes to its setting, ecstasy and divine possession and madness naturally fall upon us. For when the Light of God shines, the human light sets; when the divine Light sets, the human dawns and rises.'[1]

With Philo the influence of Hebrew tradition was too strong to allow him to use the language of deification, like the Hermetic writers. He speaks instead of the attainment of an intermediate condition. The soul which is lifted up to the vision of God 'is superior to man but less than God ... We may say, quite properly that it is neither God nor man.' In this higher state the soul is 'possessed of divine love', it enters 'the inmost shrine', it forgets itself, and 'fixes its thoughts and memories on God'. But it only retains this intermediate rank until the moment when it leaves the state of ecstasy, and returns to the normal conditions of the body.[2]

III. THE HERMETIC MOVEMENT

The group of writings known as 'Hermetic' represent a most interesting variety of Hellenistic mysticism. They owe their name to the fact that they are attributed mainly to Hermes Trismegistus ('thrice-greatest Hermes'), whom their authors regard as a sage or prophet of ancient Egypt who was deified after his death in the form of Thoth, taken as identical with the Greek Hermes. The books consist chiefly of dialogues between Hermes and his son Tat, or between Hermes and Asclepius. They appear to have originated in Egypt in the first three centuries of our era. The Egyptian element, however, is only superficial; the authors were, no doubt, Greeks settled in Egypt. The movement from which they sprang is doubtless earlier in its beginnings than the writings. We have no independent evidence of its existence as a movement, and it has been suggested that the books are 'a purely literary phenomenon'.[3] On the other hand, Reitzenstein, whose work on

1. *Who is the Heir?*, 264–6.
2. *On Dreams*, ii: 229f., 232.
3. A. J. Festugière, *La Révélation d'Hermès Trismégiste* (i: 84). Festugière, however, admits that the writings may have served as books of edification for groups (i: 428). He speaks later of 'Hermetic conventicles' (iv: 199).

the *Poimandres* did so much to draw attention to their importance half a century ago, regarded them as owing their origin to religious communities in Egypt formed by prophetic leaders. There are certainly indications in the books of the Hermetic Corpus that the religion had a social as well as a purely individual aspect. There are hymns and prayers, and in one instance (*Asclepius* 41a) there is a rubric directing men to face the South when they pray at sunset and the East when they pray at sunrise. There was, moreover, evidently a tradition of public preaching. At the close of the *Poimandres* – the first treatise in the Corpus – the prophet prays: 'Empower me that I may enlighten with this grace those of the race who are in ignorance, my brethren and Thy sons' (I, 32). Yet the books contain no suggestion of ceremonies or sacraments or of a hierarchy. Their emphasis is throughout on personal experience, mediated by private instruction, which is expressed in the dialogues. In the *Asclepius*, Hermes says that gifts of incense are unfit for God, who 'is filled with all things that exist and lacks nothing. Let us rather adore Him with thanksgiving, for words of praise are the only offering that He accepts.' The Hermetists, it seems, constituted an esoteric brotherhood, consisting of small groups of men gathered round a teacher, like the Hindu guru or the Muslim murshid, who sought to lead them to the knowledge of God.

The Hermetic writings are intended to guide men to mystical experience. They do not present us with a systematic philosophy or a completely uniform mode of thought. Yet they stand in the main for a common outlook, which is closely similar in essentials to that of Philo and of Plotinus, and which has certain points of contact with that of the Gnostics. Their philosophy is, broadly, that of Platonism in its later development, as influenced by Aristotle and the Stoics. There was also a certain Jewish influence. The writer of the first tractate was acquainted with the Greek version of the Old Testament (the Septuagint), and used the story of Creation and the Fall as the groundwork of his teaching.[1] There is no evidence of Christian influence, but it is significant that the hymn of praise with which this writer ends his work is

1. See C. H. Dodd, *The Bible and the Greeks.*

found in a collection of Christian prayers in a papyrus of the third century.

For the Hermetists God is ineffable: 'Of Him no words can tell, no tongue can speak, silence only can declare Him' (I: 31). He is the supreme Reality outflowing all concepts – 'transcending all pre-eminence, excelling all praise', most fittingly described as the Good and the Beautiful, as Mind (*nous*) and as Light. 'We may dare to say that the essence of God ... is the Beautiful and the Good' (VI: 4). *Nous* is 'of the very essence of God' (XII: 1) and so are Light and Life (I: 21). In the *Poimandres*, the prophet sees in vision the infinite divine Light which is the ultimate Source of all things, and he sees within the Light the archetypal universe. The light consists of countless divine Energies or Powers, which constitute the ideal world. Creation is sometimes, as in the *Poimandres*, attributed to a secondary divine Being, the Demiurge, generated by the Primal Mind; sometimes the Primal Mind is Himself the Demiurge. These differing tendencies correspond to the differences of view characteristic of the 'middle Platonism' which was contemporary with many of the Hermetic writers.

The relation of God to the universe is conceived at once in terms of creative Will and of immanental presence or inner identity of being. God is the Creator and Father of the cosmos, which is His image and His offspring (VIII: 2). By His Will He framed the things that are, so that all things are from Him (IV: 1). He does not separate Himself from His works, hence there is nothing in which God is not (XII: 21). All that is, He contains within Himself as His thoughts (XI: 20).[1] He who is beyond all name, the Unmanifest, is yet the most manifest, since 'there is nothing which He is not, for all things that exist are even He' (V: 10).

Man is 'a being of divine nature' (X: 24). He who knows himself passes into God, because 'the All-Father is Light and Life, whereof man is made' (I: 21). In his essential being man is *nous*, which is divine, 'wherefore some men (who know their true nature) are divine, and their humanity is nigh unto divinity' (XII: 1). But commonly men do not know themselves or God, and

1. In 'middle Platonism' the Ideas became thoughts of God.

it is this ignorance or blindness which is the root cause of evil.
'The evil of the soul is ignorance. The soul that has not come to
know Reality or the nature of things or the Good, but is blind,
is tossed about by the passions of the body; and the wretched
soul, not knowing itself ... carries round the body like a load,
not controlling it, but controlled by it' (x: 8). In the *Poimandres*
we have the myth of the Fall. The Primal Mind, it is said, gave
birth to a man in His own image – i.e. to a heavenly man. He gave
him authority over all creatures, and man conceived the desire
to create, and entered the created world. Nature saw him and
loved him, and he returned her love. Through his union with
Nature man lost his purely celestial character, and became a
twofold being – mortal by his attachment to matter, immortal by
his inmost being. The Fall of the heavenly man is thus at the same
time the origin of earthly man. It is the essential significance of
the myth that it points to the way which man must tread, if he is
to fulfil his true destiny: he must liberate himself from the bonds
of matter, and lay hold upon his deeper self.

The myth of the Fall is found only in the first tractate of the
Corpus Hermeticum, but the outlook which it symbolizes is
typical of the other writings. 'It is not possible, my son,' says
Hermes in another treatise, 'to attach yourself both to things
mortal and to things divine. There are two sorts of things, the
corporeal and the incorporeal. That which is mortal is of the one
sort, and that which is divine is of the other sort; and he who
wills to make his choice is left free to choose the one or the other'
(iv: 6). If we are to be born in *nous*, it is said elsewhere, we must
purge ourselves of 'the irrational torments of matter' – which are
specified as ignorance, grief, intemperance, incontinence, in-
justice, avarice, deceitfulness, envy, guile, anger, rashness,
malice (xiii: 7). Festugière has said that the *Poimandres* is
pre-eminently Gnostic,[1] and Dodd has compared its teaching with
that of the second century Gnostic, Valentinus, while he admits
that the Valentinian system of mythology is much more complex
and elaborate.[2] But there is this important distinction between
the two – that while in the *Poimandres* it is man who has fallen,
in the Valentinian system the whole world as it exists is the result

1. op cit., ii: 64.   2. op cit., pp. 207f.

of the Fall of Sophia (Wisdom), who is herself an Aeon or divine emanation. The standpoint of the Hermetists may not be altogether consistent, but in general their attitude is the same as that of Plotinus, who, while he emphasized the need of freeing the soul from the bond of matter, recognized at the same time that the material world is a divine creation, and criticized the Gnostics for their failure to honour it as such.[1]

For the Hermetists, as for Plotinus, it is through mystical experience that man attains liberation. In that experience, at its greatest intensity, the soul is wholly absorbed in the vision of God.

'Father,' says Tat to Hermes, 'you have given me my fill of this good and most beautiful sight, and my mind's eye is almost blinded by the splendour of the vision.' 'Nay,' Hermes rejoins, 'the vision of the Good is not a thing of fire, as are the sun's rays. ... It shines forth much or little according as he who gazes upon it is able to receive the inflow of the incorporeal radiance. ... He who has apprehended the beauty of the Good can apprehend nothing else; he who has seen it can see nothing else. ... He forgets all bodily sensations and all bodily move-ments, and is still. But the beauty of the Good bathes his mind in light, and takes all his soul up to itself, and draws it forth from the body, and transforms it wholly into the essence of God' [x: 4-6].

In the ecstatic vision of the divine, man's being is deified; he passes into the divine Light.

In another tractate the writer suggests that it is possible to rise to the knowledge of God, which implies identification with Him, by the application of the principle that 'like is apprehended by like' (xi: 20). 'If thou canst not make thyself equal to God, thou canst not know God.' Such equalization to God can be attained by the illimitable extension of our being. 'Expand thyself into the immeasurable greatness, passing beyond all bodily limits; raise thyself above all time, become eternal. Then thou shalt know God.' A man is to transcend all spatial and temporal limits – to 'become higher than all height, lower than all depth', to take to himself 'the qualities of all creatures', to conceive himself to be in every place, in the living and the dead. By such an expansion of the range of his consciousness man may rise into oneness with God, who is Himself the Whole. In Book XIII this experience of

1. *Enneads*, ii: 9: see p. 165 below.

expanded consciousness is presented, not as a condition, but rather as a result of union with God. Although certain conditions are necessary in man – the desire for God, the conquest of the lower self, the practice of inner silence – union comes, not simply through the will of man, but by the grace and mercy of God. It is the Will of God which impregnates the soul with the seed – 'the true Good', the essence of God – from which man is reborn. Hermeticism is typically a religion of grace. 'Pray [says one writer] that you may find favour, and that but one ray of God may flash upon your mind' (v: 2). The divine grace is embodied in the 'Powers' which are included in the Being of God.[1] These 'Powers' (in C. H. XIII) are ten in number; they are principles contrary to the 'irrational torments of matter', described, e.g. as divine Knowledge, Joy, Temperance, Justice, Truth. When these divine Powers enter in to possess a man's being, he is reborn. A new and divine self is formed within him. 'He is a god, and son of God; he is the All, and is in all; he is composed wholly of Powers.' Henceforth his true self lies beyond the reach of the bodily senses. 'I have gone forth from myself [Hermes says] into an immortal body; I am born in *nous*.' He is no longer, in his real nature, 'a thing of spatial dimensions'; he is not visible to earthly sight. He sees now, not merely with the vision of his eyes, but with the spiritual activity given him by the Powers. Since he is made one with God, he shares the life of all things; he is present in all beings. 'I am in Heaven, in the earth, in the water, in the air; I am in every living creature; I am everywhere.' His life is infinitely expanded in space and in time. He is 'in the womb, before the womb, and after the womb'. He sees his oneness with the All; he sees himself in *nous*. Being reborn in *nous*, he shares the divine Joy. The prophet closes with a hymn of praise. He renders thanks to God for His greatness and His glory – for His blessings in creation and in the life of the spirit. And he is conscious that, as he is united with the divine Powers, it is they who sing praise in him.

Ye Powers that are within me [Hermes cries], praise ye the One and the All. . . . O holy Knowledge, by Thee am I illumined, and through

1. In the *Poimandres* there are countless Powers, which are equivalent to the Ideas, i.e. thoughts of God.

Thee do I sing praise to the incorporeal Light. ... O Good that is in me, praise the Good; O Life and Light, from You comes the song of praise, and to You does it go forth.

It is God in him who rejoices through His Powers in His own eternal Glory.

The Hermetic mystic sees his unity with all beings. The purgation and illumination of the soul which he attains brings him the consciousness of universal fellowship, and it is his task to do good to all. The soul which *nous* enters, and leads into the light of divine knowledge, 'never tires of hymning praises to God, and of pouring blessings both in word and in deed to all men, in imitation of the Father' (x: 21).

IV. THE GNOSTICS

One of the most significant products of the Hellenistic age is the movement known as Gnosticism. The word is sometimes used in an extended sense to cover all varieties of Hellenistic mysticism, even that of Plotinus, in spite of his criticism of the Gnostics. That usage rests on the assumption that the distinctive feature of the movement is *gnosis* in the sense of mystical knowledge. But *gnosis*, as applied to religious knowledge, is not necessarily mystical. The Christian Apologists of the second century laid great stress on *gnosis* as implying knowledge of divine truth, but in their use of the term there is no suggestion of mystical experience. Among those commonly described as Gnostics the word sometimes has that significance, but its reference is also to the mysteries of life and destiny, the origin of the world, the nature of man, the way of salvation – mysteries which the Gnostics claimed to solve by means of a highly complex series of myths given by revelation to their prophets or (in the case of Christian Gnostics) handed down from Jesus or his disciples by a secret tradition.

Formerly little was known of the Gnostics at first hand; men were dependent for their knowledge on the testimony of Church Fathers like Irenaeus, Hippolytus, Epiphanius, and on the extracts from Gnostic writings which they gave. The Fathers were unhappily by no means impartial witnesses. In the nineteenth century certain Gnostic treatises, like the *Pistis Sophia* (third century A.D.), were discovered. More recently – in 1945 – forty-four treatises belonging to a Gnostic library were unearthed at Nag Hammadi (formerly Chenoboskion) in Egypt. The latest manuscripts go back to the fourth century, but their contents are in general of much earlier origin. Most of the documents are still unpublished, but accounts of them have been issued, and some have been translated.[1] The discovery serves to emphasize the Jewish background of Gnosticism. In this connexion account must also be taken of another recent discovery – that of the *Dead Sea Scrolls*, on which a voluminous literature has already arisen.[2] It is almost universally agreed that the sect of the Scrolls – the community of Qumran by the Dead Sea - was a branch of the Essenes, who originated in the second century B.C. and whose life is described by Philo and Josephus. The Essenes represent a type of Judaism which was particularly subject to external influences. In *The Manual of Discipline*, for example, the origin of evil is explained in terms of Zoroastrian dualism; it is said to be due to the activity of the two Spirits of Truth and Perversity, which God created in the beginning. It is significant that in the newly-discovered writings of the Gnostics Zoroastrian influence played a notable part. (One of the treatises is the so-called *Apocalypse of Zoroaster*.) The world-drama is presented as a conflict between the Powers of Light and Darkness; but the dualism is not absolute, since at the root of all things is the supreme and everlasting God. This doctrine is set forth, not only in the original Zoroastrian Scriptures (the *Zendavesta*), but in the Greek writings of the Magi (Zoroastrian priests) in Asia Minor in the second century B.C. It appears to have been the influence of these writings in their penetration of mystical Judaism which gave rise to the Gnostic movement.

How far Gnosticism is found in the Scrolls is a disputed question. Certainly the claim is made to the possession of mystical knowledge resting on the vision of God.

1. See J. Doresse, *Les Livres secrets des Gnostiques d'Égypte*; R. M. Wilson, *The Gnostic Problem*; R. M. Grant, *Gnosticism and Early Christianity*.

2. See, e.g., K. Schubert, *The Dead Sea Community*; M. Yadin, *The Message of the Scrolls*; *The Scrolls and the New Testament*, edited by K. Stendhal; A. Dupont-Sommer, *The Essene Writings from Qumran*.

Through His marvellous mysteries [says the writer of *The Manual of Discipline*] my eye has gazed upon the eternal Being – a saving knowledge which is hidden from the man of knowledge [in the ordinary sense], a wise insight which is hidden from the sons of men, the wellspring of righteousness, the reservoir of strength and the place of glory. . . . Among mortals God gave it as an eternal possession to those whom He has chosen [xi: 5-7].

With this we may compare the ecstatic cry of *The Revelation of Dositheus* in the Nag Hammadi library: 'Let us rejoice! Let us rejoice! Let us rejoice! We have seen; we have seen; we have seen That which truly was at the beginning, That which truly was, That which was the first Eternal, the Unbegotten.'[1] The mystical aspect of the Scrolls finds expression also in the fragments of a heavenly liturgy found in one of the caves of Qumran, which is said to be related to the Chariot-mysticism characteristic of the early phases of Jewish mystical tradition.[2] The Apocalyptic literature, significant in the history of Jewish mysticism for its account of the ascent of chosen souls to the heavenly sphere (see p. 176 below), was held in the highest regard among the Essenes. The Gnostics of Chenoboskion made frequent use of Apocalyptic writings, and the heavenly Chariot is described in two of their treatises.[3] The Essenes and the Gnostics are thus at one in their expression of mystical experience and in the form which it assumes among them. But the elaboration of myth characteristic of developed Gnosticism is not to be found among the Essenes.

There was a considerable variety of Gnostic sects in the first three centuries of the Christian era, but they borrowed their writings from one another quite freely. It was common ground among them that the physical world was not a divine creation, but the outcome of a pre-mundane Fall – the Fall of the Demiurge into matter, or the Fall of Sophia or another of the numerous Aeons (Powers emanated from the supreme God) with whom the

1. J. Doresse, *Les Livres secrets des Gnostiques d'Égypte*, p. 206.
2. See K. Schubert, *The Dead Sea Community*, p. 70; and pp. 176-9 below.
3. Doresse, op. cit., p. 320.

Gnostics peopled the invisible world.[1] In man – or rather in certain men, since the Gnostics in general limited the divine principle to a few – there was a spark of divinity, and it was their aim to secure its release from the sphere of matter, to which it was bound by the chain of rebirth, and its return to the higher realm from which it came. As in the Mystery-religions (see p. 155 below), the soul was believed to pass through the spheres of the planets in its ascent to the celestial world. The spirits which ruled these spheres were conceived as hostile to man. In order to overcome their resistance, it was necessary to know their names. To win salvation, it was necessary also to know the nature of the soul and the secrets of the higher worlds. 'Not baptism alone sets us free,' said a Gnostic writer, 'but *gnosis* – who we were, what we have become, where we were, whither we have sunk, whither we hasten, whence we are redeemed, what is birth and what rebirth.'[2] The myths which provide this information tell in some instances of a Redeemer whose help is needed to bring man deliverance. In the Christianized *gnosis* of the second and third centuries, which was the object of attack from the Church Fathers, the Redeemer is identified with Christ.

The piety of the Gnostics varied considerably in its quality. Their morality was generally ascetic, but in some of the sects it was held that once a man had gained salvation he was free from the obligations of morality. It is evident that this antinomian attitude, on which the Fathers lay such stress, was by no means representative. In the newly discovered books, which are said to comprise the texts most commonly in use, there is no suggestion at all of licentious rites, and such practices were strongly denounced by the great majority of sects. As we have seen, the Gnostics were not typically dualists in the sense of believing that ultimate Reality itself was dual. The two opposed elements of Light and Darkness have a common root in the one ultimate

1. An ancient Gnostic sect, the Mandaeans (Nasoraeans), which may have originated before the rise of Christianity in heterodox Jewish circles, held that the world was created by archetypal man (Adam Qadmaia). Their dualism is less pronounced than that of most Gnostics. They still survive in Mesopotamia. See E. S. Drower, *The Secret Adam.*

2. *Excerpta ex Theodoto*, 78 : 2. The *Excerpta* were compiled by Clement of Alexandria in the third century, from Gnostic writings.

divine Power, who is Himself – as Hellenistic philosophy commonly declared – beyond the reach of intellectual knowledge. Thus in the *Apocryphon Johannis* (*The Secret Book of John*), included in the Chenoboskion collection, the creation of the lower world is ascribed to Ialdabaoth, an evil power comparable to the Persian Ahriman, but the latter, so far from being ultimate, is the offspring of Sophia, who herself came into being as the last of a series of Aeons. God is Himself utterly inconceivable. He is described as 'the true God, the Father of all, the Invisible who is above all, who exists in His incorruptibility, and dwells in pure light which no eye may behold'.[1] It is said that He contemplates His own image in the waves of the pure light which surrounds Him. He brings forth by His thought the perfect Power, Barbelo, who becomes the primordial man, and produces the first thought of the universe. The *Apocryphon* describes the course of events in the lower world in a number of myths based on a re-interpretation of the stories of Genesis, Yahweh being identified with Ialdabaoth. Its outlook is typical of Gnostic teaching in at once affirming the absolute perfection of divine Reality, and condemning the lower world as a sphere of error and darkness, which owes its origin to a Power seeking to frustrate the divine purpose.

Another work of special interest found in the Chenoboskion library is *The Gospel of Truth*, which is to be attributed most probably to Valentinus, perhaps the greatest of the Gnostics, who taught at Rome in the middle of the second century. *The Gospel of Truth* ascribes creation to Error personified, but it is otherwise lacking in the mythical element so prominent elsewhere. It is concerned, above all, with the higher gnosis. It was evident from the fragments of his work previously known that the central feature of the religion of Valentinus was the mystical contemplation of God. He said in a letter that the soul of man is inhabited by many evil spirits; 'but when the one good Father visits it, then it is sanctified and gleams with light. And he who possesses such a heart is so blessed that he shall see God.'[2] It is the vision or knowledge of God which is the central theme of *The Gospel of*

1. R. M. Wilson, *The Gnostic Problem*, p. 150.
2. Legge, *Rivals and Forerunners of Christianity*, II: 125.

Truth. Men are alienated from God because of their spiritual ignorance, their forgetfulness of Him. He has enlightened those who were in darkness through His revelation of Himself in Christ, the Word or Son of God. Christ brings men into the knowledge of God which is union with Him. This is the goal to which they are called. 'The Father knows the beginning of them all [i.e. of all men] and their end . . . The true end is the taking of *gnosis* concerning Him who is hidden . . . Him to whom to whom all shall return who came out of Him' (37: 35–8: 3). Of those who have received this saving knowledge it is said: 'They are themselves the Truth (through their identification with Christ). And the Father is in them, and they are in the Father, being complete (perfect), being indivisible in the truly Good' (42: 25–30).

One of the few Gnostic works discovered in the last century is the *Pistis Sophia*, written in Egypt probably in the latter part of the third century. The book consists of teaching supposed to have been given by Jesus to the disciples after the Resurrection. A prominent feature of it is the emphasis laid on the 'mysteries' (i.e. the rites of the Gnostic Church) and their power to purify the soul. It reflects in this respect the influence of the Mystery-religions so widespread in its time. *Gnosis* is conceived as the knowledge which solves the problem why things exist as we know them – why there are darkness and light, good and evil, tears and laughter, cold and heat, wild beasts and birds and precious stones. The writer is preoccupied with the question who will be saved, and who will be finally lost. If they are to be saved, men must renounce the whole world and all its associations. If they participate in the Gnostic 'mysteries', and follow the pure ethic of compassion and love, their being will be transformed, and they will become rays of the divine Light. Here and now, indeed, the Gnostic, though he is a man in the world, is higher than all the host of invisible Powers; he is identified with Jesus. It is here that we see most truly the mystical quality of the writer's outlook. 'Though he be a man in the world,' Jesus says, 'yet shall he be a king with me in my Kingdom. He is a man in the world, but a king in the Light. . . . Amen, I say unto you, that man is myself, and I am that man' (Section 230).

Gnosticism found a new expression in the third century with

the rise of the Manichaean religion, founded by Mani in Persia. Mani is said to have received a spiritual illumination in his early manhood, which brought him the immediate knowledge of divine Reality. He claimed to be the manifestation of the Para-clete, the last and greatest of the prophets, who brought to its completion the work of the founders of other religions, Zoroaster, Jesus, Buddha – he travelled in India and so doubtless knew Buddhism at first hand. It was his aim to establish a universal religion. His teaching was derived to a great extent from that of the Gnostics; he was also influenced directly by Zoroastrianism. It has commonly been supposed in the West that he was a thorough-going dualist in the metaphysical sense, but recent study has made it clear that his outlook was substantially the same as that of the Gnostics.[1] There are two opposed principles at the root of all things, two Kingdoms of Light and Darkness in perpetual conflict; but there is one sole God over all. The conflict began with time itself, and will cease when time is done away. Matter is a force of blind desire opposed to the force of Light, but Light will in the end prove victorious; matter will be completely dissolved. All souls now subject to matter will finally be saved.

Manichaeanism spread widely both in the East and in the West in the fourth century. In the West it gained support largely from the adherents of the Gnostic sects. In the early Middle Ages it gave rise to new sects (Bogomils and Paulicians) in Eastern Europe, whose teaching was extended to Italy and France in the tenth century. Under the name of Cathari or Albigenses the sectaries established themselves widely in the South of France, until the movement was destroyed in the thirteenth century by the Albigensian Crusade.

V. THE MYSTERY-RELIGIONS

The syncretistic tendency characteristic of the Hellenistic period found expression in certain cults originating in Egypt and the Near and Middle East, which are known as 'Mystery-religions'. As with the Eleusinian and Dionysiac Mysteries, which themselves continued to exist, these religions centred in the initiation

1. See Puech, *Le Manichéisme*; Roché, *Études manichéennes et cathares*.

of individuals into a sacred 'mystery', through which men attained rebirth, being 'changed', 'enlightened', 'deified'. In one aspect the 'mystery' consisted in the portrayal of a myth concerning the struggles, sufferings, and triumph of a deity. It was thus a sacramental drama. But its essential aim – achieved, naturally, in very different degrees – was the inner experience of the initiates, gained through their participation in the drama. 'They could rise to a mysticism which attained the heights of contemplation, or they might remain at a level of ecstatic emotion.'[1] The Mysteries were, in any case, concerned with the life and destiny of the individual, and, being so concerned, they ignored the barriers of race and class. They were broadly monotheistic in their outlook, but their monotheism was of an inclusive, not an exclusive, type. Each particular deity was regarded as a special form of the ultimate and universal God. The Egyptian goddess, Isis, is represented as saying: 'The whole earth worships my godhead, one and individual, under many a changing shape, with varied rites and by many divine names.'[2] Men sometimes received initiation into a number of different cults. The cults were in practice in some cases closely allied to one another. They achieved a widespread popularity throughout the Roman Empire in the second and third centuries of our era.

In considering the nature of the Mysteries, it is necessary to remember their differences as well as their unity. The chief Mysteries were those of Isis and Osiris, of the Great Mother and her consorts (Attis and Adonis), and of Mithras. The Mystery of Mithras is strikingly different from the first two, each of which, again, has its distinctive character. In the old Persian religion, Mithras was a god of light. The prophet Zoroaster ignored him, in the interests of his monotheistic teaching; but under the Persian Empire his worship took firm root in Asia Minor, and from there it made its way eventually, as a Mystery-religion, to Rome. Mithraism came to prevail widely in the Roman Empire, through the influence especially of the Roman armies. The myth related how Mithras slew a wild bull (the first creation of the supreme God, Ahura-Mazda), from whose blood

1. W. L. Knox, *St Paul and the Church of the Gentiles*, p. 101.
2. Apuleius, *Metamorphoses*, XI: 5.

sprang the rest of living Nature. The central rite in Mithraic temples was thus the ritual slaughter of a bull. There was also a sacrament of bread and water mixed with wine, the wine being said to spring from the blood of the bull. The sacrament celebrated the last meal which Mithras took, along with Helios, the sun-god, and other companions.[1] From the bread and wine initiates gained the power to conquer evil spirits; they were also penetrated by a divine substance which gave them the assurance of immortality. The religion was marked by its strongly ethical emphasis – its inculcation, in particular, of manly virtues in the struggle against evil, its stress on self-control. Alone among the Mysteries, it confined initiation to men. There were seven grades of initiates, corresponding to the seven planetary spheres through which the soul descended at birth from the eternal world of light, and through which again it must pass on its upward way to perfection and eternal bliss. Mithras himself was the constant helper of the soul; it was by his grace that the soul might return to the world of light.

The religion of Mithras was closely allied to the cult of Cybele, the Great Mother, although the two were remarkably different in character. The Great Mother cult prevailed in Asia Minor from the sixth century B.C. It was brought to Rome in the third century B.C., although it was not officially recognized until the first century A.D. It centred in the myth of the Mother-goddess and her lover, Attis, who died, and was restored to life by the goddess. Like the myth of Dionysus and of Osiris, it symbolized originally the decay and death of vegetation in the winter and its revival in the spring; but in the Mystery-religion it stood for the experience of the initiate, who in his union with the god died to the old life and was reborn to a higher and immortal being. One form of the myth told that Attis was unfaithful to the goddess, and in a frenzy of remorse he castrated himself and died. The goddess, however, brought him back to life, and he became immortal. In the festival of Attis, in the spring, his devotees entered soul and body into his tragedy. They lacerated their flesh with knives, thus identifying themselves with him in his

1. Helios was sometimes described as the son of Mithras, who was himself probably regarded as the vicegerent of the supreme Power.

sufferings. At a later stage, the revivification of Attis was celebrated with wild rejoicing; the devotees shared the joy of his new
and immortal life. One feature of the Mystery was the Tauro-
bolium - often mistakenly associated with Mithraism. A platform
of perforated planks was placed over a pit. A bull was killed on
the platform; in the pit was a devotee, who was drenched by the
blood of the bull. The primary idea seems to have been the magical
prolongation of physical life, but the rite came to be interpreted
in a spiritual sense, as a cleansing from sin. The votary was said
to be 'born again' - 'reborn into eternity'.

The Mystery of Isis had its basis in the Egyptian myth of
Isis and Osiris. The myth told of the murder of Osiris by his
enemy, Set; the lamentation of his sister-wife, Isis, and her
wanderings; the triumph of her son, Horus, over Set; and the
resuscitation of Osiris. In ancient Egypt this was a fundamental
aspect of the national religion. The Mystery was instituted
through Greek influence under the Ptolemies, successors of
Alexander the Great. In the cult Osiris was worshipped in a new
form, as Serapis, with the intention of uniting Egyptians and
Greeks in his worship. Serapis was identified with Asclepius
(Aesculapius), the divine Healer, and also with Zeus, Dionysus,
and Helios. The religion became widely established in the Roman
Empire, at first in the East and later in the West. In this instance
we are fortunate in having an account of the experience of an
initiate, in the *Metamorphoses* (Book XI) of Apuleius (second
century A.D.). Apuleius is telling the adventures of Lucius, the
hero of his story, but there can be no doubt that in this matter he
is drawing on his own memories. The central feature of the
ceremony of initiation appears to have been a ritual death and
resurrection, involving the identification of the initiate with
Osiris, though much remains obscure in detail. As one with
Osiris, Lucius claims to have visited the realms of the dead,
where he 'saw the sun gleaming with bright splendour at dead of
night'. He declares that he 'approached the gods above and the
gods below, and worshipped them face to face'. In the culminating experience of the rite he was placed on a daïs - like the image
of a god - beside the image of Isis, with a flaming torch in his
hand and a crown of palm leaves on his head, and displayed to

the assembled worshippers. This is a rite of deification. The initiate is treated as Osiris-Re (Osiris in his identity with the sun-god). Lucius 'has been purged of his mortality, reconstructed as an immortal being, filled with divine power, and is worshipful. He receives worship only at this point, not afterwards; it is the recognition by the faithful of what has been wrought in him.'[1] Henceforth he is pledged to the service of Isis, the 'holy and eternal Saviour of the human race'. In his prayer of farewell to Isis, he cries: 'My voice is too poor in utterance to tell what I feel concerning Thy majesty ... I will guard the memory of Thy divine Countenance and of Thy most holy godhead deep hidden within my heart's inmost shrine, and their image shall be with me for ever.'

Even with this record before us, it is not easy to judge the precise nature of the initiate's experience. Certainly the Isis-cult embodied a genuinely spiritual piety. How far it carried with it an actual heightening or extension of consciousness it is hard to say. Yet it is clear that for some initiates the rites of the Mysteries were the vehicle not only of a genuine devotion to the divine, a real inner change of heart and mind, but of an actual experience of mystical apprehension and mystical union. The possibility of such an experience was commonly recognized at this time. Thus Aelius Aristides, a devotee of Asclepius (identified, as we have seen, with Serapis), records in his *Sacred Discourses* that it was once revealed to him by Asclepius that 'my mind was to be rapt from my present state of life; that when it was so rapt I should be made one with God, and, being made one with God, I should have transcended our mortal state'.[2] We have the testimony of Proclus, the Neo-Platonist philosopher of the fifth century, that the Mysteries were a fertile ground for such experiences. 'Who will not agree [he asks] that the Mysteries and the initiations lead the souls upward from this life of matter and mortality, and bring them into contact with the gods?' Some initiates, he says, 'are placed in harmony with the holy symbols, and, completely getting out of themselves, take up their abode with the gods and are filled with God'. Those who make themselves fitted for it

1. A. D. Nock, *Essays on the Trinity and the Incarnation*, p. 105, note 1.
2. A. J. Festugière, *Personal Religion among the Greeks*, p. 96.

'suddenly receive into their bosoms the divine illumination itself, and naked, as they would say, are partakers of the divine'.[1]

VI. PLOTINUS AND NEO-PLATONISM

Hellenistic mysticism may be said to have reached its culminating point in the work of Plotinus (A.D. 205–c. 270). Plotinus was a native of Egypt, and he spent his formative years at Alexandria. There he eventually became a pupil of the Platonic teacher Ammonius Saccas, in whose philosophy he found the satisfaction which he had sought in vain elsewhere. Nothing is known directly of the thought of this teacher, but it appears to have provided at least the groundwork of the philosophy of Plotinus. At the age of forty Plotinus settled in Rome, and there he composed the treatises which were afterwards collected and arranged as the *Enneads* – consisting of six books, each of which is divided into nine sections.

The Neo-Platonism of which Plotinus is the outstanding representative was expounded by a succession of teachers down to the closing of the schools in Athens in A.D. 529. But among the successors of Plotinus its character underwent a notable change. For Plotinus, the experience of mystical union was the basic fact, and it was the central purpose of his teaching to lead men to it. His successors in the school, chief among whom were Porphyry, Iamblichus, and Proclus, stood on a lower level of spiritual insight. Their interest was genuinely religious, and in their religion there was an element of mysticism. But it was their main concern to revive the traditional pagan worship, to which Plotinus himself attached little importance, and to formulate a scheme of thought capable of defending it in face of Christian hostility. The Emperor Julian, who attempted to restore the pagan cultus in the fourth century, was a Neo-Platonist, a follower, in particular, of Iamblichus (d. c. A.D. 330). In the teaching of Iamblichus, the gods came to hold the central position. Along with the gods came the practice of magic, based on the principle of universal 'sympathy' – the interconnexion of all things in

1. W. R. Halliday, *The Pagan Background of Early Christianity*, pp. 274, 262f.

Heaven and earth – as a means of invoking their aid.[1] Proclus (d. A.D. 485) elaborated the philosophy of Plotinus, and transformed it into a highly complex and rigid system of thought, by means especially of a host of 'Henads' springing from the One, each of which has the character of absolute Being. Thus Neo-Platonism, which began as a fresh and vital impulse of spiritual life and experience, ended its career in the pagan world as a scholastic system steeped in magic. But this was by no means the end of its influence. With Augustine and the pseudo-Dionysius, the wisdom of Plotinus passed into the sphere of Christian teaching, and became a potent factor in the growth of Christian mysticism. No single man outside the Bible has exerted, directly or indirectly, so great an influence as Plotinus on the thought of the Christian mystics. With the re-discovery of classical literature in the sixteenth century, that influence was renewed in Protestant mysticism. Outside Christian circles, moreover, it played a great part in the thought and experience of the Sufis. It is therefore of the utmost importance to understand the teaching of Plotinus, not only for the light which it casts on the nature and implications of mystical experience, but for the influence which it has exercised on the whole development of mysticism in Christianity and Islam.

Plotinus was the heir of Plato. His own philosophy is presented as an exposition of Plato's teaching. But the Platonism which he imbibed from Ammonius Saccas must have been the 'middle Platonism' taught by such men as Plutarch, Numenius, and Albinus in the first two centuries. 'Middle Platonism' was marked by its doctrine of the hierarchy of being. Between the supreme and absolute Reality and the world there was a series of intermediary Powers, differently conceived by different thinkers. Plotinus accepted the doctrine of the hierarchy of being, but he transformed it. For him there are three Hypostases or divine Essences – three distinct, but not separate realities within the unity of the Godhead. His conception is comparable to, though

1. Plotinus himself believed in the efficacy of magic, and advocated the use of 'counter-incantations' in order to ward off the harmful effect of spells. See *Enneads*, IV: 41–3.

not identical with, the Christian doctrine of the Trinity. It is essential to the understanding of Plotinus to remember that the three Hypostases are not three separate beings, but three phases of the one divine Triad. Confusion sometimes arises because Plotinus, in naming one Hypostasis, may be referring to the Triad as a whole, or even to one of the two not named. The divine Triad consists of a hierarchy of descending degrees or levels of reality. The fountain-head of being is the One or the Good; the One eternally engenders *nous*; *nous* eternally engenders Soul, which is the Creator of the universe in time and space.[1] There is thus an eternal process of engendering or emanation. Plotinus finds an analogy of this process in the physical world. Fire gives out heat; fragrant substances diffuse perfume; the sun generates the light encircling it. In fact, all existences (he says) tend to produce 'some necessary outward-facing nature, an image of the engendering archetype'. So *nous* is 'a circumradiation produced from the Supreme'. Or, again, *nous* is 'an act and utterance of the One', as Soul is 'an act and utterance of *nous*' (v: 1: 6).

The One is God in His transcendent aspect, though God in His transcendence is also immanent in all being – God as the ultimate Source and the final Goal of all being. He is 'That on which all depends, towards which all existences aspire as to their source and their need, while itself is without need, sufficient to itself ... the measure and term of all' (i: 8: 2). In His transcendent aspect, God is utterly beyond the range of human thought – 'a nobler Principle than anything we know as being, fuller and greater; above reason, mind, and feeling' (v: 3: 14). By virtue of its very depth and greatness the One is 'beyond all statement'. 'Its nature is that nothing can be affirmed of it.' It transcends even the categories of existence, or essence, or life. 'We can but try to indicate, in our feeble way, something concerning it' (v: 3: 13; iii: 8: 10). The One is 'fount of all that is best'; 'great beyond anything great'; 'infinite in fathomless depths of power'; 'good in the unique mode of being the Good above all that is good' (vi: 9: 5f.); 'the fountain and principle of beauty' (vi: 8: 13).

1. The creation of the world is also ascribed to *nous* as the outcome of its dynamic contemplation of the One.

'The Good' as so described as the object of desire, the goal and fulfilment of all life in its quest for self-completion.

For Plotinus, transcendence is not opposed to immanence; it is not identified with externality or otherness. In his book, *The Evolution of Theology in the Greek Philosophers*, Edward Caird contends that if the One is connected with the world, 'it must be only as its external cause or source, and not as a principle which manifests itself therein' (II: 231). But, as Bréhier shows in his account of the philosophy of Plotinus (*La Philosophie de Plotin*), it is in his stress on immanence that we have the distinctive feature of his thought. The many are immanent in the One, and the One in the many. In the hierarchy of being, there is no separation of the lower from the higher, but rather absorption in it. The Soul, as we shall see, coincides at its highest point with *nous*, and *nous* enters into union with the One. There is thus a continuous interpenetration of being. 'The universe is in the Soul; Soul is contained in *nous*. ... *Nous* in turn is contained in something else [the One] ... The One contains all' (v: 5: 9). And the One, which contains all, is immanent in all. 'God is outside of none, present unperceived to all.' In Him, all otherness is done away with. 'The Supreme as containing no otherness is ever present with us, and we with Him when we put otherness away' (VI: 9: 8). There is a reciprocal indwelling of the One in all beings and of all beings in the One. And it is as the expression of this fundamental fact that there arises that desire for the Good, that return to the Unity which contains all and dwells at the heart of all, which is the goal of life.

Nous, the second Hypostasis, is the highest reality in the realm of being – i.e. of individual and differentiated existence. It is the reflection in that realm of the absolute unity of the One. *Nous* has commonly been rendered '(divine) Mind' or 'Intelligence'. Stephen MacKenna translates it 'the Intellectual Principle', although he suggests that 'Spirit' may often convey its quality more adequately, and that is the term employed by Inge in his *Philosophy of Plotinus*. *Nous* has been defined as 'intuitive thought which is always united with its object';[1] and it is the quality of union with its object which is its distinctive characteristic.

1. Armstrong, *Plotinus*, p. 36.

'Its very essence [says Plotinus] is vision' (v: 1: 10). And vision here implies both distinctness and identity. *Nous* represents the ideal of knowledge, in which, while there is a distinction between knower and known, subject and object, there is also identity – in which the knower becomes one with the known. For *nous* the object of knowledge or vision is twofold. On the one hand, it sees the One, and in the vision is identified with it. On the other hand, its gaze is directed to the many; and the many to which it looks are not external to it, but within it, as aspects of its own being. The 'many' here are not the 'many' as we know them in space and time, existing in division and conflict. The world of *nous* is the world of reality, not the world of shadows and appearances which alone we see as long as we live in Plato's Cave. It is Plato's world of Forms or Ideas, which are for Plotinus living beings, distinct and yet united, making up an eternal order, with which *nous* itself is one. '*Nous* is itself the very things on which its intuition acts ... They are itself and the content of itself ... *Nous* and being [the real world] are one' (v: 9: 5).

In the archetypal world, all things exist in their ideal form, distinct yet in unbroken unity; all spirits have their individual being, yet all are one in mutual interpenetration in the Eternal Now.

A pleasant life is theirs in Heaven [as Inge translates] ... They see all things, not the things that are born and die, but those which have real being; and they see themselves in others ... Every one is manifest to every one internally ... Every one has all things in himself, and sees all things in another; so that all things are everywhere, and all is all, and each is all, and the glory is infinite [v: 8: 4].[1]

Nous is both individual and universal; it is 'a plurality-in-unity', so that as between the individual and the universal there is a mutual indwelling. *Nous* in its wholeness is transcendent to the individuals whose life is included within it; it is enthroned above them, and gives them all they possess. Yet it lives in each centre of life, so that each is one with the Whole; each is the Whole in a particular aspect.

It involves them as members of its universality, while they in turn involve the universal *Nous* in their particularity ... Each particular

1. *The Philosophy of Plotinus*, 1st edition, II: 85f.

individual is actually what it is – its individual self – potentially the totality [vi: 2: 20].

It is in this eternal world of *nous*, this world of achieved perfection and glory, that man (like all things that are) has his true home and his abiding immortality. We ourselves, living in time and space, live also in the Eternal.

Even our human soul has not sunk entire; something of it is continuously in the spiritual world [iv: 8: 8].

The higher soul of each of us is one with *nous*.

Soul is the third Hypostasis, emanating eternally from *nous* as *nous* emanates from the One. Through Soul the eternal world of true being is linked with the world of time and space and imperfection. In one phase of its nature Soul belongs to the world of *nous*, remaining unchangeably there. It 'circles about *nous*, on the upper level united with it, filled from it, participant in its nature' (v: 1: 8). It is 'an image or representative of *nous*', its 'idea and act'; it 'takes fullness by looking to its source' – engaged in ceaseless contemplation (v: 2: 1). Soul is thus in one aspect eternally transcendent. Although it 'ensouls' the cosmos, it does not belong to it.

So far as the universe extends, there Soul is; and if the universe had no existence, the extent of Soul would be the same; it is eternally what it is [iv: 3: 9].

But, while Soul has its eternal being in the archetypal world, in another phase it goes forth continuously to generate the material universe on the model of the Forms which it contemplates, to give order and unity to the cosmos, and to enter into it as its indwelling life. Soul is 'the author of all living things'; it is the Maker of the sun and the heavens, giving law and movement and life to all. 'Each separate life lives by the Soul entire ... entire in unity and entire in diffused variety. By the power of the Soul the manifold heavenly system is a unit' – a living, organic whole (v: 1: 2).

Like *nous*, Soul is both universal and individual. The universal Soul is manifested in a multiplicity of individual souls. In one aspect, the relation between the soul of each and the Soul of all is that of identity. 'There is one identical Soul, every separate manifestation being that Soul complete' (IV: 3: 2) – the Soul in its fullness is in each centre of life. 'The Soul in all the several forms of life is one Soul, an omnipresent identity' (IV: 9: 1). That being so, the separate souls must also be one. That does not mean that we are purely and simply identical. It does not imply that we share one another's feelings, our experience, our character. Soul is 'simultaneously one and many'. The fact of sympathy in face of suffering bears witness to our unity. But unity is compatible with variety, and variety involves a certain apartness, a certain separation of soul from soul.

The variety does not abrogate the unity; the souls are apart without partition ... They are no more hedged off by boundaries than are the multiple items of knowledge in one mind. The one Soul so exists as to include all souls [VI: 4: 4].

In the individual man there is both a higher and a lower soul. Just as the universal Soul is on its upper level united with *nous*, and has its being in the eternal order, so it is with the soul of each individual. In its deeper region, each soul has its being before its embodiment, and is itself eternal (IV: 7: 12). Each belongs by its inmost nature to the world of *nous*. Each is the expression (logos) of a spiritual principle contained in that world, and each remains for ever 'attached to its own spiritual original by that point of its being which least belongs to the partial order' (IV: 2: 5).

The souls of men are not cut off from their origin ... Though they have descended even to earth, yet their higher part holds for ever above the heavens [IV: 3: 12].

In the higher soul there can be no such thing as evil. 'All evil is accretion' (IV: 7: 10): it is something alien to the inmost nature of the soul, which arises in the course of its embodied life. It is as though another man has foisted himself upon the primal man that we were (and are) in the spiritual world. Through his life in the world of the senses, man has come to include 'an inner rabble' of pleasures, fears, desires, and it is from the dominance of these over the inner man that evil comes to be (VI: 4: 14f.). It is the entry into matter that brings about the fall of the soul, for matter 'encroaches upon the soul's territory, and crushes it back' (I: 8 : 14). The soul thus comes to be like a child taken away from its home and brought up far away, which forgets both its father and itself as it originally was. 'So the souls no longer discern either God or their own nature ... All their awe and admiration is for the alien ... the mundane' (v: 1: 1). The soul 'descends from the universal to become partial and self-centred ... Severed from the whole, it nestles in one form of being; for this it abandons all else, entering into, and caring for, only the one ... With this comes what is known as the casting of the wings, the enchaining in the body' (IV: 8: 4). Through its imprisonment in the body the soul is bound to the wheel of transmigration, in which it reaps in the experience of suffering the fruits of its own wrongful deeds.

It is necessary here to guard against a twofold misunderstanding. Plotinus does not wish to suggest that the physical world in itself is evil, or that physical existence as such is tantamount to 'imprisonment'. In his polemic against the Gnostics (II: 9) he maintains with the greatest emphasis that the creation of the material world is not a thing to be deplored; it is not the outcome of any fall of the Soul of the All. The universal Soul creates the world 'from the things it knew in the divine'. 'The universe is a life organized, effective, all-comprehensive, displaying an unfathomable wisdom.' The world of sense is full of beauty; it contains 'forms whose beauty must fill us with veneration for their Creator, and convince us of their origin in the divine'. We must not, like the Gnostics, 'cavil against the universe' or cherish 'hate for the corporeal'. We must rather 'accept meekly the constitution of the whole'. We must be content, as long as we have bodies, to 'inhabit the dwellings prepared for us by our good sister Soul [the All-Soul] in her vast power of labourless creation'. All this is not incompatible with what Plotinus says elsewhere of the necessary imperfection of the physical world and of the need to awake from the 'slumber' which befalls the soul while it takes for actualities 'the figments of its sleeping vision' (III: 6: 5). The evils of life have their root in the principle of matter – 'the cause at once of the weakness of the soul and of all its evil' (IV: 8: 14). Matter is for Plotinus the principle of negation or non-being – 'the utterly unordered', 'the absence of being', something which does not actually exist, though it underlies material existence. (It may be compared with the Hindu maya.) In the thought of Plotinus, the Good is the absolute Reality, the fullness and perfection of being. The highest degree of reality is the highest degree of good: correspondingly, the lowest degree of reality is the lowest degree of good. Matter therefore as the principle of non-being is identified with the principle of evil (1: 8). In so far as material things have a measure of reality, in so far as they are the image of the higher world which is the world of true being, they are good and not evil. But since the material world lacks the fullness of reality which belongs to the world of *nous*, it is necessarily imperfect. The life of man shares that imperfection. Yet imperfection is not the same thing as evil. In man evil arises through the choice of the will, subjecting itself to matter, allowing the body to dominate the soul. The evil that has overtaken the souls, alienating them from their own true nature, 'has its source in self-will, the desire for self-ownership' (v: 1: 1). Imprisonment in the body does not come about automatically through life in the body, since it is possible while we live in the body to transcend its range – to assert the power and freedom which are inherent in the soul.

'A soul which has never deeply penetrated into the body, and is not a slave, but a sovereign ruling the body,' need not 'be expectant of evil with regard to such a body ... It remains always intent upon the Supreme' [IV: 8: 2].

The true way of life, for Plotinus, is the way which leads the soul to itself in its unity with *nous* and so to the One. He recognizes the necessity of the 'civic virtues' (prudence, fortitude, temperance, justice) as a stage. But they relate primarily to life in the physical world, and if the soul is to find itself, it must look beyond; it must free itself from the bondage of matter and from all that is external to its own essential being. The soul will thus be inwardly detached from the activity of the senses which is necessary to life in this world. The higher life is therefore a life of purification – the purification of the soul from all that it has put on in its descent from the higher world. Plotinus draws the analogy of a sculptor carving a statue, who cuts and smooths the stone, 'until a lovely face has grown upon his work'. So he bids us cut away all that is external, so that 'nothing from without may cling to the authentic man' (I: 6: 9). He sums up his doctrine of mystical purification in the injunction: 'Cut away everything' (V: 3: 17).

The mystic way is for Plotinus the way of inner freedom and detachment from external things. It is also the way of introversion. Since the One is 'within, at the innermost depth' (VI: 8: 18), we must turn our gaze within, closing our eyes to the world about us, retreating inwards, and seeking there the divine vision. In one passage he refers directly to his own experience. He tells how it has happened many times to him that he has been lifted out of the body into himself, 'becoming external to all other things and self-encentred, beholding a marvellous beauty . . . acquiring identity with the divine' (IV: 8: 1). This is what he describes in an oft-quoted passage as 'the flight of the alone to the Alone' (VI: 9: 11) – when the soul 'has in perfect stillness attained isolation' and is 'caught away, filled with God'. There is no suggestion here, as is often supposed, of moral isolation or of an experience which cuts us off from contact with other souls. On the contrary, there is an infinite enlargement of our being, a breaking down of the barrier of separation which is characteristic of the soul in its descent. To find the central Unity, in which we are one with all, we must enter the inner sanctuary, each in the solitude of his individual being. That is a necessary law of the inner life. But the fulfilment of this necessity does not of itself ensure attainment. All that we can do, as Plotinus says, is to 'fit ourselves for the vision, and then wait tranquilly for its appearance, as the eye waits on the rising of the sun' (V: 5: 8).

The vision, when it comes, is an experience of unity – a unity so close, so immediate, so complete, that it transcends even the intuitive perception uniting subject and object which is distinctive of *nous*. The experience is one which cannot be adequately expressed in words.

The vision baffles telling: for how could a man bring tidings of the Supreme as detached, when he has seen it as one with himself? [VI: 9: 10].

The term 'vision' is itself insufficient, since it implies the duality of seen and seer.

In this seeing we neither hold an object (external to ourselves), nor trace distinction, nor are there two. The man is changed, no longer himself nor self-belonging; he is merged with the Supreme, sunken into it, one with it.

The experience is one of identity. In this experience, moreover, not only is the seer lifted into oneness with the object of his vision; the act of vision is itself identical with the object.

The vision floods the eyes with light, but it is not a light showing some other object; the light is itself the vision [VI: 7: 36].

The light by which we see the One is the radiance of the One.

This light is from the Supreme, and is the Supreme. . . . This is the true end set before the soul, to take that light, to see the Supreme by the Supreme; for That by which the illumination comes is That which is to be seen, just as we do not see the sun by light other than its own [V: 3: 17].

The vision of the One carries with it the transformation of our being, the deification which is our goal.

One that shall know this vision, with what passion of love shall he be seized, with what pang of desire, what longing to be molten into one with This! . . . This, the Beauty supreme, the absolute and the primal, fashions its lovers to beauty, and makes them also worthy of love [I: 6: 7].

In a well-known passage, Plotinus likens us to the members of a choir standing round the conductor, but sometimes singing out of tune because their attention is diverted from him. 'We are always before the Supreme, but we do not always attend. When we look, our goal is attained; . . . we lift a choral song full of God.' When it has been filled with God, the soul 'brings forth beauty, righteousness, all moral good'. Through the vision of God, the self is 'wrought to splendour, brimmed with the spiritual light, become that very Light . . . raised to Godhood, or, better, knowing its Godhood' (VI: 9: 8).

Life in its fullness and perfection can only be lived in the spiritual world.

> How comes the soul [Plotinus asks] not to keep that ground? Because it has not yet wholly left its earthly abode. But the time will come when it will enjoy the vision without interruption, no longer vexed by any hindrance of the body [VI: 9: 10].

It is the limitations of life in the flesh that stand in the way of a continuous vision of the One. While we are in the physical world, the ecstatic vision which lifts us into the divine union is a rare experience; but in the eternal order, to which even now we belong in our deeper being, it is a normal and necessary condition. The choir which sings in harmony because its members fix their gaze uninterruptedly on the conductor is an image of life in that sphere.

> *Nous* [we are told] has two powers, first that of grasping intuitively its own content, the second that of advancing and receiving, whereby to know its Transcendent [VI: 7: 38].

The first power Plotinus describes as that of knowing; it involves both identity and difference. The second he describes as that of loving – the ecstatic love whereby the soul is 'molten into one' with the One. Through this second power, the soul is raised out of the realm of being – the sphere of diversity in unity which is the eternal order – into the undifferentiated unity of the One. In this unity the soul 'is no longer in the realm of being; it is in the Supreme' (VI: 9: 11). In the higher life, it is implied, the two phases co-exist. In ecstasy, the consciousness of self is lost, absorbed in the consciousness of the divine. But the world of *nous* is an eternal reality, and there, while separation is broken down and the soul is freed from its limits, individuality and individual consciousness remain in the all-inclusive unity of the Spirit.

CHAPTER 6

Hebrew and Jewish Mysticism

I. MYSTICISM IN THE OLD TESTAMENT

THE most widely differing views have been held as regards the relation of the religion of the Old Testament to the attitude and experience of the mystics. It is sometimes said that the Old Testament knows nothing of this attitude and experience; it stands for a type of religion altogether foreign to mysticism. On the other hand, it has been maintained that mysticism 'prevailed in varying degrees of intensity throughout the centuries comprised in the Old Testament history'.[1] It is certainly true that mysticism does not hold the central place in Hebrew religion, as it does in the higher phases of Hinduism or of Mahayana Buddhism. It has been said, indeed, that Hebrew religion stands for a doctrine of God which lays exclusive stress on the divine transcendence and so allows no scope for the growth of mysticism. In his classic work, *Prayer*, Heiler has drawn a sharp contrast between the religion of the prophets, which represents the highest phase of Hebrew piety, and the religion of the mystics. He identifies mysticism with a monism which excludes all duality, and prophetic religion with a dualism which denies union. For prophetic religion, he declares, 'God and man are never mingled' (p. 169). In forming this conclusion, Heiler ignores a fundamental aspect of prophetic experience. In his account of mysticism he says a good deal about ecstasy. To be in ecstasy, he observes, is to be 'obsessed and engulfed by the superhuman and the divine' (p. 8). In the ecstatic experience 'the barriers between man and God disappear' (p. 169). But ecstasy is not an experience which can be confined to those whom Heiler describes as mystics. Among the early Hebrews, certainly, it belonged to the prophetic tradition. The prophetic movement in Israel was influenced by the religion of Canaan, one feature of which was the work of prophets, conceived as intermediaries possessed by

1. Abelson, *Jewish Mysticism*, p. 7.

the god in ecstasy; through them the god expressed his will. So in early Israel it was held that in ecstasy the Spirit of Yahweh entered the prophets and spoke through them.[1] In I Samuel 10:6 Samuel tells Saul that when he meets a band of prophets, the Spirit of Yahweh will come mightily upon him, and he will prophesy along with them. Prophecy was an organized movement, represented by the 'sons of the prophets' or guilds of prophets, and later by a body of official court prophets at Jerusalem. It is true that the canonical prophets dissociated themselves from such men. Amos rejected the very name of 'prophet' given to them (7:14). Jeremiah denounced them as false (23:16ff.). But that was because of their unfaithfulness – their failure to convey the word of God as the great prophets understood it, in its demand for personal righteousness and social justice and in its proclamation of coming disaster to Israel.

The great prophets stood apart from the organized 'prophecy' of their time. They were solitary individuals who felt that they had received a personal call to their work. But in the very nature of their call we see the continuity of their experience with that of their predecessors. The main fact here is their receptivity – their passivity in face of the divine. Undoubtedly they were men of great energy and activity. Yet the message which they gave was a thing they felt to be laid upon them; they spoke and acted under a sense of sheer compelling necessity. 'Yahweh took me from following the flock,' says Amos (7:14). 'Yahweh put forth his hand to touch my mouth,' says Jeremiah (1:9). 'The hand of Yahweh was upon me,' says Ezekiel (1:3). Brunner has emphasized the divine calling of the prophets as an illustration of his view of revelation as something totally unrelated (unlike mystical experience) to the spiritual state or capacity of the men who were called. The prophets, he says, are 'not saints, not mystics who by their own inner life find their way to God'; they are 'chosen for no other reason than God's will'[2] – which apparently works in a quite arbitrary fashion. Actually it is clear that the great prophets

1. The Spirit of Yahweh is a divine energy sometimes conceived as an aspect of his being, sometimes as a power separable from him.
2. *The Theology of Crisis*, pp. 33f.

were men of an unusual spiritual sensitiveness, men deeply
conscious of the challenge of the times. They were men also who
shared the mystics' capacity for ecstasy. Brunner suggests that the
mystics find their own way to God. Yet the mystics everywhere
recognize that, while it is possible to prepare the way for inner
vision by spiritual training, no such training can ensure its
attainment. And the man who follows the inner way seeks above
all to become receptive to the divine. He seeks, as Boehme says, to
'cease from the thinking of self and the willing of self'. Prophetic
experience is certainly akin to that of the mystic in the essential
attitude which underlies it. In mystical ecstasy, as Heiler says, a
man is 'engulfed by the divine'. But that is precisely the experience of the prophets. 'The hand of Yahweh was upon me,' they
say; and that phrase implies that they were in a state of ecstasy
or trance, unconscious of their surroundings. Ezekiel says that
after a particular visitation he remained for a week 'in a state of
utter stupefaction, dumb and motionless' (3: 15). It seems to
have been in the ecstatic state that the messages of the prophets
were received. T. H. Robinson has suggested that the recurring
phrase traditionally rendered 'Thus saith the Lord' should
probably be translated in the past tense – 'Thus said the Lord' –
the reference being to an ecstatic experience now past in which
the oracle in question was received.[1] The experience of the prophets in this respect is closely similar to that of some of the
mystics. St Teresa, for example, was largely guided in her later
life by 'locutions' – messages giving her direction or warning,
which she interpreted as divine commands. An illuminating
account of similar experiences is given by Nicholas of Basel,
who says: 'I heard a voice which came not from myself, but yet it
came to me as one who spoke within me; but it was not my
thoughts that it spoke.'[2] It is evident from the authority which
the prophets claim for the words they utter that it was not their
thoughts that the oracles expressed; it was a revelation which
they received.

Evelyn Underhill has described the higher phases of the life
of the mystic as 'theopathic' – it is God who is felt to live and

1. *Prophecy and the Prophets*, pp. 33f.
2. Quoted by Willink, *The Prophetic Consciousness*.

act in him. The mystic is led at times to identify himself with the divine. And it is these very claims which are implied in prophetic utterance. The prophet is 'a man of the Spirit' (Hosea 9: 7). He is 'full of power by the Spirit' (Micah 3: 8) which has 'entered into him' (Ezekiel 2: 2). 'The prophet [says Rowley] was conscious of a real union with God ... He believed that in him God was speaking, since He had gathered the prophet's personality into His own.'[1] Among the Hebrews, as A. R. Johnson has shown in his book, *The One and the Many in the Israelite Conception of God*, personality is something fluid, and not sharply marked off. The members of a man's household are regarded as an extension of his own being. Thus in Genesis 44, Joseph's steward is identified with Joseph himself; he speaks in his person. The social unit (the 'kin-group') is a corporate personality. Yahweh himself is a member of a corporate body – the heavenly Council – and according to Jeremiah the prophet belongs to this Council (23: 22). He is thus an extension of the personality of Yahweh; as Yahweh's messenger, he is identified with him, so that he can speak and act in his person.

It is true that there is a certain distinction between the experience of the prophets and that of the mystics generally. Hocking has said that the prophet is 'the mystic in action'.[2] The revelation which he claims to receive is a message specifically related to the circumstances and events of his time. He is called as a prophet to proclaim that message. His union with God is a functional union; he is identified with God as His messenger to men. With mystics generally, the case is different. What they seek is union with God as an end in itself. Such union carries with it the transformation of their being, but it does not involve a specific task or type of work. But if the prophet's union with the divine is a functional union, if (as he believes) he is made one with God as His messenger for a particular end, his experience has none the less an essentially mystical quality. It involves a quickening of the spiritual consciousness, an awareness of the supreme reality of the Transcendent. Prophetic experience, says Harold Knight, is 'a variety of that immediate and experimental knowledge of God

1. *The Servant of the Lord*, pp. 119f.
2. *The Meaning of God in Human Experience*, p. 511.

which is claimed by all the mystics'.[1] Two of the prophets, Isaiah (in Ch. 6) and Ezekiel (in Ch. 1), give an account of the vision of God which came to them in ecstasy at the time of their call. What is chiefly significant is not the details of the vision, which are clearly symbolical, but the consciousness of the divine Presence which underlies the whole. For both Isaiah and Ezekiel the vision was overwhelming in its majesty. Beneath the sense-imagery in which their experience clothed itself is the outstanding fact that they had encountered the numinous; they had come into immediate contact with God. That contact, whether conveyed through visions or voices, was the essential feature of the prophets' experience. It was that which brought them the inspiration, the illumination, the unshakeable assurance, which were the secret of their strength.

It is significant that the prophets' experience of the numinous, like the mystics' experience generally, is of a universal Reality. It may be true, as Wheeler Robinson contends, that in the Old Testament God is always transcendent rather than immanent in any proper sense, 'revealing Himself by His Spirit in particular occasions and through particular people, not by any universal presence'[2] The striking fact, in any case, is this: that to the prophets God reveals Himself as a Presence freed from the limitations commonly set upon Him. Ezekiel sees the visions by the river Kebar in Babylonia, although (as Peake remarks) 'the God who came into his experience with such illuminating and quickening power was popularly supposed to be confined to Canaan'[3] 'The whole earth [cries Isaiah] is full of His glory' (6: 3). 'Am I a God at hand, and not a God afar off? [in the words of Jeremiah] ... Do not I fill Heaven and earth?' (23: 23). In one of the very greatest of the Psalms, the poet extends the divine Presence to Sheol, the under-world, commonly conceived as a realm of darkness where no man can praise God (Psalm 139: 8). Here, as in other passages in the Psalms, we have an evident indication of the experience of contact with God characteristic of the prophets. The Psalms were written for the most part in the

1. *The Hebrew Prophetic Consciousness*, p. 109.
2. *Inspiration and Revelation in the Old Testament*, p. 248.
3. *Commentary on the Bible*, 1st edition, p. 504.

post-Exilic period, after the work of the great prophets was done, at a time when the central feature of religion was the sacrificial worship of Yahweh in the Temple at Jerusalem. The Book of Psalms represents the inner and spiritual side of this worship. At its highest point, the piety of the Psalmists rises to the level of a veritable passion for God. They give expression in burning words to the yearning of the soul for the renewal of the immediate experience of God which they have enjoyed in Temple-worship.

O God, thou art my God, I yearn for thee. ... As I have seen Thee in the sanctuary, with visions of Thy power and majesty, so will I bless Thee while I live [Psalm 63 : 1, 2, 4, in Moffatt's translation]. As the hart pants after the water-brooks, so pants my soul after thee, O God [Psalm 42 : 1].

And the Psalmists are not only moved by a mystical passion for the re-awakening of God-consciousness; they give evidence again and again of an abiding communion, a sense of the divine Presence not confined to time or place, which links them with God in an enduring unity.

Whom have I in Heaven but Thee? And there is none upon earth that I desire beside Thee ... God is the strength of my heart and my portion for ever [Psalms 73 : 25f].

Jeremiah, the greatest of the prophets, looked ahead to the coming of a time when his own immediate consciousness of God would become a universal possession of the house of Israel (31 : 34). In the fullness of its scope, the dream has not hitherto been realized. But this, at least, can be said : the mystical tradition, embodied in its own way in the life and experience of the prophets, was renewed among the Psalmists, and through the living power of their words has been a potent factor in the quickening and nurture of the spiritual consciousness in the religion of Israel and in Christianity.

II. JEWISH MYSTICISM

(a) Early Jewish Mysticism

As we have seen, there was a mystical element in the experience of Hebrew prophets and psalmists. In later centuries there arose within the sphere of Judaism a specifically mystical movement, which attained its fullest development in the medieval Kabbalah. The early history of this movement is obscure, but there are indications of its existence in the Apocalyptic literature, in the teaching and experience of some of the early Rabbis recorded in the Talmud, and among the Essenes and the Therapeutae, whose mode of life is described by Philo. (See p. 139 above.) The latter was himself a representative of early Jewish mysticism, but his teaching was so largely coloured by Hellenistic influence that it falls most naturally into the sphere of Hellenistic mysticism. Jewish mysticism generally was affected by this influence, but it drew more largely upon Jewish tradition than did Philo.

The Apocalyptic writers are primarily concerned with the revelation of things to come, like the end of the present age and the advent of the Messiah. But they set out also to make known the secrets of the unseen world; and the revelation which they bring is presented as having its basis in a certain experience. That experience is substantially identical with the central feature of the type of mysticism known as Merkabah (Chariot) mysticism, which was inspired by the prophetic vision described in Ezekiel 1. The Apocalyptic books are ascribed to ancient seers, like Enoch, Abraham, or Baruch, who ascend to Heaven, where they see the divine glory and receive a revelation of things to come. Thus in the *Apocalypse of Abraham*, written in Palestine towards the end of the first century, Abraham ascends to Heaven with the angel Yahoel, his celestial guide. There he sings a song of adoration and praise.

Thou art He whom my soul hath loved [he cries to God], eternal Protector, shining like fire ... Thou, O Light, shinest before the light of the morning upon Thy creatures. And in Thy heavenly dwelling-places there is no need of any other light than that of the unspeakable splendour from the light of Thy countenance [Ch. 18].

Abraham then sees the divine Throne, covered and encircled with fire, and a chariot with fiery wheels. His visionary experience reproduces the main features of Ezekiel's vision, but it is evident that we have here something more than a literary composition.

The imagery of fire and light is constantly employed by the mystics – often in a quite realistic sense – to describe their apprehension of the intensity and the splendour which character-ize the divine Presence. It is said in the Talmud that a certain Rabbi – Eliezer ben Arach – was once expounding the mysteries of the Merkabah to his master, Rabbi Yohanan ben Zaccai – a leader of Palestinian Judaism in the first century, who is said to have been the father of Merkabah mysticism. No sooner had Rabbi Eliezer begun his exposition than fire came down from Heaven, and encompassed all the trees of the field. An angel called out from the fire: 'Truly these, even these, are the secrets of the Merkabah'[1]. We have here an indication, in legendary form, of the ecstatic consciousness of the divine Presence associated with the mysteries of the Merkabah. A similar story is told of another Rabbi of the first century, Jonathan ben Uziel. He was once, it is said, sitting and studying the Torah – by which is meant, no doubt, in this instance, the lore of the Merkabah – when every bird that flew above him was burnt by fire.[2]

In another case, it is related in the Talmud that when Rabbi Yohanan heard of the marvels which attended a discourse on the Merkabah, ministering angels came in companies to listen to the words, and he cried out: 'Blessed are the eyes that see such things; I saw myself with you in a dream, seated upon Mount Sinai, and I heard a heavenly voice exclaiming *Ascend hither; ascend hither ... You and your disciples are destined to be in the third set ...* ' – that is, as Abelson explains, the third of the three classes of angels who stand continually in the divine Presence.[3] It was the aim of the mystics of the Merkabah to ascend to Heaven, as it was believed that Enoch and Abraham and other seers had done during their lifetime, and there to be-hold the Presence of God. In the Hebrew Book of Enoch (3 Enoch) it is related that Rabbi Ishmael ascended into the highest Heaven, and it is implied that 'such an ascension was the regular aspiration of the mystic of the circle'.[4] A Talmudic tradition tells of four Rabbis of the first and second centuries who entered

1. Abelson, *Jewish Mysticism*, pp. 42f.   2. ibid., p. 41.
3. ibid., pp. 43f.   4. Odeberg, *The Fourth Gospel*, p. 72.

Paradise during their earthly life. Such men were known as
'Merkabah-riders' or 'descenders of the Merkabah'. (The journey
of the soul to Heaven, at first described as an 'ascent to the
Merkabah', came later to be known as the 'descent to the Merkabah', although the metaphor of ascent was still employed in
the detailed description of the process.) It seems that there were
organized groups of mystics so described. A body of literature,
known as *Hekhaloth Books*, was written to describe their experiences – containing descriptions of the Hekhaloth or heavenly
palaces through which they passed in their journey to the Throne
of God in the seventh palace. These documents appear to have
been edited in the fifth and sixth centuries, having originated at
an earlier date. The ascent of the soul to its heavenly home is a
conception familiar in Hellenistic culture. It plays an important
part in the teaching of the Gnostics.   Mystery of
                                                      i Books the
                                                      's' – corres-
                                                      's. In order
                                                      a pass – a
                                                      stage of its
ascent. Jewish mysticism is thus intermingled with magic in this
phase of its growth.

The 'Riders of the Merkabah' had to fit themselves for their
ascent by moral training and ascetic practices like fasting and
ablutions. They achieved their end by the vision of the Hekhaloth,
and finally of the Merkabah, in a condition of mystical ecstasy.
This condition was induced by the invocation of the divine name
or by the recitation of hymns, many of which are recorded in the
Hekhaloth Books.

His Throne radiates before Him [we read in one of the hymns] and
His palace is full of splendour ... With a gleam of His ray He encompasses the sky, and His splendour radiates from the heights. Abysses
flame from His mouth, and firmaments sparkle from His body.[1]

In a tract known as the *Shiur Komah* ('the Measure of the
Body of God') the body of the Creator is described in detail,
enormous figures being given for the length of each organ. The

1. Scholem, *Major Trends in Jewish Mysticism*, p. 59.

description resembles that of the body of the beloved in the fifth chapter of the Song of Solomon. Whatever its original intention, it is interpreted in the *Hekhaloth Books* as a representation of the 'hidden glory' of God. It is the vision of this divine glory, symbolized in the Merkabah, which (as we have seen) is the goal of the mystic. The divine glory 'encompasses the sky', but it is not conceived in immanental terms; it is something essentially transcendent. In the *Hekhaloth Books* God is conceived as above all the 'holy King'. With this school of mystics there appears to be no thought of the union of the soul with God. The mystic stands before the Throne: the essence of his experience is illumination or vision. Scholem indeed has said that 'the infinite gulf between the soul and God is not even bridged at the climax of mystical ecstasy'.[1]

But is the gulf actually 'infinite'? Is the division between God and man absolute? In the Enoch literature so closely associated with Merkabah mysticism, we are presented with the experience of a man who, when he ascends to Heaven, is transformed into an angelic being. In *The Book of the Secrets of Enoch* (known as *2* or *Slavonic Enoch*, and written in Egypt in the first century), we are told that when Enoch entered the seventh Heaven, God commanded the archangel Michael to take from him his 'earthly robe' and to 'clothe him with the raiment of My glory'. When this was done, Enoch said, 'I gazed upon myself, and I was like one of His glorious ones, and there was no difference' (22: 8–10). In the *Hebrew Enoch* (written in the second century) he is identified with Metatron. Now, Metatron – the meaning of the name is obscure – holds a distinctive position among the angels. He is described as 'Prince of the Presence' and 'Prince of the world'. According to the medieval philosopher, Judah Ha-Levi, while some angels were created, others are eternal, and constitute in their totality 'the glory of God' together with the Throne, the Chariot, and other eternal things.[2] These angels are thus a divine emanation. In Merkabah mysticism, this is certainly the case with Metatron. He is actually described as 'the lesser Yahweh'. The Rabbis declare that he is the angel of whom Yahweh said to Moses: 'Behold, I send an angel before thee. ... My name is in

1. ibid., p. 56.   2. Abelson, op. cit., p. 64.

him' (Exodus 23: 20f.). The name of God is not merely a word. As Abelson says, it is 'a kind of essence of the Deity Himself'; so that the essence of the Deity is to be found in Metatron. He is 'a link uniting the human with the divine ... a heavenly co-worker with God'.[1] The significant fact is this, that in his ascension to the celestial sphere Enoch is identified with Metatron. But in his exaltation to the heavenly world Enoch typifies the experience of the mystic in his ecstasy. Is it not therefore implied that in his ecstasy the mystic also shares the measure of deification which is attributed to Enoch? Jewish mystics may indeed have shrunk from drawing that conclusion explicitly, but at least it may be said that there was for them no 'infinite gulf' between the soul and God, no absolute division between the world of living beings and the Creator. It was not only Metatron, and not only Enoch in his identification with Metatron, who participated in the divine essence. It was held that Adam was at first a spiritual being, and that the divine Spirit of the first Adam 'descended from Heaven into, and joined itself with, the spirit of prominently righteous men of subsequent ages such as Enoch, Abraham, Moses, Elijah'.[2]

The best-known book belonging to the early phase of Jewish mysticism is the *Sefer Yetsirah* (*Book of Creation*), which was composed most probably between the third century and the sixth, and which exercised a very considerable influence on the later development of mystical speculation. Its connexion with Merkabah mysticism is indicated by the frequent references which it contains to the 1st chapter of Ezekiel. As the title suggests, the book is concerned with the problem of creation and so with the constitution of the universe. Its interest is therefore purely theoretical, although its theories were utilized in the practice of magic. (In Talmudic legend it was possible to obtain magical powers by the use of the book.) The *Sefer Yetsirah* opens with the statement: 'By means of thirty-two mysterious paths did the Eternal, the Lord of Hosts, engrave and establish His name and create His world.' The 'thirty-two paths' are the twenty-two letters of the Hebrew alphabet and the ten 'Sefiroth'. The original

1. ibid., pp. 68, 71f.   2. Odeberg, op. cit., p. 265.

meaning of this word is uncertain. In the Kabbalah, as we shall see, the Sefiroth play a great part as the personified attributes of God. Here their significance is different: they are the ten elementary numbers, conceived as living powers and regarded as divine emanations. The word may be connected with the Hebrew *sappir* (sapphire), which is used in the description of the Throne in Ezekiel 1: 26.

'Their appearance [says the author] is like a flash of lightning, and their goal is without end; God's word is in them when they come forth and when they return; at His bidding they speed swiftly as a whirlwind, and before His Throne they prostrate themselves.'[1]

The first of the Sefiroth (one) is said to be 'the spirit of the living God'. It is the source from which the others spring. The second, third, and fourth are the elements (air, water, and fire), regarded as non-material entities, water being the basis of the earthly world and fire of the heavenly. The others are the six dimensions of space – the four points of the compass together with height and depth. The Sefiroth represent form rather than matter. It is the twenty-two letters which are the primal cause of matter. The world of corporeal things arises from the conjunction of the two. The letters, like the Sefiroth, are a divine emanation. The writer defines their function in creation in these words: 'God drew them, hewed them, combined them, weighed them, interchanged them, and through them produced the whole creation and everything that is destined to be created.'[2] The formation of words from letters is called 'the building of houses', and the building up of things out of their elements is regarded as akin to this process. It was taught traditionally that the world was made by the word of God: the letter-mysticism of *The Book of Creation* represents in essence simply an elaboration of this conception, the assumption being that Hebrew is a sacred language and so the language of creation.

(b) Medieval Hasidism

The early centres of Jewish mysticism were Palestine, Babylonia, and Egypt. In the ninth century, mystical teaching was introduced

1. Scholem, op. cit., p. 76.   2. ibid.

into the Jewish community in Italy, and Merkabah mysticism flourished there for a while. The members of the Kalonymus family, who migrated from Italy to the Rhineland in the following century, carried mystical teaching and aspiration with them, and there a new movement arose under their influence. Its creative period extended from the middle of the twelfth century to the middle of the thirteenth. (Had it some connexion with the Rhineland mysticism of the Christian Church?) There were three chief leaders of the movement – Samuel the Hasid, his son Judah the Hasid, and Eleazar of Worms, disciple and relative of Judah. Their writings are found in the *Sefer Hasidim* (*Book of the Devout*). All these men, and especially Judah, exerted a profound influence on the Jews of Germany. In contrast with that of the early leaders of the Kabbalah, the work of the Hasidim affected the life and thought of virtually the whole of German Jewry, and its influence remained for centuries. Scholem has said, indeed, that 'the rise of Hasidism was the decisive event in the religious development of German Jewry'.[1]

The name 'Hasid' (plural, 'Hasidim') indicated the distinctive quality of the movement. It is found in the Book of Psalms in the sense of 'pious', 'godly', 'devout'. In the second century B.C. it was applied to that section of the Jews which was most intensely devoted to the teaching and practice of traditional piety, and so most strongly opposed to the tendency to compromise with foreign influence; the Pharisees and Essenes were its offshoots. Among the Hasidim of the Middle Ages, the essential fact was the cultivation of a mystical piety leading to a constant sense of the divine Presence. Whereas in Merkabah mysticism stress was laid mainly on the training of the visionary and ecstatic faculties, so that the soul might be caught up into the celestial world and perceive the divine glory, among the Hasidim the emphasis was on the living of a life of devotion which found its fulfilment in the vision and the love of God. In this emphasis, and in the general nature of its outlook, medieval Hasidism was closely akin to the movement known by the same name which was founded by Baal-Shem in the eighteenth century.

1. op. cit., p. 81.

As in the teaching of Baal-Shem and his disciples, and in marked contrast with the attitude of Merkabah mystics, the dominant thought of German Hasidism is the divine immanence. 'God fills the whole ether', says Moses Azriel, a Hasid of the thirteenth century, 'and everything in the world ... Everything is in Him, and He sees everything ... for He has the power to see the universe within His own Being.'[1] Eleazar of Worms dwells upon the fact, stressed by Christian mystics, that God is nearer to the universe and to the human soul than the soul is to the body. A later writer interprets the saying of Deuteronomy 7: 21, 'the Lord thy God is in thy midst', as applying to the individual soul rather than to the community, as the context implies – God is the Soul of the soul.[2] This thought finds significant expression in the interpretation given by the Hasidim to the divine 'glory' so fundamental to the mysticism of the Merkabah. The Hasidim drew a distinction between two kinds of glory (kavod). There is the visible glory appearing on the Throne of the Merkabah and seen in the vision of the prophets; but there is also an inner glory whereby God speaks to the soul. In the *Book of Life* (*c.* 1200), this inner glory is identified with the Will or Word of God, the Holy Spirit, and is conceived as inherent in all beings.[3] The inner glory of God, His hidden presence in all things, is also identified with His 'holiness' as distinct from His 'greatness' (or 'Kingdom'), which is equated with His visible glory. The 'holiness' of God is said to be infinite, whereas His 'greatness' is finite. The distinction is held to be of particular significance in the practice of prayer. According to Eleazar of Worms, the Hasid addresses his prayer to God as King, in His visible glory, but his true intention is directed rather to His 'holiness' – His infinite and formless glory. It is this which he seeks as a mystic to contemplate. 'Everything is in Thee [in the words of the Hymn of Unity, composed by a follower of Judah the Hasid, and incorporated in the liturgy of the synagogue], and Thou art in everything; Thou fillest everything, and Thou dost encompass it.'[4]

The teaching of the Hasidim was in part a reflection of the

1. ibid., p. 109.   2. ibid., p. 110.
3. ibid., p. 112.   4. ibid., p. 108.

thought of Saadia, sometimes called the 'father of Jewish philosophy', who was head (Gaon) of a Babylonian academy in the early tenth century. Another influence was that of Neo-Platonism, which expressed itself particularly in the doctrine of archetypes. This doctrine was taught by Eleazar, and it finds a place in *The Book of the Devout*. It has its prototype in the conception of a heavenly Curtain spread before the Throne of God, which is found in *3 Enoch* and in the Hekhaloth tracts.[1] The Curtain is said to contain the images of all things from the creation of the world. This idea was taken over by the Hasidim. For them:

> The archetype is the deepest source of the soul's hidden activity. The fate of every being is contained in its archetype. ... The prophet is able to perceive it, and thus to read the future. Of Moses it is expressly said that God showed him the archetypes.[2]

There is, according to the Hasidim, a hierarchy of five invisible worlds. The highest is the 'world of light', which they identify with the 'holiness' or invisible glory of God.[3]

In its practical aspect, the new movement found expression in a distinctive attitude and way of life, summed up as the ideal of Hasiduth or devoutness. One feature of this ideal is a certain otherworldliness or asceticism. The Hasid must turn his back on ordinary life: he must shun profane speech and innocent pleasures like playing with children or keeping birds for ornament. He must avert his eyes from women, to avoid temptation. There is, however, no sexual asceticism in the stricter sense. *The Book of the Devout*, in fact, emphasizes the value of married life. This attitude is typical of Jewish mysticism generally. Apart from the Essenes and the Therapeutae in early times, it did nothing to promote monasticism. Yet the Hasidim laid the greatest stress, no doubt under Christian influence, on the practice of penance. An elaborate system was drawn up, and codified by Eleazar. Men

---

1. The Curtain appears in the newly discovered Gnostic writings (p. 148 above), where it divides the world of light from the world below (Doresse, op. cit., p. 320).

2. ibid., p. 118.

3. Boehme and Law likewise identify 'eternal nature' with the divine 'glory' (see pp. 271, 276).

would sometimes sit in snow or on ice for an hour every day in winter; they would expose their bodies to the sting of ants or bees in summer. In the case of mortal sins, they would submit themselves to far more painful penalties. In some instances they imposed suffering on themselves, not for their own sins, but for those of their fellows. 'Those who are truly just', said one Hasid, 'take sufferings upon themselves for their generation.'[1]

The Hasid must cultivate a complete indifference to praise or blame. He must be utterly impervious to the scorn evoked by his way of life among worldly-minded people. The importance attached to this attitude is shown by the fact that the very word 'Hasid' was apt to be interpreted as 'one who bears shame'. Yet the Hasidic ideal was very far from being one of mere aloofness or detachment. The mystic must not ignore his duties to the community or the need of loving his fellow-men. The ruling principle of his life is the love which is forgetful of self. He must therefore not insist on the letter of the Torah in his own interest. The Hasidim speak of a 'heavenly law', which exceeds the requirements of the Torah. As Scholem points out, there was 'a latent antagonism between the two conceptions. ... The Hasid, who in his outward behaviour submits to the established law in all its rigour, at bottom denies its absolute validity for himself'.[2] The love of God conquers his egoism and fills him with joy.

The soul [says Eleazar] is full of love of God and bound with ropes of love in joy and lightness of heart. ... When the soul thinks deeply about the fear of God, then the flame of heartfelt love bursts in it, and the exultation of innermost joy fills the heart. ... Everything is nothing to him except that he may do the Will of his Creator, do good to others and keep sanctified the name of God. ... And all the contemplation of his thoughts burns in the fire of love for Him.[3]

To describe his relation to God, Eleazar makes use of the analogy of human love, freely employing erotic language, after the fashion of Christian and Muslim mystics.

Medieval Hasidism represents at its best a highly developed spirituality. At the same time, as with Merkabah mysticism, it contains a magical element based on the mysterious power of sacred names. This appears to have been a factor in the practice

1. ibid., p. 106. 2. ibid., pp. 94f. 3. ibid., p. 95.

of prayer. A contemporary Jewish writer, Jacob ben Asher, says that the Hasidim 'were in the habit of counting or calculating every word in the prayers, benedictions, and hymns, and they sought a reason in the Torah for the number of words in the prayers'. The number of words in a prayer was linked with Biblical passages of the same numerical value and with names of God and the angels. The linkage may have been devised to promote mystical meditation, or it may have had a magical significance. In popular legend, the Hasid was presented as one who was vested with power over the forces of Nature, and in the writings of Eleazar there may be found tracts on magic and the power of the secret names of God side by side with discourses on the way of life and the divine nature.

(c) Abulafia and Prophetic Kabbalism

Hasidism, as we have seen, was the form which Jewish mysticism assumed in Germany in the twelfth and following centuries. During the same period, mysticism of another type was developing in Provence and Spain. This variety of mysticism came to be known as 'Kabbalism'. 'Kabbalah' is literally 'tradition'. The term implies that mystical teaching represents the true interpretation of the Scriptures, having been handed down by word of mouth from time immemorial. The word is sometimes used to cover medieval Hasidism, but it is best to restrict its application, with Scholem, to the movement which began in Provence in the twelfth century, and was developed in Spain, receiving its culmination in one phase in the work of Abraham Abulafia in the thirteenth century, and in another phase, contemporaneously with this, in the *Zohar*. This second line of development was continued, with important modifications, in the work of Isaac Luria and his followers in the sixteenth century.

The importance of Abulafia is often overlooked. His works remained unpublished until the nineteenth century, when some of his lesser writings and extracts from others were issued. Yet in his own day and later his influence was considerable. He had little contact with Rabbinic learning, but was widely read in

1. ibid., p. 100.

contemporary Jewish philosophy, and was influenced especially by Maimonides (eleventh century), perhaps the greatest of all Jewish philosophers. On account of the boldness of his thought, and his prophetic claims, he was assailed by some of the more orthodox Kabbalists. 'They called me heretic and unbeliever [he said] because I had resolved to worship God in truth.'[1] He was born at Saragossa in 1240. He travelled in the Near East in his early manhood, and spent much of his life in Italy and Greece. Most of his works were written in Italy towards the end of the thirteenth century.

It was the essential aim of Abulafia to open the way for men to the perception of divine Reality. What he sought, in particular, was an object of meditation which would free the soul from the normal limitation of its range of vision to the world of the senses. He found this object in the letters of the Hebrew alphabet. The contemplation of the name of God would, as he taught, lead to mystical ecstasy. He was notably influenced here by the teaching of the *Sefer Yetsirah* (see pp. 180f. above). Divine language was for him, as for Kabbalists generally, the substance of reality. The pure thought of God is expressed by a spiritual language, the letters of which are the elements of spiritual being. Every language, and not Hebrew only, may be a medium whereby the language of God is apprehended by human consciousness. In mystical meditation men practise the permutation and combination of letters. This activity Abulafia compares with that of a musical composer. At its culmination it leads a man to see the name of God and His angels in his heart. His soul will then leave his body in ecstatic joy, and he will receive an influx of spiritual life. Through training and experience of this nature he is prepared for the final stage – that of prophetic vision – when his soul is lit up by the radiance of the world of divine light, and comes to belong to that world. The man of prophetic vision is also the true lover of God, and conversely the man whose service is inspired purely by love is on the path which leads to prophecy.

In his early life, as has been mentioned, Abulafia travelled in the Near East, and in the course of his travels he may have

1. Scholem, op. cit., p. 130.

become acquainted with the theory and practice of Yoga. An important part of the training which he prescribes is the technique of breathing as taught by the practitioners of Yoga in India. He also sets forth rules of bodily posture. His system thus represents in one aspect a Judaized Yoga. We see its Indian affinities, moreover, in his conception of the place which is held in spiritual development by the 'master' (the *guru*), and in his interpretation of the goal of attainment. He says that the man of vision sees the image of his master confronting him at the hidden gates of his soul. The master, however, is not merely a human being; he personifies the angel Metatron, a semi-divine principle (see pp. 179f. above), or even (as is sometimes said) God Himself. A man is indeed not merely confronted by his master: he is identified with him, and so with Metatron or with God.

> The man who has felt the divine touch and perceived its nature [he says] is no longer separated from his Master [here evidently meaning God], and behold, he is his Master, and his Master is he, for he is so intimately united to Him that he cannot by any means be separated from Him.[1]

In this doctrine of identification with the divine, familiar to us in certain phases of Christian, Islamic, and Indian mysticism, Abulafia stands alone among Jewish mystics.

In the prophetic Kabbalism of which Abulafia is the outstanding representative, it is also taught that in the state of ecstasy a man encounters his own self detached from him.

> The complete secret of prophecy [says one writer] consists for the prophet in that he suddenly sees the shape of his self before him talking to him, and he forgets his self, and it is disengaged from him, and he sees the shape of his self before him talking to him and predicting the future.

Another writer is quoted as saying:

> I call Heaven and earth to witness that one day I sat down and wrote a Kabbalistic secret; suddenly I saw the shape of my self standing before me and my self disengaged from me.[2]

Such experiences, it appears, were more highly valued than the

1. ibid., pp. 140f.   2. ibid., p. 142.

visions of light which were the usual accompaniment of ecstasy.

Unlike the great majority of Kabbalists, Abulafia was definitely opposed to the practice of magic. He recognized the possibility of achieving power over the forces of the world by such means, and his own teaching concerning the use of divine names in meditation was applied by his successors to this end. But Abulafia himself was rootedly hostile to it. He issued a specific warning against the employment of the *Sefer Yetsirah* for this purpose.

(d) The 'Zohar' and Speculative Kabbalism

At the very time when Abulafia was expounding his doctrine of prophetic Kabbalism, a book was being written (or compiled) in Spain which was destined to hold a unique position in Jewish mysticism. So far as its influence on Jewish mysticism is concerned, the *Zohar* (literally 'brightness' or 'splendour') has been compared with the writings of the pseudo-Dionysius in relation to Christian mysticism. It resembles those writings in another respect. Like them, it purports to represent the work of an ancient worthy. The *Zohar* is in form a record of the discourses of Rabbi Simeon ben Yohai (who lived in the second century) and of his disciples. It is written chiefly in a form of Aramaic which is based largely on the Babylonian Talmud. It is for the most part a commentary on the Pentateuch, which it interprets on the basis of mystical symbolism. It cannot, as a whole, have originated before the thirteenth century, since it draws upon mystical writings of the time. It was first circulated between 1280 and 1300 by Moses de Leon, who was living in Castile, and who issued numerous Hebrew works under his own name. It is sometimes said that the *Zohar* cannot be the production of a single writer, owing to its enormous bulk and the varied character of its contents. Scholem, however, after a careful study of the Hebrew writings of Moses de Leon, has come to the conclusion that he was the author of the book, save for certain sections like the Raya Mehemna ('Faithful Shepherd'), which were added somewhat later.[1]

The *Zohar* expresses the outlook of a school of Kabbalists whose earliest production was the *Bahir* ('Brightness'), issued in

1. *Major Trends in Jewish Mysticism*, Ch. 5.

Provence in the twelfth century, but containing much older material. The teaching of the *Zohar* represents the development of its ideas concerning God, human destiny, and the significance of the Torah. The *Zohar* takes as its starting-point the assumption common to all Kabbalists that underlying all things is the creative power of speech. That power is embodied, not only in the written word of Scripture, but in all that exists in the seen and the unseen worlds, and in the deepest mysteries of the life of God, which Scripture unfolds. The essential meaning of the Torah is thus its symbolical or mystical meaning. What it conveys to us, above all, is a divine mystery – the development of forces working outwardly in time and space, but inwardly in the Being of God Himself. Language, and in particular the language of Scripture, is the clue which unlocks the hidden mysteries of being. This fact indicates the hidden unity of all things. 'God's essence [says Moses de Leon in one of his Hebrew writings] is linked and connected with all worlds, and all forms of existence are linked and connected with each other.'[1] In this universal linkage there is a constant interaction between the lower and the higher phases of being – between 'the above' (the Kingdom of Heaven) and 'the below' (the Kingdom of earth).

The central feature of the teaching of the *Zohar* is the conception of the Sefiroth. In the *Sefer Yetsirah*, as we have seen (pp. 180f.), the Sefiroth are living numbers, conceived as divine emanations. In the *Zohar*, their numerical significance disappears; they are commonly described as 'grades' – i.e. degrees of creative power or divine manifestation. They are at once qualities or attributes and agencies of God – the creative names which God gave Himself. The world of the Sefiroth is the hidden world of divine language which underlies the phenomenal universe. They represent both phases of the hidden life of the Godhead and means of His self-revelation to man. They are channels or 'flowings forth' (emanations) of the divine Light whereby the transcendent God becomes immanent in the world. They are active in the soul of man – itself an emanation from them – and so they enable man in his turn to play a creative part in the divine order and to unite himself with them.

1. ibid., p. 223.

In Himself God is En-Sof ('without end') – the Infinite. As such He is devoid of qualities; His Being is utterly beyond all knowing. In a certain sense He is Ayin ('Nothing') – the undifferentiated background of being. Yet He may be described as Or En-Sof – 'the infinite Light' – and from the unutterable radiance of His Light there spring the ten lights of the Sefiroth which illuminate the minds of men. Taken as a whole, the Sefiroth form 'the one great Name of God', Yahweh, which is equivalent to the divine Presence as it is manifested in the order and harmony of creation. In themselves they constitute 'the world of union' – the highest of the four unseen worlds intermediate between En-Sof and 'the world of separation' in which man exists in his fallen state. They are described also as 'the Face of God', 'the Garments of God', 'the Tree of God' which grows throughout creation – it is only through the power of the Sefiroth living and acting in them that created things exist. They form, moreover, the figure of Adam Kadmon, the original spiritual form of man. All the Sefiroth are united with one another in an interpenetrating unity. Though each is marked by the predominance of a particular quality, all participate in the qualities of the rest. All are subject to common influences, so that whatever affects one affects the others.

The Sefiroth are divided into three triads, with a tenth representing the harmony of them all. The highest, Kether, the 'Crown' of God, is indistinguishable from En-Sof. It is the mystical 'Nothing', 'the primordial point' – 'an absolute indivisible unity baffling all analysis and description'.[1] From Kether proceeds Hokhmah, the divine 'Wisdom', in which is enshrined the ideal existence of all things in undifferentiated unity; and from Wisdom comes Binah, the divine 'Intelligence', in which all forms pre-exist in the Mind of God which sees them in itself. It is said that the divine Wisdom is the 'Father', the active principle producing all things, while the divine Intelligence is the 'Mother', the passive or receptive principle. The second triad consists of Hesed, the 'Love' or 'Mercy' of God; Din, the 'Power' of God, which is manifested mainly as the power of judgement or punishment, and so is equivalent to 'Justice'; and

1. Abelson, op. cit., pp. 146f.

Tifereth, 'Beauty', or alternatively Rachamin, 'Compassion'. Strangely, as it seems to us, Hesed is a male principle, and Din a female. 'Mercy is the life-giving, ever-productive because ever-forgiving power', while 'Justice is the necessarily opposed faculty holding in check what would otherwise prove to be the excesses of Mercy'.[1]

The third triad consists of Netsah, 'Victory', the lasting endurance of God, taken as masculine; Hod, the 'Glory' or 'Majesty' of God, regarded as feminine; and Yesod or 'Foundation', the ground of stability in the universe. Finally, there is a tenth principle which unites and harmonizes the rest – Malkuth, the 'Kingdom' of God, which is also called the Shekhinah, signifying the Presence of God in the universe, including His special manifestation in the lives of men and in hallowed places. Among the Hasidim the Shekhinah is identified with the inner Glory of God, whereby He reveals Himself to men (see p. 183 above). As Abelson has shown, the thought of the Shekhinah plays a prominent part in Rabbinical literature, where it is often identified with the Holy Spirit.[2] In the *Zohar*, the Shekhinah receives a feminine character. It is described as the Queen, and is conceived alternatively as the daughter and the bride of God. The Sefiroth as a whole are said to be the offspring of the union between God and the Shekhinah, which is also regarded as the mother of each individual Israelite. She is the archetype of the community of Israel, and she is at the same time present in the actual community. We are reminded of the place held by Sophia in the teaching of the Gnostics. The Sefiroth in general may be compared with the Aeons of the Gnostics and the ten 'powers' of the Hermetic literature.

It has been mentioned above that in its unity and totality the world of the Sefiroth is represented in one aspect by the figure of Adam Kadmon. In his original form man, like the universe as a whole, was of a purely spiritual nature, existing in unbroken unity with God in the higher celestial earth (the Garden of Eden). His body was of the nature of light, and he was endowed with all wisdom. There was thus complete unity between God and

1. ibid., p. 150.
2. *The Immanence of God in Rabbinical Literature.*

the Shekhinah, His manifestation in the world. In consequence of the Fall, this unity was broken, and throughout creation harmony was replaced by discord. Since that time the Shekhinah has been in exile, revealed only in individuals here and there, or at particular places. She is 'Rachel weeping for her children'. It is the essential nature of sin that it brings division and separation, just as in the primal sin of Adam the fruit was separated from the tree. One Kabbalist says that the Sefiroth were first revealed to Adam in the Tree of Life and the Tree of Knowledge taken together, but Adam separated one from the other, and so introduced the principle of division and isolation into the world, worshipping the Shekhinah only (here identified with the Tree of Knowledge), apart from the rest of the Sefiroth. The union of God and the Shekhinah was thus impaired, and what is called 'the exile of the Shekhinah' was brought about. Evil is traced also to the introduction of disharmony among the Sefiroth in another way. Din, the quality of stern judgement, became detached from Hesed, the quality of love or mercy. How this came about the *Zohar* does not explain – whether through the sin of man or through the intrinsic working of factors inherent in the divine life. In any case, the attribute of stern judgement was held to become independent of the divine mercy, and so to break loose from the divine life and to be transformed into what is radically evil – Gehenna and the world of Satanic forces. The fire of wrath, which in God was tempered by His mercy, became the fire of Hell. In this matter the teaching of the *Zohar* was reiterated by Jacob Boehme in the seventeenth century (see p. 271 below).

Although man has fallen into separateness and mortality, he is still in his essence a spiritual being. His body is 'an outer covering', a 'veil', not the man himself. Yet the human form has a cosmic significance. It is a microcosm, which includes all things, higher and lower, in itself. 'The different parts of our body [the *Zohar* says] correspond to the secrets of the divine wisdom' but 'the real part of man is his soul' (ii: 76a). The soul, while essentially a unity, is threefold in its nature, and the three elements are themselves an emanation from the world of the Sefiroth. The lowest element is nefesh, the principle of life. Above this is ruach, sometimes rendered 'spirit', but representing in the *Zohar* the normal exercise of self-conscious activity – the soul as the seat of the moral attributes and of the intellect or reason. Highest of all is neshamah, the 'holy soul' or 'super-soul', the inner or deeper self, the 'spirit' or 'divine spark of the soul', which stands high above ruach, and provides it with its light. Neshamah is literally 'breathing': it is 'the breath of higher spirituality, the bridge which connects man with the heavenly world'.[1] It is an emanation of Binah, the divine Intelligence, and unites man with God. Like the German mystics, the *Zohar* recognizes that the 'spark' is incapable of sin. It is an individualized expression of the divine. As the *Zohar* says, it is in its essence 'the Supernal Soul, the Soul of all souls, inscrutable and unknowable, veiled in a covering of exceeding brightness' (II: 245a). In entering into the depths of his own being, man thus becomes aware of the presence of God.

As an emanation from the Sefiroth, the soul pre-exists in the heavenly world, 'hidden in the divine Idea'. Before its descent to earth, it vows to fulfil its task – to re-unite itself with God. During its earthly life, it weaves the garment of light which it is to wear after death in the 'realm of radiance', from its righteous acts. In its final blessedness, when it has completed its growth, the soul ascends to its source, and is re-united with God. This union is described in terms of love. The soul is united with 'the Queen', the Shekhinah, or with the 'heavenly King, the Holy One', in 'the Palace of Love'. But it is only 'if a man is drawn towards the Holy One, and is filled with longing for Him in this world' that the soul is 'carried upwards towards the higher realms' (I: 99). Otherwise men have to undergo reincarnation on earth, or to be purified in 'the fiery stream of Gehenna', or even destroyed. Reincarnation, first taught in the *Bahir*, is apparently an exceptional destiny in the *Zohar*, though regarded by later Kabbalists as universal (see p. 199 below).

It is the aim of the mystic to attain union with God. Such union receives its culmination in the world to come, but it is possible for a man during his earthly existence to enter into a state of union (devekuth) – to be joined or united with God in mystical ecstasy, and to be one with Him in a continuous attachment or adhesion.

1. Müller, *History of Jewish Mysticism*, p. 102.

Unlike Abulafia, the *Zohar* lays little stress on ecstasy. Its emphasis is rather on devekuth as a permanent condition of being. This state of being has a social aspect in the glorification of poverty which is characteristic of the *Zohar*, perhaps through the influence of the contemporary Spiritual Franciscans (see pp. 261f. below). It is said that the Shekhinah is poor, since 'she has nothing from herself', but only what she receives from the stream of the Sefiroth (i: 249b). In the *Zohar* there is no trace of sexual asceticism. Marriage is not regarded as a concession to the weakness of the flesh: it is a sacred mystery reflecting the union of God with the Shekhinah.

For the mystic, two things are supremely necessary, according to the *Zohar* – the love of God and the practice of prayer. The love of God is identical with true fear, which springs from the sense of His greatness as 'the Rock and Foundation of all worlds, before whom all existing things are as naught'. Fear, so understood, carries love with it. 'A man should love his Master with a perfect love ... which remains steadfast in both affliction and prosperity.' Affliction, indeed, arises 'in order that there might be this perfect love' (i: 11b, 12a). As the writer says elsewhere, God crushes the body of the righteous man 'in order to give power to his soul, so that He may draw him nearer to love' (ii: 180b). The love of the soul for God is not interpreted in erotic terms, save in the case of Moses, of whom it is said that he had intercourse with the Shekhinah (i: 21b, 22a). With other men, the love of God is likened to the love of a child for its father. In the Palace of Love, where the heavenly King unites Himself to holy souls, the soul receives the kiss of its Father 'like a daughter' (ii: 97a, 146b). The *Zohar* looks upon prayer, if it is offered with concentrated devotion (kawwanah), as a powerful instrument of good, not only leading men towards union with God, but bringing about in the world above a new measure of peace and joy, which descend to earth and are distributed to all receptive souls. In its essence prayer does not consist of spoken words.

Prayer consists in another voice attached to the voice which is heard. It thus behoves men to pray silently with that voice which is inaudible – to pray 'with proper concentration of the mind on the unity of God' [ii: 209b].

It is man's task, as the *Zohar* understands it, not only to seek after union with God as the goal of his individual being but, in doing that, to strive also after the restoration of the universal harmony which sin has destroyed, and so to bring to an end the exile of the Shekhinah. 'The impulse from below', it is said repeatedly, 'calls forth that from above.' The power of man thus extends to the higher realms of being. 'He who worships God out of love lifts everything to the stage where all must be one' (II: 216a). It is not only through individual activity consecrated to God that unity can be restored, but through the concerted activity of the community of Israel, which was chosen for this very purpose. By virtue of this election, the Shekhinah attached itself peculiarly to Israel. It was for the restoration of unity that the divine revelation in the Torah was given to Israel. The commands and prohibitions of the Torah correspond by a species of numerical symbolism to the limbs and sinews of the human body; and the observance or breach of these regulations brings about a reaction through the body in the corresponding part of the world of the Sefiroth and so in the whole. Far from diminishing the importance of the detailed observance of the Torah, the Kabbalism of the *Zohar* had the very opposite effect. A particular significance was attached to the festivals ordained by the Torah and to the Sabbath. Each day in the week was subject to the influence of one of the Sefiroth, and the Sabbath was related in this way to the tenth (Malkuth or the Shekhinah) which unified the potencies of them all. The Sabbath was therefore a day of holy joy. Its meals had a mystical value. 'They served to set in motion from above the blessings of the day for the world below.'[1]

The joy which it brought was not confined to men. It was –

– 'a day of joyful reunion in the supernal worlds. On that day the rigours of Judgement are shut out, and give way to the healing power of love, enfolding with its blessings the whole of creation. Even the denizens of Hell find respite on that day from the expiating pangs of their sins.'[2]

The Sabbath was thus an anticipation of the day when the

1. Epstein, *Judaism*, p. 241.   2. ibid., pp. 240f.

Messiah himself should come, when the exile of the Shekhinah should be ended, and all beings in Heaven and earth should again be made one.

(e) *The School of Isaac Luria and Messianic Kabbalism*

An event of decisive importance in the development of Jewish mysticism was the expulsion of the Jews from Spain in 1492. As the result of this event, the Messianic element present in Kabbalism (as in all forms of Jewish religion) received a new emphasis, and it became the great object of the mystics to play their part in hastening the coming of the Messianic Age. The 'birthpangs' of that Age had, as they believed, already begun. At the same time Kabbalism, being so closely linked up with the national aspirations of the Jewish people, came to enjoy a widespread popularity. It was, indeed, for a time the dominant form of Jewish religion. In the Kabbalah the doctrine of transmigration, which taught men to regard earthly life as a condition of exile from the soul's true home in God, and set forth the various stages of that exile, came to the forefront and was widely accepted among the Jews.

Many of the Jews who were driven out of Spain migrated to the East and expecially to Palestine, and there in 1534 the leader of the new movement, Isaac Luria, was born. Eventually he settled at Safed, and there, along with Moses Cordovero and other Kabbalists, he founded the Community of the Devout, which became the centre of the movement. Luria was above all a visionary. His teaching was given as an interpretation of the *Zohar* on the basis of revelations from the prophet Elijah; he is also said to have received a celestial guide in the person of Simeon ben Yohai, who advised him to settle at Safed (near which town the sage was buried). He wrote little himself, but his sayings were compiled and expounded by his disciples, chief among whom was Hayim Vital (d. 1630).

Although its most distinctive feature is its Messianic or redemptive emphasis, Luria's teaching, like that of the *Zohar*, is highly speculative. His conception of the origin of the universe is in fact far more complex than that of the *Zohar*. He rejects by implication the divine all-inclusiveness postulated by the *Zohar*, which declares that God 'comprises all creatures in Himself' (II: 19b). That was also the teaching of the Hasidim, and the same doctrine was held by Luria's fellow-worker, Cordovero, who said of En-Sof: 'everything that exists is contained in His substance ... Nothing exists outside of Him.'[1] To avoid this conception, Luria developed the idea of Tsimtsum ('contraction' or 'withdrawal').[2] The existence of the universe rests on a process of divine contraction or withdrawal. In other words, God must have initially withdrawn from some part of His own Being, and so have formed a kind of primal vacuum or empty space, so that later He might return to it in His creative work. At every stage of the cosmic process this dual act of withdrawal and manifestation is renewed: light first flows back into God, and then flows out of Him. Always there is ebb and flow in the divine life – inhalation and exhalation. Along with this conception goes Luria's explanation of the origin of evil – the doctrine known as 'the Breaking of the Vessels'. The divine Light flowed into primordial space in the form of the Sefiroth. From the lights of the Sefiroth was formed the primal man, Adam Kadmon. The light then flowed forth from Adam Kadmon into certain vessels which were intended to serve as media for its manifestation. The vessels corresponding to the three highest Sefiroth gave shelter to the light. But the light corresponding to the other seven shattered the vessels containing it. The Breaking of the Vessels was the turning-point in the cosmic process: as the outcome of it, the harmony of the universe was destroyed. The light streaming from God was broken up into sparks, which illuminated only certain parts of creation, leaving other parts in darkness. In this way light and darkness, good and evil, became opposed forces contending for mastery.

The discord and confusion arising from the Breaking of the Vessels were accentuated by the Fall of Adam, which repeated it on a lower plane. After the first disaster, a process of restitution (Tikkun) began. A new stream of light flowed forth from En-Sof, and issued from the forehead of Adam Kadmon. The lights of

1. Scholem, op. cit., p. 253.
2. Tsimtsum is a doctrine taught by some of the Gnostics. See Doresse op. cit., p. 323.

the Sefiroth were organized afresh. Each Sefirah became a Partsuf or 'countenance' of God – a manifestation of the whole divine Personality. The Shekhinah, which had entered into exile with the Breaking of the Vessels, became Rachel, the celestial bride. But with the Fall of Adam she was exiled anew. Before the Fall (as in the *Zohar*) Adam was a spiritual being embracing the whole world. His Fall therefore affected everything: the universe fell with him, and the material world, where all things are in exile, came into being. But this condition is not final: the process of Tikkun, whereby the scattered lights and sparks may once more be united, and the Shekhinah may be brought back to God, is renewed in man. It is within his power to play an active part in the process. Luria thus shared the hope and aspiration of the *Zohar*, and gave it a new emphasis. The whole life and work of man receives its meaning from its relation to the cosmic and super-cosmic goal.

For Luria the doctrine of transmigration (Gilgul) has a fresh significance. As we have seen, in the *Zohar* it represents an exceptional destiny. With the school of Safed it became a fundamental law – a necessary part of the process of Tikkun. The experience of the Jews in exile typified the exile of the soul. Transmigration was conceived, not only as a means of retribution for past offences, though this thought remained (especially in relation to rebirth in the form of animals and even plants or stones); it was regarded as providing men with new opportunities of gaining salvation. The process was interpreted, moreover, not only as involving a series of separate journeys through time, but as in the last resort a unity. All souls are contained in the universal soul of Adam, so that all transmigrations are 'migrations of the one soul, whose exile atones for its fall'.[1] Within the whole, again, there are particular groups or families of souls, the members of which can help one another on their way. Transmigration continues for each soul until it has won its way to union with God. Such souls will be finally re-united with the soul of Adam, when the exile of the Shekhinah is ended at the coming of the Messiah.

For Luria, the whole practice of religion finds its meaning in

1. ibid., p. 282.

relation to the Tikkun. It is the Tikkun which provides the purpose of the Torah: the commandments are to be fulfilled so that the spiritual nature of man and the harmony of the universe may be restored. Like the *Zohar*, Luria's teaching lays the greatest stress on the potency of mystical prayer. Before any act of worship is performed, the devotee must engage in concentrated meditation (kawwanah) on its deeper significance. Such meditation is at once a means to the union of the soul with God, and an instrument whereby man's influence is brought to bear on the higher orders of being. A new liturgy was composed, consisting of mystical meditations and prayers. (The 'Prayer-Book of Isaac Luria' was later adopted by the Hasidim of the eighteenth and nineteenth centuries.) Luria also advocated fasting and other forms of self-mortification as an aid to spiritual growth, although he remained true to the Jewish tradition which emphasized the sanctity of bodily life. He laid the greatest stress on the principle of love. Since in all human beings there is in the last resort one universal soul, which strives to recover its unity, all are organically interrelated. As Cordovero says: 'In every one there is something of his fellow-man. Therefore whoever sins injures not only himself, but also that part of himself which belongs to another.' One must love one's neighbour as oneself, 'for the other is really oneself'.[1] Love must be nurtured by the constant exercise of meditation and prayer. On retiring at night, one should pray:

> Lord of the universe, I forgive all who have made me angry and harmed me. ... whether wittingly or unwittingly, whether in deed or thought. May no man be punished for my sake or because of me.[2]

Love must be universal, extending to all human beings without restriction of nationality. It was, indeed, believed by the mystics of Safed that the exile and dispersion of the Jews was itself designed to bring about the salvation of all human souls.

> This is the secret why Israel is fated to be enslaved by all the Gentiles of the world: in order that it may uplift those sparks which have fallen among them ... It was necessary that Israel should be scattered to the four winds in order to lift everything up.[3]

1. ibid., p. 289.   2. Epstein, op. cit., p. 250.
3. Scholem, op. cit., p. 284.

(f) Sabbatianism, a Mystical Heresy

Under the influence of Luria, Kabbalism was widely identified with apocalyptic hopes and expectations. Luria himself looked to the coming of the Messiah in his own lifetime. It was the widespread excitement produced by such beliefs which gave rise to the Sabbatian movement in the seventeenth century. The central figure of the movement was Sabbatai Zevi, a Jew of Spanish descent born at Smyrna in 1626. Zevi was an unbalanced and neurotic personality, subject to alternating exaltation and depression. He claimed that in his early manhood he had received a great illumination, and in moments of exaltation he thought of himself as the Messiah. It was not, however, until he met Nathan of Gaza (born in 1644) that he was definitely convinced of his Messianic mission. Nathan was a student of the *Zohar* and of Luria's teaching. He underwent a mystical experience which led him to believe that he was endowed with the gift of prophecy. 'The Spirit came over me [he said in a letter] and I saw the Merkabah, and I saw visions of God all day and all night, and I was vouchsafed true prophecy like any other prophet.'[1] Nathan felt that he possessed the power of reading men's souls and giving them spiritual direction. Zevi, it seems, felt himself in need of spiritual help, and he came to Nathan for this purpose. During his periods of depression he was subject to severe temptation, and sometimes fell into sin. But when he came to Nathan, the latter was assured that in spite of his lapses Zevi was indeed the Messiah, and he induced him to proclaim himself. He was led, in fact, to modify the teaching of Luria in accordance with Zevi's experience. Nathan was the foremost theologian of the Sabbatian movement. In his *Treatise of the Dragons*, he taught that the soul of the Messiah had fallen into the abyss together with some of the sparks of the divine Light, after the Breaking of the Vessels. Along with the soul of the Messiah there are certain serpents or dragons which torment it and seek to lead it astray. The soul of the Messiah struggles with the serpents in the endeavour to win perfection, and when the process is accomplished, the Messiah will become incarnate on earth. Nathan makes it quite clear that

1. Scholem, op. cit., p. 295.

his mythical theory was based on the struggles of Zevi. 'The serpents [he says] always endeavoured to allure him [the Messiah] . . . and they were able to take possession of him when the state of illumination had departed from him.'[1]

Zevi proclaimed himself Messiah at Gaza in 1665, and his claim became known and widely accepted throughout the Jewish world. He was hailed with enthusiasm as 'King of the Jews', and it was believed that the day of universal salvation was at hand. Zevi, however, was arrested by the Turkish authorities, and brought before the Sultan. He was presented with the choice of conversion to Islam or death. He chose conversion. Ten years later (in 1676) he died in obscurity in Albania. The Sabbatian movement did not end with his denial of the Jewish faith. Large numbers of his followers continued to believe in him, regarding his apostasy as a sacred mystery, and expecting him to return in triumph to Palestine as Messiah. After his death it was hoped that he would be reincarnated in this capacity. In Salonica a prophet arose in the person of Berukyah (or Baruch Kunio), who claimed that he was Sabbatai Zevi reborn, a 'living Messiah' or 'God-man'. Berukyah's followers in Turkey, like Zevi himself, made an outward profession of Islam. (They were known as Doenmeh or Dormeh.) The Sabbatian movement generally changed its character: it was henceforth propagated in secret. In order to avoid persecution at the hands of the Jewish leaders, its adherents professed orthodox Judaism. At a later time a group of Sabbatians in Poland, under the leadership of Jacob Frank, joined the Roman Catholic Church. Poland was the centre of the movement in Europe. From there missionaries were sent to Galicia, Moravia, Prague, and the towns of Germany. Contact was established with the disciples of Berukyah, and the latter was worshipped as 'true God, eternal King, our living Messiah, who hast been in this corporeal world, and hast re-ascended to thy place'.[2] From time to time other prophets appeared, each of whom was looked on as a reincarnation of Sabbatai Zevi. Like the Zaddik of the later

1. ibid., p. 298.
2. Scholem, 'Le Mouvement sabbaïste en Pologne' (*Revue de l'Histoire des Religions*, 43: 227).

Hasidim, each prophet was the centre of a community of believers over which he enjoyed a boundless authority.

The most remarkable feature of Sabbatianism was its paradoxical character. As Christianity rests on the paradox of a Messiah who was crucified, Sabbatianism was based on the paradox of a Messiah who became an apostate. It therefore sought to glorify apostasy. Strangely enough, the strength of its appeal lay partly in this very fact. In the fifteenth century, the Jews of Spain had made an outward profession of Christianity to avoid persecution. Their descendants – the Marranos – returned to the fold after they had fled from Spain, yet they still had an uneasy conscience, and the doctrine of an apostate Messiah brought them relief.

A leading theologian among the Sabbatians was Abraham Miguel Cardozo (d. 1706), who was himself by birth a Marrano. It was his teaching that through the sins of Israel all Jews were originally destined to become Marranos, but they were delivered from this fate by the grace of God, which imposed the sacrifice of apostasy on the Messiah, who alone was capable of enduring such a destiny without harm. Cardozo departed from the tradition of Lurianic Kabbalism. His doctrine of God, like that of most Sabbatian teachers, represents a new departure in Kabbalism. It is a revival of Gnostic dualism, with its distinction of the hidden God or First Cause and the God of Israel, who is the revealed God. Unlike the Gnostics, however, Cardozo and the Sabbatians laid all their emphasis on the latter, while regarding Him as ontologically secondary or derivative – the effect of the First Cause. The hidden God has no relation to the world or to man. Traditionally, it is held, Israel has confused the two. That is its error. The God with whom men are concerned in religious worship is the God of Israel, whose union with the Shekhinah is the goal of prayer. Not unnaturally, both Rabbinic and orthodox Kabbalists reacted strongly against this conception.

In contradistinction to the attitude of Cardozo, Nathan of Gaza advanced his teaching as an interpretation of the doctrine of Isaac Luria. His book, the *Treatise of the Dragons*, was written prior to Zevi's apostasy, but there was clearly nothing contrary to its tenets in that event. His later works came after it (he lived until 1680). In these he sought to show that the Messiah's apostasy is a necessary part of the mission laid upon him: he must enter into the realm of evil for the purpose of liberating the sparks of divine Light from their captivity, and he must perform actions, like apostasy, which are condemned as wrong.

It is easy to see that the glorification of apostasy, and the justification of other acts contrary to the Law, could readily lead to an antinomian position. Nathan of Gaza and other leaders of the more moderate wing of Sabbatian thought avoided this tendency by insisting that the 'strange actions' of the Messiah were not examples to be followed. These actions symbolize the freedom of the Messianic Age, when the traditional Law would no longer be binding; meantime men must accept its restrictions. Side by side with moderate Sabbatians, there were extremists like Berukyah and the Doenmeh of Salonica, who took the opposite view. All men, they taught, must follow Zevi's example and descend into the realm of evil, that evil may be overcome.

The outstanding leader of the extreme Sabbatians in Europe was Jacob Frank (1726–91), who towards the end of his life became Baron Offenbach. Frank was said to be a reincarnation of Berukyah and so of Zevi, and at the same time an incarnation of the Sefirah Tifereth (Beauty, see pp. 191f. above), and thus a God-man and an object of worship. With him, as with Zevi, we enter the sphere of mystical pathology. Frank has been described as an impostor. He was certainly obsessed by the love of power. Yet, as Scholem has said, 'there is no reason not to believe that he had his hours of savage enthusiasm, of ecstasy and vision'.[1] He claimed that it had been revealed to him in a dream that he had been chosen as the apostle of Poland. For him Poland, and not Palestine, was the promised land. He called upon his followers to declare their faith openly. Those who did so were excommunicated. In order to escape persecution, Frank and many of his disciples accepted baptism into the Catholic Church (in 1759), while maintaining their own organization in secret.

Frank's teaching was quite definitely antinomian. 'I came', he said, 'to deliver the world from every law and every statute which

1. *Revue de l'Histoire des Religions*, 44: 47.

were in force until now. .... I came only to destroy everything.'[1]
His disciples practised secret rites of an orgiastic nature. The
elect were beyond good and evil; they must not be judged by
prevailing moral standards. Sin of every kind was actually sacred,
provided that it was committed with religious fervour. He held
out to his followers the promise of world-conquest, if they would
take up arms. Happily nothing was done to put his teaching into
practice in this direction. The sect which Frank founded retained
its identity as a clandestine organization within the Catholic
Church for seventy or eighty years. The greater number of
Sabbatians did not accept Frank's authority; they remained
within the Jewish community. Many were in course of time won
over to Hasidism.

(g) Modern Hasidism

The modern movement known as Hasidism is similar in its main
emphasis to the medieval movement of which an account has
been given in the second section of the present chapter, yet the
one has no historical connexion with the other. More than any
other movement in Jewish mysticism, modern Hasidism has
made its appeal to the common people. Its popular character is
evident from the prominent place held in the presentation of its
teaching by religious tales – stories of the deeds of the saints.
Hasidism belongs to the Kabbalist tradition, although its emphasis has been not on doctrine but on personal life and experience. Its leaders have accepted much of the teaching of
Isaac Luria, but they have in general departed from his Messianic
emphasis. The movement took its rise in the Ukraine, where
Sabbatianism had flourished, and many of its supporters were
adherents of that movement. It seems that the founder treasured a
mystical manuscript written, unknown to himself, by a prophet
of moderate Sabbatian views. In spite of the wide differences between the two movements, they agreed in ascribing
leadership to the prophet or illuminate rather than to the
learned Rabbi.

The founder of modern Hasidism is known as Israel Baal
Shem. He was born in 1700 on the border of Volhynia and

1. ibid., p. 61.

Podolia. He spent his early life in humble occupations such as digging lime in the Carpathian mountains and keeping an inn for peasants – the inn being actually managed by his wife, while he spent his time in meditation in the woods. In the last twenty years of his life (1740–60) he became the centre of a band of disciples attracted by his mystical message. His influence was exerted almost entirely by his oral teaching, as with Luria. He was regarded as a holy man and a wonder-worker, many miracles being attributed to him. The name Baal Shem ('master of the name' of God) is itself an indication of his reputed power in that direction. In the sixteenth century and later the name had been given to a number of men claiming to exercise such powers, especially in Eastern Europe. In the case of the founder of Hasidism the name is one more proof among many of the close connexion between mysticism and magic which forms part of the Jewish mystical tradition. Among the followers of Baal Shem, it was held that magical power is the normal accompaniment of mystical ecstasy.

Baal Shem and his disciples were the heralds of a new quickening of the religious consciousness. The founder was succeeded in the leadership of the movement by Rabbi Baer of Meseritz, known as 'the great Maggid' ('preacher'), who sent out missionaries to all parts of the Ukraine. Through their work Hasidism spread rapidly in Eastern Europe. It was Rabbi Baer who introduced the conception of the Zaddik (or 'perfectly righteous man'), which played so great a part in the later development of the movement. In its early stages the main emphasis of the Hasidim was on the divine immanence. They saw the living Presence of God as the dynamic essence of all things; and the vision was to them a constant source of joy, of exaltation, of ecstatic fervour. What chiefly mattered in all religious acts was the spirit of intense devotion with which they should be performed. The Hasidim were opposed to all forms of asceticism, such as penance and fasting beyond what the Law enjoined. Men must avoid all gloom of spirit, and enjoy the good things of life in purity of heart. The whole of life must be consecrated to God. Life should be lived between the two poles of service (avodah) and ecstasy (hithlavuth). 'Hithlavuth is embracing God beyond time and space. Avodah is the service of God in time and space.'[1] What gives service its significance is the spiritual intention (kawwanah) which underlies it. For Luria, as we have seen, kawwanah is an act of concentrated meditation engaged in prior to the offering of worship (see p. 200 above). With the Hasidim it becomes rather the direction of the whole being to God, so that the divine purpose may be accomplished, the exile of the Shekhinah may be ended, the scattered sparks may be re-united. The exile and deliverance of the Shekhinah is the chief concern of prayer. While they no longer cherished apocalyptic dreams, the Hasidim looked to the ultimate goal of the restoration of unity in the universe and in the life of God, and they believed that it was in the power of man to further that end through consecrated striving, and above all through the force of prayer. The hasid 'prays [it was said] that the want of the Shekhinah may be satisfied, and that through him, the praying man, the unification of God with His Shekhinah may take place'.[2] Prayer is a means whereby unity may be restored; it is also a means of realizing unity here and now between the praying soul and the whole community of Israel, and so of giving help to others and receiving help from them. One leader said with reference to prayer:

I bind myself with the whole of Israel – with those who are greater than I, that through them my thoughts may ascend, and with those who are lesser than I, that they may be uplifted through me.[3]

It is essential in prayer to forget oneself. Such forgetfulness reaches its highest point in ecstasy, in which a man is wholly absorbed in God, losing the consciousness of himself and his surroundings, and attaining what is described as 'the extinction of [separate] existence'. It is said that the man who is in ecstasy is 'above Nature and above time and above thought'.[4] One master had to look at a clock in order to keep himself in the world, another had to put on spectacles when he wanted to see particular things, 'for otherwise he saw all the things of the

1. Buber, *The Legend of the Baal-Shem*, p. 23.
2. ibid., p. 27.   3. ibid., p. 29.
4. ibid., p. 19.

world as one'.[1] The state of ecstasy was so highly valued that sometimes the Hasidim made use of artificial stimuli, like loud chanting or dancing, to achieve it.

Since the goal of endeavour was in one aspect the annihilation of the separate self in God, it was natural that the Hasidim should consider the two qualities of humility and love as supremely necessary. Love must be universal; it must be directed to men as men irrespective of their attitude or character. A man must love his enemies just as much as his friends. Such charity was displayed, above all, by the founder. Baal Shem, like Jesus, consorted freely with those whom others despised – those who were poor and neglected or cast out of respectable society. Unlike other teachers, he chose especially to associate with women, and so was accused by his opponents of immoral conduct. 'Let no one think himself better than his neighbour,' he said, 'for all serve God, each according to the measure of understanding which God has given him.'[2] Love itself, it was recognized, implies humility.

Only the truly humble man in heart will not feel it a hardship to love one of the wicked, thinking 'for all his wickedness, he is better than I am'.[3]

This attitude to wrong-doers is related to the universal immanence of God. Since God is present in all beings, there is a measure of good in all, and it is our duty always to look to the good, and not to judge that which appears to be evil. We must therefore, to the greatest extent possible, think well of others. Evil differs from good, not absolutely, but only in degree. There is no separate sphere of evil. Evil is 'but a lower grade of the good, owing to the diminution of the divine Light illumining it'.[4] The very vitality of evil springs from God. Even the greatest sinner need never despair of the divine forgiveness. There is no bound to the possibility of repentance. It is well to observe in this connexion the transformation of Luria's doctrine of Tsimtsum effected by the Hasidim (see p. 198 above). For Luria, as we have seen, this meant the withdrawal of God from some part of

1. Buber, op., cit. p. 20.   2. Schechter, *Studies in Judaism*, I: 28f.
3. Newman, *Hasidic Anthology*, p. 186.
4. Epstein, op. cit., pp. 273f.

His own Being, and the formation of a dark vacuum, in order to make room for the universe. For the Hasidim it indicates, on the contrary, the very Presence of God in the universe – 'an adaptation of the power of His infinite Light to the capacity of endurance of His creatures' and so 'a diminution in the intensity of the divine Light'.[1] The sparks of divine Light are present in all things.

Hasidim was essentially a movement of religious revival. It found its centre in the life and experience of the saint, rather than in any defined body of doctrine. A leader of the movement once said: 'I did not go to the Maggid of Meseritz to learn Torah from him, but to watch him tie his boot-laces.'[2] This emphasis on personality found particular expression in the conception of the Zaddik, which the Maggid himself introduced, and which became the distinctive feature of the movement. Rabbi Baer said that it is only the man who has become one with God who is capable of that complete concentration of the mind on God which is the secret of effective prayer. Other men must attach themselves to a Zaddik, who is able to help them to develop their latent powers and to secure divine favours for them. The Zaddik thus became, like the guru and the sheikh, a mediator between God and men, a channel of divine grace, empowered to raise men to God by virtue of his own God-consciousness – possessing an authority equal to that of the Torah, the guide of men's lives and the centre of the communal life of his followers. Each local band of disciples had its own Zaddik, and each Zaddik was marked by the special qualities which he stressed and by which he was himself distinguished. Some were renowned for ecstatic visions, some for psychic powers or miraculous deeds, others for intense humility or boundless charity or self-forgetting love. It is said that one was so completely self-effacing that he became altogether impervious to bodily suffering, yet so tender to sinners that he took their guilt upon himself. In the early period of its existence the movement gave birth to many true saints and mystics. Yet, as the Zaddik became more and more dominant, Hasidism tended to lose its original spontaneity. The principles for which it stood

1. Scholem, op. cit., p. 344.   2. ibid., p. 273.

were overshadowed by the claim to personal power. The Idea of the Zaddik was one which obviously lent itself to abuse. Its whole validity was dependent on the integrity of the individual, and with the passing of time this was often lacking. Men claimed a spirituality which they did not possess, and battened on the credulity of their followers. Mysticism was too often replaced by obscurantism and superstition.

In their early days the Hasidim were often brought into conflict with established religious authority. Baal Shem and his disciples denounced the Rabbis much as Jesus had done. Many changes were introduced in the liturgy, and the prescribed hours of prayer were sometimes neglected. When the Hasidim gained the upper hand in a community, they were apt to depose the Rabbi and to appoint a leader of their own in his place. The authority attributed to the Zaddikim was felt to undermine the position of the Torah. In many places the wrath of the orthodox gave rise to persecution: the leaders of the Hasidim were scourged, their books were burnt, their synagogues were closed. Such measures proved completely futile, serving only to enhance the popularity of the sect and to intensify the devotion of its adherents. At the same time Rabbinical opposition was not without its effect. In the nineteenth century there was a revival of Rabbinical learning within the movement, accompanied by a repudiation of the emotionalism to which it had given rise and producing works of casuistry altogether alien to its original spirit. Hasidism thus became allied to the very Rabbinism to which it had at first been so markedly opposed. Apart altogether from this particular reaction, a new type of Hasidism, marked by its intellectual emphasis and known as Habad Hasidism, grew up in Lithuania under the leadership of Shneur Zalman of Ladi (d. 1813). Shneur Zalman sought to systematize the teaching of the movement. The name 'Habad' itself indicates the nature of his emphasis: it is derived from the Hebrew initials of the second and third of the Sefiroth, Hokhmah (Wisdom) and Binah (Understanding) and their offspring, Daath (Reason or Knowledge). In this school of thought the conception of the Zaddik was transformed. From being a mediator between God and man, characterized (as he was in the common view) by wonder-working power, the Zaddik became above all a teacher, venerated not only for his holiness, but for his knowledge of the Torah. The movement none the less retained the mystical character of Hasidism, laying particular stress on the ecstatic nature of prayer. After the death of Shneur Zalman, Habad Hasidism found its centre for a century in northern Russia. Today its headquarters are in New York, where it has its own schools, and sends out missionaries to many places, especially to North Africa and Israel.[1]

1. See Epstein, op. cit., p. 281.

CHAPTER 7

Christian Mysticism

I. MYSTICISM IN THE NEW TESTAMENT

(a) *The Mysticism of Jesus*

WE have seen that the outstanding feature of the experience of the Hebrew prophets was the sense of immediate contact with God. Now, it is clear from the gospels that the prophetic tradition was renewed in Jesus – hence his conflict with the legalism of the Scribes and Pharisees – and it is natural to infer that he shared the distinctive prophetic experience. The inference is confirmed by the records. The story of his life begins in Mark with his baptism in the Jordan, when 'he saw the heavens opened and the Spirit descending upon him [or 'into him', as an ancient MS. has it] like a dove' and he heard a voice from heaven proclaiming his divine sonship (Mark 1: 10 f.). In the Western text of Luke 3: 22 the words are said to have been: 'Thou art my Son; this day I have begotten thee.' It was widely held in the early Church that, as this version was held to imply, it was through the descent of the Spirit, possessing him and penetrating his being, that the divine life was born in Jesus. The event was sometimes described as 'Christ's second nativity'. Whatever its precise significance, the main fact, from our present point of view, is that the story, with its visionary and auditory features, is closely similar to the records of the call of Isaiah and Ezekiel. And just as, with the prophets of old, it is manifest that underlying the sense-imagery in which their experience was clothed there was the immediate apprehension of the divine Presence, breaking in upon them and consecrating them to their appointed task, so it was with Jesus. It is no rash conjecture to suppose that beneath the details of the gospel story there lay a profound and overwhelming experience of God, binding Jesus to Him in a continuing unity.

The story of the Baptism, whatever its historical basis,

represents the spiritual illumination of Jesus which was the inspiration of his work. The Transfiguration appears to rest on an
experience of ecstasy.

> He was transfigured before them; his face shone as the sun, and his
> garments became white as the light [Matthew 17: 2].

A similar story is told of the Buddha shortly before his death.
It is a frequent experience among the mystics that they have been
aware of the divine Glory as of a blinding, dazzling light; and the
divine radiance, it seems, has sometimes shone through their
bodies. Bonaventura tells of St Francis that once his whole body
was 'wrapped in a shining cloud'. It may well be such an event,
as Evelyn Underhill suggests,[1] which was the kernel of the gospel
story.

The experience of God expressed itself for Jesus in the consciousness of the divine Fatherhood. 'The experience of God as
Father', says T. W. Manson, 'dominates the whole ministry of
Jesus.[2] In the Fourth Gospel the evangelist presents this consciousness as one of divine indwelling:

> I am in the Father, and the Father in me. The words that I say to
> you I do not speak of myself, but the Father who dwells in me does His
> works [John 14: 10].

In the manner of the Fourth Gospel, the words probably represent an interpretation of the attitude of Jesus rather than an
actual utterance of his own, but they rest upon a true insight into
the nature of his experience. Jesus, as we have seen, revived the
tradition of the prophets. Underlying that tradition was the
sense of the presence and power of the Spirit living in them and
working through them. At the Baptism, it is said, the Spirit
descended upon Jesus (or into him). Like the prophets, he spoke
with the authority which the Spirit within him gave. Like them,
he had the courage and independence, and at the same time the
utter humility, which are the outcome of the divine inworking
power. He is said to have told his followers that in the hour of
trial it would not be they who spoke, but 'the Spirit of your
Father speaking through you' (Matthew 10: 20). These words
are evidently the reflection of his own experience. The fact shines

1. *The Mystic Way*, p. 117.   2. *The Teaching of Jesus*, p. 103.

out through the record of the words and deeds of Jesus that it was the consciousness of the 'Spirit of the Father' living in him which was the inspiration of his life. An illustration of this fact is the peculiar power of Jesus to cure disease – 'by the finger of God', as he said (Luke 11: 20); that is, by the power of the Spirit in him (cp. Acts 10: 38). Paul similarly speaks of the gift of healing as one of the manifestations of the power of the Spirit (I Corinthians 12: 9). A modern Indian mystic has told how he came to possess the power of healing by touch quite spontaneously, as the outcome of the growth of his spiritual consciousness.[1] So also the healing gift of Jesus would appear to have been a by-product of his God-consciousness.

A Christian mystic, Gerlac Petersen, has said of the soul which is made one with God: 'It worketh all its works in God, or rather God doth work His own works in it.'[2] No words can more aptly convey the essential secret of Jesus. Although there is little in the teaching of Jesus in the Synoptic Gospels which bears a specifically mystical character, yet the total impression which the gospel story leaves upon us is of one who lived in the constant awareness of the divine Presence. It is significant that Arthur Drews, the author of *The Christ Myth*, who regarded the gospel story as purely mythical, recognized its value as a symbol of the union of man with God. Union with God is in one aspect an entire self-giving to the divine; and it is that entire self-giving which we see in Jesus, and which is reflected in his ethical demands. The supreme law for him is the love which makes us one with God – by which we may share the divine perfection (Matthew 5: 48). The great sin is the self-seeking and self-exaltation which above all things stand in the way of that attainment. Jesus, like the Buddha, was moved by a boundless compassion. He identified himself with his fellows in their sufferings. The words of the Son of Man in the parable of Judgement are, clearly, an expression of his own attitude:

Inasmuch as you did it to one of the least of these my brethren, you did it to me [Matthew 25: 40].

1. See *An Indian Monk*, by Shri Purohit Swami.
2. From *The Fiery Soliloquy*, quoted by Evelyn Underhill in *The Golden Sequence*, p. 57.

In a special way Jesus identifies himself with his followers. They are to rise with him into the universal love which makes men sons of God. As his followers, they are an extension of his own personality, as he himself, being the messenger of God, is an extension of the divine Personality:

He who receives you receives me, and he who receives me receives Him who sent me [Matthew 10: 40].

In words like these we have an anticipation of the 'Christ-mysticism' of Paul and John.

(b) Pauline and Johannine Mysticism

In the religion of the Christian Church as it is represented in the New Testament there was a mystical element from the Day of Pentecost onwards. What underlies the story of Pentecost is evidently an experience of ecstatic possession by the Spirit, finding expression in what was felt to be inspired utterance or 'speaking with tongues' (I Corinthians 14). The 'rushing of the mighty wind' and the 'tongues of fire' symbolize the sense of a new transcendent energy at work in men which marked the birth of the Christian Church. The sense of the presence and power of the Spirit which began with Jesus was renewed among his followers after his death.

The outpouring of the Spirit at Pentecost is associated in the narrative with the resurrection and exaltation of Jesus (Acts 2: 33). Otto has suggested that the belief in the resurrection rested on an experience of a mystical character.[1] The earliest witness to the resurrection is Paul, whose experience, like that of Isaiah and Ezekiel at their call and that of Jesus himself, combined sense-perception and spiritual apprehension. Paul says that Christ 'appeared' to him (I Corinthians 15: 8 and cp. 9: 1). According to the Acts of the Apostles 'a light from heaven shone round about him' (9: 3) but it is implied in verses 17 and 27, as well as in Paul's own words, that he saw Jesus himself. It may be that he saw him, in Otto's phrase, 'as a royal figure of radiant glory'. The vision was, in any case, the outer expression of an inner and continuing assurance of the living presence of Jesus in the new

1. *The Idea of the Holy*, 4th edition, pp. 226f.

and more glorious mode of being into which (as Paul came to believe) he had passed. Paul was one given to ecstatic experience. He possessed the power of 'speaking with tongues' and of prophecy. In one instance he felt himself to be caught up into Paradise, where he heard 'ineffable things' (II Corinthians 12: 2–4). His vision of the risen Christ was doubtless an experience of the same order. It is significant that in the account of his conversion and the events which followed it, attributed to Paul in Acts 22, he says that after he had returned to Jerusalem he fell into a trance in the Temple, and again saw Jesus (verse 17). Presumably his initial experience was of the same character. It is significant also that in I Corinthians 15 Paul equates his experience with that of Peter and the others to whom Christ appeared. Peter also was an ecstatic gifted with visionary powers, as we see from the story of Acts 10. It seems likely therefore that for the primitive Church the resurrection was in the first instance an experience of a mystical order, a vision of Christ exalted and glorified – 'transported into the glory of God'[1] – and so, in accordance with current belief, raised to the right hand of God. In Acts 2: 32 f. – as also in Hebrews 12: 2 – the exaltation of Jesus is virtually identified with his resurrection.

The religion of the early Church appears to have been rooted, like the religion of the prophets and of Jesus, in the visionary and ecstatic experience whereby men have been brought again and again into contact with the Transcendent. It is in the epistles of Paul and in the gospel of John that the mystical aspect of primitive Christianity finds its fullest and most definite expression. The distinctive quality of the mysticism which is the essence of Pauline and Johannine Christianity is indicated in the term 'Christ-mysticism'. The experience in which it centres is union with Christ. It is its particular characteristic that it mediates the sense of the Transcendent through a historical person, Jesus of Nazareth. An attempt has been made by Drews, Couchoud,[2] and others to show that Jesus was for Paul a purely mythical figure, like the divine heroes of the Mystery-religions (see pp. 153ff. above). But the attempt has broken down completely. If one thing can be

1. Guignebert, *Jésus*, French edition, p. 651.
2. *The Enigma of Jesus.*

regarded as a certainty, it is that for Paul the Christ with whom he sought to be united had lived and suffered and died in the person of Jesus. It is true that the Mystery-religions were a living influence in the Roman world in Paul's time. They provided part of the framework in which Paul set his teaching. Yet in essence Paul's faith and experience were his own; and the basis of that faith was, in one aspect, the historical actuality of the life and death of Jesus. It has, indeed, been said that Paul knows nothing of 'God-mysticism' – of the immediate knowledge of God in His eternal reality which has been the typical experience of the mystics, Christian and non-Christian alike. That contention can scarcely be sustained, in view of the ecstasy of which Paul speaks in II Corinthians 12. Yet it is 'Christ-mysticism' which is typical of him.

'Christ-mysticism' is itself a form of transcendental experience. It is the essence of the early Christian faith, as we have seen, that Jesus has been transported into the divine Glory. The limitations attendant on his life in the flesh have been done away. In Paul's conception he belongs wholly now to the spiritual order. Paul speaks interchangeably of 'the Spirit of Christ' and 'the Spirit of God'. He thinks of Christ in his exaltation 'in terms of the Spirit which is immaterial and omnipresent.[1] Since Christ is Spirit, he can live in men – can possess them, and speak through them, and become the inner principle of their being – and they can live in him. It is here that we have the core of Paul's 'Christ-mysticism'. His essential aspiration is to be 'found in Christ', to know him and the power of his risen life (Philippians 3: 9f.) 'It is no longer I that live [he can say] but Christ that lives in me' (Galatians 2: 20). The recurring phrase 'in Christ' implies this personal union. And union involves a breaking down of barriers, a blending of personalities, an identity of experience.

As one with Christ, Paul makes his own the experience through which Christ has passed. He suffers with Christ, he dies and rises with him, he sits with him in the heavenly places. He shares Christ's status before God, his character and his destiny.[2]

While Paul lays the greatest stress on the historical actuality of

1. C. Anderson Scott, *Christianity according to St Paul*, p. 154.
2. Peake, *The Quintessence of Paulinism*, p. 22.

the life and death of Jesus, in the light of his 'Christ-mysticism' the historical facts become symbols of inner experience. The Christian shares the fellowship of Christ's sufferings, that he may share his glory (Romans 8 : 17). He dies with him, to the life that centres in self, that he may rise with him into his oneness with God.

Albert Schweitzer has said that the fundamental thought of Pauline mysticism is the sense that through union with Christ men are 'raised above this sensuous, sinful, and transient world, and already belong to the Transcendent'.[1] Christ has entered the eternal order, and through their union with him Christians already share his exalted life, while they live in time and space (Ephesians 2: 6 and Colossians 3: 1). It is a token of this exaltation, on which Schweitzer lays considerable emphasis,[2] that Christians share the glorified form of Christ. They have already, as Paul implies, received beneath their garment of flesh a new 'corporeity', which will be manifested at the consummation to which Paul looks ahead in the body of divine effulgence (the spiritual body) which is the actual body of Christ (I Corinthians 15 : 35 f). It is because he is 'grafted into the corporeity of Christ', in Schweitzer's view, that the Christian is united with Christ, and in Christ with all who share this union, so that in a quite literal sense the Church forms a single body of which Christ is the head and the animating spirit. Schweitzer is certainly right in stressing the organic unity of those who share the new life in Christ as an essential feature of Pauline mysticism. Christians are 'one person in Christ Jesus' (Galatians 3: 28). They make up together 'one new man' (Ephesians 2: 15). They are to become members of the one 'full-grown man' in whom all are to be gathered up (Ephesians 4: 13 f). The mysticism of Paul is essentially a corporate mysticism. But this feature, while it is reinforced by the thought of a new 'corporeity' common to those who are united with Christ, is not in any way dependent on it. Indeed, it is the logic of the mystical experience that it makes for unity. So far as a man is one with the Spirit, he is one with all who share a like experience. It is noteworthy that in I Corinthians 12, where Paul develops more

1. *The Mysticism of Paul the Apostle*, p. 3.
2. ibid., pp. 121ff.

fully than in any other passage the thought of the unity of the 'body of Christ', his emphasis is on the unity of the Spirit which dwells in the body and makes it one.

Paul has an exalted conception of human destiny. It is true that he is the champion of an uncompromising moral dualism. While man in his true being is 'the image and glory of God' (I Corinthians 11: 7), he has fallen into sin, so that in his actual nature he is a 'child of wrath' (Ephesians 2: 3). In every man the flesh – 'man's emotional and intellectual nature as perverted by sin'[1] – wars against the spirit. If therefore man is to rise into his true heritage, the 'old man' – the narrow self – must be slain; he must die to self, that he may 'put on the new man, created after the likeness of God' (Ephesians 4: 24). His nature will then be transformed and divinized. In his union with Christ he shares the life of the Spirit which is the life of God. Christ, as Paul implies in his later epistles, is himself divine. He is 'the image of the invisible God, the first-born of all creation – [born first, before all the creation (Moffatt)] – for in him all things were created' (Colossians 2: 5 f). Paul here identifies Christ with the pre-existent principle of Wisdom (Proverbs 8: 22 f) which is virtually identical with Philo's conception of the Logos – the 'first-born' or 'eldest Son of God'[2]. 'By nature [he says] Christ was in the form of God' (Philippians 2: 6); that is, he shared in the divine essence. And he imparts this essence to men. Through union with him they are lifted out of the sphere of what is merely human into the divine. It is the goal that lies before them, to be wholly transformed in God. As the fullness of divine perfection dwelt in Christ (Colossians 1: 19 and 2: 9), so they are to be filled with that same fullness (Ephesians 3: 19).

We all, with unveiled face, reflecting as a mirror the glory of the Lord, are being transformed into His likeness from glory to glory [II Corinthians 3: 18].

It is clear that the early Fathers and the medieval mystics were in full accord with the teaching of the Apostle when they used the term 'deification' to describe the ultimate destiny of the soul

1. C. H. Dodd, *The Meaning of Paul for Today*, p. 60.
2. Cp. W. D. Davies, *Paul and Rabbinical Judaism*, Ch. 7.

which becomes 'one spirit with the Lord' (I Corinthians 6: 17).

The 'Christ-mysticism' of Paul finds renewed expression, in its main features, in the Fourth Gospel. Modern students are in general agreed that this gospel presents us not with the actual teaching of Jesus but rather with a series of meditations designed to indicate what the evangelist regarded as the spiritual significance of his life and work. We can scarcely doubt that beneath those meditations there lies a basis of personal experience similar to that which underlay and inspired the work of Paul. The gospel may, indeed, be regarded as in one aspect a re-interpretation of the person and work of Jesus in the light of 'Christ-mysticism'.

Jesus is presented in John as the incarnation of the Logos – the 'Word' or 'Thought' of God, conceived, as in Philo, as at once an immanent principle and a personal being, the Son of God, who shares the divine essence. The Logos is the eternal Life manifested in the world. And this divine Life is 'the Light of men' (1 : 4), 'the true light that enlightens every man' (1 : 9). It is the work of Christ as the incarnate Logos to bring to men the life and the light which are the inmost principle of their being.

The mysticism of the Fourth Gospel is most fully expressed in the Farewell Discourse (Chs. 14–17), where Jesus speaks of his impending death and departure from his followers, and of his return in the Spirit to be with them and to unite them with himself. We have here a re-statement of Paul's conception of the exaltation of Christ and all which that involves. The death of Jesus is presented as involving his return to the Father. 'I go to the Father,' Jesus says; and he bids his disciples rejoice in the fact. To 'go to the Father' is to pass into a new mode of being, to enter into a perfect union with the Father, untrammelled by the limitations of earthly life. His being will henceforth be immeasurably enlarged, so that he will come again to his disciples as an inner and abiding presence.

His 'going' is itself a 'coming'. For he goes to the Father, to whom all things are present, so that by his departure he becomes more accessible than ever before.[1]

1. Temple, *Readings in St John's Gospel*, ii: 228.

Christ will, in fact, be in his disciples, and they will be in him. As an inner presence, living and working in and through them, doing greater things through their instrumentality than he himself was able to do, Christ is one with the Spirit whose divine energy he liberates into the world. John speaks of the Spirit as the 'Paraclete' – the Helper or Counsellor. As with Paul, the Spirit is conceived now as distinct from Christ, now as one with him in his exalted life. Christ sends the Paraclete, or the Father sends him in Christ's name; yet in the person of Christ the Paraclete already dwells with the disciples, and His coming to live in them is the coming of Christ – 'I will not leave you desolate; I will come to you.' For John, as for Paul, the inner presence of Christ is a mystical experience which may alternatively be described as the inner presence of the Spirit with whom Christ is one.

It is the essential feature of 'Christ-mysticism' that Christ as a divinely-human person unites men with himself in God. Johannine mysticism, like Pauline, is a corporate and not merely an individual fact. It receives its culminating expression in the prayer of Jesus in Chapter 17. Jesus prays that all who follow him may share his union with God – that all may be one, as a living and interpenetrating unity of souls, 'even as Thou, Father, art in me, and I in Thee, that they also may be in us'. The divine destiny which Christ has attained, the divine glory which belongs to him in his perfect union with the Father, he seeks to share with all his followers – 'that they also may be with me where I am'; 'that they may be one even as we are one, I in them and Thou in me, that they may become perfectly one'.

II. MYSTICISM IN THE EASTERN CHURCH

The history of the Christian Church falls naturally into two great divisions, Eastern and Western. It is convenient, in considering the nature of Christian mysticism, to follow the line which this fact indicates, and to describe separately the characteristic features of mysticism as it developed in the East and in the West respectively. There is, of course, no hard-and-fast distinction between the two phases of mystical life and thought. In fact, there is much common ground between them. Mystics everywhere share the same essential experience, and Christian mystics draw upon a common heritage of faith and devotion. Apart from the specifically Christian tradition of which they are the heirs, Christian mystics, in the East and West alike, have been subject to a further common influence. As it developed under the Roman Empire, Christianity came increasingly to adopt the thought-forms provided by Greek philosophy. The theology and the mysticism of Paul and John already express that influence. As we have seen in Chapter 5, Platonism had a pronounced mystical aspect, which was paramount in Neo-Platonism, and the developed mysticism of the Christian Church in both its branches reveals a definitely Platonic influence. As we shall see, moreover, medieval Western mysticism was indebted to an incalculable extent to the teaching of a great Eastern Christian mystic, the pseudo-Dionysius. At the same time, Western mysticism grew up in its own setting, and gave rise to a rich profusion of varied forms.

(a) 'Dionysius' and the Way of 'Unknowing'

Of all the mystics of the Christian Church, the one who has exercised the greatest influence is the author of *The Mystical Theology*, *The Divine Names*, and other writings which became known in the East in the sixth century. The supposed author of these works is Dionysius the Areopagite, St Paul's convert at Athens. For centuries they enjoyed a considerable authority owing to this fact. They are often regarded today as the work of a Syrian monk living in the sixth century, though they are sometimes assigned to an earlier date – from the third to the fifth century.[1] 'Dionysius' was a Neo-Platonist. God is for him beyond being (as we know it) and so beyond the possibility of intellectual knowledge – nameless and ineffable. Nothing that we can say of Him can be adequate to express the infinite mystery of His life. This is a truth fundamental to all profound religious insight. We have seen the part which it plays in Indian, Chinese, and Hellenistic mysticism. In the Christian tradition, many of the Fathers – from Clement of Alexandria in the second century onwards – shared the vision of 'Dionysius'.

The attitude of 'Dionysius' is not exclusively negative. In *The*

1. Lossky, *The Mystical Theology of the Eastern Church* pp. 23f.

Divine Names he dwells on the symbolical value of divine attributes like 'life', 'wisdom', 'goodness', 'power'. But his main stress is on the utter insufficiency of all our concepts in face of the unfathomable depth and greatness of divine Reality. 'The One who is beyond thought surpasses the apprehension of thought, and the Good which is beyond utterance surpasses the reach of words'; the transcendent Godhead 'dwells in a region beyond us, where our feet cannot tread'.[1] Therefore his preference, as he says, is for the 'negative way'. In *The Mystical Theology* he says (in Ch. 1) that 'while God possesses all the positive attributes of the universe, being the universal Cause, yet in a stricter sense He does not possess them, since He transcends them all ... He is super-essentially exalted above created things'. Not even the highest of human categories can be properly applied to Him – neither soul nor mind nor spirit ('as we understand the term'), not even essence or eternity or unity or godhead (the quality of deified men).

The reason cannot attain to Him or name Him or know Him ... nor can any affirmation or negation be applied to Him ... He transcends all affirmation as the perfect and unique Cause of all things, and all negation by the pre-eminence of His simple and absolute nature, free from every limitation and beyond them all [Ch. 5].

The 'negative way' has been subject to a good deal of criticism. Even writers as sympathetic to mysticism as Inge and Rufus Jones have regarded it as a baleful influence. But its critics have commonly failed to do any real justice to it. The 'negative way' – the way of 'unknowing' – is in reality based on an essentially positive insight. It is because of the immeasurable greatness and glory of God that He transcends our knowing. And 'unknowing' is in itself a positive attitude – the attitude of inner stillness which brings into play the deeper powers of the soul. In a passage at the opening of the *Mystical Theology* which has been quoted again and again by mystical teachers, 'Dionysius' bids us:

In the exercise of mystical contemplation leave behind the senses and the activities of the intellect, and all things sensible and intellectual ... that thou mayest arise, as far as thou mayest, by unknowing towards union with Him who transcends all being and all knowledge.

1. *The Divine Names*, I: 1; XIII: 3.

Here 'Dionysius' is concerned to emphasize the necessity under which we are laid, by the nature of the case, if we are to approach God by way of mystical contemplation: we must close the doors of the senses, and still the activity of thought.

We pray [he says again] that we may come unto this darkness which is beyond light, and through the loss of sight and knowledge may see and know That which is above vision and knowledge [Ch. 2].

The 'darkness which is beyond light' is the vision of the divine Glory, which to us seems dark through excess of light. This vision or knowledge is also described as union or absorption. 'Leaving behind us all human notions of divine things, we still the activities of our minds, and reach (as far as this may be) into the super-essential Ray';[1] 'there God joins us to Himself, in so far as the power of union with Him is possessed even by us men',[2] and we become 'wholly absorbed in Him who is beyond all'.[3] In mystical contemplation the soul is no longer conscious of itself; it is made one with the divine Light, merged or absorbed therein. It is thus 'deified'.[4] For 'Dionysius', deification is an experience to which the soul attains in ecstasy; it is also the goal of our being. God is for him not only transcendent; He is immanent in all things. He 'dwells indivisibly within the separate and individual things'.[5] Creation is a process of emanation whereby God, while remaining one, brings forth the many existences from Himself. 'The Creator [says 'Dionysius'] is transported out of Himself, and drawn from His transcendent Throne above all things' through an ecstasy of divine Love.[6] There is thus an outgoing from God in creation; and there is also a return to Him, realized in the ascent of the soul to deification or union with Him. The ultimate Reality, symbolically termed 'God', is (as we have seen) ineffable. The names applied to it are not merely means whereby we conceive its nature; they are energies or effluences radiating from it. The super-essential Mystery is called 'Being' or 'Life', because it bestows being and life; it is called 'Light', because it illuminates the mind; it is called 'God', because through our participation in its outflowing energy it makes us divine.[7]

1. *The Divine Names*, I: 4.   2. ibid., XIII: 3.
3. *The Mystical Theology*, Ch. 1.   4. *The Divine Names*, I: 5.
5. ibid., II: 11.   6. ibid., IV: 13.   7. ibid., II: 7.

Deification is the goal of our being. We may reach it in moments of mystical ecstasy (or 'unknowing'), but as a permanent state of being it can only be attained by the utter conquest of self-love and attachment to the things of time and space. 'Dionysius' says little of the mystic way, but what he says amounts to an uncompromising demand for self-renunciation. Just as in mystical contemplation the consciousness of self is lost, so in life as a whole self must be completely surrendered to God.

We must go out of ourselves to give ourselves entirely to God, for it is better to belong to Him than to ourselves, and thus God can give Himself to those who abandon themselves to Him.[1]

If we are to be 'led upwards into the super-essential radiance of the divine Darkness', it can only be 'by the unceasing and absolute renunciation of ourselves and of all things'.[2]

(b) Eastern Mysticism and the Divine Light

The mysticism of 'Dionysius' is in its main features typical of that of the Eastern Church as a whole. The central fact is the experience of God. To Eastern mystics this experience comes typically as a vision of the divine Light, which transforms and deifies the soul. In mystical ecstasy, says Maximus the Confessor (seventh century), 'the mind is ravished by the divine boundless Light, and loses all sensation of itself or of any other creature, and is aware of Him alone, who through love has produced this illumination.'[3] St Simeon, known as 'the New Theologian', a Byzantine poet of the eleventh century – one of the greatest of all Orthodox mystics – tells of a young man who received a vision of the Light in an apparently sensible form. While he was at prayer, 'a brilliant divine radiance descended on him from above, and filled all the room. Thereupon the young man forgot that he was in a room or beneath a roof, for on all sides he saw nothing but light. ... Love and the cleaving of his heart to God brought him into ecstasy, and transformed him wholly into the Light of the Holy Spirit.'[4]

1. ibid., vii: 1
2. *The Mystical Theology*, Ch.1
3. *Early Fathers from the Philokalia*, p. 300.
4. *Writings from the Philokalia on Prayer of the Heart*, pp. 145–7.

This type of experience was familiar to many of the Eastern Christian mystics. St Simeon himself declares: 'I am filled with light and glory; my face shines like that of my Beloved, and all my members glow with heavenly Light.'[1] This Light was regarded as 'the visible quality of the Divinity, of the energies or grace in which God makes Himself known'.[2] Gregory Palamas (fourteenth century) spoke of it as 'that Light which is the Glory of God, without end, and the splendour of Divinity, divine and eternal, uncreated, being itself the Majesty of God'.[3] It was for him 'beyond all description', and perceived not by the senses, but by the 'eyes of the heart'.[4] Those who see the Light are deified by it, since in their vision of it the Light penetrates their being, and so lifts them into union with God.

The divine Light which the mystics saw was identified in their interpretation with the Glory of God which appeared in the theophanies of the Old Testament (as in Moses' vision of the Burning Bush) and which was revealed to the three disciples of Jesus at the Transfiguration and to St Paul on the road to Damascus. Particular emphasis was laid on the Transfiguration. Among Eastern mystics generally, no such stress was laid as was commonly laid in the West on the imitation of the earthly life of Jesus. What we have to do, it was taught, is not to imitate the example of Jesus, but to share, so far as may be, the divine radiance which illuminated him, by following the path of prayer and contemplation. That radiance was made visible to the apostles on Mount Tabor. At the Transfiguration, it was held, there was no change whatsoever in the earthly form of Jesus, for he lived perpetually in the light of his divinity. The change occurred in the consciousness of the disciples, who then saw him as he truly was. The mystics sought to identify themselves with Christ in his divine glory. There is no parallel among Eastern saints to the stigmatization of St Francis, but again and again Eastern saints have felt themselves to be transfigured by the divine Light which shone through Jesus. As Berdyaev has said:

1. Quoted by Berdyaev: *Freedom and the Spirit*, p. 244.
2. Lossky, op. cit., p. 222.
3. Quoted by R. Payne, *The Divine Fire*, p. 314.
4. ibid., p. 319.

'The idea of the divinization of man is the fundamental concept of Orthodox mysticism.'[1]

The doctrine of the divine Light became a subject of acute controversy in the Eastern Church in the fourteenth century. It was attacked as heretical and blasphemous by Barlaam, a Calabrian monk who came to Constantinople and taught for a time at Thessalonica. He regarded the doctrine as polytheistic, since it implied two eternal substances – a visible and an invisible God. Gregory Palamas defended the doctrine with the utmost vigour, maintaining that the divine Light pertained not to the essence but to the outflowing energy of God. Finally, at the Synod of Constantinople in 1351, the doctrine was recognized as an article of faith in the Orthodox Church.

(c) Prayer and Ecstasy; 'Hesychasm' and the 'Jesus-Prayer'

The greatest stress was laid among Eastern mystics on the practice of meditation and prayer as the means of lifting the soul to the consciousness of God. It was this practice which formed the centre of the life of the hermits and monks of the Egyptian and Syrian deserts from the third century. The *Conferences* of John Cassian, who spent some years in his early life in the monastery of Bethlehem, and later lived for a time among the ascetics of the desert in Egypt (towards the close of the fourth century), form a classical exposition of the life of prayer, widely influential in both East and West. 'Through constant meditation on things divine and through spiritual contemplation', Cassian says, 'the soul is caught up into an ecstasy';[2] and it enters at length into a union with God so close and continuous that 'whatever we breathe or think or speak is God'.[3] According to Maximus the Confessor, it is the mark of the highest state of contemplative prayer that 'in the very act of rising in prayer the mind is ravished by the divine boundless Light'.[4] In prayer, says 'Dionysius', we draw near to 'the primal Goodness', which in its 'all-embracing infinitude' is never absent from us. It is, he suggests, 'as if a resplendent cord were hanging down from the height of Heaven to this world below, and we appeared to pull it down; but in very truth,

1. op. cit., p. 255.   2. *Conferences*, III: 70.   3. ibid., x: 7.
4. *Early Fathers from the Philokalia*, p. 300.

instead of drawing down the rope ... we were ourselves being drawn upwards to the higher refulgence of the resplendent rays'.[1]

A particular method of prayer, which has played a great part in the life of the Orthodox Church, was adopted by the monks of Mount Athos (in Macedonia) under the influence of St Simeon. The method, known as 'Hesychasm' (from the Greek *hesychia* or 'stillness'), consisted in the practice of inner stillness or concentration of the mind on the divine Presence, induced by the repetition of the 'Jesus prayer' (*O Lord Jesus Christ, Son of God, have mercy on me, a sinner*), which was accompanied by controlled respiration – the prayer being repeated at each drawing of the breath. It was held that the name of Jesus contained within itself a divine energy, which constant repetition brought into play, so that it came to penetrate the soul and to render it divine. The practice, as Berdyaev says, 'lies at the very heart of Orthodox mysticism'.[2] The prayer culminated in the experience of ecstasy, in which men attained a vision of the divine Light. Gregory Palamas taught that in repeating the Jesus-prayer 'man was performing the supreme act for which he was created, for he found himself at last within the same Light which shone on Mount Tabor during the Transfiguration'.[3]

(d) Deification and the Unitive Life

In Eastern Christian mysticism, a fundamental place is held by the thought of deification. In the experience of contemplation, says Gregory of Sinai (fourteenth century), the mind is 'ineffably merged with God into one spirit'.[4] In speaking of the experience of union, St Simeon uses an analogy which is often employed by Western mystics.

Suddenly [he says] God came, and united Himself to me in a manner quite ineffable. Without any 'confusion of persons' He entered into every part of my being, as fire penetrates iron, or light streams through glass.[5]

St Simeon says, again, as St John of the Cross said later:

1. *The Divine Names*, III: 1.   3. R. Payne, op. cit., p. 298.
2. op. cit., p. 256.   4. *Writings from the Philokalia*, p. 63.
5. Quoted by Berdyaev, op. cit., p. 244.

'Through grace we become gods and sons of God.'¹ The analogy
of iron and fire was used in the fourth century by John of Lycopolis, who lived in the Thebaid (the Egyptian desert). John of
Lycopolis works out the analogy in detail:

As, when iron is placed in the fire, and the fire passes into it and
becomes one substance with it, the iron partakes of the fire, and assumes
its likeness and colour, and no longer appears as it formerly did, but
takes on the aspect of the fire, because it has become absorbed in the
fire and the fire in it, and so they become one; so, when the love of
Christ comes into the soul as a living fire which consumes the seeds of
sin from the soul, it becomes of one substance with Him and He with
it. . . . From the likeness of its own nature it is changed into the likeness
of God . . . and it is absorbed in His love for all men.²

The soul being thus united with God in an inseparable union,
it enters upon the 'unitive life'. By the continual practice of contemplative prayer, it is possessed by the divine Love, conceived
as a divine energy flowing forth from God to deify the soul. 'Love
the divine gift', says Maximus the Confessor, 'perfects human
nature, until it makes it appear in unity and identity, by grace,
with the divine nature.'³ (Grace, for the Eastern Church, is
equivalent to the divine energies.) Eastern mystics, following
the tradition of the Desert Fathers, were rigidly ascetic, yet the
unitive life was for them not only a life of renunciation; it was a
life permeated by the positive power of love.

'When the soul reaches the perfection of the Spirit,' says Macarius
(a Coptic hermit of the fourth century), 'being completely purified from
passion, and is joined and commingled with the Holy Spirit . . . then it
becomes all light, all exultation, all heartfelt love, all goodness and
lovingkindness.'⁴

Such love is altogether incompatible with ill-will. As St
Maximus observes:

He who sees in his heart a trace of hatred towards another for some
fault of his is a complete stranger to love of God, for love of God can
in no way tolerate hatred of man.⁵

1. *Writings from the Philokalia*, p. 107.
2. Quoted by Margaret Smith, *Studies in Early Mysticism in the Near
and Middle East*, p. 92.
3. Quoted by Lossky, op. cit., p. 214.   4. M. Smith, op. cit., p. 65.
5. *Early Fathers from the Philokalia*, p. 288.

In his union with God, man participates in the divine Love which flows out to all beings. Eastern mystics therefore rise at times into a compassion which is truly cosmic in its scope, consciously embracing all creatures. Isaac the Syrian (sixth century), who spent the greater part of his adult life in a lonely cell in the wilderness, speaks of the sympathy which the saint naturally feels for the whole living creation. 'A charitable heart [he says] is a heart which is burning with charity for the whole of creation – for men, for the birds, for the beasts, for the demons.' He who has such a heart 'cannot bear to see, or to learn from others of any suffering being inflicted upon a creature'. He is moved to pray, St Isaac continues, for all beings – for evil-doers and enemies of truth, and for the animals. 'He will pray even for the reptiles, moved by the infinite pity which reigns in the hearts of those who are becoming united to God.'[1]

As he grows towards God, the scope of man's being is enlarged. St Simeon says of a certain ascetic that 'he possessed Christ wholly, and was himself like Christ ... He was, in fact, entirely Christ'; and being thus united with Christ, he felt himself to be one with all men. 'He had, as it were, not only his own limbs or members, but those of every other human being as well, having both one and yet many bodies.'[2] This sense of oneness with other human beings, as a phase of the unitive life, was emphasized in the nineteenth century by the Russian mystic, John of Cronstadt, for whom it became the basis of intercessory prayer. Such prayer he defined as 'holding all men in our hearts through love, the descent of Heaven into the soul'.[3]

When you pray [he said], endeavour to pray more for others than for yourself alone, and during prayer represent to yourself vividly all men as forming one body with yourself, and each separately as a member of the body of Christ and your own member ... Why has sincere prayer for each other such great power over others? Because of the fact that by cleaving to God during prayer I become one spirit with Him, and unite myself by faith and love with those for whom I pray. For the Holy Ghost, acting in me, acts at the same time in them.[4]

1. Lossky, op. cit., p. 111.
2. Berdyaev, op. cit., p. 245.
3. *A Treasury of Russian Spirituality*, edited by G. P. Fedotov, p. 351.
4. ibid., pp. 361f.

III. MYSTICISM IN THE WESTERN CATHOLIC CHURCH

(a) The Mysticism of St Augustine

In Western, as in Eastern, Christian mysticism the main influence, in addition to the inner logic of the Christian life of faith and love, has been Neo-Platonism, which found its climax in the vision of the One. In the Western Church it was through Augustine that this influence was chiefly exercised until the twelfth century, when the works of 'Dionysius' began to be widely known. The case of Augustine is particularly significant, not only because it was through the acceptance of Neo-Platonism that he was led to Christianity, but because it was while he was a Platonist that the mystical experience first came to him. As Kirk remarks, his descriptions of the vision of God 'are all but wholly Platonic'.[1] 'I had come to Thee [he says] from among the Gentiles, and I set my mind upon the gold which Thou didst will Thy people to take from Egypt' (Confessions, VII: 9). Augustine is evidently referring here to the Enneads of Plotinus, which had been recently translated into Latin by Victorinus, who was himself converted to Christianity. As a Platonist, he practised the way of contemplation, and so attained the mystic vision.

I entered into my inward self, Thou being my Guide ... And I beheld with the eye of my soul above the same eye of my soul, above my mind, the Light unchangeable. It was not this ordinary light, which all flesh may look upon, nor as it were a greater of the same kind. ... Not such was this Light, but other, yea far other than all these. Nor was it above my soul as oil is above water, nor yet as heaven is above earth, but above my soul because it made me ... He who knows the truth knows that Light, and he who knows it knows Eternity [VII: 10].

The divine Light which Augustine saw in the moment of vision – when 'with the flash of one trembling glance' he 'arrived at That which is' (VII: 17) – confirmed the essential faith which he had come to hold as a Platonist. In a later passage, itself notably influenced by the phraseology of Plotinus, he attributes a similar experience to his mother Monica and himself, when

1. The Vision of God, p. 354.

together they raised themselves in thought towards 'the Self-Same', and passed beyond thought, reaching out of themselves and 'touching by a flash of insight the eternal Wisdom which abides above all' (IX: 10). The experience is of God as at once transcendent and immanent, eternal and unchangeable, yet the inmost life of the soul. 'Thy God is ever unto thee', he cries, 'the life of thy life' (X: 6). 'Too late have I loved Thee, O Thou Beauty of ancient days, yet ever new. . . . And, behold, Thou wert within, and I abroad' (X: 27). In the opening passage of the *Confessions* he dwells on the unsearchableness of God – the paradox of the divine Presence which fills all things, yet is contained by nothing; without which no being can exist, yet whose entrance into the soul is man's deepest quest. God is, indeed, for Augustine 'above all that can be said of Him . . . He is best adored in silence, best known by nescience, best described by negatives'.[1] 'Negative theology' thus has its place in his teaching, although he does not attribute to it the same primacy as does 'Dionysius'. As a mystic, in any case, he recognizes the necessity of transcending thought in the quest for God.

Augustine nowhere speaks explicitly of union with God. He speaks in terms of vision and contact rather than of union. None the less it is plain that the experience is in fact one of union. The 'Light unchangeable' which he sees, the divine Wisdom which he touches, is not external to him; it is the inmost life of his being. He feels and knows God, in Poulain's phrase, as 'something interior which penetrates the soul'.[2] Yet, while from the first Augustine knew the divine Presence as a reality with which in his deepest being he was one, the union which he experienced initially was a fleeting state of consciousness. He was unable to fix his gaze on the Light which he saw. 'I perceived myself to be far off from Thee in the region of unlikeness' (*Confessions*, VII: 10). His conversion to Christianity, he implies, has brought him a new strength and stability of soul. But from the first he saw the goal which lies before him. Even as he felt his distance from the divine Light in the actual nature of his being, there came to him a voice which said: 'I am the food of grown men; grow, and thou

1. Inge, *Christian Mysticism*, 2nd edition, p. 128.
2. *Graces of Interior Prayer*, p. 90.

shalt feed on Me; nor shalt thou transform Me, like the food of thy flesh, into thee, but thou shalt be transformed into Me.' The goal is deification – transformation into God. He prays that God, who is the Life of his life, will enter into his heart and inebriate it, 'that I may embrace Thee, my sole Good ... Narrow is the mansion of my soul; enlarge Thou it, that Thou mayest enter into it' (I: 5).

In the teaching and experience of Augustine as indicated in the *Confessions* there are already laid down the main lines of Western mysticism. The Platonism which he accepted became an essential feature of the mystical tradition. Through him the Platonic doctrine of the Ideas or archetypes of all that exists in the world, regarded as elements of the eternal Being of God, passed into the current of mystical thought. Yet in the developed system of teaching which Augustine worked out there is a marked duality. Many of his ideas, such as human depravity and the fore-ordination which doomed a great part of mankind to everlasting Hell, are altogether inconsistent with his insight as a Platonist and a mystic. He illustrates strikingly the difficulty which has always confronted the orthodox Christian mystic, of combining the illumination which comes to him as a mystic with a dogmatic tradition radically divergent from it.

(b) The Mysticism of Gregory the Great and St Bernard

During the early Middle Ages the dominant influence on Western mysticism was that of Augustine. The teaching of Cassian on prayer (see p. 227 above) also played an active part in nourishing the inner life fostered in the Benedictine monasteries. The leading exponents of early medieval mysticism were Gregory the Great at the beginning of the period (he became Pope in 590) and Bernard of Clairvaux (1091–1153) at the end. Cuthbert Butler has described the type of mysticism which they represent as 'purely and solely religious' and 'non-philosophical'.[1] He admits, however, that the mysticism of Augustine is 'coloured by his Neo-Platonism'; and through Augustine, Neo-Platonism was certainly a factor in the thought and experience of his successors in the mystical tradition. In the very 'endeavour to mount to God in

1. *Western Mysticism*, 2nd edition, p. 187.

prayer, and seek union with Him', which was (as Butler observes) the practical motive-force of their mysticism, we see (as with Augustine himself) the outcome of the impact of Platonism on the spiritual life of the Christian Church. Yet it is undoubtedly true that in the interpretation of mystical experience the Platonic philosophy played a lesser part in early Western mysticism than it played in the Eastern Church and in the developed mysticism of the West.

Gregory, like Augustine and the Easterns, expresses mystical experience in terms of illumination. God is the boundless Light, and contemplation is the endeavour to 'fix the eye of the heart on the very ray of the unencompassed Light', and so to 'pass into the Light'.[1] He dwells on the limitations which beset men in that endeavour. In the present life we can only see the divine Light 'scantily' and in a passing glimpse. The disability which for Gregory limits our vision of God is wholly distinct from the Dionysian 'darkness of unknowing'. His attitude is not altogether consistent. For, while he suggests that God is never seen 'as He is' by those who contemplate Him in this life, he also declares that 'by certain ones still living in this corruptible flesh . . . the eternal Brightness of God is able to be seen', and he makes it clear that the divine 'Brightness' is identical with the divine essence.[2] St Bernard falls into a like inconsistency. On the one hand, he maintains that 'no wise man, no saint, no prophet is able to see God as He is, nor has been able in this mortal body'; on the other hand, he says that Benedict in a well-known vision (to which Gregory also makes reference) was rapt to see Him face to face, as in the Beatific Vision in Heaven.[3]

St Bernard brings us nearer, in point of content as well as of time, to the developed mysticism of the Middle Ages. He speaks of mystical experience, as later mystics constantly speak of it, in terms of union. The culmination of contemplation lies for him in ecstasy, in which the soul 'loses itself wholly in God', and is 'emptied of itself'. 'To be thus affected is to be made divine.'[4] He uses the analogy continually repeated by medieval mystics, of water poured into wine and taking upon itself the taste and

1. Western Mysticism, pp. 110f.   2. ibid., pp. 129f.
3. ibid., pp. 175f.   4. *On loving God*, Ch. 10.

colour of the wine; of iron made hot and glowing in the fire; of air suffused with the light of the sun and transformed into light. 'If in man [he asks] aught of the human were to remain, how should God be all in all? The substance of human nature will indeed remain, but in another form, with another glory, with another power.' In this consummation of mystical experience, man is deified – lifted wholly out of himself in his individual being, and made one with God. St Bernard says at the end that the soul can only hope to attain this state in the life to come. But he implies earlier that it is possible for a man to enter into such experience in the present life, even though it be 'but once suddenly, for scarcely one moment'. St Bernard did not, however, adhere consistently to his own insight. He continued, it is true, to seek union with God. In his *Sermons on the Song of Solomon* he says that a soul filled with ardent love of God naturally desires to be united with Him. 'Such a soul desires that God ... should enter in and possess her.'[1] But union with God, as he interprets it in the *Sermons*, does not involve a unity of 'substance' or essential being. Man and God may be called 'one spirit', 'if they adhere to one another by the glue of love'. There is thus a mutual indwelling, but there is no identification of being. They remain apart even in the closest union, 'separate in their own wills and substances ... not blended in substance, but consentaneous in will'.[2] In such a passage, we see the triumph of theological orthodoxy over mystical insight.

(c) The 'Divine Dark' in Western Mysticism

In developed Western mysticism the dominant influence was that of 'Dionysius'. His works were translated into Latin in the ninth century by John Scotus Erigena, the Irish philosopher and theologian, who taught in Paris. Erigena himself worked out a scheme of thought based on the teaching of 'Dionysius'. His book *On the Division of Nature* was condemned as heretical early in the thirteenth century, and was almost wholly lost sight of for several centuries. His translation of 'Dionysius', however, became widely known in the twelfth century, and henceforth coloured the teaching of nearly all Western mystics. The doctrine

1. *Sermons on the Song of Solomon*, 31.   2. *Sermon* 71.

of the 'divine Dark' thus passed into the currency of Western mystical thought.

One of the most representative works of medieval mysticism is a tract, *Of Cleaving to God* (*De Adhaerendo Deo*), traditionally attributed to Albertus Magnus (thirteenth century), but actually written after his time.[1] The negative way is for the writer the means to the concentration of the soul on the knowledge and love of God. We must cast out of our minds 'the impressions, images and forms of all things which are not God', that we may look upon God within our own self (Ch. 4); for He is the indwelling Life of all things, 'more intimately and more closely present to each thing than each thing is to itself' (Ch. 9). When we enter deeply into ourselves, 'the eye of inner vision is opened, and a ladder is prepared by which the soul may ascend to the contemplation of God'. In approaching God, we must deny 'all that may be fathomed by our understanding ... even the idea of being as it is found in created things'. God is beyond all that we can feel or understand; but He is 'perfectly accessible to our secret, inmost love' (Ch. 7). We must 'summon up the whole heart and power of our love, and pour ourselves into God with all the strength of our inmost soul', that we may be 'absorbed into His Being' (Ch. 1). It is the distinctive quality of love to change the lover into the object of his love, for love has a 'unitive and transforming power'. So far therefore as the love of God possesses us, it 'transforms us into God, so that we become one spirit with Him' (Ch. 12).

A work closely similar in its emphasis to this tract is *The Cloud of Unknowing*, written by an English mystic in the fourteenth century. A translation of the *Mystical Theology* of 'Dionysius' (under the title *Dionise hid Divinite*) is usually attributed to the same author. He speaks again of the twofold necessity which lies upon us as we follow the way of contemplation. We must put 'a cloud of forgetting' between us and all created things, so that we may fix our mind on God. We must at the same time enter into the 'cloud of unknowing' which lies between us and God. 'Of God Himself can no man think' (Ch. 6). We may, indeed, think of the attributes of God – of His

1. A new translation was issued by the Blackfriars Press in 1947.

kindness and worthiness – but in the higher work of contemplation such things must be 'covered with a cloud of forgetting'. It
is love alone that can pierce the darkness that lies upon us. 'We
must smite upon that thick cloud of unknowing with a sharp dart
of longing love.' If we persevere in the quest, God may then 'send
out a beam of ghostly light' to pierce the cloud that divides us
from Him, and to reveal to us the divine mystery 'which man
may not, nor cannot speak' (Ch. 26). We shall then be 'inflamed
with the fire of divine love', and so be 'oned with God in
spirit and in love', and thus in fact be 'made a God in grace'
(Ch. 67).

Christian mystics in general do not embark upon any direct
expression of their inner experience. Among the exceptions to
this statement is Angela of Foligno, a Franciscan mystic of the
thirteenth century. In her *Book of Divine Consolations* she has
given us an extensive account of her religious life. The influence
of 'Dionysius' was introduced into the Franciscan movement by
Bonaventura, widely known as a theologian and a biographer of
St Francis. Angela adopts the Dionysian approach.

Those persons who do best know God [she says], who is infinite and
unspeakable, are those who do the least presume to speak of Him,
considering that all which they do say of Him, or can possibly say, is as
nothing compared with that which He truly is ... Because God is so
much greater than the mind and all other things, we are not able by any
means whatsoever to measure or speak or think of Him [p. 29].

She recognizes, however, the place of thought in leading us on
to the mystic vision. Meditation or 'mental prayer' is a necessary
stage in the ascent of the spirit. 'Mental prayer is when the meditation of God fills the mind so entirely that it thinks on naught
else save on God.' With the mystic, mental prayer is succeeded by
inner vision, which she describes as 'supernatural prayer', when
the soul is suddenly exalted into God.

Supernatural prayer is that during which the soul is uplifted above
its own nature. And understanding, it knows; but that which it knows
it cannot explain, because all that it perceives and feels is above its
own nature.

The fruit of divine knowledge is the fullness of love, and such love produces deification, 'for he who loves with not only a part of himself, but the whole, transforms himself in the thing beloved' (pp. 99f.).

In certain passages Angela speaks directly of her vision. The vision was preceded by auditory experience.

Upon a certain time when I was at prayer, and my spirit was exalted, God spoke to me many gracious words full of life. And when I looked, I beheld God, who spoke with me. . . . I beheld a fullness and a clearness, and felt them within me so abundantly that I can in no wise describe it . . . I beheld a Beauty so great that I can say naught concerning it, save that I saw the supreme Being, which contains within itself all goodness [p. 169].

On another occasion:

The eyes of my soul were opened, and I beheld the plenitude of God, whereby I did comprehend the whole world, both here and beyond the sea, and the abyss and all things else; and therein I beheld naught save the divine Power in a manner assuredly indescribable, so that through excess of marvelling the soul cried with a loud voice, saying: 'This world is full of God' [p. 172].

In the thirteenth and fourteenth centuries, mysticism exerted a marked influence on the religious life of Germany and the Low Countries. The founder and the most distinguished member of what is called the Rhineland school of mysticism was Meister Eckhart, a leading member of the Dominican order in Germany and the most influential German preacher in the Middle Ages – one of the profoundest of all mystical teachers. Other adherents of the school were Eckhart's younger contemporaries, Suso, Tauler, and Ruysbroeck, and the authors of the *Theologia Germanica* and *The Book of the Poor in Spirit* (known also as *The Following of Christ*).[1] In the fourteenth century, some time after Eckhart's death in 1329, those who accepted the teaching of the school formed a loose association known as the Friends of God, some of whom were laymen.[2] The doctrine of 'Dionysius' is fundamental to this school. 'When the soul utters the name of God [says Eckhart], the word does not bear within itself the real

1. Issued in a new translation by C. F. Kelley in 1954.
2. See Kelley's Introduction to *The Book of the Poor in Spirit*.

truth of His Being. ... Whatever one says that God is, He is not; He is what one does not say of Him rather than what one says that He is.'[1] The infinite glory of the divine Presence transcends all words. 'God is better than anything we can conceive. ... Our highest aspirations are but grovelling things falling hopelessly short of God.'[2] It is because of the very fullness or perfection of His Being that God transcends our intellectual knowledge. 'The things which are in part', says the *Theologia Germanica*, 'can be apprehended, known and expressed; but the Perfect cannot be apprehended, known or expressed by any creature as creature' (Ch. 1). The writer adds that for this reason 'we call the Perfect "Nothing"'. The use of this term is characteristic of German mysticism. (We are reminded of the Taoist 'Nothing' and the Buddhist 'Void'.) Eckhart says in his vivid way: 'God is as high above being [i.e. finite being] as the highest angel is above a midge. ... God is neither this nor that.'[3] Yet he adds that he does not intend to deny being to God – to suggest that He is non-existent. In fact, God is the one Reality, and created things are 'a mere nothing', since their existence depends wholly on the presence of God within them.[4]

The statement that 'all creatures are a mere nothing' belongs to the list of propositions drawn from Eckhart's sermons which were condemned by the Pope. Another of his sayings which came under the Papal ban was 'That God is neither good nor better nor best'.[5] Here again we have an illustration of 'negative theology'. Eckhart proceeds in his sermon to quote the words of Jesus, 'No one is good save God alone' (Matthew 19: 17). God is good, since He communicates Himself to those who will receive Him. Yet in the essence of His Being He lies beyond all the qualities we can assign to Him. Being and goodness are garments or veils under which He is hidden, and in mystical experience it is possible to contemplate God unveiled. What Eckhart calls the 'intellect' (i.e. the power of intuitive knowledge)

1. *Meister Eckhart: an Introduction to the Study of his Works with an Anthology of his Sermons*, by J. M. Clark, pp. 158f.
2. *Meister Eckhart* (F. Pfeiffer), English translation by C. de B. Evans, I, 133.
3. *Sermons* (Clark), p. 206.   4. ibid., p. 173.   5. ibid., p. 207.

'apprehends Him naked', in His essential and ineffable glory, 'divested of all names'. Another way of putting this is to say that the soul rises beyond the thought of 'God' to the vision of 'the Godhead'. Eckhart does not adhere consistently to the distinction, but he sometimes uses the term 'God' to indicate the triune God of Christian theology, God as defined by qualities like being and goodness, God as an active Power, the Creator of the universe. In this sense, he says, 'God and the Godhead are as different as Heaven and earth'.[1] So far as we apprehend the divine from the standpoint of will, of active effort, of striving after the good, God 'as distinguished from the Godhead' is necessary to us. 'The will is well satisfied with God in so far as He is good.' But from the standpoint of 'intellect' or vision, we cannot be satisfied with anything short of the ultimate or absolute Reality. Evelyn Underhill suggests that the contrast is between 'the absolute and unconditioned Godhead and the God of religious experience',[2] but Eckhart's point is in fact that religious experience finds its culmination in the vision of God as the Godhead. 'The intellect is truly as little satisfied with God as with a stone or a tree. ... She breaks into the ground out of which goodness and truth break forth.' She attains that union with divine Reality whereby alone true knowledge is possible to man. 'What God is in Himself (as Godhead) no man can tell except he be ravished into the Light that is God Himself.'[3]

In his union with the divine Essence, man transcends the limitations of his finite being. In the words of the *Theologia Germanica*, the apprehension of the Perfect is 'impossible to the creature in virtue of its creature-nature and qualities, that by which it says "I" and "myself"'. If we are to know the Perfect, 'the "I", the self and the like must all be lost and done away' (Ch. 1). Such transcendence of creatureliness is possible, because man in his deepest being is one with God. 'The word "man" [says Eckhart] means something that is above Nature, above time, and raised up above everything that is inclined to time and

1. ibid., p. 181.
2. *The Mystics of the Church*, p. 134.
3. *Meister Eckhart* (Pfeiffer), I: 134.

place and corporeality.'[1] Man must therefore seek to become that which he eternally is. He must follow the way of detachment from self and from the things of time – the way of self-surrender, of love, of humility; he must learn to dwell in eternity, where his true being lies. He will then be deified. 'Through knowledge', as Eckhart says, 'I receive God into myself, and through love I enter into Him. ... We are transformed into God, so that we may know Him as He is.'[2]

The doctrine of the divine Dark finds notable expression in the teaching of Nicholas of Cusa (Cues, on the Moselle) in the fifteenth century. Nicholas became a Cardinal in 1449, and he played an active part in ecclesiastical politics on the side of reform. He renewed the tradition of German and Flemish mysticism, and was influenced especially by Eckhart, defending him, in spite of the Papal condemnation, against orthodox attack. He read 'Dionysius' in Greek. His best-known work is *De Docta Ignorantia* (*Of Learned Ignorance*), of which a new translation has recently appeared. He also wrote a mystical treatise, *The Vision of God* (translated into English in the seventeenth century and again in 1928). Like 'Dionysius', he uses the term 'ignorance' to indicate both the negative approach – the fact that God as 'the summit of all perfection', 'the absolute Being of all being', transcends intellectual knowledge – and the positive power of vision whereby God may be known. 'Sacred ignorance has taught us that God is ineffable, because He is infinitely greater than words can express.'[3] God can only be approached by him 'who knows himself to be ignorant of Him'.[4] In all our thought concerning God and His relation to ourselves and to the world, Nicholas sees, there is bound to be an element of paradox. Since the divine Essence pervades all things, we are led to say that God 'moves with all that move, and stands with all that stand'; yet, being exalted over all, He neither moves nor rests. Motion and rest, and the opposition between them, 'and whatever may be

1. *Meister Eckhart: Selected Treatises and Sermons* (J. M. Clark and J. V. Skinner), p. 155.
2. *Sermons* (Clark), p. 190.
3. *Of Learned Ignorance*, p. 60.   4. *The Vision of God*, p. 60.

uttered or conceived', are to be found 'on the hither side of the Infinity' which is the Being of God.[1] All contradictions are resolved in Him. One application of this principle is the coincidence in God of unity and otherness. It was the failure to grasp his teaching in this aspect which made possible the charge of Pantheism sometimes brought against Nicholas, as also against Eckhart. God, he teaches, is immeasurably transcendent, but He is immanent in all things, and so in one aspect one with all. 'He is in Himself the absolute Ground, in which all otherness is unity, and all diversity is identity' (p. 13). Since God is infinite, there can be nothing which is outside His life, nothing which is finally separate from Himself. 'The Infinite brooks not otherness from itself, since, being Infinity, naught exists outside it. ... Infinity is alike all things and no one of them all' (p. 62).

What Nicholas is specially concerned to emphasize in *The Vision of God* is that God is Himself the absolute Vision, 'the true unlimited Sight', in which all lesser modes of vision are included. It was a familiar Neo-Platonic thought that the universe owes its being to the divine activity in contemplation. So Nicholas says 'I am, because Thou dost look at me' (p. 16). God beholds us and all things, and in beholding us He gives Himself to us, that we may see Him. To attain the vision of God, to see His Face unveiled, we must put away the pretensions of intellectual knowledge, and 'enter into a certain secret and mystic silence' (p. 26). In this silence or 'ignorance', the divine Vision, which is the divine Love, may possess us.

None can see Thee save in so far as Thou dost grant a sight of Thyself, nor is that sight aught else than Thy seeing him that sees Thee [pp. 19f].

Our vision of God is at the same time God's vision of us; it is a participation in the divine and eternal Vision which is God Himself. As Eckhart said:

The eye with which I see God is the same eye as that with which God sees me; my eye and God's eye are one eye, and one sight, and one knowledge, and one love.[2]

1. ibid., p. 42.
2. *Sermons* (Clark), p. 227.

(d) God and Man: the 'Spark of the Soul'

A fundamental aspect of the teaching of all Christian mystics is the universal indwelling Presence of God. (It is on this account that Emil Brunner in our time is so rootedly hostile to mysticism.) In an illuminating passage in her *Life*, St Teresa, the great Spanish mystic of the sixteenth century, tells us that she was led by her own experience to recognize this truth, although it had been previously quite unfamiliar to her – it was admitted but not emphasized in Catholic theology.

> In the beginning it happened that I was ignorant of one thing – I did not know that God was present in all things; and when He seemed to be so near [i.e. in her own illumination], I thought it impossible. Not to believe that He was present was not in my power, for it seemed to me, as it were, evident that I felt there His very Presence.[1]

St Teresa's Spanish contemporary, St John of the Cross, draws an important distinction in connexion with the conception of union with God. In one sense God is united with all beings. He dwells in every soul, 'even that of the greatest sinner in the world'. But 'this way of union, or presence of God, in the order of Nature', is something quite distinct from the conscious experience of union which is the 'union and transformation of the soul in God by love'.[2]

The immanence of God in the soul is closely associated in mystical teaching with the conception of a particular phase or aspect of the soul which is, so to say, the seat of the divine Presence. In *The Interior Castle*, St Teresa speaks of the different 'mansions' which constitute the life of the soul. God Himself, she says, owns one of these mansions as His dwelling place – the mansion of the Empyrean Heaven in the centre of the soul (p. 192). This is 'the little Heaven of the soul, where dwells the Creator of Heaven and earth' (p. 160). An English mystic, Julian of Norwich (fourteenth century), speaks of two parts into which the soul is divided – the lower part of man's nature and the higher. The lower part is the soul as expressed in normal human

1. *The Life of St Teresa, written by Herself*, Lewis's translation, p. 147.
2. *Ascent of Mount Carmel*, II: 5: 3.

experience. 'In the lower part are pains and passions, mercies and forgiveness.'[1] In the highest part 'there is but one high love and marvellous joy' (p. 134). The highest part of the soul is eternally united with God. The soul of Christ is 'full high in the glorious Godhead, and verily where the blessed soul of Christ is, there is the substance [the essential being] of all the souls that shall be saved with Christ' (p. 130). Since Julian cherishes the hope of the final salvation of all mankind (p. 20), she implies that this is true of all. The higher soul is in one aspect 'a godly will that never assented to sin, nor ever shall' (p. 76). It is the source of all that is good in our life. 'The life and the virtue that we have in the lower part ... cometh down to us from out of the natural love of the high Self, by grace.' By the working of grace in our lower part we shall be 'oned with the high Self above' (p. 126).

One of the outstanding mystics of the sixteenth century was Louis de Blois (Blosius), Abbot of Liessies in the Spanish Netherlands. In his *Book of Spiritual Instruction*[2] he says that God, who is wholly present in all things, 'dwells in the human mind and in the centre of the soul in a very special manner' (p. 26). The centre of the soul is a 'divine temple from which God never departs' (p. 100). It is 'the abyss of the soul and its intimate essence'; it is irradiated incessantly by the uncreated Light; it 'remains constant in cleaving to God, its Origin'; it is thus 'above place and time', and is 'lifted up above all created things' (p. 99). The soul is thus in its essence uncreated, as Julian of Norwich implies. It is, as E. I. Watkin says with reference to Julian's teaching, 'outside the time series in the eternal Now of God'.[3] This conception was explicitly taught at an earlier date by the Rhineland mystics. Eckhart, indeed, was condemned for saying (as was alleged): 'There is something in the soul that is uncreated and uncreatable.' In his sermon at Cologne in reply to the charge of heresy which was brought against him, he repudiated this particular assertion. 'I never said, so far as I know, that there is something in the soul which is uncreated or uncreatable, because

1. *Revelations of Divine Love*, edited by Grace Warrack, p. 126.
2. Translated into English in 1900, and issued in a revised edition in 1955.   3. *Poets and Mystics*, p. 87.

then the soul would be composed of created and uncreated.'[1] The soul, he implies, is an indivisible unity, not something partly created and partly uncreated, as Julian taught by implication. Yet Eckhart had said in fact: 'There is something in the soul that is so akin to God that it is one with Him. . . . It has nothing in common with anything that is created' (ibid. p. 225). His defence in this respect is wholly unconvincing. It is true that his teaching concerning the deeper element in the soul – the 'spark' or 'apex' or 'ground' of the soul – is not entirely consistent. He says in one passage that 'the spark of the soul', which is 'a light pressed in from above', 'the image of the divine nature', was 'created by God' (p. 159). Yet that is certainly not in harmony with his more typical teaching. In one sermon, for example, he says: 'There is a power in the soul which touches neither time nor flesh. . . . The eternal Father eternally begets His eternal Son in this power without intermission' (p. 135). Here Eckhart gives us the clue to the real nature and significance of his thought and that of the Rhineland mystics generally. Man, as they conceive him in accordance with their Neo-Platonic outlook, belongs in his essential being to the eternal order, which comprises the ideal archetypes of all things. The ideal archetypes are elements in the eternal Being of God; in their totality they are the Word or Son of God, who is eternally begotten by the Father. As Suso puts it, they have 'an existence identical with God's life, God's knowledge and God's essence'.[2] So the Flemish mystic, Ruysbroeck, says: 'Through the eternal Birth all creatures have come forth in eternity, before they were created in time. So God has seen and known them in Himself.'[3] It is man's ideal archetype, the divine image of himself, which is in God eternally, that is the spark or ground of the soul. Man is thus eternally united with God in his deepest being. He 'receives without intermission the impress of his eternal archetype', and it is this 'union between God and our spirit in the nakedness of our nature' which is 'the first cause of all holiness and blessedness' (ii: 57).

1. *Sermons* (Clark), p. 252.
2. *The Life of the Blessed Henry Suso by Himself*, p. 243.
3. *The Adornment of the Spiritual Marriage*, iii: 3.

(e) The Imitation of Christ in Western Mysticism

Among Western, in contradistinction to Eastern, Christian mystics we find a constant emphasis on the following of Christ, the imitation of his example, as the way to perfection and union with God. The words of the well-known treatise, *The Imitation of Christ*, are typical: 'We ought to imitate Christ's life and conduct, if we will be truly enlightened and delivered from all blindness of heart' (I: 1). *The Imitation of Christ* was the product of the piety of the Brethren of the Common Life – a mystical brotherhood widespread in Holland and Germany in the fifteenth century. The same principle which underlay that Brotherhood had two centuries before inspired St Francis and his followers. The endeavour to reproduce the life and follow the example of Jesus was, indeed, common to all Western mystics.

In his compendium of mystical teaching, *Holy Wisdom* (seventeenth century), Augustine Baker quotes Suso as saying that 'the one desire of perfect souls is to imitate the example of our Lord Jesus in simple faith' (IV: 6). Men sought to follow the way of Christ as himself the perfect mystic, who was one with God. 'If man follows Christ as he has gone before us,' says a Rhineland mystic, 'his spirit also becomes one with God. For Christ is one with God, and hence it is necessary that he who desires to be one spirit with God should first unite himself with Christ.'[1] The writer uses the language of 'Christ-mysticism', but for him, as for Christian mystics generally, the centre of aspiration and experience is union with God, to which the life of Christ points the way. To be one with Christ is to share his spirit, to live as he lived. 'This union of man with Christ implies [or, in Morell's rendering, "consists in this"] that he do all things as Christ did them when he was man. ... Man is one with Christ when he has one action with him.' The author of the *Theologia Germanica* refers to the person of Jesus as an example of a deified man in whom God fully dwells. 'Christ's human nature was so utterly bereft of self and of all creatures as no man's ever was, and was nothing but a house and habitation of God' (Ch. 15). He tells us that a deified man loves all men, even though they may do him the utmost wrong,

1. *The Book of the Poor in Spirit*, p. 121.

'the proof and witness whereof may be seen in Christ' (Ch. 33). The whole matter is well summed up by John Tauler: 'As Christ was united in spirit with the Father, so also must we strive to be, as far as possible in this life'.[1] In the words of Ruysbroeck:

> Let us turn inward to our Lord Jesus Christ, and contemplate his passion and death. ... Then shall Christ carry us with himself into that exalted life wherein we are united to God, and our pure souls cleave by love to the Holy Spirit and dwell in Him.[2]

The imitation of Christ, as the mystics conceive it, involves fundamentally a dying to self, a giving up of ourselves wholly to God. 'Purgation' is a necessary phase of the contemplative life, and that necessity is clearly illustrated in the teaching and example of Jesus. As Suso says, we must practise 'a perpetual giving up of self, and make God's honour and glory our sole aim, just in the way that the dear Christ acted towards his heavenly Father'.[3] In this way we strike at the root of sin, which is the principle of self-love and self-seeking. The assumption of the mystics that there is a hidden core of divinity in the soul does not in any way diminish their realization of the fact of sin. Evil is a negative fact; it has no place in the sphere of the ultimately real, since it is essentially a denial of truth and reality. Nevertheless it is a fact deeply rooted in human life and human nature as we know it. And it is only through an utter detachment from self, such as we see in its fullness in Christ, that sin can be overcome. Detachment from self was sometimes taken to involve an entire renunciation of human ties, and here again appeal was made to the teaching and example of Jesus. The tract *Of Cleaving to God* (see p. 236 above) suggests that we should be utterly indifferent to the affairs of the world, so that we may be wholly absorbed in the love of God. 'Grace', says Eckhart, 'draws man away from temporal things, and purifies him from all transient things.'[4] Yet Eckhart repudiates 'world-flight': 'One must learn an inner solitude [in which, it is implied, one may be conscious of God],

1. *The Inner Way*, p. 230.
2. *The Seven Steps of the Ladder of Spiritual Love*, p. 22.
3. op. cit., p. 66.
4. *Selected Treatises and Sermons* (Clark and Skinner), p. 164.

wherever one may be.'[1] What is essential is the inner poverty of spirit in which we are emptied of self and filled with God.

In the imitation of Christ the mystics lay special stress on humility and love. 'The Saviour of the world,' says Angela of Foligno, 'has verily shown meekness and lowliness of heart to be the root and foundation of all virtue.'[2] Augustine Baker traces the humility of Christ to his realization of 'the nothingness of creatures and the absolute totality of God'. Christ 'remained continually plunged in the abyss of his own nothing. . . . He considered all his own perfections as not his own, but God's.'[3] The humility of Christ was matched by his compassion, his charity, his universal love, flowing out of the love of God which possessed him. So St Catherine of Siena (fourteenth century) taught that we must love our fellows with the love of God Himself.[4] Such love, as the mystics see, is altogether incompatible with hatred or enmity. 'The love of Christ,' says Augustine Baker, 'will not permit us to exercise enmity towards any person in the least degree, since charity is to be universally extended to all.'[5] St Francis is said to have found 'perfect joy' in the patient endurance of abuse and anger. 'Above all the gifts and graces of the Holy Spirit that Christ gives to his beloved is that of overcoming self and for love of him willingly to bear pain and buffetings and revilings and discomfort.'[6] St Bernard, unhappily, excepts from the rule of universal love those 'who, it is clear, will not return to the love of God'[7] – referring presumably to obdurate heretics. Among the mystics some – like St Francis, St Catherine of Genoa, Angela of Foligno, Margery Kempe – were inspired by Christ's spirit of universal love to extend their compassion to all living things. Margery Kempe, an English mystic of the fourteenth century, says of herself:

1. *Talks of Instruction* in Blakney's *Meister Eckhart*, a *Modern Translation*, p. 9.
2. op. cit., p. 114.
3. op. cit., p. 313.
4. *The Dialogue of St Catherine of Siena*, pp. 193f.
5. op. cit., pp. 262f.
6. *The Little Flowers of St Francis*, Ch. 8.
7. A. C. McGiffert, *A History of Christian Thought*, ii: 232f.

If she saw a man with a wound or a beast ... or if a man beat a child before her, or smote a horse or other beast with a whip ... she thought she saw our Lord being beaten or wounded.[1]

(*f*) *Ecstasy and Deification*

We have seen in section (*c*) that Western mystics typically describe the culmination of inner experience as 'deification'. The state of being so described is commonly associated with ecstasy, in which the soul is 'ravished out of fleshly feeling' and absorbed wholly in the consciousness of God. One of the best accounts of mystical experience in this aspect is found in the writings of the Scholastic theologian, Richard of St Victor (twelfth century) – the first author to give a systematic statement of mystical theology. In his short treatise, *Of the Four Degrees of Passionate Charity*, he says:

> The third degree of love is when the mind of man is ravished into the abyss of divine Light, so that the soul, having forgotten all outward things, is altogether unaware of itself, and passes out completely into its God.

While the soul is in this state, he adds:

> When it is surrounded on every side by the divine fire of love ... it sheds its very self altogether, and puts on that divine life, and, being wholly conformed to the beauty it has seen, passes wholly into that glory.[2]

In this exalted state, says Walter Hilton, 'God and the soul are no longer two, but one. ... In this union a true marriage is made between God and the soul, which shall never be broken.'[3] Suso contrasts the union with God which the soul attains in ecstasy with the experience of earthly lovers. 'Earthly lovers, however greatly they may love, must needs bear to be distinct and separate from one another; but Thou, O unfathomable fullness of all love ... in virtue of Thy being absolutely all in all, pourest Thyself so utterly into the soul's essence that no part of Thee

1. *The Book of Margery Kempe* (World's Classics), p. 88.
2. Richard of St Victor, *Selected Writings on Contemplation*, p. 228
3. *The Ladder of Perfection* (translated by L. Sherley-Price), 1: 8. Walter Hilton was a contemporary of Julian of Norwich and of the author of *The Cloud of Unknowing*.

remains outside.'[1] In the experience of union, at its highest point, the soul is lifted so fully into the consciousness of God that no awareness of distinction remains. When self-consciousness returns, Ruysbroeck says, 'we find a distinction and an otherness between ourselves and God', since our created being persists; but in the actual experience of union 'we feel ourselves to be swallowed up in the fathomless abyss of our eternal blessedness, wherein we can never find any distinction between ourselves and God'; 'whenever we feel this union, we are one being and one life and one blessedness with God'.[2]

Eckhart speaks of this experience of identification with the divine as the birth of the Son (or the Word) in man. In Eckhart there is a twofold begetting or birth of the Son. On the one hand, there is the process of emanation whereby the ideal universe, which is the Son, comes forth eternally from the Father; on the other hand, there is the ascent of the soul to its eternal being in God, whereby the Son (that is, the divine consciousness) is born in man. Eckhart repeats again and again with the utmost emphasis the identity of man in his higher consciousness with the Son. 'When the soul is free from time and place, the Father sends His Son into the soul';[3] 'when the Father begets His Son in me, I am the same Son, and not another' (p. 174); 'He makes me His only-begotten Son without any difference. ... I am transformed into Him in such a way that He makes me one with His being, and not just similar to it. By the living God, it is true that there is no difference' (p. 189). It is typical of Eckhart's boldness as a mystical thinker that he ranks the birth of the Son in the soul – the continued incarnation of God in man – above the historical incarnation in Jesus.

It is more worthy of God that He should be born spiritually of every virgin, or of every good soul, than that He should have been born physically of Mary [p. 212].

Among the Spanish mystics of the sixteenth century, we find a similar stress on the experience of deification. St John of the

1. *The Life of Blessed Henry Suso by Himself*, p. 227.
2. *The Sparkling Stone*, Chs. 10, 12.
3. *Sermons* (Clark), p. 175.

Cross, for example, says that in uniting the soul with Himself, God 'communicates His own supernatural being in such a way that the soul seems to be God Himself. . . . The soul seems to be God rather than itself, and indeed it is God by participation'.[1] The same affirmation is made by John of the Angels, Diego de Estella, and Luis de Leon. The last-named says that in the state of union the divine Word penetrates the soul wholly, and absorbs it into Himself, 'so that in very truth the soul not only has God dwelling in it, but is indeed God'.[2] The Spaniards repeat the metaphor, so familiar in mystical tradition, of iron and fire. 'As iron, when it is greatly heated in the forge [says Diego de Estella], becomes fire, so my heart, O God, as it burns in Thy divine and sacred fire, is wholly transformed by love: it is deified, and becomes as God.'[3]

(g) The Dark Night of the Soul

A phase of the inner life often experienced by mystics of the Western Church is the state of darkness and dereliction known as 'the Dark Night of the Soul'. This condition has, indeed, often been regarded as a necessary stage of spiritual progress. But in the Eastern Church, while it is not altogether unknown, it holds no such place; and it is not in fact universal in the West. None the less it is a widespread phase of experience. Among those who refer to it are Angela of Foligno, St Catherine of Siena, St Teresa, Suso, Tauler, Ruysbroeck, and St John of the Cross. It seems to be in essence a reaction against the rapture and exaltation of spirit known in ecstasy. 'An extraordinary consolation', says Augustine Baker, 'is usually attended by succeeding anguish and desertion': so especially ecstasy 'is commonly followed by a most terrible unexpected desolation'.[4] Here the soul so far loses the sense of oneness with God attained in ecstasy that it is completely deprived of the consciousness of the divine Presence, and is apt to regard itself as finally lost. Thus, as Berdyaev observes: 'For the mystics, both the identity between the creature and the

1. op. cit., II: 5: 69.
2. E. A. Peers, *Studies of the Spanish Mystics*, I: 334.
3. E. A. Peers, *Spanish Mysticism*, p. 152f.
4. op. cit., v: 4: 5.

Creator, and the gulf which separates them, are equally facts of experience.'[1]

The 'Dark Night' varies in its quality according to the particular temperament and outlook of the person concerned; but the primary fact is the temporary cessation of the divine union. Augustine Baker says of the soul which is in this condition: 'If she would elevate her spirit, she sees nothing but clouds and darkness; she seeks God and cannot find the least marks of His Presence. . . . Her prayers and meditations are most grievous to her, because infinitely difficult' (loc. cit.). The soul falls into a state at first of emotional lethargy, accompanied by the stagnation of the will. As Ruysbroeck says: 'The man begins to complain of his wretchedness: whither has gone the ardent love, the inwardness, the joyful praise? And the inward consolation, the intimate joy, the sensible savour – how has he lost them?'[2] Torpidity is followed by despair. Men lose their peace and tranquillity; they are tormented by sinful thoughts and desires, and they are sometimes troubled by the vision of fiends. They feel, perhaps, that by some great unknown sin they have brought their dereliction upon themselves. Such a state of wretchedness may last for months or years, although it may be relieved by occasional renewals of the mystic consciousness. In any case, the 'great desolation' comes only to the man who has progressed far along the inner way. He does not, therefore, allow it to divert him from his purpose. By the effort of his will he cleaves to God, and he learns to accept his trials with patient resignation. The soul, as Baker says, 'yields herself as a prey to almighty God, to be cast into this most sharp Purgatory of love'. It feels that it shares the dereliction of Christ, and thus it attains the utmost transcendence of self-willingness to be deprived of the greatest of all the blessings of life. 'In order to raise the soul from imperfection,' said the divine Voice to St Catherine of Siena, 'I withdraw Myself from her sentiment, depriving her of former consolations, which I do in order to humiliate her and cause her to seek Me in very truth, and to prove her in the light of faith.'[3]

1. op. cit., p. 242.
2. *The Adornment of the Spiritual Marriage*, ii: 28.
3. *Dialogue*, Ch. 63.

Having endured the severest of all imaginable woes, the soul enters at last into 'a state of most perfect confidence in God, not to be disturbed by any possible future affliction. For what has a soul left to fear that can with a peaceable mind support, yea, and make her benefit of, the absence of God Himself?'[1]

(h) The Spiritual Marriage

In ecstasy, as we have seen, the mystic feels himself to be deified – lifted out of the limitations of his creaturely being into oneness with the divine. For Western as for Eastern mystics, however, deification is not merely a passing experience; it is a permanent state of life, commonly known in the West as 'the Spiritual Marriage' or the 'transforming' or 'deifying union'.

'Now that we have attained through love to Thyself,' says Diego de Estella, 'we are converted into Thyself ... so that we work divine works and are spiritual men.'[2]

The union with God experienced in ecstasy gives rise to a new spiritual condition, acquired by many in its permanence only after the soul has passed through the temporary loss of the divine consciousness in the 'Dark Night'. In the experience of union (Ruysbroeck says) 'we and all our selfhood die in God. And in this death we become hidden sons of God, and find a new life within us, and that is eternal life'.[3]

This new life, or Spiritual Marriage, has two main characteristics. In the first place, it is marked in many mystics by a continuous, or almost continuous, sense of union with God. It is said of St Catherine of Genoa that for twenty-two years – during the central period of her life – 'she lived in the almost unbroken consciousness of the divine Presence'.[4] All this time she was living an active life of service to the sick poor – she founded the first hospital at Genoa (in 1477). So also, in the seventeenth century, the French mystic, Marie de l'Incarnation, said with reference to her own experience:

1. Baker, loc. cit.
2. E. A. Peers, *Spanish Mysticism*, p. 152.
3. *The Sparkling Stone*, Ch. 9.
4. Evelyn Underhill, *The Mystics of the Church*, p. 164.

My soul has dwelt in her centre, which is God. . . . One can read, write, work, do what one will, and nevertheless this fundamental occupation always abides, and the soul never ceases to be united with God.[1]

Another and better-known French mystic of the same period, Brother Lawrence, said that while he was at work in the kitchen of the monastery to which he was attached, 'I possess God in as great a tranquillity as if I were upon my knees at the Blessed Sacrament'.[2]

The Spiritual Marriage carries with it, secondly, a transformation of the soul so complete that it becomes wholly God-possessed; it is a 'theopathic' state – the individual is in all his activities the living organ or instrument of God. The soul, says Mme Guyon, the seventeenth-century mystic (who was accused, as we shall see, of Quietism), 'no longer lives or works of herself, but God lives, acts and works in her, and this grows little by little, till she becomes perfect with God's perfection, rich with His riches, and loves with His love'.[3] The Spanish mystic, Luis de León, sometimes speaks of this 'theopathic' state in terms of Christ-mysticism:

Christ's very Spirit comes and is united with the soul – nay, is infused throughout its being, as though He were soul of its soul indeed. And thus, infused and absorbed by the soul, this Spirit takes possession of its faculties and powers.[4]

Of those who are thus possessed and transformed, he says: 'Christ looks out from their eyes, speaks from their tongues, works through their senses.' They are so fully identified with Christ that He 'occupies them wholly'.[5] It is evident that 'Christ' is to be taken as equivalent to God, for what Luis de León says here of Christ he says elsewhere of God: 'God, when He is united with the soul, penetrates it wholly and enters into its secret chambers, till He is made one with its inmost being'; 'in very truth the soul not only has God dwelling within it, but is indeed God'.[6]

1. ibid., p. 203.　　2. *The Practice of the Presence of God*, Ch. 4.

3. *Les Torrens*, I: 9: 3 (quoted by Evelyn Underhill, *Mysticism*, 6th edition, p. 516).

4. E. A. Peers, op. cit., p. 160.　　5. ibid., p. 159.

6. E. A. Peers, *Studies of the Spanish Mystics*, I: 334.

The divinization of the soul which comes about in the Spiritual Marriage is, clearly, to be distinguished from its identification with God in ecstasy. The soul is not here lifted into a consciousness of divine Glory in which it is no longer aware of itself; its conscious selfhood remains, but it remains as a thing transfigured by the divine Presence, a manifestation of the divine Life. 'My being is God,' says Catherine of Genoa, 'not by simple participation, but by a true transformation of my being'; 'God is my being, my "me", my strength, my beatitude'; 'man by love makes himself one single thing with God, and finds there every good'.[1] For Catherine, as Von Hügel says, 'God, loving Himself in and through us, is alone our full true self'.[2] The French mystic of the later nineteenth century, Elizabeth de la Trinité, speaks of the same experience. 'The soul [she says] has endured the mystical death in which she annihilates herself, and forgets herself, so completely that she dies in God to be transformed into Him'; 'all her movements become divine, and, though they are God's, they are just as much the soul's. For our Lord performs them in and with her'.[3] It is Elizabeth's aspiration to become completely identified with the divine, 'until she is wholly a receptacle of God, living with His life in her, knowing with His knowledge, loving with His love'.[4]

It is the essential feature of the 'theopathic' life that, as Augustine Baker says, the will is deified – 'so closely united and hidden in the divine Will that God may be said to will and do all things in and by it'.[5] It is the proper end, he tells us, of a contemplative life to attain 'a habitual union with God', so that for perfect souls God becomes 'the principle of all their actions, internal and external, being the Life of their life and the Spirit of their spirits', and they become 'one spirit, one will, one love with Him'.[6] In the Sermons of John Tauler there is a constant emphasis on this attainment. 'In the measure that a man comes out of himself, in that measure does God enter in with His divine grace.' To every man who walks in this way God will say: 'Thy

1. Von Hügel, *The Mystical Element in Religion*, I: 265, 282.
2. ibid., II: 39.
3. *Souvenirs*, pp. 195, 313 (quoted by Watkin, op. cit., pp. 267f.).
4. Watkin, op. cit., p. 268.   5. op. cit., III: 4: 2.
6. ibid., 1: 1: 3.

will is swallowed up in Mine, and thou hast become one with Me by grace.'[1] It is above all in the *Theologia Germanica* that the deified life is interpreted in terms of will. The author does not, indeed, ignore the element of vision, the illumination of the soul by the divine Light, which brings us the knowledge of God. The deified man is 'he who is imbued or illuminated by the eternal or divine Light, and inflamed or consumed with eternal or divine Love' (Ch. 41). But the writer is concerned chiefly with this latter aspect – the divine Love as possessing the will. He finds the meaning and purpose of the universe in the expression of the divine Will through created beings. The essence of sin is self-will, and the cure of it is in the incarnation of God in man, whereby God takes to Himself all that is in us, 'so that He alone may do all things in us' (Ch. 3). In the deified man, the very root of sin is destroyed – not automatically or once for all, but in the continuous cleaving of the soul to God, the dying to self which must be perpetually renewed. So Ruysbroeck says that the 'hidden sons of God', who live the 'God-seeing life', must 'die in love ever anew' (loc. cit.). The *Theologia Germanica* speaks sometimes of the unitive life as involving the destruction or cessation of the human will. The 'humble and enlightened man' is to 'become as naught in himself, having no will' (Ch. 51). But it is plain that what the writer has in mind is the destruction of self-will. The will inevitably remains, but, as Tauler says, it is to be 'swallowed up' in the Will of God; it is (says the *Theologia*) to be 'one with the eternal Will and to flow out into it' (Ch. 54). Through this unification with the divine – which is the essence of the Spiritual Marriage – God dwells in a man so fully that 'nothing is left in him but what is God's or of God. ... And thus God Himself, that is, the one eternal Perfect, alone is, lives, knows, works, loves, wills, does, and refrains in the man' (Ch. 53). In the same way, St Teresa said that in the final state of her life 'my life is the life which God has lived in me. ... May our Lord be praised, who has delivered me from myself.'[2]

1. *Sermon for the Second Sunday in Lent.*
2. *The Life of St Teresa written by Herself*, p. 197.

IV. HERETICAL MOVEMENTS IN WESTERN CATHOLIC
MYSTICISM

(a) The Heresy of the 'Free Spirit'

The mystics whose work we have been considering adhered to the dogmatic, ceremonial, and moral traditions of the Western Catholic Church. It is true that the teaching of Eckhart was in some respects condemned by the Pope, but he himself repudiated any heretical intentions. Yet it is clear that there was in fact a certain tension between mystical thought and experience and the established system of ecclesiastical religion. The experience of the soul in its union with God has no essential relation to the dogmatic traditions of the Church. It is not surprising, therefore, that in medieval times there arose a type of mysticism which rejected existing rites and formulas. At the same time it was only to be expected that heretical mysticism, in emancipating itself from the limitations of orthodoxy, should give rise to distortions and extravagances to which orthodox mystics were immune.

The heresy known as 'the Free Spirit' attained a wide popular influence in the later thirteenth century, but its beginnings go further back.[1] The outlook characteristic of the movement was elaborated early in the thirteenth century by a group of men trained at the University of Paris, who were known as 'Amaurians', since they were followers of Amaury (Amalric). Amaury lectured on the teaching of Erigena, who had translated the works of 'Dionysius' into Latin. (See p. 235 above.) It was the Neo-Platonism of 'Dionysius' which formed the philosophical groundwork of the heresy – as it formed the philosophical groundwork of medieval mysticism generally. Amaury himself was condemned for heresy in 1204, and five years later eleven of his disciples were burnt. The Amaurians were ardent propagandists of anti-ecclesiastical mysticism. They claimed to be inspired 'prophets', endowed with supernatural powers. They taught that the whole existing Church-order was destined to pass away, and that it was their task to inaugurate a totally new era in the spiritual life of mankind, based on the inner consciousness of God

1. See Norman Cohn, *The Pursuit of the Millennium*, Chs. 7–8.

which they had themselves attained. There were three 'dispensations', they said, in the religious life of the world – that of the Father, that of the Son, and that of the Holy Spirit. The Father was incarnate in Abraham, the Son in Jesus, the Spirit in themselves. The Spirit was, indeed, present in all things and in all men, but He was incarnate peculiarly in themselves, through their own God-consciousness. As the outcome of their work the incarnation of the Spirit would soon become universal. But before that happened, the world would be devastated by the Messianic 'Woes' foretold in the gospels, and the greater part of mankind would perish. There is a strange intermingling in their teaching of spiritual faith and apocalyptic fanaticism. Within five years, they taught, the 'Woes' would light upon the world in the shape of war and famine and fire, but at the end of that time the surviving remnant would be deified; every man would know himself to be divine. 'All men [they declared] will be Spirituals, so that each will be able to say "I am the Holy Spirit" and "Before Abraham was, I am".'[1] The incarnation of the Spirit would free the world from all existing laws and commandments, and those in whom that incarnation has taken place are already free; they have no need of external forms – of baptism or confession or eucharist.[2] The Amaurians were accused, like their successors, of an antinomianism which disregarded all moral restraint. But they were certainly sustained by an exalted spiritual faith quite incompatible with a mere selfish amoralism – a faith which enabled them to face persecution and death with dauntless courage. It is significant that of the fourteen men condemned at the Synod of Sens in 1209 only three recanted.

Thanks to the rigorous policy of the Church in burning heretics, the doctrine of the Free Spirit as the Amaurians proclaimed it was soon suppressed; but before the end of the century the same tendency re-asserted itself on a much larger scale. Its protagonists were now adherents of the lay orders known as 'Beghards' and 'Beguines' – men and women who, like the Tertiaries of the Franciscan and Dominican orders, were dedicated to a religious life, but continued to live in the world, either

1. Cohn, op. cit., p. 160.
2. R. M. Jones, *Studies in Mystical Religion*, pp. 187f.

in communities or as wandering mendicants. These pious laymen and laywomen for the most part held no distinctive doctrines, but among the men (Beghards), who were often unauthorized preachers, some were missionaries of the Free Spirit, while the women (Beguines) sometimes accepted Brethren of the Free Spirit as their spiritual directors. They were so commonly suspected of heresy that the Council of Vienne (1311) decreed the abolition of the orders, and they were subject to constant persecution. In spite of persecution, however, the heresy continued to exert widespread influence. There was no hard-and-fast distinction between Beghards and Friends of God (see p. 238 above), and consequently some of the Friends of God were associated with the heretical movement. The leader of the heterodox wing was Nicholas of Basel, who travelled widely as a missionary on behalf of its teaching; he was eventually burnt at Vienne in 1397. The principles of the heresy were attacked by other Friends of God, like Tauler, Suso, and the author of the *Theologia Germanica*.

The heresy of the Free Spirit was known traditionally as 'the Pantheist heresy', but in its later phase, as in its earlier, its outlook was in fact Neo-Platonic. Its adherents cherished the aspiration after deification which was common ground among the mystics.

The Free Spirit is attained [an adept said] when one is wholly transformed into God. ... In this union one is restored to one's original state, before one flowed out of the Deity.[1]

What marked out the mystics of the Free Spirit appears to have been the boldness with which they made the claim to have attained such a transformation and the incautious inferences which they were apt to draw from it. The precise significance of sayings attributed to them, taken out of their context, is not always easy to gauge, but we can readily understand that in their revolt against Church tradition, with its emphasis on the weakness and sinfulness of man, the adepts of the Free Spirit fell at times into a fanatical disregard of their human limitations. The *Theologia Germanica* says that in their claim to deification they failed to distinguish between the life of God as it is in

1. Cohn, op. cit., p. 183.

eternity, with its unchangeable perfection, and the life of God as it is lived in deified men (Ch. 40). The writer adds that they declare that they have 'got above conscience and the sense of sin'; they are 'above all works, customs, laws, and order', and so even above 'that life which Christ led in the body'. This agrees with other testimonies. Thus, according to a letter written by the Bishop of Strasbourg to his subordinates (in 1317):

They say that every man can by virtue of his nature become as perfect as Christ, and can acquire even greater merit than Christ. . . . Many among them have attained such a degree of perfection that they say they cannot sin. . . . They hold themselves unmovable on the Summit of the Ninth Rock [the highest point in the soul], and neither rejoice nor lament.[1]

Among the Brethren of the Free Spirit it was the highest grade – the adepts – who claimed to have reached the goal of perfection or deification, after having first undergone a prolonged course of spiritual training. The rest were disciples, who owed an absolute and unquestioning obedience to the adepts. The spiritual authority attributed to the adepts was reinforced by the social teaching of the Brethren. All things, it was taught, belonged of right to the adepts, and they might therefore take for themselves in practice whatever they chose without scruple. Such claims to power and privilege obviously lent themselves to grave abuse, and there can be no doubt that such abuse occurred. The heretics were commonly accused of sexual licence, and it appears that promiscuity did sometimes happen among them – associated, as it would seem, with a controlled method of intercourse. The sexual act itself, performed with due control, was regarded in some circles as an actual means of mystical experience. It was natural that in their reaction against ecclesiastical tradition, with its ascetic bias, heretics should be led to favour markedly contrasted opinions.

Although the adepts of the Free Spirit, in their claims to perfection and to infallible authority, betray a certain lack of balance and a certain fanaticism, there were among them indications of a very genuine enlightenment. There were doubtless considerable differences in the quality of their inner life, but

1. R. M. Jones, op. cit., pp. 207f.

they had, at least, the insight to distinguish between the life of the spirit and the established dogmatic and ecclesiastical system. It was their essential offence in the eyes of the orthodox that for them, in the words of the Bishop of Strasbourg, 'the soul's inward voice is safer than the truths preached in the church'.[1] They displayed a particular insight in matters of eschatology. According to the Chronicler Caesarius of Heisterbach, the Amaurians 'denied the resurrection of the body. They taught that there is neither Heaven nor Hell as places, but that he who knows God possesses Heaven, and he who commits a mortal sin carries Hell within himself.'[2] The Bishop of Strasbourg includes among the tenets of the Free Spirit the belief that in the end 'nobody will be lost, not even Jews or Saracens, because their spirits will return to God?'

(b) The Spiritual Franciscans and the 'Eternal Gospel'

In the Franciscan order a heresy grew up in Italy and France in the thirteenth century which sprang, like the heresy of the Free Spirit, from the widespread feeling of discord between the established ecclesiastical system and the claims of the mystical consciousness. The basis of the heresy was the theory held by the Amaurians of three ages in the history of the world – that of the Father, that of the Son and that of the Holy Spirit. This theory was formulated (independently of the Amaurians) in the later twelfth century by Joachim of Fiore, a theologian and a mystic, who founded an order of monks in Calabria. The age of the Father, characterized by servile obedience and fear, lasted from Adam to Jesus; that of the Son, marked by filial subjection and faith, from Jesus to the thirteenth century; the age of the Spirit was about to dawn. Its main features would be liberty, love and contemplation. In it God would be immediately apprehended by all men in mystical vision. 'Human beings would possess only spiritual bodies ... The world would be one vast monastery, in which all men would be contemplative monks, rapt in mystical ecstasy.'[3] It was the coming of this new spiritual condition, in which the Church of the East would be re-united with the Church

1. R. M. Jones, loc. cit.
2. ibid., p. 187.　　3. Cohn, op. cit., p. 100.

of the West,[1] that constituted for Joachim the 'Eternal Gospel'.

As Joachim himself proclaimed it, the Eternal Gospel was not a heresy. Yet it clearly contained the seeds of heresy. The teaching of Joachim was adopted by a group of disciples belonging to the Franciscan order. After the death of St Francis (1226) the order was divided on the question of the strictness with which the ideal of poverty which he had taught was to be fulfilled. The party which stood for the literal observance of the Rule was known as the 'Spirituals'; and it was among them that the teaching of Joachim took root. Joachim's followers regarded him as an inspired prophet, and among them there grew up a school of prophets claiming a like inspiration and producing prophetic works in his name. The Spirituals looked upon St Francis as the founder of the age of the Spirit and upon themselves as members of the new order which would replace the existing Church, and would lead the world to the realization of its final destiny. They sought to justify their claims by means of prophecies attributed to Joachim. This new rendering of the Eternal Gospel naturally brought its advocates into collision with the ecclesiastical authorities. In 1254 there was issued in Paris a book known as the *Introduction to the Eternal Gospel*, which has been described as 'the manifesto of the final Church of the Holy Ghost'.[2] It comprises three works actually written by Joachim, together with an introduction and notes by a Spiritual Franciscan, Gerard of San Donnino. In the introduction and notes, which are known to us only indirectly, through orthodox denunciation, Gerard declared that the Eternal Gospel had been entrusted to the Franciscan order, and that in that order the ideal of the age of the Spirit was fulfilled. Through its work the prevailing sacerdotal system would be removed, and the religion of the Spirit would replace it. It is not surprising that the book was condemned by a Papal commission and ordered to be burnt, while Gerard was deprived of his priestly office and imprisoned.

1. For Joachim the monastic life was best represented by the hermits of the desert.
2. Gebhart, *Mystic Italy*, p. 183.

(c) Quietism

Another movement which illustrates the conflict between mystical religion and ecclesiastical authority is Quietism, which exercised a considerable influence in Italy, France, and Spain in the seventeenth century. The leading figures in the movement were Miguel de Molinos, Mme Guyon, and Fénelon, Archbishop of Cambrai, all of whom received, in varying degrees, official condemnation. Molinos became widely known in Rome as a spiritual director. His book, *The Spiritual Guide* (published in 1675), enjoyed enormous popularity. It was, however, attacked by the Jesuit preacher, Segneri; but when the matter was referred to the Inquisition, the book was at first declared to be entirely orthodox. The Jesuits continued to be hostile, and Molinos was arrested (in 1685). Two years later he admitted and abjured his heresy, but was imprisoned for life. He died in prison at a date unknown. His recantation cannot be taken at its face value. The Pope condemned sixty-eight propositions drawn from *The Spiritual Guide* and the unpublished writings of Molinos. In France, meanwhile, Mme Guyon, in conjunction with Father Lacombe, conducted an energetic campaign on behalf of Quietist principles. Her companion was sent to the Bastille in 1687, and she was herself later imprisoned there for several years. Mme Guyon won great influence over Fénelon, who was involved in a bitter controversy with Bossuet, Bishop of Meaux. Bossuet attacked his book, *Maxims of the Saints* (1697), and shortly afterwards the book was condemned by the Pope. It is indicative of the growth of ecclesiastical opposition to Quietist tendencies that a work of the Spanish mystic, Antonio de Rojas, *The Life of the Spirit*, was placed on the Index in 1689, half a century after its publication. When first published, it won warm approval in high quarters, and in *Holy Wisdom* Augustine Baker commends the method of prayer which it advocates to the attention of his readers.

The main factor in securing the condemnation of Quietism appears to have been the fear of mysticism, with its stress on inner experience, as a popular influence – especially on the part of those militant champions of ecclesiastical authority, the

Jesuits. The fear was doubtless accentuated by the fact that the Flemish Quietist, Antoinette Bourignon (1611–80), broke away from the Church altogether. She rejected ecclesiastical authority of any kind and all set forms of worship.

> The resignation of our will to God [she said] supplies all things. We no longer need any means of devotion, such as fasting, public worship and the sacraments, because God works in us what pleases Him.[1]

Neither Molinos nor Mme Guyon, and still less Fénelon, had any such subversive thoughts. Molinos did, however, deprecate frequent confession (on which the Jesuits laid such stress), save for beginners in the 'interior way'. While he insisted on daily communion when possible, he declared that to the interior soul 'all days are alike, all are solemn festivals'; and so with sacred places – 'to it all places are alike'.[2] It is easy to see the danger of such an emphasis from the standpoint of the rigid guardians of ecclesiastical discipline; and apparently Quietism did have some effect in loosening the bonds of external observance. For Bishop Burnet records that at the height of the Quietist revival in Rome those affected by the movement 'were observed to become more strict in their lives, more retired and serious in their mental devotions, yet there appeared less zeal in their whole deportment as to the exterior parts of the religion of the Church'.[3]

The essential feature of Quietism was its emphasis on what St Teresa called 'the prayer of quiet' – the stillness of the soul in the presence of God, which mystics have always regarded as a fundamental condition of the birth of the higher consciousness. 'By not speaking, not desiring, and not thinking,' says Molinos, 'one arrives at the true and perfect mystical silence, wherein God speaks with the soul, and communicates Himself to it.' He adds that it is 'by means of perfect resignation and internal silence' that we can attain to the perfection of the soul, which consists in 'loving God sufficiently'.[4] Molinos is very far from imagining that the inner quiet which brings union with God is an easy

---

1. Quoted by W. L. Hare, *Systems of Meditation in Religion*, p. 187.
2. Condemned Proposition 33 (Hare, op. cit., p. 189).
3. Quoted by Inge, *Christian Mysticism*, 2nd edition, p. 233, note 1.
4. *The Spiritual Guide*, I: 17.

attainment. On the contrary, he emphasizes the difficulties which it involves. The soul which treads the interior way must pass through the 'dark night' of bitter sorrow – of aridity, of wearisomeness for the things of God, of the sense of desertion, of temptation. It is only through constant effort and struggle that the state of 'internal recollection' or contemplation can be won. In that state, as he insists, it is an entire mistake to suppose that the soul is 'idle and wholly inactive'.

To be attentive to God, draw near to Him, to follow His internal inspirations, receive His divine influences, adore Him in His own intimate centre ... are true acts, though simple, wholly spiritual, and in a manner imperceptible through the great tranquillity wherewith the soul exerts them [1: 5].

The state of inner quiet is a state of intense, but tranquil activity.

Quietism is often misunderstood by its modern critics as well as by its contemporary antagonists. One source of misunderstanding is the doctrine of the 'One Act' taught by Molinos. Fénelon himself, who has been described as 'a semi-Quietist', condemned that doctrine, in a letter to the Pope, as 'a poisoned source of idleness and internal lethargy'.[1] Whatever may have been its effects among his followers, it was by no means the intention of Molinos to promote 'idleness and lethargy'. The One Act is for him the expression of continuity in the inner life.

A man having once made the resolution of doing the Will of God, and of being in His Presence, he still perseveres in that act, so long as he recalls not the same, although he be taken up in hearing, speaking, eating, or in any other external good work [1: 15].

The fixing of the will on God, once performed in contemplative prayer, goes on through life in the soul which 'walks continually in God's Presence', and does all things 'through God'.

From what has been said, it is evident how misleading is Evelyn Underhill's assertion that 'pure passivity and indifference' were the Quietist ideal.[2] The 'indifference' here referred to can only be the 'Holy Indifference' – indifference as to one's own destiny in this life or in the life to come – which was for Quietists an out-

1. Inge, op. cit., pp. 239f.
2. *Mysticism*, 6th edition, p. 389.

come of the disinterested love of God. In the second condemned proposition of Fénelon he says that in the unitive life 'every interested motive of fear or hope is lost'.[1] We must renounce self so completely, and love God so purely, that we are ready to be damned for His glory. It is said that on his death-bed a young priest even prayed to be sent to Hell, 'so that the divine justice and the divine glory might be more fully confessed'.[2] We have here an illustration of the extravagances to which Quietism gave rise. As Ronald Knox observes, it led to a scrupulosity in which a man would 'torture himself with scruples to make sure that he is not loving God because he hopes to get anything out of it'.[3] Molinos even said (according to Condemned Proposition 13) that a man 'ought not to have a desire of his own perfection, of his sanctification or his salvation'.[4] What he meant by that was that we must banish the thought of self altogether, and set our mind wholly on God. Fénelon said very much the same thing. It was his teaching that we must not think of ourselves or our individual relation to God. Similarly Molinos rejected petitionary prayer. 'It does not become him who is resigned to the Will of God to ask of Him, because to ask is an imperfection, being an act of the personal will or of personal choice' (Condemned Proposition 14).

The Quietist seeks to live a life, not of inactivity, but of an activity wholly dependent on God. In the words of Mme Guyon: 'Instead of promoting idleness, we promote the highest activity by inculcating a total dependence on the Spirit of God.'[5] It is 'self-action' and 'self-exertion' which must be overcome – action and exertion springing from ourselves in our separateness, not from God, who is the inmost centre of our being. We must give up self and the activity of self to the 'annihilating power of divine Love', so that the divine activity may supplant our own. We must seek to be 'susceptible of divine impressions', so that we may be 'wholly moved by the divine Spirit, who is infinitely active'. Father Knox has said that 'the root of the Quietist error' is 'a kind of ultra-supernaturalism. . . . The Quietist wants to do away

---

1. Baker, op. cit., p. 492.
2. R. A. Knox, *Enthusiasm*, p. 350.
3. ibid., p. 351.
4. Hare, op. cit., p. 189.
5. *A Short and Easy Method of Prayer*, Ch. 21.

with human effort as such, so as to give God the whole right of spiritual initiative. ... God alone must do everything' (p. 350). But it is the aim of mystics generally in the unitive life to let God act through them. In the words of the *Theologia Germanica*: 'I would fain be to the eternal God what a man's hand is to a man' (Ch. 10). The author of *The Book of the Poor in Spirit* declares that 'if man is really to attain God, he must empty himself of all self-action, and permit God alone to act in him. For all that is good is the work of God' (p. 168). Molinos quotes the seventeenth-century French mystic, St Jeanne Chantal, who was not herself a Quietist, as saying: 'It is God's will and pleasure that a total stop should be put to the operations of my soul, because He would have all things done by His own activity' (1: 13). It was not, as Mrs Herman remarks, that Quietism is 'the mystical expression of the doctrine of the total depravity and helplessness of human nature',[1] since it was a cardinal point in its teaching that the soul is the dwelling-place of God. It was rather that the Quietists sought to live and act, not from the superficial self, but from the deep inner centre of their being, and to receive light and inspiration continually from this source. Such a course certainly lent itself to error and self-deception. In particular, they were apt to confuse impulses springing from their own subconscious minds with divine light and guidance. De Caussade, a French mystic of the eighteenth century, observes that Quietists suppose 'that every thought that comes to them in the repose and silence of prayer is a light and inspiration from God'.[2] The same criticism has been made, rightly enough, of the adherents of the Group Movement in our time. It is only at the summit of the inner way that God can indeed become 'the principle of all men's actions, a Light to direct all their steps and to order all their workings'.[3] Molinos was accused of saying (in Condemned Proposition 57) that 'by acquired contemplation we reach a state in which we commit no more sin'; and it was the essential mistake of the Quietists to ignore the degrees of growth in the mystical life, and so to assume that they were immune to the possibility of sin and

1. Article on 'Quietism' in the *Encyclopaedia of Religion and Ethics*.
2. *On Prayer*, English translation, p. 13.
3. Baker, op. cit., 1: 1: 3.

error – that they had 'already attained' and were 'already made perfect'.

V. PROTESTANT MYSTICISM

In the religion of the Roman Catholic Church, mysticism holds a recognized though subordinate place. It is commonly acknowledged that the experience of union with God is the natural outcome of contemplative prayer, which is a prominent feature of the tradition of Catholic piety. In breaking away from the Catholic system, Protestants have to a great extent discarded this practice, and to that extent Protestant religion has cut itself off from the roots of mystical experience. On the other hand, it may be said that mysticism finds a foothold in Protestantism which it does not find in Catholicism, through the emphasis which Evangelical Protestants lay on personal experience. But for the Evangelical what is essential is experience of salvation through faith in the atoning sacrifice of Christ; and that experience has in itself no mystical quality. It may, indeed, be associated with 'Christ-mysticism'; and in Evangelical circles, with the attempt to return to New Testament Christianity, there has been a certain revival of the mysticism of Paul and John. But that, in any case, is a secondary and incidental feature of Evangelical piety. In the main stream of Protestant orthodoxy, mysticism of any sort holds no necessary place. It is characteristic of Protestant mysticism that it has flourished among those who have departed, not merely from Catholic dogma, but in one way or another from the new orthodoxy of the Reformation churches. It serves thus to reveal far more clearly than does Catholic mysticism the liberalizing tendency of mystical experience.

(a) The Mysticism of Jacob Boehme

By far the greatest and most original of Protestant mystics was the Silesian cobbler, Jacob Boehme (1574–1624). In view of its distinctiveness, his teaching requires separate treatment in these pages. Boehme came to mysticism spontaneously and in a highly unfavourable environment. He was brought up as a Lutheran at a time when the Lutheran Church had fallen away from its original freshness and fervour into a system of barren dogma, which laid particular emphasis on the literal word of Scripture. At an early age he rebelled against this system, and was moved to seek an immediate experience of divine Reality. He enjoyed a mystical illumination in his youth; but the crucial experience of his life occurred when he was twenty-six. Looking one day at the surface of a polished pewter dish which reflected the sunlight, he suddenly felt himself suffused with the divine Light and seeing into the very heart of the universe. To test the reality of his experience, he went out on to the public green at Görlitz, and there his vision was intensified. 'I reached to the innermost birth of the Deity,' he says in *Aurora*, 'and there I was embraced with love as a bridegroom embraces his bride. ... In this light my spirit suddenly saw through all, and in all created things, even in herbs and grass, I knew God, who He is, how He is, and what His Will is' (xix: 12f.).

It is characteristic of Boehme that for him the mystic experience was not only an experience of union with God; it was at the same time a revelation which contained in itself the solution of the deepest problems of the universe.

In one quarter of an hour [he said] I saw and knew more than if I had been many years together at a university. ... I saw and knew the Being of beings, the Byss and Abyss, the eternal generation of the Trinity, the origin and descent of this world and of all creatures through divine Wisdom.[1]

It is impossible to say how far the teaching of Boehme was actually the outcome of his own illumination, and how far it was the expression of the influence of other teachers. Both factors were certainly involved. Before his illumination, he held the popular belief that Heaven was a place above the stars, where God had His abode. Through the mystical insight which came to him he saw that God dwells in all things, and that His Presence itself is Heaven. (We may recall that it was through her own mystical awakening that St Teresa also was led to see the divine indwelling; see p. 243 above.) On the other hand, there is no doubt that Boehme was indebted for much of the detail of his scheme of thought to earlier teachers. He was influenced, in particular, by

1. Second Epistle.

the sixteenth-century German mystics, Schwenckfeld and Weigel (see pp. 275, 285f. below), and by the mystical Nature-philosopher and alchemist, Paracelsus. His own writing is often highly obscure, and it owes its obscurity mainly to the frequent use which he makes of the language of alchemy.

In Boehme's teaching concerning God there are two main distinctive features. In the first place, there is the doctrine of the Ungrund, the primal Ground of being – which has been revived in our time by Berdyaev. Boehme knew nothing directly of the Catholic mystics or of Plotinus and 'Dionysius'. But the Ungrund represents for him the negative aspect of Deity; it may be compared with the 'Godhead' of Eckhart. It is 'the great Mystery', 'the Abyss', 'the eternal Stillness' – the undifferentiated totality of the Absolute, the ultimate Source of all things, in which there is neither light nor darkness, neither good nor evil. Boehme dwells mainly on the positive aspect of the divine nature. God is for him absolute Personality, universal Love, which 'infinitely transcends all that human sense and reason can reach to'.[1] In the Being of God there is an eternal process of generation or becoming, whereby God as Person, as Light and Love, arises out of the Ungrund. Becoming is the foundation of all positive being. It would be a complete distortion of Boehme's position to suppose that for him God is subject to any temporal process of becoming. God, he teaches, is eternally complete, eternally perfect; but eternally He makes Himself what He is, eternally He assumes His nature of goodness and love.

Boehme teaches, secondly, that there is no manifestation without the interplay of opposites. 'In yes and no all things subsist.'[2] He applies this thought to the nature of God and His relation to the world. Underlying all reality, as he sees it, there are three fundamental principles – fire or wrath, light or love, and the realization of them in body and form. The third principle he sometimes calls 'body', and sometimes 'spirit', i.e. the dynamic activity which creates bodily form. In God Himself these three principles are found, corresponding to the three Persons of the Trinity. What he calls the 'fire-ground' in God is the root of all

1. *Of the Supersensual Life*, Dialogue 1.
2. *Theosophical Questions*, III: 2.

things. Without it there would be no evil in the world; but neither would there be any positive good – there would be no mobility, no energy, no life. 'All would be a nothing.' As Stephen Hobhouse has put it: 'Potential wrath is the foundation of all good life, even in Heaven itself.'[1] The principle of fire or wrath Boehme identifies with the Father. That does not mean that for him God is ever in Himself a wrathful being. The first principle exists in God only to engender the second – the principle of light and love. In God the wrath remains potential – a principle of strength, of majesty, of ceaseless energy. So it should be in ourselves and in all beings. The essential fact underlying evil is the separation of qualities which naturally belong together – the separation of the qualities of fire and energy from those of light and love, with which they should be united. (There is a remarkable parallel, if it is only a parallel, to Boehme's philosophy in this aspect in the teaching of the Jewish mystic, Luria; see p. 193 above.) Good and evil exist not only in man; they are found in unceasing conflict throughout the natural world. The world as we know it, with its rigid exclusive materiality and its separation of life from life, represents a Fall. The primal tragedy lay in the act of Lucifer, who willed to centre in himself, to exalt himself against God. The primal Fall was renewed in a lesser degree with Adam, who sought the enjoyment of physical Nature, and so actually brought about its materialization. There is a close affinity here between the teaching of Boehme and that of the Gnostics and the Jewish mystics of the Kabbalah.

Over against the world of time and space, of materiality and separateness, there is for Boehme, as for the mystics who follow the Platonic tradition, an ideal universe, which he calls 'eternal Nature' or 'the uncreated Heaven' – the 'body' or the 'glory' of God. He sometimes personifies it as a maiden – the embodiment of the divine Wisdom. 'Eternal Nature' is other than God, yet inseparable from Him. In it all things exist in a state of perfection and harmony. There man himself exists in his eternal essence in unbroken unity with God. The world in which we live, while it is a fallen world, is yet in its essential nature an outbirth of this ideal universe, not a creation out of nothing. 'If God made all

1. *Selected Mystical Writings of William Law*, p. 376.

things out of nothing, then the visible world would be no revelation of Him, for it would have nothing of Him in it; He would still be off and beyond and would not be known in this world.'[1] Boehme speaks in terms both of creation and of emanation. The creation of the world is 'a manifestation of the unsearchable God', as an apple which grows on a tree is not the tree itself, but grows from the power of the tree. So all things have sprung from the divine desire for manifestation. Boehme also uses the analogy of play or sport, familiar in Indian teaching; and he likens creation to 'a great harmony of manifold instruments which are all tuned into one harmony'.[2]

Much of Boehme's teaching appears to us as highly speculative, yet it is illuminated by a profound mystical insight. He laid great stress on the fact of evil and of man's actual separation from God, but he never lost sight of the divine Presence which dwells in our inmost being or of the union with God which is our rightful goal.

The true man [he said] whom God created is still hidden within that which is fallen. .... The true holy self, that lies hidden within the other, is as much in Heaven as God Himself, and the Heart of God is born within it.[3]

The eternal essence of man, belonging to the Uncreated Heaven, is a divine theophany – a manifestation of the divine Glory. And it is man's task on earth to incarnate that greater self, and so to incarnate God.

Incarnation can only be achieved by the imitation of Christ, who represents God in the world, revealing in his life and death the divine nature of love. In Christ 'Love became man, and put on our human flesh and our human soul'; 'one who is Love itself was born of our own very birth'.[4] The divine Love may likewise be born in us. 'I have brought His life into mine [Boehme says], so that I am made one with Him in His love.'[5] Like Eckhart, he

1. *Aurora*, XXI: 60–2.
2. *The Signature of All Things*, XVI: 1–3.
3. *First Epistle*.
4. *The Three Principles*, XXV: 43: 6.
5. *The Signature of All Things*, IX: 64.

speaks of the birth of God in the soul: 'the Son of God, the eternal Word of the Father, must become man, and be born in you, if you will know God.'[1] We thus participate in the life of Christ, so that he lives in us and unites us with himself. We die with Christ to the fallen self, that we may rise with him into union with God. The mysticism of Boehme is thus, in one aspect, identical with the 'Christ-mysticism' of Paul and John. As a Protestant, he rejects the ideal of the monastic life, but he uses language as strong as that of any Catholic concerning the necessity of the negative way in its ethical aspect.

It is not meant that one should run from house and home, from wife and children and kindred, and flee out of the world, or forsake his goods so as not to regard them; but he must kill and make as nothing his own self-will.[2]

Self as a separative principle, dividing us from God, must be wholly destroyed, so that the Love of God may possess us and work in us. It is because we break ourselves off with our own willing from God's willing, and with our seeing from God's seeing, that we are not united with Him. And if we are to attain that union, we must 'stand still from the thinking of self and the willing of self', and become 'quiet and passive to the impressions of the eternal Word and Spirit', so that 'the eternal hearing, seeing and speaking may be revealed' in us. By this 'quiet introversion of the spirit' we can 'sink into the great Love of God', and be 'penetrated and clothed upon with the supreme splendour of the divine Glory'.[3] We thus enter into the unitive life, in which our will is united wholly with the Will of God.

So then it is no longer thy will, but the Will of God, no longer the love of thyself, but the Love of God, which moveth and operateth in thee.[4]

For Boehme, as for the Catholic mystics, the goal of man is deification. 'God has become that which I am, and has made me that which He is.'[5] Love is itself a divinizing power:

The height of love is as high as God Himself is; its greatness is as

1. *The Threefold Life*, III: 31.　　2. *Mysterium Magnum*, XII: 55.
3. *Of the Supersensual Life*, Dialogue 1.　　4. ibid., Dialogue 2.
5. *The Signature of All Things*, XII: 13.

great as God. ... It brings Thee to be as high as God Himself is by
uniting thee with God, as thou canst perceive in the humanity of our
dear Lord Jesus, whom love has raised to the highest Throne.[1]

(b) Divine Immanence and Transcendence in Protestant Mysticism

The teaching of Boehme was in some respects highly distinctive.
In particular, his conception of duality as grounded in God and of
the law of polarity as essential to all manifested being are a
contribution of his own. But in fundamentals his thought is one
with that of Protestant mystics generally. It is significant that,
although there were for a time separate groups of his followers
('Behmenists') in England, they were eventually absorbed by the
Quakers. Protestant mystics are naturally more diversified in
their outlook than Catholic mystics; they include Anabaptists,
Lutherans, Anglicans, Quakers. Yet the main fact which strikes
us, when we review their teaching, is its essential unity. And,
while as Protestants they are deeply divided from the Catholic
system in some aspects, as mystics they are united in the essentials
of thought and experience with Catholic mystics. Protestant
mystics were themselves in general profoundly influenced by the
writings of medieval mystics – more especially by the *Theologia
Germanica* – directly or indirectly. [2] (Boehme knew nothing of the
Catholics, but was influenced by Weigel, who often quotes them.)
The Protestant mystics were also affected to a marked extent by
the revival of Platonism, which occurred as an outcome of the
Renaissance in the fifteenth and sixteenth centuries. It was, indeed,
the new vogue thus given to the works of the Neo-Platonists
which was the main intellectual factor underlying the growth of
Protestant mysticism.

One of the earliest of the Protestant mystics was Sebastian
Franck (1499–1542), who entered the priesthood of the Roman
Church, but soon broke away, and was for a time a Protestant
preacher. Franck was a thoroughgoing adherent of the 'Dionysian' tradition. God is for him above all notions, all definitions,

1. *Of the Supersensual Life*, Dialogue 1.
2. The *Theologia Germanica* was translated into Latin by Sebastian
Franck and by Castellio, and from the latter's rendering it was translated
into English by John Everard and Giles Randall. Weigel wrote a commentary on it.

all determinations; it is negative assertions alone which are strictly true of Him. It is only in relation to ourselves that He can be described as personal. He is the Source and the inmost Essence of all things, expressing Himself in the world and so, in one sense, identifying Himself with it, yet remaining eternally transcendent. The world of essential reality is the supersensible world, which denies and opposes the world of the senses. The influence of Franck is seen most notably in the Lutheran pastor, Valentine Weigel (d. 1588), whose writings were not printed until after his death. By signing the various 'confessions' of his day, he professed an orthodoxy to which he did not inwardly adhere. When his books were published (at Halle, 1609–12), they were banned, but they were afterwards printed secretly. Weigel refers repeatedly to the works of 'Dionysius', Eckhart, Tauler, and the *Theologia Germanica*; he was also indebted to the teaching of Nicholas of Cusa. For him God is beyond all determinate being and all thought. He is the ultimate Essence of all things. He incarnates Himself in man, knows Himself in and through man, and so becomes Person, Consciousness, and Will. All things were in God eternally – in His Thought and His divine Wisdom, which Weigel describes as the 'heavenly Eve'. (Cp. Boehme's conception of the divine Wisdom as a heavenly Maiden: see p. 271 above.)

Among English mystics the 'Dionysian' tradition was renewed by John Everard, rector of St Martin-in-the-Fields in the early seventeenth century, who translated the *Mystical Theology*, also the *Theologia Germanica*, selections from Eckhart and Tauler, and a book of Sebastian Franck (*The Knowledge of Good and Evil*). For Everard, again, God is the One, the absolute and perfect Reality, and so beyond the range of thought. Created things are beams or rays of that supreme Reality, who is the Soul of all being. Together they form 'one mighty sweet-tuned instrument', a harmonious choir of being, 'guided by one Spirit'.[1] The Cambridge Platonists, profoundly influenced as they were by Plotinus, emphasize in general the positive rather than the negative aspect of divine Reality. But in his work, *Of the*

1. R. M. Jones, *Spiritual Reformers*, p. 247; cp. Boehme and the 'harmony of manifold instruments' (p. 272 above).

Existence and Nature of God, John Smith, the most deeply mystical member of the school (save perhaps for Peter Sterry), refers to the experience of the 'divine Dark'. The soul which looks beyond the material universe, he says, 'may fly upwards from one Heaven to another, till it be beyond all orb of finite being, swallowed up in the boundless Abyss of divinity. . . . This is that divine Darkness of which the Areopagite speaks, which the higher our minds soar into, the more incomprehensible they find it.'[1] As a Christian Platonist, John Smith recognizes both the divine transcendence and the divine immanence in all things. 'God hath never thrown the world from Himself, but runs through all created essence, containing the archetypal ideas of all things in Himself.'[2] In the writings of William Law (eighteenth century) we find a similar emphasis. The mystical teaching of Law was largely based on that of Boehme, although he was also acquainted with the works of 'Dionysius' and the medieval mystics. Like Boehme, he rejected explicitly the traditional notion of creation out of nothing, on the ground that it leaves no room for the divine indwelling. 'The fiction of the creation out of nothing separates everything from God, for if it is created out of nothing, it cannot have something of God in it. Nature, so far from being out of nothing, is 'the manifestation of all that in God which was before unmanifest'.[3] A cardinal feature of Law's doctrine, as of Boehme's, is the conception of 'eternal Nature' or the archetypal universe, which he describes as 'the unbeginning Majesty of God, the Kingdom of God or visible Glory of the Deity, the beatific manifestation of the triune God'.[4] As with the Cambridge Platonists, Law's constant stress is on the positive aspect of Deity. God, as he repeatedly insists, is 'an eternal Will to all goodness', 'an immense Ocean of divine Love'. But he recognizes that in Himself, and apart from His manifestation in eternal Nature and the created universe, God is 'inconceivable'. In one of his letters he says that the attributes of God 'are only so many

---

1. op. cit., Ch. 1 in *Select Discourses*.
2. *The Excellency and Nobleness of True Religion*, Ch. 8.
3. *The Spirit of Prayer*, II: 1.
4. *An Appeal to All that doubt*, in *Selected Mystical Writings of William Law*, pp. 46f.

human ways of conceiving that abyssal All which can neither be spoken nor conceived by us'. We may rightly speak of God in terms of different qualities, but the ultimate fact underlying all such distinctions is 'that unity of God which we can neither conceive as it is in itself nor divide into this or that'.[1]

In the seventeenth century a movement arose in England during the Civil War which had remarkable affinities to the medieval heresy of the Free Spirit. Its supporters are known as the Ranters. Like the medieval movement, it came to be held in bad odour, owing to the antinomian tendencies associated with it (see pp. 292f. below); but the essential root from which it sprang was mystical experience dissociated from the traditions of the Church, whether Catholic or Protestant. Just as with the heresy of the Free Spirit, the outlook of the Ranters has been commonly described as 'Pantheism', but actually it appears to have been in essence Neo-Platonic. One of the leaders of the movement was Jacob Bauthumley, who wrote in a profoundly mystical vein of the relation between the soul and God. In his book, *The Light and Dark Sides of God* (1650), he says that we can speak of God only in terms of paradox.

If I say I see Thee, it is nothing but Thy seeing of Thyself; for there is nothing in me capable of seeing Thee but Thyself. . . . My seeking of Thee is no other but Thy seeking of Thyself.[2]

Bauthumley speaks at times as though intending to imply a pure and simple identification of God with the universe, but that is quite evidently not his meaning. He does, indeed, identify God in one aspect with all things – as does Sebastian Franck – because (as he says) 'there are no distinctions in God, He being one undivided essence'.[3] But the divine transcendence is essentially involved in his teaching, since 'all things were [he says] let out of God' into the world of time and space. 'As all things had their subsistence and being in God, before they were ever manifested in the world of creatures: so in the end whatever is of God . . . shall be rapt up into God again.'[4]

The teaching of other Ranter leaders is the same, and is simi-

1. Letter iv in *Selected Mystical Writings*, p. 202.
2. Quoted by Cohn, op. cit., p. 336.
3. ibid., p. 337.   4. ibid., pp. 339f

larly based on mystical experience. Thus in his tract, *Heights in Depths, and Depths in Heights*, Joseph Salmon says:

> I appeared to myself as one confounded into the abyss of eternity, nonentitized into the Being of beings, my soul spilt and emptied into the fountain and ocean of divine fulness.[1]

Salmon speaks, in truly Neo-Platonic vein, of our life in time and space as a descent into multiplicity 'from oneness or eternity'. Our true life is in unity: 'in one we are, from one divided we are no longer.' And it is the aim of the mystics to return to the Unity from which we came – 'to contract our scattered spirits into their original centre, and to find ourselves where we were before we were'.[2] As the Presbyterian, Thomas Edwards, says in the course of his hostile account of Ranter teaching, in his book, *Gangraena*, it was the belief of the Ranters that 'every creature that hath life and breath is an efflux from God, and shall return to God again, to be swallowed up in Him as a drop is in the ocean'.[3]

(c) *The Divine Light in Man*

The central feature of Protestant mysticism is the doctrine of the divine Life and Light in man. In the sixteenth century there was in Germany a group of exponents of mystical religion, sometimes known as 'Spirituals' or 'Spiritual Reformers', of whom Franck and Weigel are leading representatives. Closely associated with Franck were Hans Denck, Bünderlin, and Entfelder, all of whom were at one time Anabaptists. They were united especially by the stress they laid on the inner presence of God as the Light of the soul, and the consequent need on our part to turn within that we may see it.

> The Kingdom of God [said Denck] is in you, and he who searches for it outside himself will never find it; God, the all-highest, is in the deepest abyss within us, and is waiting for us to return to Him. ... Men flee from Thee, and say they cannot find Thee; they turn their backs, and say they cannot see Thee; they stop their ears, and say they cannot hear Thee.[4]

1. R. M. Jones, *Studies in Mystical Religion*, p. 476.
2. Cohn, op. cit., p. 341.   3. ibid., p. 319.
4. R. M. Jones, *Spiritual Reformers*, pp. 24f.

Bünderlin, like the Quakers, dwells on the voice of conscience as a witness to the inner Presence, which is as near to the heart of our being as light is to the eye. Man is linked to God by his higher self, which is the image of God planted in our nature 'like the Tree of Life in Eden'.[1] Franck's teaching is the same: there is a divine element in us, which is the inmost essence of the soul.

> No man can see or know himself, unless he sees and knows, by the Light and Life that is in him, God, the eternally true Light and Life. Wherefore no man can ever know God outside of himself, outside that region where he knows himself in the ground of himself. ... He must find God in himself, and himself in God.[2]

In the seventeenth century a little book called *Light on the Candlestick* was issued by a member of the Dutch group known as the Collegiants.[3] The Collegiants were an offshoot of the Remonstrants in Holland, who broke away from the Reformed Church through their rejection of the Calvinist dogma of unconditional predestination. The Collegiants were bodies of people who met together for worship, like the Quakers in England, without a professional ministry, and practised silent waiting on God. It was a member of the Collegiant group meeting at Rynsburg – with which Spinoza was associated for some years – who wrote *Light on the Candlestick*. Its message is a call to the inward apprehension of the divine Presence.

> Without thyself, O man, thou hast no means to look for by which thou mayest know God. Thou must abide within thyself; to the Light that is in thee thou must turn thee. ... God is nearer unto every man than himself, because He penetrates the most inward and intimate parts of man, and is the Life of the inmost spirit. Mind therefore the Light that is in thee.[4]

Soon after its publication (in 1662) this little book was translated into English, and circulated as a Quaker tract.

The Quaker movement owed its origin to the work of George Fox; but the ground was prepared by the existence up and down the country of groups of people known as 'Seekers'. Prior to

1. ibid., p. 36. 2. ibid., pp. 53f.
3. The word is derived from the Latin *collegium* or gathering.
4. R. M. Jones, op. cit., pp. 130f.

the mystical experience described in the first chapter of his *Journal*, when he saw the 'endless and eternal Love of God', the attitude of Fox himself was that of a Seeker. The people so described were, like the Spiritual Reformers of the sixteenth century, dissatisfied with all existing churches and forms of religion. They were waiting for a further revelation, through which the true Church of Christ should be re-born. In Fox they found a leader to whom that revelation came, and in many places they formed the nucleus of the Society of Friends. The central message of Fox was the doctrine of the Inner Light. 'The Lord God opened to me by His invisible power', said Fox in his *Journal*, 'that every man was enlightened by the divine Light of Christ' (1: 2). The Quakers, like Franck and the other 'Spirituals', describe the divine Light by many names – 'the Word of God', 'the grace of God', 'the Spirit', 'that of God in man', 'the Christ within'. They speak of it also as 'Seed', since it is the power within us which quickens the higher life in the soul. In his statement of Quaker teaching in the *Apology for the True Christian Divinity* (1676), Robert Barclay says:

By this Seed, Grace and Word of God we understand a spiritual, heavenly, and invisible Principle in which God, as Father, Son and Holy Spirit, dwells – a measure of which divine and glorious Life is in all men as a Seed, which of its own nature draws, invites, and inclines to God [Proposition v, section 13].

It was sometimes said – as Fox records – that the Light of which the Quakers spoke was 'a created, natural light', an aspect of the nature of man in his creaturely being. William Penn, second only to Fox as a leader of the movement, declares emphatically that the Light is 'something else than the bare understanding which man hath as a rational creature'. He maintains, indeed, that the Light is 'natural' in the sense that it 'comes along with us into the world', and is the Light of our nature, of our minds and understandings, and is not the 'result of any revelation from without. ... For it is natural to man to have a supernatural Light, and for the creature to be lighted by an uncreated Light.'[1] George Keith, another leader of early Quakerism, calls the Light

1. *Primitive Christianity Revived*, Ch. 3.

'the birth of God (or Christ) in us', and distinguishes it from the soul. 'The soul of man is capable of corruption and defilement by sin, but the divine Seed and Birth is not capable of the least corruption.' It is in itself eternal and uncreated, as an aspect of the divine nature, and it 'had its being in us ever since we had a being'; but it 'is hid and wrapt up, or imprisoned in us', because of our sins.[1] The Inner Light is thus identical with the 'Spark' of the medieval mystics; and, like the 'Spark', it is the source of all that is good in our life, and in particular of the knowledge and love of God. The Quakers often refer to conscience as a witness to its universal presence. As Penn observes, it is 'the root of all true religion in man, and the good seed whence all good fruits proceed'.[2]

The divine Light in man may be regarded from two points of view – as an aspect of human nature, and as an aspect of the Life of God. It is both human and divine. The group of Anglican divines known as the Cambridge Platonists (since they were trained at Emmanuel College, Cambridge) refer to it as 'reason'. They lay great emphasis on the exercise of reason in the ordinary sense in matters of religion. (That emphasis is characteristic of Platonism.) 'I oppose not rational to spiritual', says Whichcote, 'for spiritual is most rational'; 'there is nothing so intrinsically rational as religion is, nothing that can so justify itself, nothing that hath so pure reason to recommend it as religion hath'.[3] On account of their opposition to the narrowness and dogmatism which were as marked a feature of Protestant as of Catholic orthodoxy, the Cambridge Platonists were described by their critics as 'Latitude-men' or 'Latitudinarians'. They were, indeed, pre-eminently 'Broad Churchmen'. But they were very far from being 'rationalists', like the Deists. We can only attain to the knowledge of God, John Smith insists, by union with Him. Reason is in its essence 'a light flowing from the Fountain and Father of lights', so that to deny reason is 'to deny a beam of divine Light'.[4] But man is a fallen being; and through the Fall

1. R. M. Jones, *Selections from the Children of Light*, p. 15.
2. op. cit., Ch. 1.   3. *Aphorisms*, 221, 457.
4. *The Excellency and Nobility of True Religion*, Chs. 1–2 (in *Select Discourses*).

reason as we commonly know it has lost its original purity and power. 'Pure and perfect reason' is in God alone, whose knowledge is immediate and all-embracing.[1] Yet we partake of the divine Reason, and it is possible for us, by shutting the eyes of sense, to open the eye of the soul – 'the brighter eye of our understanding', which is the intuitive knowledge of divine truth. 'This is the way to see clearly; the light of the divine world will then begin to fall upon us, . . . and in God's own Light shall we behold Him.' Reason will thus be 'raised by the mighty force of the divine Spirit into a converse with God', and so 'turned into sense', and what was before only faith 'now becomes vision'.[2]

For the Cambridge Platonists reason is in its higher aspect the vision of God. (It is the equivalent of *nous* in the Neo-Platonic sense.) In a similar way Castellio in the sixteenth century speaks of the image of God as the divine Reason which existed before the foundation of the world.[3] More commonly mystics, accepting the normal view of reason as essentially discursive, are apt to distinguish it from the divine Light. So Francis Rous (a contemporary of the Cambridge Platonists and a member of Cromwell's Council of State) says:

> The soul has two eyes – one human reason, the other far excelling that, a divine and spiritual Light. . . . By it the soul doth see spiritual things as truly as the corporal eye doth corporal things.[4]

Weigel distinguishes between reason (Vernunft), which perceives the truths of natural science, and understanding (Verstand), which sees the divine. The eye of the understanding is the spark of the soul, which is in God eternally as the uncreated essence of man. Since man in his deepest being is one with God, our knowledge of God is God's knowledge of Himself in us. And, in contradistinction to the knowledge of Nature, where the human mind plays an active part, divine or supernatural knowledge is purely passive. It is a Light which man receives from God,

1. *Of the Existence and Nature of God*, Ch. 2.
2. *The True Way or Method of attaining Divine Knowledge*, section 2.
3. R. M. Jones, op. cit., p. 101.   4. ibid., p. 268.

who is Himself the eye and light of the soul. Among the Cambridge Platonists, Peter Sterry speaks much of this deeper self, where God and man are one. 'There is [he says] a spiritual man that lies hid under the natural man as seed under the ground' – the root and bottom of the soul, which belongs to the eternal world.[1]

For William Law, in the eighteenth century, the fundamental fact in religion is the divine Life and Light in man. 'Consider the treasure thou hast within thee: the Saviour of the world, the eternal Word of God, lies hid in thee, as a spark of the divine nature which is to overcome sin and death and hell within thee, and generate the life of Heaven again in thy soul.'[2] Law lays constant emphasis on the necessity of our turning to the Inner Light – the 'Light and Spirit and Power of God in the soul'. In his teaching concerning the 'Spark' there is a certain duality, due, as it would seem, to a certain lack of clarity in his thought. On the one hand, he conceives of the Spark as 'the deepest and most central part of the soul' – 'the centre, the fund or bottom of the soul' – which is the particular seat of the divine indwelling, the root or depth in us where God is immediately present, and where alone He is to be found.[3] He speaks of it as 'the abyss of the heart, an unfathomable depth of eternity within us'.[4] On the other hand, he says that the Spark has 'come forth from God ... and therefore it is always in a state of tendency and return to God'.[5] There is here a confusion between the Spark and the soul: it is the soul which has come forth from God into a finite and temporal mode of being, and which tends to return to Him – to 'reach after the eternal Light and Spirit of God from whence it came forth'. The Spark, which is in the soul as its inmost being, has not 'come forth' from God; it is that in us which is one with God eternally. What Law is seeking to emphasize is that the divine element in our nature is there, not only as a mysterious depth to be discovered, but as a dynamic principle to guide and inspire and transform us – to quicken in us the desire of the soul for God which brings us into union with Him.

1. ibid., p. 283.   2. *The Spirit of Prayer*, I: 2 (Hobhouse, p. 81).
3. ibid.   4. *Letter* XI (Hobhouse, p. 212).
5. *The Spirit of Prayer*, I: 2 (Hobhouse, p. 85).

(d) The Birth of Christ in the Soul

Among Protestant mystics it is sometimes said that when the divine Light comes to penetrate a man's being, there is a 'birth' of God, or of Christ, within his soul. As we have seen, Eckhart speaks of union with God in such terms (see p. 250 above). The Quaker, George Keith, refers to the divine Light as itself the birth of God in man. In that sense the birth of God is a fact common to all. But Keith also speaks of 'the spiritual birth of Christ in us' as an event or a process rather than an immanent principle – an event which occurs when 'the life and spirit of Christ is united unto the soul'.[1] And it is this use of the expression which is typical. Thus Boehme says that, if we are to know God, the Son of God must become man and be born in us (see p. 273 above). Similarly John Smith says of the man who lives the unitive life: 'This life is nothing else but God's own breath within him, and an infant-Christ formed in his soul.'[2]

Protestant mystics recognize to the full the historic revelation of God in the life and death of Jesus. They interpret that revelation in terms of the love which, as Boehme says, raised Jesus 'to the highest Throne'.[3] Hans Denck declares that 'God was so completely identified in love with Christ that all the Will of God was the will of this person'.[4] So also Sterry says that in Christ the divine and the human spirit are 'twined into one'; in him 'God and man are one – one love, one life, one likeness'.[5] It is therefore the value of the life of Jesus that it shows us the way to God, so that in the outer facts of that life we have symbols of the life of the spirit which is perpetually renewed. 'God has once become flesh in Christ', says Entfelder, 'and has revealed thus the hidden God; and, as happened in a fleshly way in Mary, even so Christ must be spiritually born in us.'[6] John Everard amplifies the symbol of Christ's birth. The life of Christ can only avail for us, he says, if he is 'spiritually conceived in our hearts by the power of the Holy Ghost' – if we feel him 'stirring to be born and

1. *Selections from the Children of the Light*, p. 15.
2. *The True Way of attaining Divine Knowledge*, section 1.
3. p. 274 above.   4. R. M. Jones, op. cit., p. 25.
5. ibid., p. 284.   6. ibid., p. 42.

brought forth in us'.[1] Likewise William Law says that if we follow the desire for God when it arises in us, 'it will lead [us] to the birth of Jesus, not in a stable at Bethlehem in Judaea, but to the birth of Jesus in the dark centre of [our] own fallen soul'.[2]

What gives this symbolism its particular significance is the fact that 'Christ' (more rarely 'Jesus') is for the mystics not merely a historical person, but a universal principle – the Word, the Logos, the Son of God, the divine Light in men. For Franck and Weigel, for example, Christ is 'the Son who from all eternity put on human nature', who 'was from all eternity the complete and perfect image of God, God made "man" and the necessary bond between man and God'.[3] This 'divine humanity' is incarnate wherever men rise into union with God. It is natural therefore that they should speak of the birth of the spiritual consciousness in man as the birth of Christ in him. The Quakers use the term 'Light of Christ' interchangeably with 'the Inner Light'. Gerard Winstanley, the leader of the Digger movement in the seventeenth century, whose teaching in its religious aspect was closely akin to that of the Friends, identifies the Inner Light with 'the mighty man, Christ Jesus'. He says:

> Every one hath the Light of the Father within himself, which is the mighty man, Christ Jesus. ... Your body is His body, and now His spirit is your spirit, and so you are become one with Him and with the Father.[4]

Similarly the contemporary preacher, John Saltmarsh, says that in the new and higher revelation now dawning upon the world Christ will be 'in all His saints and people, shining in them as an inward Light and Glory for the immediate revelation of truth'.[5] Here, as with Boehme, the mysticism of the Inner Light passes into Christ-mysticism in the Pauline and Johannine sense.

The chief representative of Christ-mysticism among Protestants is Caspar Schwenckfeld (d. 1561), the Silesian reformer. In

---

1. ibid., p. 244.   2. *The Spirit of Prayer*, I: 2 (Hobhouse, p. 104).
3. Koyré, *Mystiques, Spirituels, Alchimistes*, pp. 91f.
4. R. M. Jones, *Studies in Mystical Religion*, p. 497.
5. ibid., p. 486.

his early life Schwenckfeld was profoundly influenced by Luther, and this influence affected his developed teaching far more than was the case with the other 'Spirituals'. Yet he was furiously denounced by Luther and his supporters for his heresies. The centre of his doctrine was his conception of the celestial body or 'spiritual flesh' of Christ. He rejected the traditional notion of the dual nature of Christ as at once human and divine. Christ, he held, was altogether divine and uncreated; he was from all eternity the God-man, and as such he possessed a body formed of 'spiritual flesh'. He lived in this body on earth, and possesses it in his exalted life in Heaven. This belief was actually held by most of the Anabaptists and by other 'Spirituals', like Weigel. It was derived from the Gnostics. Schwenckfeld taught, like Luther and Calvin, although on a different basis, that man is totally corrupt by nature – as a created, and therefore finite and imperfect, being. To be saved, we must be delivered from our creaturely nature; we must receive into ourselves 'a divine and spiritual life, having its source in the Being of God, and mediated to the soul by the living, inward-working flesh and blood of Jesus Christ'.[1] Salvation thus comes to man only from Jesus Christ. In his exalted life Christ unites himself inwardly with the souls of men, and imparts to them his own divinity. Men are mystically united with Christ by faith. For Schwenckfeld, faith has itself a mystical significance. It is not a merely human act of trust and self-giving. It is (in his own words) 'a penetrating stream of light flowing out from the central divine Light and fire which is God Himself, into our hearts'; it is 'an emanation from the eternal Life of God, and is of the same essence and substance as God Himself'.[2]

For Protestant mystics generally 'Christ' is less closely identified with the historical or the exalted Jesus than for Schwenckfeld. For William Law, for instance, 'Christ' is the divine Life in the soul – the Son or Word of God incarnate in Jesus, but manifested also wherever men turn to God in faith and love. It is true that the life of Jesus, as the incarnate Son, is the perfect expression of the Word, so that 'all our salvation consists in the

1. R. M. Jones, *Spiritual Reformers*, p. 71.
2. ibid., pp. 77f.

manifestation of the nature, life, and spirit of Jesus Christ in our inward new man', and we are to 'do all in a desire of union with Christ'.[1] But 'Christ' is a universal principle, 'the life and light and holiness of every creature that is holy'.[2] And it is the uprising of that principle within us which is 'the birth of Christ' in our souls.

(e) Sin and Salvation; Deification; the Last Things

Protestant, like Catholic, mystics are by no means blind to the fact of sin. The sense of the divine Life and Light in man does not in any way serve to obscure for them the darker phases of human experience. We have seen how great a part is played by the problem of evil in the thought of Boehme, and it is true of Protestant mystics generally that they are acutely aware of the problem. The case of George Fox is typical. He was 'ravished with the sense of the Love of God', but he was also 'under great suffering in his spirit' because of men's cruelty and inhumanity to their fellows. The attitude of mystics to the fact of evil is finely summed up in his words:

I saw that there was an ocean of darkness and death; but an infinite Ocean of light and love, which flowed over the ocean of darkness.[3]

George Keith says, as we have seen, that the divine element in man is 'hid and wrapt up or imprisoned in us' because of sin (see p. 281 above). It is, in fact, the very nature of sin for the mystics that it separates us from God.

The kingdom of self [says Law] is the Fall of man or the great apostasy from the life of God in the soul; and every one that lives unto self is still under the Fall and great apostasy from God.[4]

For the mystics, the Fall, like the drama of redemption, is a symbol of experience, but it is also an event. For Paracelsus, and through him for Boehme, and so for Law, it was the Fall of Lucifer which brought about the existence of the world as we

1. loc. cit. (Hobhouse, p. 76).
2. *The Spirit of Love*, I (Hobhouse, p. 143).
3. *Journal*, I: 1.
4. *The Spirit of Prayer*, I: 2 (Hobhouse, p. 94).

know it, with its hard materiality, its separation and mutual exclusiveness of objects and individuals. The Fall is essentially a lapse from unity and interpenetration.[1] The mystics naturally lay very great stress on the fact of evil and its manifestation in human life.

All sin, death, damnation and hell [says Law] is nothing but this kingdom of self, or the various operations of self-love, self-esteem and self-seeking, which separate the soul from God.[2]

Yet, with their recognition of the universal presence of the divine Light in man, they reject the Lutheran and Calvinist dogma of total corruption. It is true that the kingdom of self is also universal. John Smith declares that 'the spirit of apostasy is lodged in all men's natures'; malice, revenge, pride, hatred, self-will are the expression of 'a hellish and diabolical nature seated in the minds of men'.[3] But these things pertain only to the temporal aspect of human nature, not to the 'holy self' or the 'celestial Light', which abides in the inmost depths of our being. To this conception Schwenckfeld's teaching appears to offer an exception. For Schwenckfeld taught that as a created being man is totally corrupt by nature. But he also maintained that in his essential being man is not a creature; he is an uncreated and eternal form of the manifestation of God.

The real difference between Schwenckfeld and the other 'Spirituals', like Franck and Weigel, lies in his understanding of salvation as a wholly supernatural event. He accepted Luther's doctrine of predestination and his denial of human freedom: if man is to be saved, it can only be through the gift of faith, conceived as a divinizing power flowing in upon us from the Life of God. Franck and Weigel, on the other hand, emphasize the fact of freedom. Of course, they do not think of salvation in purely moralistic terms. It is man's part to renounce his 'Adamic' self, that God, or the inner Christ, may be born within him. It may be said that we are saved by grace alone; but the grace that trans-

1. This is the view taught in the Kabbalah. It has evident Gnostic affinities.
2. loc. cit. (p. 92).
3. *A Christian's Conflicts and Conquests*, Ch. 3.

forms us and unites us with God is itself the inner Christ, the divine Light within us, with which we are one in the depths of our being. For Franck and Weigel, sin exists for man alone, and not for God. Sin is the attempt of the finite being to separate itself from God. By the nature of the case there can be no such separation in reality. As an act of the created will sin possesses a relative truth; but it cannot affect man's essential being, or destroy his freedom. It is therefore possible for man to abandon self, to penetrate to his deeper being, and so to be united with God.

The necessity of self-abandonment is common to the mystics. As we have seen with Boehme, Protestants are apt to state the negative way in its ethical aspect as strongly as any Catholics.

All that thou callest 'I' [says John Everard], all that selfness, all that propriety that thou hast taken to thyself, whatsoever creates in us I-ness and self-ness, must be brought to nothing.[1]

Self must be renounced, as Law emphasizes, that God may be all-in-all in us.

Where this All of God is truly known and felt in any creature, there its whole breath and spirit is a fire of love. ... All that is in God is opened in the creature, it is united with God, and has the life of God manifested in it.[2]

By the denial of self, John Smith affirms:

The soul loves itself in God, and lives in the possession not so much of its own being as of the Divinity; desiring only to be great in God, to glory in His Light, and to spread itself in His fulness ... triumphing in nothing more than in its own nothingness and in the all-ness of the Divinity.[3]

For the mystics, salvation is the birth of Christ in the soul or union with God. Through the life-giving power of faith, Schwenck-feld taught, the soul is saved from its creaturely being; it participates in the 'heavenly flesh' of Christ; it is progressively transformed and spiritualized; it is restored, in Christ, to its original

1. R. M. Jones, op. cit., p. 249.   2. loc. cit. (Hobhouse, pp. 101f.).
3. *The Excellency and Nobleness of True Religion*, Ch. 2.

unity with God. For Franck and Weigel also, although the process of salvation is differently conceived, it has the same objective. Through the birth of Christ within him, man is brought back into that unity with the divine Life which was his before the Fall. It is Christ born in us who redeems us, not Christ given for us on the Cross as an objective sacrifice. That is the teaching of Law.

> Christ given for us is neither more nor less than Christ given unto us. He is in no other sense our full, perfect and sufficient atonement than as His nature and spirit are born and formed in us.[1]

Union with God thus becomes the very essence of living religion. As John Smith puts it:

> This is the very soul and essence of true religion, to unite the soul in the nearest intimacy and conjunction with God. . . . The spirit of a good man is always drinking in fountain-goodness, and fills itself more and more, till it is filled with all the fulness of God.[2]

Union with God involves deification. Hans Denck declares that the Inner Word, which dwells in all, is always seeking to unite us with the Father. 'The Word', he adds, 'was in human beings for this purpose, that it might divinize them, as happens to all the elect.'[3] Salvation, as John Smith says, 'is nothing else but a true participation of the divine nature'; a good man becomes 'the tabernacle of God wherein the divine Shechinah does rest'.[4] He is freed from the self-seeking and self-love which 'imprison the soul and confine it to its own home'; he shares the Life of God, who is 'that infinite fulness that fills all in all'. Living wholly to God, and living the life of God, 'in a sober sense a man becomes deified', the soul and God being united together 'in the unity of affections, will, and end'.[5] In his *Centuries of Meditation*, Thomas Traherne, the seventeenth-century Anglican poet and mystic, dwells on the same thought. In its true nature, Traherne maintains, the soul of man shares the infinity of God; and by the love which unites us to Him we may participate in

---

1. *The Spirit of Love*, II: 1 (Hobhouse, p. 163).   2. loc. cit.
3. *Spiritual and Anabaptist Writers* (edited by G. H. Williams), p. 101.
4. op. cit., Ch. 5.   5. ibid., Chs. 4, 3.

His universal Life. 'That which does love wisely and truly ...
is the shining light and temple of Eternity and one spirit with the
Holy Ghost.'[1] Thus we may become in act what we are in power.

> You are to remember always the unsearchable extent and illimited
> greatness of your own soul. ... Because it is the house of God, a living
> temple and a glorious throne of the Blessed Trinity ... yea, a person
> that in union and communion with God is to see Eternity, to fill His
> omnipresence, to possess His greatness.[2]

It is our destiny 'to sit in the Throne of God'. But 'to sit in the
Throne of God' is to transcend the limitations of our finite and
temporal being.

> To sit in the Throne of God is to inhabit Eternity. ... God's Throne
> is His Omnipresence, and that is infinite. ... The Omnipresence and
> the Eternity of God are our Throne, wherein we are to reign for ever-
> more.[3]

Reference has been made above to the Ranters, whose teaching
closely resembles that of the medieval Brethren of the Free
Spirit.[4] According to Thomas Edwards, the Ranters revived the
notion of three stages of revelation, the stage now beginning being
that of the Holy Spirit, who rules men from within.[5] It is, of
course, everywhere the belief of the mystics that it is possible for
men to live by the Inner Light. Jacob Bauthumley was expressing
the universal aspiration of the mystics when he said that he sought
'to live no other life than what Christ lives spiritually in me'.[6]
The belief attributed to the Ranters by the contemporary writer,
John Holland, that they were 'living in God, and God in them',[7]
was common ground. To live a God-centred life is naturally to
transcend external rules and ordinances. According to Winstanley, 'outward ordinances' are forms and customs which pass
away when men enter the stage of spiritual religion.[8] But to
transcend external forms and rules is not to set aside the obligations of moral conduct or to ignore the possibility of sin. It is
true that the mystics sometimes maintain that it is possible in this

1. *Centuries of Meditations*, II: 50.   2. ibid., II: 92.
3. ibid., IV: 72.   4. See pp. 277f. above.
5. Cohn, op. cit., p. 319.   6. ibid., p. 338.
7. ibid., p. 323.   8. R. M. Jones, *Studies in Mystical Religion*, p. 498.

life to attain perfection. That was the teaching of George Fox. In a discussion with a priest of the Church of England who denied such a possibility, 'I told him [Fox says] there is a perfection in Christ, above Adam and beyond falling, and that it was the work of the ministers of Christ to present every man perfect in Christ.'[1] Men are 'renewed by Christ [Fox says in an *Epistle to Friends*] into the image of God which man was in before he fell'.[2] The possibility of perfection was inculcated also in the mystical movement known as the Family of Love, which was founded in Holland in the early sixteenth century by Henry Nicholas. (The movement was brought to England about 1550, and flourished here in the seventeenth century.) Nicholas says: 'God anointed me with His godly Being, manned Himself with me, and godded me with Him to a living tabernacle or house for His dwelling and a seat of His Christ'[3]; and it is the essence of his teaching that men may be incorporated into the Life of God, and so become 'godded' in union with Christ. The Familists held that it was possible for men to attain a state of perfect obedience to the Inner Light. Yet Nicholas warned his followers not to take it for granted that they had reached this condition, but 'to look steadily for the increase of God [within them], abiding steadfast in the service of love'.[4] The Familists were accused by their orthodox opponents of antinomianism and immoral conduct; and it is possible that there was a certain basis for the charge in the behaviour of some of their adherents, but it is certainly not true of the movement as a whole. Nicholas laid the greatest emphasis on the need of a Christian righteousness. Like the Collegiants, he followed the great majority of the Anabaptists in rejecting war and the taking of oaths, thus anticipating Fox and the Friends. He explicitly repudiated the antinomian position.

The law [he said] is not abolished; it is fulfilled in love. ... No one ever transcends righteousness, for the entire work of God towards salvation has been making for the fruits of righteousness.[5]

It was distinctive of the Ranters, among Protestant mystics, that many of them rejected the very idea of sin, save as a purely

1. *Journal*, II: 6.   2. ibid., II: 7.
3. R. M. Jones, op. cit., p. 439, note 2.
4. ibid., p. 440.   5. ibid., p. 436.

personal or subjective thing. In the year 1650 an Ordinance was passed by Parliament against their 'blasphemous and execrable opinions'. Among these is the belief 'that there is no such thing really and truly as unrighteousness, unholiness or sin, but as a man or woman judgeth thereof'.[1] Not all Ranters adopted this view. Bauthumley in his book, *The Light and Dark Sides of God*, says that sin represents 'the dark side of God, which is a mere privation of light'. God 'appears more gloriously' in goodness than in wrong-doing, but 'the wrath of man praises God as well as his love and meekness'. Sin is in itself 'a nullity' (as Neo-Platonists in general held), since God alone truly is. God must therefore not be regarded as its Author, and it does not fall within His decree. At the same time, he says inconsistently: 'All things are as that supreme Will acts, and brings them forth.' He adds that it is not his intention 'to countenance any unseemly act or evil in any man'.[2] Other Ranters held a different position. Laurence Clarkson, for example, says in his autobiography *The Lost Sheep Found* (written after he had ceased to be a Ranter) that as a Ranter he had practised sexual promiscuity with no qualms of conscience.[3] All things, he taught in his tract *The Single Eye*, are done by God, so that 'there is no act whatsoever that is impure in God, or sinful with or before God. ... Sin hath its conception only in the imagination. ... If thou judge not thyself, thou shalt not be judged.'[4]

Like the Brethren of the Free Spirit, the Ranters set aside traditional beliefs concerning the Last Things. Jacob Bauthumley speaks of Heaven as a state of soul.

Then men are in Heaven, or Heaven in men, when God appears in His glorious and pure manifestations of Himself, in love and grace, in peace and rest in the spirit. ... I find that where God dwells, and is come, and hath taken men up, and wrapped them in His Spirit, there is a new Heaven and a new Earth, and all the Heaven I look to enjoy is to have my earthly and dark apprehensions of God to cease, and to live no other life than what Christ spiritually lives in me.[5]

1. Cohn, op. cit., p. 326.   2. ibid., pp. 338f.
3. See Fox's reference to the Ranters at Southampton in his *Journal* (II: 2).
4. Cohn, op. cit., pp. 349–51.   5. Cohn, op. cit., p. 338.

He looks to a final consummation when this shall be a universal experience, and God shall be all in all.

As all things had their subsistence and being in God, before they were ever manifested in the world of creatures; so in the end whatsoever is of God ... they shall all be rapt up into God again.[1]

So Thomas Edwards records among the tenets of the Ranters the belief that 'there shall be a general restoration, wherein all men shall be reconciled to God and saved'.[2]

Among Protestant mystics, apart from the Ranters, it is only in the writings of William Law that we have an explicit formulation of this belief. Law himself at first accepted the traditional doctrine of everlasting Hell, although he extended the scope of salvation to include the pious heathen. But in his later mystical writings he came to express a radically different view. In *The Spirit of Love* he says that suffering is necessary as a means of purifying the soul and saving it from sin, and that this redemptive suffering will continue after death[3] – as in the Catholic conception of Purgatory. But he does not limit Purgatory, as Catholics do, to those who are already saved. Nothing can defeat the final Purpose of God. 'All that is fallen in Adam into death must rise and return into a unity of an eternal life in God.'[4] The same outlook is implied in the teaching of Paracelsus. As we have seen, Paracelsus regarded the physical universe as the outcome of the Fall. He held that in course of time the world, with its conflict of forces, will inevitably perish, and earthly life will pass away. The world will be replaced by a spiritualized or deified universe, in which all things will be transformed and perfected. The spiritual body which Christ assumed after the Resurrection is a symbol of this regenerated world. In such a universe there could be no place for an everlasting Hell.

The logic of the doctrines of Franck, Weigel, and Schwenckfeld is the same. But there is no indication in their writings that they drew the inference to which reason naturally led. Boehme certainly did not. In his dialogue *Of Heaven and Hell* he makes his belief clear that Hell remains, along with Heaven, in the spiritual

1. ibid., pp. 339f.   2. ibid., p. 319.
3. *The Spirit of Love*, ii: 2.   4. ibid., ii: 3.

world. It is true that for the Protestant mystics both Heaven and Hell are states of soul, not places in a spatial sense. There is no 'place', as they insist, in the world of spirit. Heaven, says Boehme in the dialogue, is 'the turning in of the will into the love of God'. The soul which is one with God 'is itself the very Heaven of God, wherein He dwells'. Likewise the soul in which the divine Light does not shine 'carries about a Hell within itself'.

That was the teaching also of the Cambridge Platonists. 'Hell's fuel', says Whichcote, 'is the guilt of a man's conscience', while 'Heaven lies in an inward reconciliation to the nature of God. So that both Hell and Heaven have their foundation within men.'[1] John Smith speaks of the absurdity of supposing – as some of the Quietists did – that a man who loves God could be content to suffer the woes of Hell, if such should be the Will of God. 'The most real Hell' is a state of self-love, pride, and arrogancy against God, and to love God and seek to be united with Him is 'the most substantial Heaven'.[2]

Thomas Traherne seeks to break down the dualism which divides Heaven and earth. He stresses the 'enjoyment of the world', which is the keynote of his thought, because he sees the world as 'the place of angels and the Gate of Heaven'.[3] We 'are in Heaven everywhere', if we 'live in God'.[4] It should be our aim to 'piece this life with the life of Heaven, and to see it as one with all Eternity, a part of it, a life within it'.[5]

(f) The Universality of the Divine Light; its Relation to the Church and to Scripture

A distinctive feature of Protestant mysticism is the stress which is laid by many of its exponents on the universality of the divine Light. Denck speaks of the witness of the Spirit in heathens and Jews. Franck finds divine revelation in the works of Cicero, Seneca, Plato, Plotinus. The same attitude is typical of the Cambridge Platonists. Fox appealed to the fact of conscience in the American Indians as a proof of the universal presence of the Inner Light. Law rejoiced in the fact that 'so many eminent

1. R. M. Jones, *Spiritual Reformers*, p. 302.
2. *The Excellency and Nobleness of True Religion*, Ch. 7.
3. op. cit., I: 31.　　4. ibid., IV: 38.　　5. ibid., IV: 93.

spirits have appeared in so many parts of the heathen world. These were apostles of a Christ within.'[1] The way of salvation, he insists, is everywhere the same – 'the desire of the soul turned to God' – and the awakening of that desire in non-Christians is an evidence of the truth that 'the new birth in Christ is found in those who never heard of his name'.[2]

This outlook naturally led to an enlarged conception of the Church. For Law 'the true Church of God, where the life of God is found and lived,' exists wherever love, which is 'the Christ of God', possesses and rules the soul.[3] It was this vision of the universal Church which was characteristic of the 'Spirituals' of the sixteenth century. For Weigel, the universal Church is made up of all faithful souls, and includes Jews, Turks, and pagans.

I believe [says Franck] in a holy, Christ-like Church, a fellowship of saints, and I hold as my brothers all men who belong to Christ among all sects, faiths, and peoples scattered throughout the whole world.[4]

Franck, like the other 'Spirituals', like Boehme and the Quakers, was highly critical of all existing Churches. He held that since the death of the Apostles the Church of Christ no longer existed as an institution. He did not seek to found a new organization, but only to serve the invisible Church of the Spirit. The same thing is true of most of the 'Spirituals'. Schwenckfeld defined the Church as 'the entire community of the children of God'.[5] He sought, however, to promote the formation of groups of 'spiritual Christians', who shared his faith. Other Protestant mystics also formed groups of like-minded souls, such as the Collegiants in Holland and the Society of Friends in England. The Family of Love, founded by Henry Nicholas in Amsterdam, is another example. Nicholas claimed, indeed, that the Family of Love was the only true Church.

Protestant mystics, like Catholic, acknowledged the authority of Scripture. But they saw that Scriptural authority is secondary: the primary and essential fact is the Inner Word.

1. *The Spirit of Prayer*, I: 2 (Hobhouse, p. 87).
2. ibid. (Hobhouse, p. 103).
3. op. cit., II: 1 (Hobhouse, p. 110).
4. R. M. Jones, op. cit., p. 52.   5. ibid., p. 78.

The Holy Scriptures [said Hans Denck] I consider above every human treasure, but not so high as the Word of God which is living, powerful, and eternal.[1]

It is the virtue of the Scriptures that they point us to the Inner Word. So Law declared that it is the function of Scripture to lead us to the eternal Word which is 'the light, life, and salvation of man'. He asks:

How is it possible more to exalt the letter of Scripture than by owning it to be a true outward, verbal direction to the one only true light and salvation of man?[2]

Franck insists on the insufficiency of the written word. Taken literally, the Bible contains all manner of mistakes and contradictions. As a written word, it gives rise to conflicting interpretations, and so splits the Church into fragments. What we have to do is to look to the Inner Word, which gives us the true, spiritual meaning of Scripture. Schwenckfeld, similarly, declares:

To understand the Scripture, a man must become a new man, a man of God; he must be in Christ, who gave forth the Scriptures.[3]

The Quakers would not allow the Scriptures to be called the Word of God. Fox was once moved to interrupt a preacher at Nottingham who was speaking on the text 'We have a more sure word of prophecy', and who 'told the people that this was the Scriptures, by which they were to try all doctrines, religions, and opinions'. Fox was led to cry: 'O no, it is not the Scriptures,' and to say that it was 'the Holy Spirit, by which the holy men of God gave forth the Scriptures, whereby opinions, religions, and judgements were to be tried'.[4] The final authority is the Inner Light which ever shines in the soul. 'I saw,' said Fox, 'in that Light and Spirit which was before the Scriptures were given forth.'[5]

It was particularly on this ground of the supreme authority of the divine Light in the soul that Fox and his followers were

1. ibid., p. 28.
2. *The Spirit of Love*, III (Hobhouse, p. 184).
3. R. M. Jones, op. cit., p. 74.
4. *Journal*, I: 3.   5. ibid., I: 2.

brought into conflict with the prevailing Calvinism. The Familists also were denounced for proclaiming this principle. Some years before the incident recorded by Fox (which occurred in 1649) John Etherington, a leading Familist teacher in London, was attacked in a sermon by Stephen Denison at St Paul's on the ground, among others, that he taught that men may be 'inspired with light and illumination as far as ever Paul or any of the prophets were', and that the Spirit is above Scripture.[1]

It is clear from what has been said in the foregoing pages that Protestant mystics are at one with Catholic mystics in their essential outlook. There was, however, naturally among them a greater freedom and boldness of thought, especially among the 'Spirituals' of the sixteenth century, with their Anabaptist and Gnostic affinities. As Protestants, they were freer than the Catholics to set aside elements in Church tradition which conflicted with their insight. Thus Boehme and Law could reject explicitly the doctrine of creation out of nothing; Law could develop a new conception of the Atonement and the belief in the final salvation of all men. While Christian mystics everywhere agree in affirming the presence of the divine Light in all souls, it is only among Protestants that we find an explicit recognition of the fact that it transcends all credal barriers, and that all who are guided and inspired by the Light form a universal fellowship which constitutes the true, invisible Church. And it is only among Protestants that the divine Light is acknowledged as the final authority in religion. The mystics were, indeed, far from denying the authority of Scripture, rightly understood. The Bible was to them as a whole a divine revelation. But they had the insight to see, on the basis of their own experience, that revelation cannot be confined to its pages. They knew that the Light which had shone in inspired men of old illuminated them; and they would not subordinate their vision to any written record. They were thus pioneers of an enlightenment and an understanding which far transcend the limitations of their thought.

1. R. M. Jones, *Studies in Mystical Religion*, p. 446.

CHAPTER 8

Islamic Mysticism

I. THE GROWTH OF SUFISM

THE growth of Islamic mysticism (or Sufism) is a significant illustration of the strength of the mystical tendency in religion. On the face of it, the religion of Mohammed can scarcely be regarded as of itself providing fruitful soil for the growth of that tendency. Yet within a comparatively short time after the Prophet's death a movement arose among his followers which has given birth to some of the greatest of the mystics. There is no doubt that Christian and Neo-Platonic influences played an important part in the development of Sufism. But the starting-point lay in the nature of Islamic piety. The Sufis have traditionally looked upon Mohammed himself as the greatest of all mystics. That is not a view which critical study sustains. There is no question in his own life and teaching of any such experience as union with God. The gulf that divides man from God in his outlook is too great to admit of any such possibility. At the same time, there are elements in his attitude and teaching which contain the germ of a mystical development. Mohammed believed himself to be the recipient of a divine revelation. God (he taught) is 'nearer to man than his neck-vein'; He is 'the light of the heavens and the earth'; wherever we turn, there is His Face, which abides, resplendent with majesty and glory, when all on earth shall pass away. Mohammed laid the greatest stress on the need of personal surrender and submission to God and on the practice of prayer. It is necessary, according to his teaching, not only to offer prescribed acts of prayer at stated times, but to remember God continually.

It was these elements in the religion of the Prophet which formed the basis for the development of a mystical piety. In its initial stages Sufism was primarily an other-worldly and quietist, rather than a definitely mystical, movement. It represented a reaction against the worldliness and luxury and the external piety of the period which followed the great Muslim conquests. The Sufis derived their name from the costume of white wool (*suf*) which they wore – in imitation, most probably, of Christian monks. 'Because of their clothes and manner of life,' says an early writer, 'they are called Sufis, for they did not put on raiment soft to touch or beautiful to behold; they only clothed themselves in order to hide their nakedness, contenting themselves with rough haircloth and coarse wool.'[1] Without any common organization, the Sufis lived a life of poverty and self-discipline, devoting themselves to meditation and prayer, and trusting in all things to the providential care of God. Their meditation took the form of the continuous chanting of such words as 'Allah! Allah!' It was their central aspiration to surrender themselves wholly to God, and for some of them the attitude of trust in God (tawakkul) which this involved carried with it a quietism so extreme that they would not seek for food or work for wages or take medicine. The story is told of one who fell into the Tigris. A man on the bank, seeing that he could not swim, cried out: 'Shall I tell someone to bring you ashore?' 'No,' he said. 'Then do you wish to be drowned?' Again the reply was: 'No.' 'What, then, do you wish?' 'God's will be done,' was the answer, 'what have I to do with wishing?'[2] The extreme asceticism of the early Sufis is illustrated by a story of al-Fudail. It is said that when one day he kissed his young child, the child rebuked him. 'Father, do you love me?' he asked. 'Yes,' the Sufi said. 'Do you love God?' 'Yes.' 'How many hearts have you?' 'One.' 'Then how can you love two with one heart?' We are told that al-Fudail saw that his child's reasoning was right; he ceased henceforth to cherish human affection, and gave his whole heart to God.[3]

Among the ascetics there emerged in course of time a specifically mystical religion. It is said that Ibrahim ben Adham, the prince of Balkh, who abandoned his life in the world, and withdrew to the desert, was taught the true inner knowledge of God by a Christian monk, Father Simeon.

1. Al-Kalabadhi, *The Doctrine of the Sufis* (translated by A. J. Arberry), p. 6; Al-Kalabadhi lived in the tenth century.
2. R. A. Nicholson, *The Mystics of Islam*, p. 41.
3. ibid., p. 109.

Spurn the world [said Ibrahim], for love of the world makes a man deaf and blind, and enslaves him. ... Devote thyself to God with a penitent heart and an undoubting resolve.[1]

Ibrahim belongs to the eighth century. In the previous century lived Hasan al-Basri, a famous preacher. In his sermons he dwelt much on the wrath of God, after the fashion of Mohammed. The motive-force of the religion which he proclaimed was largely fear of the consequences of sin. It is said that once he was told of a man who was destined to spend a thousand years in Hell, but in the end would be saved. (It was commonly believed that all true Muslims would eventually be delivered from the pains of Hell.) When Hasan heard this he wept, and cried: 'Would that I might be like that man!'[2] But his religion had a deeper and more positive aspect. The relation of God to the soul as he conceived it was not merely that of a Judge, nor was it simply that of an external Deliverer through whose mercy men might be saved.

When My servant becomes altogether occupied with Me [God says, as he imagines], then I make his happiness and his delight consist in remembrance of Me, and when I have made his happiness and delight consist in that remembrance, he desires Me, and I desire him; and when he desires Me, and I desire him, I raise the veils between Me and him and I become manifest before his eyes.[3]

In such words as these we have the keynote of the piety which came increasingly to characterize the Sufis. Their religion became centred in the quest of the soul for God, which found its fulfilment in the breaking down of the barriers that divide men from Him.

An outstanding figure among the early Sufis was the woman saint, Rabi'a, who was born a few years before the death of Hasan al-Basra (which occurred in 728 A.D.).[4] Rabi'a's attitude, like that of the early Sufis in general, was marked by extreme other-worldliness. It is said that she was once asked: 'Whence have you come?' She replied: 'From that world.' 'Whither are

1. A. J. Arberry, *Sufism*, p. 38.
2. Margaret Smith, *Early Mysticism in the Near and Middle East*, p. 175.
3. ibid., p. 177.
4. The account of Rabi'a's attitude and teaching which follows is based on Margaret Smith's work *Rabi'a the Mystic*.

you going?' 'To that world.' 'What are you doing in this world?'
'I am sorrowing.' 'In what way?' 'I am eating the bread of this
world, and doing the work of that world.' In contrast to the
attitude of the later Sufis, who saw the divine Beauty shining
through the veil of outer things, Rabi'a appears to have paid no
regard to the beauty of Nature. One evening in spring her servant
bade her: 'Come out to behold the works of God.' 'Come you
inside [she rejoined], that you may behold their Maker. Contemplation of the Maker has turned me aside from contemplating
what He has made.' For Rabi'a, devotion to God carried with it
the renunciation of earthly ties. It is said that several times her
hand was sought in marriage by fellow-Sufis. (Asceticism did not
normally involve celibacy for the Sufis.) In one instance she is
said to have replied: 'My existence is in God and I am altogether
His. I am in the shadow of His command. The marriage contract
must be sought for from Him, not from me.' Dying to self and
surrender to God meant for her a quietistic resignation to sickness and suffering. She refused to pray for relief. 'Do you not
know', she said, 'who it is that wills this suffering for me? ...
It is not well to oppose one's Beloved. That should be willed
which He wills.'

In one direction the Sufis, from the beginning, emphasized
the need of active endeavour – in the inner life of the spirit.
Rabi'a was marked by a constant sense of sin, which is said to
have found expression in continual weeping. 'Why do you weep
like this?' someone asked her. 'I fear [she said] that I may be cut
off from Him to whom I am accustomed, and that at the hour
of death a voice may say that I am not worthy.' Yet in her piety,
fear was something altogether secondary. The dread of Hell was
part of her religious heritage rather than a living aspect of her
own experience. What characterized her above all else was her
passion for God. Her religious life was not merely – as we might
suppose from the story of her constant weeping – one of contrition for sin. It was also one of joy. In her prayers we come again
and again on the note of thanksgiving. She expresses gratitude
even for suffering and adversity, but above all she rejoices in the
consciousness of the divine Presence. 'Thou art my joy [she
cries to God], firmly established within me.'

In the development of Sufism Rabi'a is chiefly notable for the doctrine of pure or disinterested love – the love of God for Himself – which played a great part in the thought and experience of the later mystics. She saw the insufficiency of such motives as the fear of Hell and the desire of Paradise.

I have not served God [she said] from fear of Hell, for I should be like a wretched hireling, if I did it from fear; nor from love of Paradise, for I should be a bad servant, if I served for the sake of what was given; but I served Him only for love of Him and desire for Him.

A classic illustration of her attitude is found in the words of her famous prayer:

O my Lord, if I worship Thee from fear of Hell, burn me in Hell; and if I worship Thee from hope of Paradise, exclude me from Paradise; but if I worship Thee for Thy own sake, then withhold not from me Thy eternal Beauty.

For Rabi'a, as for the later Muslim mystics, love was the way to the divine vision which was the goal of her quest. In a passage sometimes attributed to her, she speaks of two types of love.

I have loved Thee with two loves, a selfish love and a love that is worthy of Thee. As for the love which is selfish, I occupy myself therein with remembrance of Thee to the exclusion of all others; as for that which is worthy of Thee, therein Thou raisest the veil that I may see Thee.

Al-Ghazzali remarks, in his exposition of these words, 'She meant by selfish love the love of God for His favour and grace bestowed and for temporal happiness, and by the love worthy of Him the love of His Beauty which was revealed to her'.

What was characteristic of Rabi'a was the experience of God and the pursuit of a way of life centred in that experience rather than the development of any distinctive interpretation or philosophy. None the less, it is evident that, with her doctrine of disinterested love and her conception of the goal of life as union with God, her attitude involved a profound modification of traditional Islamic teaching. Among the later Sufis the change became more fundamental and far-reaching. Yet, however far they may have departed from Islamic orthodoxy, the Sufis in general claim to adhere closely to the teaching of the Koran, which for all Muslims represents a divine and infallible revelation of truth. Along with the words of the Koran they are apt to cite the so-called 'Traditions' (Hadith) – supposed sayings of the Prophet and incidents concerning him collected in later centuries, but claiming to rest, through a chain of witnesses, on the authority of one or other of his Companions. Actually many of the 'Traditions' to which the Sufis appeal are rejected by the best-known Muslim authorities. Sufi teachers were often accused of heresy; some were condemned – their books were burnt, they were imprisoned, a few suffered martyrdom. Yet nearly all of them claimed that their teaching was in full accord with the original revelation.

It is true that some teachers have adopted a far more radical position. Afifuddin al-Tilimsani, the author of a commentary on the writings of the tenth century Egyptian Sufi, Niffari, declared that the whole Koran is polytheism. Abu Sa'id, a Persian mystic of the tenth and eleventh centuries, whose teaching exercised considerable influence, adopted a less extreme attitude, which was yet far freer and more liberal than that of the majority of Sufi authorities. He did not reject the inspiration of the Koran, but he denied that it is to be regarded as a final and absolute standard of truth. While the Sufis generally looked upon the inner light of the soul as serving to interpret the written revelation, for him the inner light possesses the authority to make new laws. 'Every moment [he said] there comes a messenger from God to the hearts of his servants.'[1] In accordance with this teaching, Abu Sa'id regarded the religious law incumbent on Muslims as a thing which the man who has entered into union with God might dispense with. He is said to have forbidden his disciples to perform the pilgrimage to Mecca.

At a later time a similar attitude was adopted by many of the 'saints' of the dervish orders who exercised supreme authority over particular bands of devotees. At certain times in the history of the movement a pronounced tendency to antinomianism has asserted itself, particularly during its decadence from the close of the Middle Ages. 'The popular "saints" exhibited the utmost

1. R. A. Nicholson, *Studies in Islamic Mysticism*, p. 59.

contempt for the ritual obligations of Islam, so that they made a boast of not performing the prayers.'[1]

In contradistinction to such tendencies, the main body of Sufi teaching adhered closely to the traditions of Islam; and it is with the main body of Sufi teaching that we are primarily concerned. Even there we find wide differences of outlook. Sufism has not stood for a single, uniform mode of thought; it includes many differing shades of belief. In the pages that follow an attempt will be made to sum up the main trends of Sufi teaching in relation to (a) the nature of God and His relation to the universe, (b) the nature of man, (c) the mystic way, and (d) the goal to which that way is held to lead.

II. MAIN TRENDS OF SUFI TEACHING

(a) God and the Universe

In the development of Sufi teaching an important step was taken when the principle of immediate intuitive knowledge of God implicit in the experience of the early mystics was explicitly recognized in its distinction from intellectual or traditional knowledge. 'Real knowledge', said Dhu al-Nun, an Egyptian Sufi of the ninth century, 'is God's illumination of the heart with the pure radiance of knowledge.'[2] In this experience of illumination, the distinction between subject and object is transcended; the barrier between man and God is done away. The knowledge of God involves oneness with Him; and that oneness becomes the central fact in life. The mystic loses the consciousness of separate existence; he knows henceforth that his life is the life of God living and acting in him.

They that know God [says Dhu al-Nun] are not themselves, and subsist not through themselves, but in so far as they are themselves, they subsist through God. They move as God causes them to move, and their words are the words of God which roll upon their tongues, and their sight is the sight of God which has entered their eyes.[3]

1. A. J. Arberry, *Sufism*, p. 120.
2. Quoted by R. A. Nicholson in *The Idea of Personality in Sufism*, p. 10.
3. ibid.

It is this experience of life in God which is the centre of Sufi religion and the basis of Sufi teaching.

In their conception of God, the Sufis adhered closely to the original Islamic recognition of the divine transcendence. In the proper sense, therefore, there is no such thing as Pantheism among them, in spite of what is commonly said to the contrary. As Professor Nicholson remarked – although he did not always adhere to his own criterion – 'So long as transcendence is recognized, the most emphatic assertion of immanence is not Pantheism, but Panentheism'.[1] God is for the Sufis absolute and eternal, all-wise, all-knowing, all-perfect, exalted above all limitations of time and space, beyond the reach of human understanding. 'Because Thou art eternal and perfect,' cries Attar, the Persian poet, 'Thou art always confounding the wise.'[2] It is the vision of the divine exaltation and glory which impels men to seek union with Him. Al-Ghazzali, the great theologian of the eleventh century, dwells much on the thought of God as Light and Beauty. The beauty of the works of God, he says, shows that He Himself is perfect Beauty. The contemplation of the divine Beauty fills men's hearts with love, so that they long to look upon the All-Beautiful. All other lights are but 'partial rays or reflections of His Light'.[3] God is immeasurably transcendent, yet infinitely near. 'When My servant calls to Me, I answer him, and to him who seeks My forgiveness I will not grudge it, for I am near at hand, ready to give ear to his request.'[4] Similarly Dhu al-Nun declares: 'Thou art the most intimate of all intimates with Thy friends.'[5]

Concerning God's relation to the world there are two main streams of tendency in Sufi teaching, often intermingling, yet in essence radically distinct. On the one hand, there is that which follows the orthodox tradition in thinking of God in terms of sovereign Will – as the Creator of the world, the almighty Ruler and Master of mankind, whose inscrutable decree determines all things. On the other hand, there is the outlook derived ultimately

1. ibid., p. 27
2. *The Conference of the Birds* (English translation, 1954), p. 4.
3. Margaret Smith, *Al-Ghazzali the Mystic*, pp. 138f.
4. ibid., p. 153.   5. op. cit., p. 232.

from the Neo-Platonic philosophy which exerted a predominant influence on later Sufism, especially in Persia. This outlook conceives of the world as an emanation from Deity and of God as the hidden essence or reality of all things. While God is thus immanent in all things, the underlying reality of all, He is yet the transcendent source and the final goal of all.

According to the orthodox tradition, God is the sole Agent in the universe, the real Doer of all deeds, whatever their quality. Muslim theologians, however, manage to combine with this conception a recognition of human freedom and responsibility which is actually quite incompatible with it. In his summary of Sufi teaching, al-Kalabadhi quotes a mystic as saying: 'Whoever believes not in predestination is an infidel, and whoever says that it is impossible to disobey God is a sinner.'[1] Ghazzali lays considerable stress on predestination. He compares the world to a marionette-show watched by children, who suppose mistakenly that the figures they see are moving of their own accord.[2] And God not only determines men's outer acts; He provides the motives for the good and evil deeds for which men are rewarded or punished.

In his account of the place of evil in the world, the Persian poet and mystic of the thirteenth century, Jalal al-Din Rumi, adopts a similar approach. The existence of evil in human experience is necessary as a foil to good. Rumi does not shrink from saying that God is the source of evil, since evil has its necessary place in the scheme of things which He has ordained. Even Hell-fire and Iblis (the Muslim Satan) are

> ... created for good ends,
> To show His perfect Wisdom and confound
> The sceptics who deny His mastery.[3]

1. *The Doctrine of the Sufis*, p. 32.
2. A. J. Wensinck, *La Pensée de Ghazzali*, p. 8.
3. R. A. Nicholson, *Rumi, Poet and Mystic*, p. 150. Rumi is speaking here in terms of the tradition which regards God as the sovereign Ruler of the world; his own distinctive approach looks upon Him rather as the underlying Reality (see pp. 309ff. below). From this standpoint evil is unreal, since it belongs wholly to the phenomenal order; it is the absence of being, as darkness is the absence of light.

Rumi maintains strongly the fact of human freedom and responsibility, while maintaining also that God is the Creator of all our
acts. Where he differs from the orthodox tradition is in holding, in
common with the Persian Sufis generally, that Hell is a temporary
state of being, and that all souls, and not merely all Muslims,
will be saved at the last. Ghazzali did not go so far as that, although he thought of Hell as in essence a state of separation
from God, and he believed that all souls capable of purification
would eventually turn to Him. The ultimate fact for him, as for
Rumi, was the goodness rather than the sheer almightiness of
God. God wills the good (he taught) as good, and the evil only
for the good which it brings. 'There is nothing which opposes
His mercy.'

In the teaching of the mystics the arbitrariness of the divine
Will, so evident in the Koran, tends to disappear; the ultimate
sovereignty of good replaces the pure and simple divine auto-
cracy of the earlier orthodoxy. At the same time the greatest
stress comes to be laid on the experience of divine grace. Man
seeks God only because God seeks man. 'The seeker is in reality
the sought,' says Kalabadhi, 'and the Sought the Seeker: for the
man who seeks God only seeks Him because God first sought
him. For the cause of everything is God's act.'[1] Rumi tells of a
devotee who ceased to call on Allah, because he received no
apparent answer to his call. After a while, however, a message
came to him which said,

> ... That 'Allah' of thine is My
> 'Here am I', and that supplication and grief
> And ardour of thine is My messenger to thee.[2]

Man's quest of God is not simply his response to God's quest
of man; it is itself the work of God within him. Kalabadhi
quotes a Sufi who said that God 'left no room for any intelligent
man to claim that anything in this world or the next is either his,
or through him, or for him'.[3] God works all things in all. But if
'the cause of everything is God's act', that is true in a distinctive
sense of the life of those who seek Him, and who, as they pursue

1. op. cit., p. 141.   2. ibid., p. 91.   3. op. cit., p. 34.

the quest, are lifted into union with Him. The virtues which men attain through their self-surrender – patience, gratitude, trust in God, love for God and for their fellow-creatures – are the fruits of divine grace no less than the divine revelations which they receive. The seeker who gives himself wholly to God 'in all that he does or leaves undone, is in the hands of God', Ghazzali says, 'like a corpse in the hands of one who prepares it for burial'.[1] The simile must not be pressed. The later Sufis were not characterized by the extremes of Quietism which marked some of the earlier devotees. Active exertion was held to be perfectly compatible with trust. It was only self-seeking which was contrary to it. The activity of the saint was the activity of God Himself living in him.

A potent influence in the development of Sufi theology was that of Neo-Platonic philosophy. (A translation of Porphyry's lost commentary on the *Enneads* of Plotinus appeared in Arabic under the misleading title *The Theology of Aristotle*, in A.D. 840, though its contents may have been known at an earlier date.) God's relation to the universe is conceived, under Neo-Platonic influence, not in terms of will, but in terms of essence – God is the one Reality which is the inmost essence of all things. From this standpoint the principle of divine Unity, fundamental to Islam, was reinterpreted. 'God [says the Koran] – there is no God but Him.' What that implies, the Sufis came to hold, was that God is not merely the sole Cause of existence and the sole Agent in existence, but that He alone has real being. Their typical name for God is al-Haqq – 'the Real'.

This means primarily that God alone is self-existent; all else is derivative, and (taken by itself) unreal. So far as anything exists at all, it exists as a ray of His light. The world is an emanation proceeding from Him, as sunbeams proceed from the sun. 'All things', says Ghazzali, 'are a ray of the essential light of God ... The one real light is God Himself.'[2] In some passages, it is true, Ghazzali uses language implying a more orthodox conception of

1. M. Smith, *Al-Ghazzali the Mystic*, p. 168.
2. ibid., p. 139.

creation. 'All that is other than God', he says, 'was created by His power out of non-existence' (p. 138). Yet elsewhere he expresses himself in terms commonly described as Pantheistic. Thus he says that 'the sum total of the visible and invisible worlds considered as a whole is called the divine Presence' (p. 141) – apparently implying an identification of God with the universe, seen and unseen. But, as was said above, God for the Sufis is always transcendent. 'He is too exalted,' Ghazzali declares, 'to be contained in any place and too holy to be limited by time' (p. 105). To the saying in question he immediately adds another, which qualifies it. The divine Presence, he adds, 'encompasses all existent things, since there is nothing existent save God and His works and His Kingdom and His servants, who are His handi-work.'

A more consistent and thorough-going doctrine of emanation was worked out by the Spanish Sufi, Ibnu al-Arabi, whose philosophy was expounded in poetic form by the Persian mystics. Arabi was the most influential of all Sufi teachers after Ghazzali. For him God is the one absolute and eternal Reality above and beyond all appearances in time and space, yet revealing Himself in and through those appearances.

We ourselves are the attributes by which we describe God; our existence is merely an objectivization of His existence. God is necessary to us in order that we may exist, while we are necessary to Him in order that He may be manifested to Himself.[1]

As Jami, the Persian Sufi of the fifteenth century, puts it:

The unique Substance, viewed as absolute and devoid of all pheno-mena, all limitations and all multiplicity, is the Real. On the other hand, viewed in His aspect of multiplicity and plurality, under which He displays Himself when clothed with phenomena, He is the whole created universe. Therefore, the universe is the outward visible expres-sion of the Real, and the Real is the inner unseen Reality of the universe.[2]

The world is thus the self-revelation of God, and it is the aspiration of the mystic that he may pierce the veil of outer

---

1. Nicholson, *Studies in Islamic Mysticism*, p. 83.
2. Nicholson, *The Mystics of Islam*, pp. 81–2.

things, and may see the hidden Reality which lies beneath. 'Make this phenomenal world', Jami prays, 'the mirror to reflect the manifestations of Thy Beauty, and not a veil to separate and repel us from Thee.'[1] The hidden Reality beneath all the forms of being is God. In a passage which is of particular interest for its implicit reference to the teaching of Jesus, attributed in a tradition to Moses, Arabi says:

> There is no existence save God's existence. . . . It is related that the Prophet declared that God said to Moses, 'O my servant, I was sick, and thou didst not visit Me, I begged of thee, and thou gavest not to Me,' with other like expressions, pointing to the fact that the existence of the beggar is His existence, and the existence of the sick is His existence . . . The existence of all created things is His existence. And when the secret of an atom of the atoms is clear, the secret of all created things, both outward and inward, is clear, and thou dost not see in this world or the next aught beside God.[2]

It is easy to see why the teaching of Arabi and his followers has been described as 'Pantheism'. 'The world visible and the world invisible', says Attar (the twelfth-century Persian Sufi), 'are only Himself.'[3] The world is an aspect of divine Reality. But it is only an aspect. There is no such absolute identification of God and the world as Pantheism properly implies. The divine Presence is hidden within the form of outer things, so that to the illuminated soul 'every atom is His throne'. Arabi describes the world as 'the breath of the Merciful'. The phenomena of the world, that is to say, are the breathing out, the exhalation, of essences or qualities contained in their ideal form in the being of God from all eternity. Thus while God 'moves under the forms of all created things', while He has 'hidden Himself within that which exists', while in that sense 'the existence of all created things is His existence', He still remains in His eternal being above and beyond the flux of Nature; He shines everlastingly in His changeless Glory. In the very affirmation of the divine Presence in the world, the Sufis constantly imply the divine transcendence of all that is finite.

1. *Jami* in the 'Wisdom of the East' series, p. 55.
2. M. Smith, *Al-Ghazzali the Mystic*, pp. 210f.
3. *The Conference of the Birds*, p. 3.

(b) The Nature of Man

In their conception of man, the Sufis (like the mystics generally) adopt a dual attitude. On the one hand, they display a vivid awareness of the imperfection and sinfulness of human nature; on the other hand, they see within the soul of man the shining of a divine Light, which reveals the deepest truth of his being. This interpretation of human nature found expression in a psychological analysis which became traditional among the Sufis. The source of evil in the nature of man is the nafs or lower soul – the principle of egoism in all its phases, which finds expression in lust, pride, envy, uncharitableness – in all that separates us from God. In early Sufism, especially, the greatest emphasis was laid on this aspect of human nature and on the battle that must be continually fought against it.

Everything which comes from the nafs [said al-Muhasibi] is deceitful, and no deed of it is praiseworthy, or tends to the truth . . . If you follow it in its desires, you will go down to Hell . . . It is the source of affliction and the origin of all evil.[1]

Side by side with the lower soul, the Sufis saw in man a deeper principle. Ghazzali compares the soul to a mirror which is soiled and covered with rust, but which may be cleansed and polished, so as to reflect the beauty of the higher world.[2]

The heart [that is, human personality as a whole] has two doors, the one turned towards outer things, the other towards the inner kingdom – this door is that of inspiration and revelation.[3]

The higher soul existed before the creation of the body. From the time of Muhasibi, the Sufis generally accepted Neo-Platonic teaching in this respect – without, however, admitting the belief in transmigration taught by the Neo-Platonists. The doctrine of reincarnation was held, exceptionally, by certain teachers. It was taught, for example, as a probable hypothesis by Ishraq Maqtul, a Sufi who was executed at Aleppo for heresy in the

1. Margaret Smith, *Early Mysticism in the Near and Middle East*, p. 226. Al-Muhasibi died in A.D. 857.
2. Wensinck, op. cit., p. 55.
3. ibid., p. 66.

twelfth century. Some souls, at least, probably come back to this world, Maqtul maintained, to overcome their deficiencies and rise higher in the scale of being.[1] Rumi explicitly rejected transmigration, while he held that the soul traverses many planes of being in the course of its pilgrimage from God to this world and back to Him.[2] The belief in the pre-existence of the soul is for the great majority of Sufis an inference from its hidden divinity. The deepest part of the soul, as Ghazzali taught, is divine, a ray of the divine Light, a spark of the eternal Flame. Its true home is in the heavenly world. In this world it is a prisoner, like a bird in a cage. Man has descended into this world owing to the Fall of Adam, who forgot himself and his Lord. In the experience of each individual the Fall is repeated. The inmost phase of man's being is commonly called the ruh or spirit, an aspect of which is the sirr or ground of the soul, an organ of spiritual sight, whereby man may rise into the immediate apprehension of God.

An interesting phase of Sufi teaching is the doctrine of the Logos and the Perfect Man developed by Ibnu al-Arabi and his contemporary Ibnu al-Farid of Cairo. The conception goes back in essentials to al-Hallaj (executed in A.D. 922), and perhaps even further. Man is conceived not only as the goal of creation, but as, in his ideal nature, the first emanation from the Absolute, who reflects all the divine attributes, and who is the archetype of the universe. The Perfect Man is identified with the Logos. He is the agent in the creation of the world and its animating and ruling principle; he is the mediator of inspiration and divine grace. The most striking feature of this whole conception is its identification with the person of Mohammed. The doctrine of the pre-existence of Mohammed arose at an early date, first among the Shi'ites and then among the Sunnis. The first thing that God created, it came to be believed, was the pre-existent form of Mohammed, conceived as a celestial light, which took up its abode in Adam and in the whole succession of prophets. The Sufis took over this conception, and identified it with that of the Logos and the Perfect Man. The 'Reality' or 'Idea' or 'Spirit' of Mohammed

1. Muhammad Iqbal, *The Development of Metaphysics in Persia*, pp. 147f.
2. R. A. Nicholson, *Rumi, Poet and Mystic*, p. 36.

is thus conceived as the creative and sustaining principle of the universe and the source of all revelation. The prophets who preceded Mohammed in time were therefore in reality, according to this belief, inspired by him. As the outcome of this development of thought, the greatest stress came to be laid on the person of the Prophet. Since he is the living source of grace and inspiration, the mystics are drawn into a personal communion – and even union – with him. Attar says that if a Muslim enjoys the vision of God, 'it comes through the light of the spirit of Mohammed ... It is in the power of the Prophet to bestow on his community a portion of that which he enjoys.'[1] In some verses written in the twelfth century by al-Buri, a Sufi of Yemen, Mohammed is besought to forgive sin and to remove its power: 'I beseech thee by thy glory to forgive the sins which I have committed ... Wilt thou not of thy grace set me free?'[2]

(c) *The Way of Life*

The way of life taught and followed by the Sufis is closely related to the goal which they seek. In its deepest being the soul is divine – 'within the heart and soul [Attar said] is the very essence of God'. But man is divided from God by his blindness to the light of Reality and by the power of his narrow self. It is the purpose of the man who enters upon the upward path to remove the veils between God and the soul. 'May God', Ghazzali once prayed for a disciple, 'anoint your inward vision with the light of Reality; may He empty your inmost self from all save His own Presence.'[3] The aim which the disciple seeks is the immediate vision of God, and the inner transformation of his being, so that God alone may live and act in him.

From an early period in the history of Sufism its doctrine and practice were inculcated to disciples either as individuals or as groups by those who had attained proficiency in the life of the spirit. Eventually convents were founded in which disciples resided for a shorter or longer time under the leadership of a director (murshid), who claimed absolute authority over his

1. R. A. Nicholson, *The Idea of Personality in Sufism*, p. 65.
2. ibid., p. 67.
3. M. Smith, *Al-Ghazzali the Mystic*, p. 149.

followers. The convents were at first separate institutions, but in the twelfth century the dervish Orders were instituted, linking together those convents which looked to a common founder, and were therefore marked by the use of a common ritual and mode of discipline.[1] One of the best-known Orders is that of the Mevlevi dervishes founded by Jalal al-Din Rumi, whose distinctive ritual is the Whirling Dance, designed (like all dervish ceremonies) to produce an experience of ecstatic union with God.

The first step in the way that leads to God is repentance or contrition, arising from the sense of sin. 'Contrition', says Ghazzali, 'results from the realization that sin intervenes between the sinner and the Beloved; it is the grief of the heart when it becomes aware of the absence of the Beloved.'[2] Rumi lays equal stress on the necessity of acknowledging sin and repenting of it.

Be ashamed of thy sins [he says], confess them humbly to God, beseech Him to pardon them, and so change thy heart that thou wilt loathe what thou hast done, and renounce it utterly.[3]

It is commonly said that repentance is the first of the 'stations' through which the soul must pass on its pilgrimage. Other 'stations' (or phases of the purgative life) are renunciation, poverty, trust in God. The aim of ethical discipline is the eradication of self-will. The aspirant must be denuded of every thought and every desire that will turn his heart away from God. For this purpose, the director would impose on his disciples particular modes of discipline – fasting, vows of silence, periods of solitary meditation – corresponding to their needs. A man who had been the governor of a province, for example, had to beg in the streets of Baghdad for a year, and afterwards to spend four years seeking out all whom he had wronged, and asking their pardon. He had then to spend another year as a beggar, and finally to occupy himself with menial duties in his first year in the convent.[4]

The 'stations' of the purgative life were followed by certain

1. 'Dervish' is a Persian word meaning 'beggar' and so 'mendicant'. In Islam generally, however, it is used for a member of a religious fraternity, whatever his mode of life.
2. M. Smith, *Al-Ghazzali the Mystic*, p. 153.
3. Nicholson, *The Idea of Personality in Sufism*, p. 54.
4. Nicholson, *The Mystics of Islam*, pp. 34–5.

'states', such as meditation, fear, hope, love, nearness to God, and finally the ecstatic contemplation of God which leads to union with Him. The greatest emphasis was laid on the practice of meditation, which Ghazzali defines as 'the state of those who have drawn near to God', and of 'recollection' (dhikr). In the Koran it is said that 'the gravest duty is the remembrance of God' (29, 44); and among the Sufis this duty was fulfilled by the repetition of the name of God or of a religious formula, like 'Glory to Allah' or 'There is no god but Allah', accompanied by intense concentration of mind.

The first stage of dhikr [said a Sufi] is to forget self, and the last stage is the effacement of the worshipper in the act of worship.[1]

Thus 'recollection' merges in contemplation, or absorption in the consciousness of God. The process was assisted from an early date by Indian methods of yoga or breath-control. Among the dervish Orders a similar result was sought by means of music and dancing.

For those who aspired after union with God, the director was not only one whose guidance must be implicitly accepted; he was sometimes also himself an intermediary in the process. The disciple, in this event, must constantly meditate on the murshid, so that he sees him in all men and in all things, and the spirit of his teacher goes with him in all his ways. He becomes at last so completely absorbed in his director that he is said to attain 'self-annihilation' in him. The same process is then applied to the founder of his Order, through the help of his guide, and later to the Prophet. The disciple is united successively with the director, the founder, and the Prophet, and comes to possess their spiritual powers. In this way the path is prepared for union with God.[2]

Islamic mystics are drawn into close unity, not only with their spiritual guides, but with one another. 'Every disciple has his own little group of intimate friends, who share his thoughts and feelings and enter with sympathy into all that concerns him.'[3] At

1. ibid., p. 48.
2. See J. P. Brown, *The Dervishes* (edited by H. A. Rose), p. 330.
3. Nicholson, *The Idea of Personality in Sufism*, p. 71.

the same time Sufis are sustained by a sense of unity extending to the whole company of aspirants and saints. In the words of Abu Sa'id: 'They are brethren who love one another for God's sake.'

The supreme actuating force of the Sufi is the love of God – the passionate devotion to God which is also a burning desire to be united, or rather re-united, with Him. And the love of God naturally carries with it the love of our fellows and of all creatures.

The sign of love to God [according to al-Muhasibi] is love of all that He loves, and it must find its expression in dealing with His creatures in that spirit of compassion in which He Himself deals with them.[1]

Ghazzali emphasizes the same fact. It is the essential nature of Sufism as he defines it 'to abide continuously in God and to live at peace with men; whoever abides in God and deals rightly with men, treating them with unfailing kindness is a Sufi ... In your dealings with others, treat them as you would wish them to treat you.'[2] It is true that for the Sufis the love of God involves, as a phase of experience, a total absorption in the divine Presence, and in that sense 'love [as a Sufi put it] is that which renders blind and deaf'. Ghazzali stresses this experience, but he stresses equally the fact that the saint comes down from the Mount of Transfiguration to live in the power of his vision.

It has been pointed out above that early Sufism was marked by an essentially ascetic, other-worldly piety. In later Sufism, as in all forms of spiritual religion, the ascetic strain remains, in the sense of a constant effort of self-conquest. The repudiation of the nafs or lower self appears sometimes to go much further than this, and to imply the complete rejection of physical desire. Ghazzali was himself, as D. B. Macdonald has pointed out, inconsistent in this respect.[3] Yet Sufism has in the main been true to the Islamic tradition. There was no compulsory celibacy for those residing in a convent, and in fact most Sufis were married. Al-Hujwiri, in his compendium of Sufi teaching, *The Unveiling of the Veiled* (compiled in the eleventh century), endorses the traditional attitude when he says: 'No companionship is equal in

1. M. Smith, *An Early Mystic of Baghdad*, p. 238.
2. M. Smith, *Al-Ghazzali the Mystic*, p. 104.
3. *The Religious Life and Attitude in Islam*, p. 279.

reverence and security to marriage, when husband and wife are well suited to each other.'[1] In the writings of Sufi poets there is a great deal of erotic symbolism. This has sometimes been misunderstood by Western readers, and taken to imply a glorification of sensuous experience. Actually what the poets celebrate in terms of sensuous imagery is the union of the soul with the divine. The symbolism, it is true, implies the recognition of a common element in divine and human love. In a commentary on one of his own poems in which reference is made to certain well-known Arab lovers, Ibnu al-Arabi says:

> Love, *qua* love, is one and the same reality to those Arab lovers and to me; but the objects of our love are different, for they loved a phenomenon, whereas I love the Real.[2]

The love of God, he contends, should be marked by the same passionate intensity, the same 'transport and rapture', as was shown by the human lovers of whom he speaks. So also Ghazzali says: 'It is reasonable to give this passionate love to that One from whom all good things have come.'[3] Human love is an analogue of the love of God; it may thus prepare the way for that greater love in which alone our soul can find final satisfaction. So Jami said,

> Even from earthly love thy face avert not,
> Since to the Real it may serve to raise thee.[4]

For the Sufis the world of the senses has no final or intrinsic reality; but it is not a mere illusion from which men must turn aside. It is a shadow, an image, a reflection of the truth, a necessary means of its manifestation, and so for us it may become a bridge or gateway to the Real. We must rejoice therefore in all that is good and beautiful in our experience and in the world about us, since, as Ghazzali says, 'All that is good and fair and lovely in this world is but a particle of the riches of God and a ray from the splendour of His glory'.[5] And so it is the true way of

1. See J. Wach, *Types of Religious Experience*, p. 361.
2. Nicholson, *The Mystics of Islam*, p. 105.
3. *Al-Ghazzali the Mystic*, p. 177.
4. *The Mystics of Islam*, p. 110.
5. *Al-Ghazzali the Mystic*, p. 177.

life for the mystic to find God in all things, and to manifest the divine in sharing the life of his fellows.

> The true saint [said Abu Sa'id] goes in and out amongst the people, and eats and sleeps with them and sells in the market, and marries, and takes part in social intercourse, and never forgets God for a single moment.[1]

(d) The Goal

For the Sufis (as for all mystics), union with God is both a present fact of experience and the goal of life. Union with God implies both a higher state of consciousness – an immediate vision of divine Reality in which the division between man and God is done away – and a transformation of human personality whereby the unification so realized becomes a permanent condition of being. From the time of Abu Yazid of Bistan in the ninth century the doctrine of fana (literally 'passing away'), which sums up the whole matter, came to hold a central place in Sufi teaching. Ghazzali explains the nature of the experience of mystical ecstasy, which the term primarily indicates, with particular clearness:

> When the worshipper thinks no longer of his worship or himself, but is altogether absorbed in Him whom he worships, that state is called fana, when a man has so passed away from himself that he feels nothing of his bodily members, nor of what is passing without, nor of what passes within his own mind.[2]

In this condition of consciousness, Ghazzali adds, the mystics 'are consumed by the glory of God's exalted countenance, and the glory of the divine Majesty overwhelms them, and they are annihilated, and they themselves are no more. They no longer contemplate themselves, having passed away from themselves, and there remains only the One, the Real.'[3]

The words of Ghazzali are typical of the thought and experience of the Sufis. 'From one who contemplates God in his heart', said Abu Sa'id, 'all else is hidden, and all things are reduced to naught, and he passes away in the presence of God's

1. Nicholson, *Studies in Islamic Mysticism*, p. 55.
2. *Al-Ghazzali the Mystic*, p. 190.
3. ibid., p. 192.

Majesty, and there remains in his heart nothing save God alone.'
Kalabadhi quotes the lines of a poet which illustrate the same
experience:

> . .. A radiance shone,
> A magical breeze breathed, and God was near.
> Then vanished selfhood utterly, and I
> Remained His only, Who with tidings clear
> Attests His Being, and is known thereby.[1]

It was a ground of offence to the orthodox that the Sufis were
sometimes led to claim that through their mystic experience they
were deified. Professor Nicholson quotes a Persian ode by the
dervish, Baba Kuhi of Shiraz (eleventh century):

> In the market, in the cloister, only God I saw;
> In the valley, on the mountain, only God I saw ...
> I opened mine eyes and by the light of His Face around me
> In all the eye discovered, only God I saw.
> Like a candle I was melting in His Fire:
> Amidst the flames outflashing only God I saw ...
> I passed away into nothingness, I vanished,
> And lo, I was the All-living – only God I saw.[2]

It was a similar sense of personal nothingness and the 'all-
ness' of God which two centuries earlier led to Abu Yazid's cry,
which was a cause of scandal to the orthodox, 'How great is My
Majesty!'[3] Abu Yazid himself explained the secret of those
words when he said 'It is God that speaks with my tongue, and I
have vanished'; 'I came forth from Yazidness as a snake from its
skin'.[4] Rumi maintains that 'the extreme of humility and abase-
ment' is to be found in the man who says 'I am God [Ana'l-
Haqq],' rather than in him who cries 'I am the slave of God
[Ana'l-'abd]', for the latter 'affirms two existences, his own and
God's', while the former 'has made himself non-existent, and
has given himself up'. In saying 'I am God' he is in effect declaring 'I am naught, He is all: there is no being but God's'.[5] For

1. op. cit., p. 125.   2. *The Mystics of Islam*, p. 59.
3. Arberry, *Sufism*, p. 54.
4. Nicholson, 'Islamic Mysticism', in *The Legacy of Islam*, p. 216.
5. *Rumi, Poet and Mystic*, p. 184.

Rumi, as for Abu Yazid, deification is equivalent to unification; to affirm self along with God is a denial of the divine Unity, which is all-embracing. It was al-Hallaj who used the phrase 'Ana'l-Haqq', and who endured martyrdom at Baghdad in partial consequence. (The matter was complicated by political and other charges.) Later Sufis interpreted these words on the ground of their own philosophy. Ghazzali takes them to be the utterance of an ecstatic love of God, identifying itself with the object of its passion. 'In love,' as Attar says, 'no longer "thou" and "I" exist, for self has passed away in the Beloved.' Ghazzali, however, evidently felt a certain reserve with regard to the affirmation of Hallaj, in view of his endeavour to reconcile Sufism with orthodoxy, for he says: 'The words of passionate lovers in the state of ecstasy should be concealed and not spoken of.'[1] Rumi ranks Hallaj with the prophets and saints in whom God has revealed Himself. He appeared as Noah, Abraham, Jesus, Mohammed.

'Twas even He that cried in human shape, 'Ana 'l-Haqq'; the one who mounted the scaffold was not Mansur (Hallaj), as the foolish imagined.[2]

The words, that is to say, were those of God Himself uttered through the mouth of the selfless Hallaj. The teaching of Hallaj himself was different. (The matter has been elucidated by the researches of Professor Louis Massignon.)[3] According to Hallaj deification is the outcome of creation in the divine image: God created man in His image, in order that man might find the divine image in himself through the transformation of his being by love, and so might become one with the divine nature. Union with God involves the infusion or incarnation (hulul) of the divine Spirit in the human body. As Hallaj puts it in his poems:

Thy Spirit is mingled in my spirit, even as wine is mingled with pure water.
When anything touches Thee, it touches me too, in every case Thou art I.[4]

1. *Al-Ghazzali the Mystic*, p. 234. 2. *Rumi, Poet and Mystic*, p. 143.
3. See especially his great work, *La Passion d'al-Hosayn ibn Mansour al-Hallaj*.
4. *The Mystics of Islam*, p. 151.

For Hallaj there is thus even in deification both unity and duality;

> I am He whom I love, and He whom I love is I;
> We are two spirits dwelling in one body.
> If thou seest me, thou seest Him,
> And if thou seest Him, thou seest us both.[1]

Incidentally, it is to be noted that for Hallaj, although Mohammed is the pre-existent Light of prophecy (see p. 313 above), it is Jesus rather than Mohammed in whom deification is perfectly realized. In using the term hulul to indicate the interpenetration of the human and the divine, Hallaj was following Muhasibi.[2] Junaid, pupil of Muhasibi and younger contemporary of Hallaj, also stresses duality. It is the meaning of Sufism, according to Junaid, that 'God should cause thee to die from thyself and to live in Him'; but, living in God, man continues to exist as an individual, and individual being involves separation from Him as well as union with Him. The lover yearns after the Beloved, yet suffers from the sense of separation.[3] Most Sufis, however, rejected the doctrine of hulul. 'In God [said Shabistari] there is no duality. In that Presence "I" and "we" and "thou" do not exist; "I" and "we" and "thou" and "he" become one.'[4] So also Attar said: 'Wherever the Sufis are, they have no separate existence, but exist only in the Unity of God.'[5]

'Unification' (tawhid) is sometimes described as ittihad or 'identity'. The mystic assumes the attributes of God, and makes them his own. 'His attributes [says Rumi] are extinguished in the attributes of God'; 'my ego has passed away, He remains alone.'[6] This doctrine was repudiated by al-Sarraj and al-Hujwiri, exponents of Sufism in the tenth and eleventh centuries. A man cannot lose his humanity, said Sarraj, 'but the inborn qualities of humanity are changed and transmuted by the all-powerful radiance that is shed upon them from the divine Realities.'[7]

1. ibid.
2. See M. Smith, *An Early Mystic of Baghdad*, p. 262.
3. Arberry, *Sufism*, p. 58.
4. M. Smith, *Rabi'a the Mystic*, p. 1.
5. *Attar* in the Wisdom of the East series, pp. 67f.
6. *Rumi, Poet and Mystic*, pp. 180, 178.
7. *The Mystics of Islam*, p. 158.

In his exposition of the conception, Ibnu al-Farid of Cairo uses a significant analogy. A woman smitten by catalepsy and possessed by a spirit utters words not her own. Similarly in the state of ittihad a man 'appears to will and act, while he is really the organ through which God wills and acts'.[1] He refers also to the story of Gabriel, who is said to have come to Mohammed in the shape of Dihya, his Companion. So through the appearance of humanity it is God who manifests Himself in the man totally at one with him.[2] For al-Farid, ittihad is a permanent state of being, comparable to the 'Spiritual Marriage' or 'transforming union' of Christian mystics. Absorption in the ecstasy of fana is not the end of his journey. The world of time and space is a necessary means to the self-manifestation of God, and so, while in ecstasy the mystic is aware only of the One, it is his task to return to the sphere of the many, and, living in unbroken union with God – with his will (as Jami puts it) 'obliterated in the Will of God' – to manifest the divine Life to men. Fana (passing away from selfhood) involves baqa (abiding in God).

What is the final meaning of this twofold condition for the soul? What is the ultimate goal of the Sufi? It is clear from what has been said that the 'passing away' from self does not in fact involve the cessation of being. The sense of separation may be done away; in any case life in God remains. For Muslim mystics as for Christian, 'self-naughting' is in its essence a positive state. The aspirant (as has been shown: see p. 316 above) is said to annihilate himself successively in his spiritual director, in the founder of his order, and in Mohammed. He identifies himself with them, and enters into their spiritual qualities. The way is thus prepared for self-annihilation in God. 'Annihilate yourselves gloriously and joyfully in Me', says the divine voice in Attar's poem, 'and in Me you shall find yourselves; so long as you do not realize your nothingness, you will never reach the heights of immortality.'[3]

What is the nature of this 'immortality'? Can it be described as in any sense 'personal'? The question is not an easy one to answer, partly because personality is an elusive concept, partly

1. Nicholson, *Studies*, pp. 223–5.   2. ibid., pp. 280ff.
3. *The Conference of the Birds*, pp. 132f.

because, for many Sufis, at any rate, the ultimate state transcends definition. Attar feels that the nature of human destiny is a profound mystery: 'This I know, that annihilation is a glorious thing, but that which I do not know is what I am yet to be.'[1] Rumi feels the same mystery. In a well-known poem he speaks of man's ascent from inanimate matter, through the world of plants and animals, to manhood. From manhood he will pass on to 'angelhood', but that is not the end.

> When I have sacrificed my angel-soul,
> I shall become what no mind e'er conceived.
> Oh, let me not exist! For Non-existence
> Proclaims in organ tones: 'To Him we shall return.'[2]

'Existence' and 'non-existence' are used by Rumi in exactly opposite senses from time to time – for the Real or the phenomenal, as the case may be. Here he is crying out for life in Eternity as opposed to life in time. Such life is a return to God. For the Sufis as has been pointed out (see pp. 312f. above), the deepest being of the soul was pre-existent; and it is man's destiny to return to his pre-existent life in God. What God willed for man, says Hujwiri, is 'that his last state should become his first again, and that he should now be as he was before he came into existence, when the spirit, not joined as yet to the body, dwelt in the Light and Presence of God'.[3] For Arabi, the pre-existent life of the soul appears to be something essentially impersonal: the soul pre-exists as an idea in the Mind of God. And this impersonal mode of being is sometimes taken to be equally characteristic of human immortality. Thus a modern Sufi writes:

Before creation the seeker was an idea in the Mind of God, and in the state of fana he becomes as he was when he subsisted in God's Mind – an idea.[4]

Such a purely impersonal conception does not in reality do justice to the typical thought and experience of the Sufis – not

1. *Attar* in the Wisdom of the East series, p. 103.
2. *Rumi, Poet and Mystic*, p. 103.
3. M. Smith, *Early Mysticism*, p. 216.
4. Munshi Fazil in *The History of Philosophy, Eastern and Western*, II: 185.

even to that of Arabi. Thanks largely to the work of Arabi, Mohammed himself came to be regarded as the Logos and the Perfect Man, in whom God and man are one. Mystics therefore claimed to enter into a direct personal union with Mohammed – to identify themselves with him. Such an experience would plainly be impossible if Mohammed were a mere idea in the Mind of God, and not a living personality. It is significant also that in Sufi tradition the saints, who have entered into an abiding union with God, are seen as again and again coming into contact after death with their disciples.

The final state, as the Sufis typically conceive it, is one neither of a purely impersonal immortality, nor of the survival of finite personality; it is one of 'absorption and transmutation'. Rumi speaks of 'the death whereby you are transmuted, and enter into the Light'.[1] That transmutation is an awakening in which man

Will laugh to think what troublous dreams he had.[2]

The main clue to the nature of man's final destiny is the breaking down of barriers which union with the Infinite involves.

Those who have passed from the world are not non-existent: they are steeped in the divine Attributes ...
The spirit everlastingly united with God is free from barriers.[3]

In his union with God, man attains an immortality in which all souls are one.

1. op. cit., p. 105.
2. ibid., p. 188.
3. ibid., p. 179.

CHAPTER 9

Mystical Religion: A Survey of Tendencies

THE study of mysticism in the various religions of the world reveals very wide differences in its forms of expression, but at the same time it reveals a certain essential unity of experience and outlook. In this final chapter an endeavour will be made to indicate some fundamental tendencies which the varied types of mysticism have in common, and at the same time to indicate some outstanding differences.

I. THE MYSTICS AND THE NATURE OF REALITY

It is recognized everywhere that through mystical experience men are brought into immediate contact with ultimate Reality, and this contact is commonly described in terms both of vision or knowledge and of union. The knowledge which direct experience brings transcends thought or intellectual knowledge, and the Reality which it apprehends is felt to be of such a nature that any attempt to express it in the categories of thought is of necessity inadequate. The typical theology of the mystics is summed up in the phrase used of the teaching of Plotinus, 'the negative theology of positive transcendence'. But if all forms of thought based on finite being are insufficient to express the nature of That which transcends such being, it is generally admitted that some terms are more, and some less, insufficient. Ultimate Reality is the supreme and infinite Perfection and Glory. The mystics differ notably among themselves regarding the use of personal language concerning the Ultimate. The terms which they use are often impersonal – Brahman, the Void, Nirvana, the Good, the One; but the implication of their experience is that the Ultimate is not impersonal in the sense that it is on a lower level of being than man himself; it is not of the nature of a mere unconscious force. It is on an immeasurably higher level – not below but above person- ality as we know it, devoid of the limitations of personality, yet not devoid of its essential qualities of life, consciousness, spirit, even though such terms may not be strictly applicable, and must be understood in an analogical or symbolical sense. Even for Shankara, Brahman is 'an ocean of pure consciousness'. The fact that man may rise into union with the Transcendent, may participate in its nature, may identify himself with it, is of the utmost significance in this connexion. We cannot be united with that which is wholly alien to ourselves. In that union, it is true, we pass into another mode of being than that of our finite personality. In its deification our being is transformed; it loses its limitations, so that it is no longer a separate self. Yet the self of man in its deeper being is one and continuous with the Infinite. In its transformation it does not cease to live, to be conscious, to possess a spiritual quality : it is only then that it enjoys the fullness of life, of consciousness, of spirituality. And it is just that fullness of spiritual being which is the distinctive nature of the Ultimate.

The language of the mystics differs according to the particular religious tradition to which they are attached, but what is most significant is the convergence of those belonging to traditions differing so widely among themselves in the same essential apprehension of truth. Thus some Christian mystics are at one with Taoists and Buddhists in speaking of the Absolute as 'Nothing'; and they are at one in the meaning which they assign to this paradoxical term. For Christians, Taoists, Buddhists the Infinite in the very fullness of its life is 'Nothing' as the negation of the finite. The most consistently negative of all the mystics was, perhaps, Gotama the Buddha (following the Pali Canon) in his avoidance of positive affirmations regarding the nature of the Transcendent. Yet it is clear that that for Gotama Nirvana is not a merely negative state; it is an eternal Reality in the attainment of which is the fullness of joy. If its nature is completely inexpressible, so also is the nature of the man who attains it. The man who enters into Nirvana is himself beyond the range of finite concepts. He is 'profound, measureless, unfathomable', because he has entered into union with supreme Reality.

II. THE MYSTICS AND PANTHEISM;
DIVINE IMMANENCE AND TRANSCENDENCE

During the course of our inquiry we have had occasion more than once to consider the familiar contention that the mystics are Pantheists. Actually, as we have seen, Pantheism, in the sense of the doctrine which identifies God purely and simply with the universe in space and time, is utterly remote from their outlook. For the mystics of all religions, divine or ultimate Reality is essentially transcendent of the world of space and time; but the affirmation of the divine transcendence is commonly accompanied by an equal stress on divine indwelling. The eternal Reality in its fullness of being is indeed the inmost essence of all. Immanence implies a certain inner oneness of the Eternal with the sphere of finite being – a certain identification of the divine with the things of time and space. It is this identification which has given rise to the impression of Pantheism. But identification is not the same thing as pure and simple identity. That is evident enough in the realm of human relationships. It is only a superficial view of personality which regards it as inherently exclusive. Personality carries with it a capacity for sympathy, compassion, 'suffering with' others; and sympathy in its intensest form involves an actual participation in the experience of others, so that they become our own, and 'otherness' is transcended. When the saint identifies himself with his fellows in their sufferings or their sins, he does not cease to be himself; his personality is enriched and enlarged. So also God in the very fullness of His Perfection and Glory identifies Himself with all beings even in their alienation from Him, dwells at their heart, becomes the universe in its seeming separation from Him.

Beyond the world of time and space, mystics have commonly recognized a higher order, characterized not by separation and conflict, like the physical realm, but by unbroken unity; there all things exist eternally in interpenetration and mutual identity. In this higher world, man himself has his eternal being in union with God. This world comes into being by an eternal process of emanation from God. In the language of Eckhart, it is the Son eternally generated by the Father. In the material world the unbroken unity and harmony of the higher order are lost. Hence it is sometimes conceived (e.g. by the Gnostics) as the outcome of a premundane Fall. More typically it is regarded as itself an emanation from the higher sphere. Mystics see the divine Presence

even in the 'world of separation'. They see that world as itself
a partial manifestation of the divine Reality which is immeasurably exalted above the level of finite, spatial, temporal being.
The finite self of man is yet in its depths one with the Infinite
and Eternal. While in one aspect God is other than all beings in
their limitation and exclusiveness, He yet identifies Himself with
all beings and lives in their life.

III. THE MYSTICS AND THE SELF

Among mystics of all schools there is a general recognition of the
high destiny of man. The human self, it is held, is capable of an
immeasurable transformation and enlargement, and this capacity
is almost universally regarded as a thing intrinsic to its nature.
The Gnostics are exceptional in limiting this capacity to men of
a certain inborn type. It is commonly believed that man, because
of the deeper life within him, may transcend the normal limits of
his nature, and may enter into oneness with God, may attain a
supreme exaltation, may be 'deified', may enter Nirvana. Yet the
mystics are thoroughly realistic in their view of human nature.
They see that the obstacle which stands in our way also lies in
ourselves – in the love and assertion of self in its narrowness and
separateness. Buddhists indeed maintain that the very notion of
self is a fantasy which we must set aside. In other forms of mystical
religion there is an equal stress on the necessity of 'self-naughting'
as a way of life. Commonly a distinction is drawn between the
lower or separated self, which finds expression in egoistic impulses of every kind, and the higher self – *nous* – or the higher
soul – neshamah – the 'spark' or ground of the soul, the Buddha-
nature, the spirit. It is this higher self which is the source of all
that is good in our life, and which must become the activating
principle of our being if we are to rise into union with God. It is
common ground among mystical teachers who adhere to this
mode of thought that the being of man in its deeper nature,
while it is in one aspect individual, is also universal – a principle
which 'pervades the universe and all other beings'.[1] The higher
self is conceived as the 'Universal Mind', the infinite Spirit, the
'eternal Buddha', living in us, or as man himself as a member of

1. Edward Carpenter, *The Drama of Love and Death*, p. 80.

the eternal order, living in an interpenetrating unity with other beings. Since in any case the higher self is in essence divine, it may be said that so far as this self comes to prevail in our life, it is God Himself who comes to possess and rule us, and to unite us with Himself. Christian mystics are apt to identify the divine principle in the soul with Christ as the eternal Son or Word of God. Similarly Sufis are sometimes led to equate the divine Life in man with Mohammed conceived as the Logos, and Jewish mystics to identify it with Adam Kadmon – the divine and universal Man.

In his union or identification with God, mystics recognize that man unites or identifies himself with other beings. A Hermetic writer says: 'I am in Heaven, in the earth, in the water, in the air; I am in every living creature.' So also Ch'eng Hao declares that to the 'man of love' there is 'nothing that is not himself'. Kabir likewise 'considers all creatures on earth as his own self'. In the language of the Upanishads, in becoming Brahman we 'become all'. It is said of an Eastern Christian mystic that he so identified himself with Christ that he felt himself to possess 'not only his own limbs or members, but those of every other human being as well'. In such identification with other beings, Jewish and Christian mystics are apt to find the secret of intercessory prayer.

In some forms of mystical religion, union with God finds anticipation or support in union with those who have themselves attained that experience. In the bhakti mysticism of India it is believed to be essential for one who seeks to follow the mystic way to offer the utmost devotion to his guru, even to worship him as one who mediates the divine Presence. Such worship is held to be itself a means to divine union. The relation of the devotee to his master may come to be felt as an actual union, whereby the disciple is able to participate in his spiritual consciousness. In the early days of their religion, the thought of union with the guru was especially prominent among the Sikhs. With them it had, not only an individual, but a corporate, aspect, since the guru was the master of an organized company of believers. The spirit of the guru was thought to live after his death in the members of his Church. We have here a close analogy to the 'Christ-mysticism' of Paul and John. The corporate aspect of Christian mysticism

finds expression in the monastic orders and in closely united
groups like the Family of Love and the Quakers. In Catholic
mysticism the spiritual director holds an essential place. So it is
also in Zen Buddhism. In the Mahayana generally, the goal which
men seek has a corporate aspect. In attaining Buddhahood men
not only transcend the limitations of finite individuality; they
enter into an organic unity with one another, so that they have
'but one being, one infinite intelligence, one united function'.
The corporate aspect of mysticism is prominent among the
Sufis, not only in the fraternities which have played so great a
part in Islam, but also in the small groups of fellow-aspirants
which form a constant feature of the Sufi movement. Among the
Sufis, union with the spiritual director is sometimes regarded as a
necessary preparation for union with God. A man learns to
identify himself first with his master, then with the founder of his
order, and next with Mohammed. He thus comes to acquire their
spiritual powers, and so is led to union with God. In certain types
of Jewish mysticism we have a strikingly similar conception. In
the Prophetic Kabbalism of Abulafia the master personifies
Metatron (a semi-divine principle) or God Himself; the disciple
identifies himself with the master, and so with Metatron or with
God. Among the modern Hasidim, the greatest emphasis came
to be laid on the person of the Zaddik, who helped men to
develop their latent powers; he was enabled by his own God-
consciousness to raise men to God. He was, moreover, the centre
of the communal life of his followers.

IV. THE MYSTICS AND THE WORLD;
THE NATURE OF EVIL

Mystical experience is always felt to be an awakening to truth and
reality. The mystic is the man of vision, the man who has attained
enlightenment, the man who sees things as they really are. Those
who do not share the vision are conversely subject to a greater or
less extent to the sway of blindness, ignorance, illusion. The notion
of Maya, as formulated by Shankara, and the Buddhist doctrine
of the Void, represent the extreme expression of this attitude. The
ecstatic experience in which men are no longer conscious of the
self or the world is here taken as the sole standard of reality;

there is no reality at all save the undifferentiated One. This position is adopted by some of the Sufis.

In general the mystics adopt a less uncompromising monism. While supreme reality belongs to the One alone, in the higher world (or worlds) there is differentiation without division or separation. For Plato the Forms, while derived from the Good, are themselves eternal. So for Plotinus *nous* and the *noeta* proceed eternally from the One. But what of time and space and the physical order? What of the souls of men in their separation from one another and from God? For Plato the world as we commonly know it is a shadow-world; it has no absolute reality, yet it is not a pure and simple illusion. Similarly for Plotinus the world of Nature has emanated from the world of *nous*, and hence it has a measure of reality, but it is the Eternal alone which truly is. The separation of soul from soul and of life from life, which marks the sphere of the finite, and fills the world with conflict, exists only on the surface. If we penetrate to the depths of being, it passes away. With this position we may compare that of Ramanuja in India. While he rejects Shankara's doctrine of Maya, he affirms avidya or ignorance as the dominating fact in the life of man. Man is like a young prince brought up among strangers; he is unaware of his origin and his true nature. (Plotinus uses essentially the same analogy.) So among the mystics generally it is taught that we cannot know ourselves as we truly are, and thus cannot know the real nature of being, unless we know our inner oneness with God.

The mystics in general are agreed in regarding evil as rooted in ignorance or blindness, and therefore as essentially negative in its nature. It is a denial of the unity of life, a loss of the true freedom and power of the soul, an assertion of the self in its imagined separateness. Mystics are acutely aware of the limitations of life in the flesh, and they sometimes regard the physical body and the world of the senses as at least a proximate cause of evil. For the Gnostics the material world is itself the outcome of a Fall – the Fall, in particular, of the Aeon, Sophia; salvation consists in the liberation of the spark of divinity which exists in man (or in certain men) from the sphere of matter and its return to God. For the Manichaeans and the Cathari matter is a force of blind desire

– a manifestation of the Power of Darkness which is in perpetual conflict with the divine Power of Light. Among the Hermetists the primeval Fall is represented in the *Poimandres* as that of the heavenly Man, who lost his celestial character through his union with Nature. For the Hermetists generally, evil qualities are 'the irrational torments of matter', from which the soul must be freed. Plotinus teaches that evil arises in the course of embodied life – through the entry of the soul into matter, whereby it is confined to a single form of being, so that it forgets its divine nature, allowing the body, which should be its servant, to dominate it. Plotinus rejects the Gnostic view that the material world is essentially evil, regarding it as a divine creation in spite of its necessary imperfection. The fullness of life can only be attained in the higher world, but it is possible while we live in the body to transcend its limitations. Among Jewish mystics the Fall is interpreted along Gnostic lines – as destroying the unbroken unity of man and all things in God through the materialization of the universe, and introducing division and discord. There is also in the *Zohar* the conception, expounded in essence by Boehme in later times, that discord arose among the divine qualities (the Sefiroth) through the separation of Judgement (Din) from Love or Mercy (Hesed) – Din breaking loose from the divine life and being transformed into the world of Satanic forces. In Luria's doctrine of the Breaking of the Vessels we have another conception of Gnostic affinities designed to account for the fact of evil through the operation of super-mundane forces. Both in the *Zohar* and in Luria we have in the conception of the Exile of the Shekhinah the idea that evil impairs the unity not only of Nature and the world of man, but of the divine world itself. Accompanying this is the belief, shared in modern times by the Hasidim, that it is man's task to play an active part, especially by the practice of mystical prayer, in the restoration of unity and harmony both in the universe and in the divine life.

V. THE MYSTICS AND THE MORAL LIFE

Among the mystics everywhere it is recognized that if we are to attain the goal of our being, there must come about in us a profound moral transformation expressing itself in the whole nature of our life. The process of moral transformation has two aspects, negative and positive.

The negative aspect is described as 'purgation' – the purification of our being by the elimination of all those qualities and attitudes which hold us back, which separate us from God, which subject us to the dominance of the narrow self and of outer things. Pride, anger, self-love, and self-assertion in all its forms, must be renounced. Humility or the absence of pride and self-assertion is sometimes said to be the foundation of all virtues. Equally essential is longsuffering, the patient endurance of wrong, the conquest of resentment or animosity in face of injury. Among Hindus and Buddhists, ahimsa or non-injury is regarded as a fundamental principle of life. Asceticism in the sense of self-discipline leading to self-conquest is commonly recognized as essential. Living as we do in the sense-world, we find in our nature, as the mystics see, a constant tendency to fall under the power which it exerts upon us, and so to lose our inner freedom. To meet this danger, we must learn detachment. Mystics sometimes go much further than this: the sense-world is felt not only to be a source of danger and temptation, but a force actually hostile to the life of the spirit. What is necessary then is complete renunciation of the world and its ties; the ideal life is the life of the hermit or the monk. So we have the rise of secluded communities practising celibacy, like the Orphics and the Essenes, and the growth of monasticism in Hinduism, Buddhism, Taoism, Christianity. Marriage, while permitted to the lay adherents of these religions (as in some Essene communities), is looked upon as a concession to the weakness of the flesh. In Hinduism, apart from the monastic orders, the strain of extreme asceticism or world-renunciation finds expression in the ideal of the sannyasi, who cuts himself adrift from the world. It must be remembered, however, that according to the fourfold scheme of life traditionally acknowledged among Hindus, the sannyasi is a man who has lived the normal life of a householder, which is thus recognized as a necessary stage of development.

In its positive aspect the characteristic principle of mystical morality is universal love. In Hinayana Buddhism love is emphasized as a necessary means of emancipation from the fetters which chain us to individual life. Among other mystics it is the outcome of the unity which binds man to his fellow-creatures, the manifestation of his divine or heavenly nature, the fruit of God-realization or of participation in the divine Love which flows out to all. Love is expressed in the compassion whereby we take to ourselves the sorrows and sufferings of others – sometimes explicitly extended to the animal creation. Compassion is pre-eminently characteristic of Mahayana Buddhism, with its vision of the eternal Buddha, the infinite Heart of Compassion embracing all creatures. The ideal of the Mahayana is the Bodhisattva, who not only feels himself as one with all, sharing the burden of others' guilt as well as of others' suffering, but devotes himself to the quest of universal salvation, dedicating even the merit he has won by his goodness to the liberation of his fellows, seeking to attain Nirvana only when all beings are redeemed.

Among those mystics who recognize that man's life in society and the family has a rightful place in spiritual growth, the moral life finds positive expression, not only in charity and compassion, but in the consecration of the tasks and relationships of the common life of the world. Even where world-renunciation is looked upon as the highest ideal, rules are prescribed for the conduct of common living. While the emphasis of Plotinus, like that of the Hermetists and the Gnostics, was mainly on the need of purgation and inward detachment, he dwelt on the necessity of the civic virtues. In his view of the physical world as a divine creation, which in its beauty and harmony is a reflection of the eternal order, he provided the basis for a richer and more positive view of the possibilities of life in this world than he himself developed. Among Muslim and perhaps also among Jewish mystics, the influence of his teaching in this aspect served to reinforce the traditions of their own religions in stressing the sanctity of earthly life. For the Sufis human love had a particular value as a symbol and an anticipation of that which is divine. While Jewish mystics avoided the use of erotic symbolism, they laid an equal stress on the value of married life. The medieval Hasidim, like Luria and his followers, practised austerity as an aid to spiritual growth, yet they maintained the sanctity of bodily life, which has been strongly emphasized in the modern Hasidic movement. In Hinduism contrary tendencies are at work. It is commonly felt that the ultimate ideal is that of the world-renouncing sannyasi, yet Hindu cults have often had an erotic aspect, and in the Tantric movement sexual union is sanctified as a symbol of the union of Shiva and Shakti. In Mahayana Buddhism the ideal of the world-renouncing monk is replaced by that of the Bodhisattva, who may be a layman. The adherents of the Pure Land sects of Japan live a normal life in the world; the priests are married men. In other Buddhist sects of the Far East the negative attitude to life in the world remained. Neo-Confucianists were thus able to challenge Buddhism on this ground, and to claim that it was the strength of their religion by contrast that it provided a way of inner detachment which sanctified the common relationships and tasks of life. In the mysticism of Catholic and Orthodox Christianity, while the dominant influence has been that of the hermit or the monk, it is recognized that the mystical life is open to the layman; and among Protestant mystics the consecration of all life is basic.

In certain forms of mysticism there is a real or apparent repudiation of moral principles. Antinomianism has prevailed on different grounds. Among the extreme Sabbatians it was believed that with the advent of the apostate Messiah, Sabbatai Zevi, the claims of the moral law could be set aside. Similarly among the Brethren of the Free Spirit and the Ranters there were some who held that since the final age – the Age of the Spirit – had dawned, sin had no meaning for those in whom the Spirit was incarnate; they were already perfect and could do no wrong. The very notion of sin, it came to be thought, was purely subjective. Similar consequences were sometimes drawn in the Tantric movement from the belief that the whole life of the world, including the distinction between good and evil, was utterly illusory. Sexual licence was even regarded as a necessary means of emancipation.

VI. THE MYSTICS AND RELIGIOUS ORTHODOXY

The great majority of mystics have been adherents of the orthodox tradition of the religion to which they have been attached, and they have normally been quite unaware of any particular difficulty or inconsistency in their attitude. Among Christian mystics, St Teresa felt the greatest horror of heresy, while St Bernard excepted hardened heretics from the application of the law of love. Now, it is true that mystical experience may arise wherever men recognize the reality of the Transcendent. But it is also true that such experience, in its more developed forms, carries with it certain implications for our thought. And it is evident that by the nature of the case there is an inevitable tension between mysticism and religious orthodoxy in its historical expressions.[1] In mystical experience there is implicit a claim to immediate revelation. Philo interpreted the experience of the prophets on the basis of mystical ecstasy; and whether or not his interpretation is justified in its details, it rests upon a certain essential insight. The experience of the great leaders of religion, whose teaching is enshrined in the Scriptures, is at least comparable to that of the mystics. Religious authority, in other words, rests in the last resort on personal insight and experience. In so far as authority is externalized and identified with the written words of Scripture or the dogmas of the Church, while it may be accepted by the mystic, there is always the possibility of conflict between its dictates and his inner vision. For the mystic, whatever his professed creed, final authority lies in his own experience. Hence come the extravagances sometimes associated with mystical religion, but hence also comes its continuing testimony to the living reality of the Spirit. And here also we have one main ground of its conflict with established authority. It was the chief, though by no means the only, offence of the Brethren of the Free Spirit that they relied on 'the soul's inward voice' rather than on 'the truths preached in the Church'. Hans Denck and the 'Spirituals' were only expressing the implication of mystical experience generally when they said that the primary and essential fact is the Inner Word. So was George Fox when he declared that he saw 'the Light and Spirit which was before the Scriptures were given forth'. John Etherington was only carrying the same principle further when he spoke of the present

1. In his *Spiritual Letters* Dom John Chapman says: 'The problem of reconciling mysticism with Christianity is difficult' (p. 269).

possibility of inspiration 'as great as that of Paul and the prophets'. The Brethren of the Free Spirit and the Spiritual Franciscans looked to the coming of a fuller revelation of truth than that of the past in the Age of the Spirit. It was the claim to the renewal of inspiration in their own experience which underlay the conflict in which Protestant mystics were again and again involved with Church authority. Hindu mystics have nearly always accepted the infallibility of the Vedas. In doing so, they have found reinforcement in the stress on mystical experience which the Vedas (the Upanishads in particular) contain. But some sects, like the Lingayats and the Kashmir Shaivas, have ventured to deny it. In its earlier phase Sufism was often involved in conflict with established authority. The most notable case was that of Hallaj, who was executed at Baghdad for his heresy. Ghazzali sought to reconcile Sufism with orthodoxy, and his attitude has been generally followed by later mystics. His contemporary, Abu Sa'id, however, while accepting the inspiration of the Koran, regarded the Inner Light as the one final authority, from which new laws may continually be given to the world. He forbade his disciples to make the pilgrimage to Mecca, and his example was followed by many of the saints of the dervish orders, who set aside the ritual obligations of Islam.

In its historical forms religious orthodoxy has a certain inevitable narrowness and exclusiveness. Mysticism, on the other hand, cannot be confined by any bounds of church or creed. It has therefore an inherent trend to universalism. So we have among Christian mystics like the 'Spirituals' of the sixteenth century, the Cambridge Platonists, or the Quakers, the explicit recognition of the universality of the Inner Light; we have Sebastian Franck's vision of the Universal Church; we have Law's grateful acknowledgement of 'heathen' saints who bore witness to the 'Christ within'. In India we have the outstanding case of Kabir, who rose above the externals both of Hinduism and of Islam, and refused to confine his vision of truth within the limits of either religion. Nanak likewise endeavoured to harmonize both religions by eliminating their external features and emphasizing the sole necessity of divine love. The modern prophet, Ramakrishna, looked upon all religions as ways to the realization of God, and his outlook has been adopted by his followers in the Ramakrishna Mission. A similar attitude is found among Sufi mystics, for whom love is the real essence of all creeds.

For the mystics the essential feature of religion is its inner quality. Doctrines, observances, institutions are secondary, and if unduly stressed, they may become a positive hindrance to the life of the spirit. Where this fact is explicitly recognized, conflict often arises with established forms and traditions. While Hindu mystics have in general accepted prevailing institutions like caste, and observances like image-worship, some have rebelled against these things. Buddhism arose in India as a movement of reform, which rejected caste distinctions as irrelevant to the inner life and the sacrificial system as inimical to it. The same thing is true of the Bhakti movement in its beginnings, and from time to time reformers have arisen within it, who have proclaimed the truth of spiritual equality. Some of its saints have denounced idolatry. Kabir and Nanak broke with Hindu tradition in these as in other matters. With the exception of the Sabbatians, Jewish mystics have always accepted the ceremonial as well as the moral Law. In modern times the Hasidim were often involved in the early days in a clash with Rabbinical authority. The clash was due in part to their criticism of the unspiritual attitude of the rabbis, in part to their indifference to such externals as the stated hours of prayer. When the Zaddik became predominant in the movement, it was felt on the side of the orthodox that his claims tended to undermine accepted authority. Under the influence of the Kabbalah, the tendency of Jewish mysticism had been rather to increase than to diminish the significance of ceremonial observances by discovering a new symbolical meaning in them. So far as doctrine is concerned, Jewish mystics have enjoyed the utmost freedom of thought, thanks to the accepted principle of the allegorical interpretation of the Scriptures. It is, of course, owing to the same principle that Christian mystics were able to harmonize their teaching with that of the Bible. With Christian mystics, where conflict has arisen on doctrinal grounds, it is on account of the challenge which their teaching carried with it to some aspect of orthodox belief. Instances are the Papal condemnation of ideas taught by Eckhart, like the uncreated essence of the soul, and Lutheran and Calvinist hostility to the teaching of the 'Spirituals'. Opposition naturally arises between the mystical conception of redemption through the life of the Spirit in man (the inner Christ) and the traditional belief in redemption as based on the historical death of Jesus.[1] William Law worked out a doctrine of the Atonement as an inner experience. In accordance with his mystical outlook, he was also led to reject the belief in everlasting Hell and to proclaim the final salvation of all souls. It is noteworthy that in this as in other respects heretics like the Brethren of the Free Spirit and the Ranters were pioneers of an enlightened eschatology. While mysticism holds a recognized place in the teaching both of the Orthodox and of the Roman Catholic Church, and adherents of both churches acknowledge the reality of mystical experience in non-Christian religions, leaders of Protestant orthodoxy like Barth and Brunner adopt a highly critical attitude to it, particularly because of the emphasis which is laid by exponents of mysticism on the universal immanence of God in the human soul.

1. On this and other grounds mysticism has been described as 'one of the subtlest enemies of Christianity' (D. Lamont, *Christ and the World of Thought*, p. 180).

Bibliography

GENERAL WORKS ON MYSTICISM

W. Winslow Hall, *Recorded Illuminates*, London, 1937.

W. L. Hare, *Systems of Meditation in Religion*, London, 1937.

F. Heiler, *Prayer*, English translation, 2nd edition, London, 1937.

E. Herman, *The Meaning and Value of Mysticism*, London, 1915.

W. E. Hocking, *The Meaning of God in Human Experience* (Part 5: *Worship and the Mystics*), London, 1912.

T. H. Hughes, *The Philosophic Basis of Mysticism*, Edinburgh, 1937.

Aldous Huxley, *The Perennial Philosophy*, London, 1946.

W. R. Inge, *Mysticism in Religion*, London, 1947.

William James, *The Varieties of Religious Experience*, London, 1902.

K. E. Kirk, *The Vision of God*, London, 1931.

J. de Marquette, *Introduction to Comparative Mysticism*, New York, 1949.

R. Mukerjee, *Theory and Art of Mysticism*, London, 1937.

R. Otto, *Mysticism, East and West*, English translation, London, 1932.

J. B. Pratt, *The Religious Consciousness*, New York, 1920.

S. Radhakrishnan, *Eastern Religions and Western Thought*, Oxford, 1939.

Margaret Smith, *An Introduction to the History of Mysticism*, London, 1930.

W. T. Stace, *Mysticism and Philosophy*, London, 1960.

A. Tillyard, *Spiritual Exercises*, London, 1927.

Evelyn Underhill, *Mysticism*, 6th edition, London, 1916.
The Essentials of Mysticism, London, 1920.
Practical Mysticism, London, 1914.

V. Vezzani, *Le Mysticisme dans le monde*, translated from the Italian, Paris, 1955.

R C. Zaehner, *Mysticism, Sacred and Profane*, Oxford, 1957.
At Sundry Times, London, 1958.

MYSTICISM IN PRIMITIVE RELIGION

N. K. Chadwick, *Poetry and Prophecy*, Cambridge, 1942.

C. Dawson, *Progress and Religion*, London, 1929.
Religion and Culture, London, 1948.

M. Eliade, *Le Chamanisme et les techniques archaïques de l'extase*, Paris, 1951.

Traité de l'histoire des religions, Paris, 1949.

Myths, Dreams and Mysteries, English translation, London, 1960.

Yoga, English translation, London, 1958.

E. E. Evans-Pritchard, *Nuer Religion*, Oxford, 1956.

E. O. James, *Prehistoric Religion*, London, 1957.

The Nature and Function of Priesthood, London, 1956.

The Beginnings of Religion, London, 1949.

Comparative Religion, London, 1938.

R. H. Lowie, *Primitive Religion*, London, 1924.

R. Otto, *The Idea of the Holy*, English translation, 4th edition, London, 1925.

G. Parrinder, *West African Religion*, London, 1949.

P. Radin, *Primitive Religion*, London, 1938.

Primitive Man as Philosopher, New York and London, 1927.

HINDU AND BUDDHIST MYSTICISM

L. D. Barnett, *The Heart of India*, Wisdom of the East, London, 1924.

J. E. Carpenter, *Buddhism and Christianity*, London, 1923.

Theism in Medieval India, London, 1921.

E. Conze, *Buddhism, its Essence and Development*, Oxford, 1951.

Buddhist Meditation, London, 1956.

The Cultural Heritage of India, vol. 4 (*The Religions*), edited by H. Bhattacharya, Calcutta, 1956.

M. C. D'Arcy, *The Meeting of Love and Knowledge*, London, 1958.

S. Dasgupta, *Hindu Mysticism*, London, 1927.

History of Indian Philosophy, 5 vols., London, 1932–55.

Mrs Rhys Davies, *Sakya, or Buddhist Origins*, London, 1931.

What was the Original Gospel in Buddhism?, London, 1938.

P. D. Devanandan, *The Concept of Maya*, London, 1950.

M. Eliade, *Yoga*, English translation, London, 1958.

Sir Charles Eliot, *Hinduism and Buddhism*, 4 vols., London, 1921–35.

E. E. Evans-Wentz, *Tibetan Yoga and Secret Doctrines*, London, 1935.

J. N. Farquhar, *Outlines of the Religious Literature of India*, London, 1920.

Modern Religious Movements in India, London, 1929.

R. Guénon, *Introduction to the Study of the Hindu Doctrines*, English translation, London, 1945.

Man and his Becoming according to the Vedanta, English translation, London, 1928.

M. Hiriyanna, *Essentials of Indian Philosophy*, London, 1949.

The Quest after Perfection, Mysore, 1952.

History of Philosophy, Eastern and Western, edited by S. Radhakrishnan and others, vol. 1, London, 1952.

C. Humphreys, *Buddhism*, Harmondsworth, 1951.

J. G. Jennings, *The Vedantic Buddhism of the Buddha*, London, 1948.

F. E. Keay, *Kabir and his Followers*, London, 1931.

A. B. Keith, *Buddhist Philosophy in India and Ceylon*, Oxford, 1923.

O. Lacombe, *L'Absolu selon le Védanta*, Paris, 1937.

G. C. Lounsbery, *Buddhist Meditation in the Southern School*, London, 1935.

J. McKenzie, *Hindu Ethics*, Oxford, 1922.

N. Macnicol, *Indian Theism*, Oxford, 1915.

G. R. S. Mead, *Quests, Old and New*, London, 1913.

P. D. Mehta, *Early Indian Religious Thought*, London, 1956.

G. F. Moore, *The History of Religions*, vol. 1, Edinburgh, 1914.

R. Otto, *India's Religion of Grace and Christianity*, English translation, London, 1930.

Mysticism, East and West, English translation, London, 1932.

L. de la Vallée Poussin, *The Way to Nirvana*, English translation, London, 1917.

Swami Prabhavananda, *The Spiritual Heritage of India*, London, 1962.

J. B. Pratt, *India and its Faiths*, Boston and New York, 1915.

The Pilgrimage of Buddhism, London, 1928.

Sri Krishna Prem, *The Yoga of the Bhagavat Gita*, London, 1938.

S. Radhakrishnan, *Eastern Religions and Western Thought*, Oxford, 1939.

Indian Philosophy, 2 vols., 2nd edition, London, 1929, 1931.

P. T. Raju, *Idealistic Thought of India*, London, 1953.

R. Rolland, *Prophets of the New India*, English translation, New York, 1930.

S. Shivapadasundaram, *The Shaiva School of Hinduism*, London, 1934.

R. L. Slater, *Paradox and Nirvana*, Chicago, 1951.

P. N. Srinivasachari, *Mystics and Mysticism*, Madras, 1951.

B. L. Suzuki, *Mahayana Buddhism*, 3rd edition, London, 1959.

D. T. Suzuki, *Outlines of Mahayana Buddhism*, London, 1907.

Essays in Zen Buddhism, 4 vols., London, 1928-34.

Mysticism, Christian and Buddhist, London, 1957.

E. J. Thomas, *History of Buddhist Thought*, 2nd edition, London, 1933.

A. W. Watts, *The Supreme Identity*, London, 1950.

Sir John Woodroffe, *Shakti and Shakta*, 4th edition, Madras, 1951.

R. C. Zaehner, *Mysticism, Sacred and Profane*, Oxford, 1957.

At Sundry Times, London, 1958.

H. Zimmer, *Philosophies of India*, London, 1951.

Texts

R. E. Hume, *The Thirteen Principal Upanishads*, London, 1931.

S. Radhakrishnan, *The Principal Upanishads*, London, 1953.

C. Johnston, *The Great Upanishads*, vol. 1, New York, 1927.

J. Mascaro, *Himalayas of the Soul*, selections from the Upanishads, London, 1938.

The Bhagavad Gita, Penguin Classics, Harmondsworth, 1962.

Sri Aurobindo, *The Message of the Gita* (text and commentary), edited by Anilbaran Roy, London, 1938.

E. J. Thomas, *The Song of the Lord*, Wisdom of the East, London, 1931.

C. Johnston, *The Crest-Jewel of Wisdom and Other Writings of Shankaracharya*, Covina, California, 1946.

Sacred Books of the East, vols. 34 and 38: *The Vedanta-Sutras*, with the Commentary by Shankaracharya, English translation, Oxford, 1890, 1896; Vol. 48: *The Vedanta-Sutras*, with the Commentary by Ramanuja, English translation, Oxford, 1904.

Patanjali, *Aphorisms of Yoga*, English translation, London, 1938.

H. H. Wilson, *The Vishnupuranas*, London, 1864-77.

J. S. M. Hooper, *Hymns of the Alvars*, London, 1929.

Songs from Prison, translations from Indian Mystics by M. K. Gandhi, London, 1934.

Selections from the Sacred Writings of the Sikhs, UNESCO Collection of Representative Works, London, 1960.

Buddhist Texts through the Ages, edited by E. Conze, Oxford, 1954.

Buddhist Scriptures, selected and translated by E. Conze, Penguin Classics, Harmondsworth, 1959.

The Living Thoughts of Gotama the Buddha, presented by A. K. Coomaraswamy and I. B. Horner, London, 1948.

S. Radhakrishnan, *The Dhammapada*, Oxford, 1950.

Buddhist Wisdom Books (*The Diamond Sutra and the Heart Sutra*), translated and explained by E. Conze, London, 1958.

Sacred Books of the Buddhists, London, 1895-1956.

S. Beal, *Catena of Buddhist Scriptures from the Chinese*, London, 1871.

Ashvaghosha's Discourse on the Awakening of Faith in the Mahayana, translated by D. T. Suzuki, Chicago, 1900; another translation by Timothy Richard, London, 1961.

Sacred Books of the East, vol. 10; *The Dhammapada and the Sutta-Nipata*; Vol. 21: *The Saddharma Pundarika*, English translation, Oxford, 1881 and 1884.

W. E. Soothill, *The Lotus of the Wonderful Law* (abridged), Oxford, 1930.

L. D. Barnett, *The Path of Light, from the Bodhicharyavatara of Shantideva*, Wisdom of the East, London, 1909.

Mahayana-Sutralamkara, edited and translated into French by Sylvain Lévi, Paris, 1911.

TAOIST AND CONFUCIANIST MYSTICISM

H. G. Creel, *Confucius, the Man and the Myth*, London, 1951.

Fung Yu-Lan, *A History of Chinese Philosophy*, 2 vols., Princeton, 1952-3.

    A Short History of Chinese Philosophy, New York, 1948.

    The Spirit of Chinese Philosophy, London, 1947.

E. Herbert, *A Taoist Notebook*, Wisdom of the East, London, 1955.

E. R. and K. Hughes, *Religion in China*, London, 1950.

H. Maspero, *Le Taoisme*, Paris, 1950.

K. L. Reichelt, *Meditation and Piety in the Far East*, London, 1953.

    Religion in Chinese Garment, London, 1952.

A. Waley, *Three Ways of Thought in Ancient China*, London, 1939.

Texts

The Analects of Confucius, translated by W. E. Soothill, World's Classics, London, 1937; another version by A. Waley, London, 1938.

Chinese Philosophy in Classical Times, edited and translated by E. R. Hughes, Everyman, London, 1941.

The Wisdom of China, edited by Lin Yutang, London, 1949.

A. Waley, *The Way and its Power*, London, 1934.

The Sayings of Lao Tzu, translated by L. Giles, Wisdom of the East, London, 1911.

H. A. Giles, *Chuang Tzu, Mystic, Moralist and Social Reformer*, London, 1889; new edition, 1961.

Musings of a Chinese Mystic (Chuang Tzu), with an Introduction by L. Giles, Wisdom of the East, London, 1906.

The Book of Lieh Tzu, a new translation by A. C. Graham, Wisdom of the East, London, 1960.

The Great Learning and The Mean in Action, edited and translated by E. R. Hughes, London, 1942.

The Book of Mencius (abridged), translated by L. Giles, Wisdom of the East, London, 1942.

GREEK AND HELLENISTIC MYSTICISM

J. Adam, *The Religious Teachers of Greece*, London, 1908.

S. Angus, *The Religious Quests of the Graeco-Roman World*, London, 1925.

The Mystery-Religions and Christianity, London, 1929.

A. H. Armstrong, *An Introduction to Ancient Philosophy*, London, 1947.

The Architecture of the Intelligible Universe in the Philosophy of Plotinus, Cambridge, 1940.

E. Bréhier, *La Philosophie de Plotin*, Paris, 1928.

R. Bultmann, *Primitive Christianity in its Contemporary Setting*, English translation, London, 1956.

E. Caird, *The Evolution of Theology in the Greek Philosophers*, 2 vols., Glasgow, 1904.

F. M. Cornford, *From Religion to Philosophy*, London, 1912.

Principium Sapientiae, Cambridge, 1952.

C. H. Dodd, *The Bible and the Greeks*, London, 1935.

The Interpretation of the Fourth Gospel, Cambridge, 1953 – on the Gnostics and the Hermetists.

J. Doresse, *Les Livres secrets des Gnostiques d'Égypte*, Paris, 1958.

E. S. Drower, *The Secret Adam*, London, 1960.

A. Dupont-Sommer, *The Essene Writings from Qumran*, English translation, Oxford, 1961.

L. R. Farnell, *The Higher Aspects of Greek Religion*, London, 1912.

E. de Faye, *Gnostiques et Gnosticisme*, 2nd edition, Paris, 1925.

A. J. Festugière, *Personal Religion among the Greeks*, California, 1945.

La Révélation d'Hermès Trismégiste, 4 vols., Paris, 1949–54.

V. Goldschmidt, *La Religion de Platon*, Paris, 1949.

E. R. Goodenough, *By Light, Light*, Yale, 1935 – Hellenistic influence on later Jewish religion.

R. M. Grant, *Gnosticism and Early Christianity*, London, 1959.

H. A. Guy, *New Testament Prophecy*, London, 1949 – on Philo, the Hermetists, and the Mystery-Religions.

C. Guignebert, *The Jewish World in the Time of Jesus*, English translation, London, 1939.

W. R. Halliday, *The Pagan Background of Early Christianity*, Liverpool, 1925.

J. E. Harrison, *Prolegomena to the Study of Greek Religion*, London, 1903.

W. R. Inge, *The Philosophy of Plotinus*, 2 vols., London, 1918.

W. Jaeger, *Aristotle*, Oxford, 1934.

Paideia, vol. 2, London, 1944 – on Plato.

E. O. James, *Comparative Religion*, London, 1938 – on the Mystery-Religions.

H. A. A. Kennedy, *St Paul and the Mystery-Religions*, London, 1913.

K. E. Kirk, *The Vision of God*, London, 1932 – on Plato, the Gnostics, etc.

W. L. Knox, *St Paul and the Church of the Gentiles*, Cambridge, 1939 – Hellenistic influence on later Jewish religion.

F. Legge, *Rivals and Forerunners of Christianity*, 2 vols., Cambridge, 1915.

G. R. S. Mead, *Fragments of a Faith Forgotten*, 3rd edition, London, 1931 – on the Gnostics.

N. P. Nilsson, *History of Greek Religion*, English translation, Oxford, 1925.

A. D. Nock, 'The Pagan Background of Early Christianity', in *Essays on the Trinity and the Incarnation*, London, 1928.

W. F. Otto, 'The Meaning of the Eleusinian Mysteries', in *The Mysteries*, Eranos Year-book, New York, 1955.

P. V. Pistorius, *Plotinus and Neoplatonism*, Cambridge, 1952.

H. C. Puech, *Le Manichéisme*, Paris, 1949.

H. Rahner, 'History of the Mysteries', in *The Mysteries*, New York, 1955.

R. Reitzenstein, *Die Hellenistischen Mysterien-Religionen*, 3rd edition, Leipzig, 1927.

    Poimandres, Leipzig, 1904.

P. Roché, *Études manichéennes et Cathares*, Paris, 1952.

E. Rohde, *Psyche*, English translation, 2nd edition, London, 1950.

P. Schmidt, 'The Ancient Mysteries', in *The Mysteries*, New York, 1955.

K. Schubert, *The Dead Sea Community*, London, 1959.

F. Solmsen, *Plato's Theology*, New York, 1942.

K. Stendahl (editor), *The Scrolls and the New Testament*, London, 1958.

E. J. Urwick, *The Message of Plato*, London, 1920 – Plato and the Advaita.

M. Wili, 'The Orphic Mysteries and the Greek Spirit', in *The Mysteries*, New York, 1955.

H. R. Willoughby, *Pagan Regeneration*, Chicago, 1929.

R. McL. Wilson, *The Gnostic Problem*, Oxford, 1958.

Texts

Aristotle, *Metaphysics*, Loeb Classical Library, London, 1933.

    Nicomachean Ethics, translated by F. H. Peters, 5th edition, London, 1893.

The Dialogues of Plato, translated and edited by B. Jowett, 3rd edition, London, 1892.

Five Dialogues of Plato on Poetic Inspiration, English translation, Everyman, London, 1910.

The Republic of Plato, English translation, Golden Treasury Series, London, 1923.

Philo, English translation, Loeb Classical Library, London, 1929–62.

W. Scott, *Hermetica*, 4 vols., Oxford, 1924–36.

The Divine Pymander, Shrine of Wisdom, London, 1963.

Gnosticism: an Anthology, edited by R. M. Grant, London, 1961.

Pistis Sophia, translated by G. R. S. Mead, London, 1896; another translation by G. Horner, London, 1924.

R. D. Casey, *The Excerpta ex Theodoto of Clement of Alexandria*, London, 1935.

A. Dupont-Sommer, *The Essene Writings from Qumran*, English translation, Oxford, 1961.

G. Vermes, *The Dead Sea Scrolls in English*, Harmondsworth, 1962.

Apuleius, *The Metamorphoses*, English translation, Loeb Classical Library, London, 1922.

Plotinus, *The Enneads*, translated by S. MacKenna, one volume edition, London, 1956.

Proclus, *Elements of Theology*, English translation, London, 1933.

The Gospel of Truth, translation and commentary by K. Grobel, London, 1960.

HEBREW AND JEWISH MYSTICISM

J. Abelson, *The Immanence of God in Rabbinical Literature*, London, 1912.

Jewish Mysticism, London, 1913.

M. Buber, *The Legend of Baal-Shem*, East and West Library, London, 1956.

I. Epstein, *Judaism*, Harmondsworth, 1959.

C. Guignebert, *The Jewish World in the Time of Jesus*, English translation, London, 1939.

A. Guillaume, *Prophecy and Divination among the Hebrews and Other Semites*, London, 1938.

A. R. Johnson, *The One and the Many in the Israelite Conception of God*, 2nd edition, Cardiff, 1961.

H. Knight, *The Hebrew Prophetic Consciousness*, London, 1947.

E. Müller, *History of Jewish Mysticism*, East and West Library, London, 1956.

H. Odeberg, *The Fourth Gospel*, Upsala, 1929 – background of the Gospel in Jewish mysticism.

A. S. Peake, *A Commentary on the Bible*, London, 1920.

H. W. Robinson, *Inspiration and Revelation in the Old Testament*, Oxford, 1946.

T. H. Robinson, *Prophecy and the Prophets in Ancient Israel*, London, 1923.

H. H. Rowley, *The Servant of the Lord*, London, 1952.

S. Schechter, *Studies in Judaism*, 2 vols., London, 1896, 1908.

G. G. Scholem, *Major Trends in Jewish Mysticism*, London, 1955.
'Le Mouvement sabbaïste en Pologne', *Revue de L'Histoire des religions*, Vols. 43–4.

M. D. R. Willinck, *The Prophetic Consciousness*, London, 1924.

Texts

G. H. Box and J. I. Landsman, *The Apocalypse of Abraham*, London, 1919.

R. H. Morfill and R. H. Charles, *The Book of the Secrets of Enoch*, Oxford, 1896.

Moses Cordovero, *The Palm Tree of Deborah*, London, 1960.

L. Newman, *The Hasidic Anthology*, New York, 1934.

H. Odeberg, *3 Enoch or the Hebrew Book of Enoch*, Cambridge, 1928.

The Zohar, translated by H. Sperling and M. Simon, 5 vols., London, 1931-4.

CHRISTIAN MYSTICISM

N. Berdyaev, *Freedom and the Spirit*, English translation, London, 1935.

H. H. Brinton, *The Mystic Will, a Study of the Philosophy of Jacob Boehme*, London, 1931.

G. Bullett, *The English Mystics*, London, 1950.

C. Butler, *Western Mysticism*, 2nd edition, London, 1922.

E. T. Campagnac, *The Cambridge Platonists*, Oxford, 1901.

E. Cassirer, *The Platonic Renaissance in England*, London, 1953.

Abbot John Chapman, *Spiritual Letters*, London, 1935.

J. M. Clark, *The Great German Mystics*, Oxford, 1949.

M. M. A. M. du Cœur de Jésus, *A Soul of Silence, Sister Elizabeth of the Trinity*, English translation, Cork and Liverpool, 1949.

N. Cohn, *The Pursuit of the Millennium*, London, 1957.

W. D. Davies, *Paul and Rabbinic Judaism*, London, 1955.

A. Deissmann, *St Paul*, London, 1912.

C. H. Dodd, *The Meaning of Paul for Today*, 3rd impression, London, 1935.
The Interpretation of the Fourth Gospel, Cambridge, 1953.

E. Gebhart, *Mystics and Heretics in Italy*, English translation, London, 1922.

M. Goguel, *The Life of Jesus*, English translation, London, 1945.

C. Guignebert, *Jésus*, Paris, 1933; English translation, London, 1935.

F. von Hügel, *The Mystical Element in Religion as studied in St Catherine of Genoa and her Friends*, 2 vols., English translation, London, 1923.

R. M. Jones, *Studies in Mystical Religion*, London, 1909.
Spiritual Reformers, London, 1914.

K. E. Kirk, *The Vision of God*, London, 1931.

R. A. Knox, *Enthusiasm*, Oxford, 1950.

A. Koyré, *La Philosophie de Jacob Boehme*, Paris, 1929.
Mystiques, Spirituels, Alchimistes, Paris, 1955.

V. Lossky, *The Theology of the Eastern Church*, London, 1957.

G. H. C. McGregor, *The Gospel of John, Moffatt Commentary*, London, 1928.

H. L. Martensen, *Jacob Boehme, his Life and Teaching*, English translation, London, 1885; revised edition, edited by S. Hobhouse, London, 1949.

J. M. Murry, *The Life of Jesus*, London, 1928.

D. H. S. Nicholson, *The Mysticism of St Francis of Assisi*, London, 1923.

H. Odeberg, *The Fourth Gospel*, Upsala, 1929.

R. Otto, *The Kingdom of God and the Son of Man*, English translation, London, 1938.
Mysticism, East and West, English translation, London, 1932 – Eckhart and Shankara.

R. Payne, *The Holy Fire*, London, 1958 – the Fathers of the Eastern Church.

A. S. Peake, *The Quintessence of Paulinism*, Manchester and London, 1918.

E. A. Peers, *Studies of the Spanish Mystics*, 3 vols., London, 1927–60.
Spanish Mysticism, London, 1924.
Spirit of Flame, London, 1943 – St John of the Cross.

A. Poulain, *The Graces of Interior Prayer*, English translation, London, 1910.

A. Schweitzer, *The Mysticism of Paul the Apostle*, English translation, 2nd edition, London, 1953.

C. Anderson Scott, *Christianity according to St Paul*, Cambridge, 1927.

E. F. Scott, *The Fourth Gospel*, Edinburgh, 1930.
The Varieties of New Testament Religion, New York, 1946.

Margaret Smith, *Studies in Early Mysticism in the Near and Middle East*, London, 1931.

C. E. Stephen, *Light Arising – Thoughts on the Central Radiance*, Cambridge, 1908 – Quaker mysticism.

Evelyn Underhill, *Mysticism*, 6th edition, London, 1916.

  The Essentials of Mysticism, London, 1920.

  The Mystics of the Church, London, 1925.

E. I. Watkin, *Poets and Mystics*, London, 1953.

Texts

John Cassian, *Works*, English translation, Nicene and Post-Nicene Fathers, Oxford, 1894.

Early Fathers from the Philokalia, selected and translated by E. Kadlonbovsky and G. E. H. Palmer, London, 1954.

Writings from the Philokalia on Prayer of the Heart, English translation, London, 1951.

Dionysius the Areopagite, *The Divine Names* and *Mystical Theology*, translated by C. E. Rolt, London, 1920.

A Treasury of Russian Spirituality, edited by G. P. Fedotov, London, 1950.

The Confessions of St Augustine, translated by E. B. Pusey, Everyman, London, 1907.

Selections from St Bernard, translated by H. Grimley, Cambridge, 1910.

Angela of Foligno, *The Book of Divine Consolations*, English translation, London, 1908.

Augustine Baker, *Holy Wisdom*, compiled by Dom Serenus Cressy, London, no date; re-issued 1950.

Louis de Blois (Blosius), *A Book of Spiritual Instruction*, English translation (revised edition), London, 1955.

The Book of the Poor in Spirit, translated by C. F. Kelley, London, 1954; another translation by J. R. Morell entitled *The Following of Christ*, attributed to J. Tauler, London, no date.

The Dialogue of St Catherine of Siena, translated by A. Thorold, abridged edition, London, 1907.

J. P. de Caussade, *On Prayer*, London, 1931; revised edition, 1948.

Of Cleaving to God (*De Adhaerendo Deo*), English translation, Oxford, 1947.

The Cloud of Unknowing, edited by E. Underhill, 2nd edition, London, 1922.

Meister Eckhart, *Anthology of Sermons*, selected and translated by J. M. Clark, London, 1957.

Meister Eckhart: Selected Treatises and Sermons, translated from the Latin by J. M. Clark and J. V. Skinner, London, 1958.

Meister Eckhart: Sermons and Tractates, translated from F. Pfeiffer's version by C. de Burgh, 2 vols., London, 1924.

Meister Eckhart, a modern translation by R. B. Blakney, Torchbook edition, New York, 1957.

Selections from Fénelon, Boston, 1879.

The Little Flowers of St Francis, translated by T. Okey, Everyman, London, 1910.

Mme Guyon, *A Short and Easy Method of Prayer*, Heart and Life Booklets, London, 1900.

Les Opuscules spirituels, 2 vols., Paris, 1790.

Walter Hilton, *The Ladder of Perfection*, translated by L. Sherley-Price, Penguin Classics, Harmondsworth, 1957.

John of Ruysbroeck, *The Adornment of the Spiritual Marriage, The Sparkling Stone, The Book of Supreme Truth*, English translation, edited by E. Underhill, London, 1916.

The Seven Steps of the Ladder of Spiritual Love, translated by F. S. Taylor, London, 1943.

Julian of Norwich, *Revelations of Divine Love*, edited by G. Warrack, London, 1901; edited by P. Molinari, London, 1958.

The Complete Works of St John of the Cross, translated by E. A. Peers, London, 1934–5.

The Book of Margery Kempe, World's Classics, London, 1954.

Thomas à Kempis, *The Imitation of Christ*, English translation, London, 1923.

Brother Lawrence, *The Practice of the Presence of God*, Epworth Press, London, no date.

Miguel de Molinos, *The Spiritual Guide which disentangles the Soul*, English translation, Library of Devotion, London, 1907.

Nicholas of Cusa, *The Vision of God*, English translation, with introduction by E. Underhill, London, 1928.

Of Learned Ignorance (De Docta Ignorantia), English translation, London, 1954.

Richard of St Victor, *Selected Writings on Contemplation*, English translation, Classics of the Contemplative Life, London, 1957.

Henry Suso, *The Little Book of Eternal Wisdom*, English translation, London, 1910.

The Life of the Blessed Henry Suso by Himself, English translation, London, 1913.

John Tauler, *Twenty-five Sermons*, translated by Susanna Winkworth, London, 1857; new edition, 1906.

The Inner Way: Thirty-six Sermons for Festivals, English translation, 3rd edition, London, 1909.

St Teresa, *The Way of Perfection*, English translation, London, 1911.

The Interior Castle, English translation, London, 1912.

The Life of St Teresa written by Herself, translated by D. Lewis, London, 1916, and by J. M. Cohen, Penguin Classics, Harmondsworth, 1957.

Collected Works, edited by E. A. Peers, London, 1946.

Theologia Germanica, translated by Susanna Winkworth, Golden Treasury series, London, 1874, reprinted 1913; new edition, 1937.

Spiritual and Anabaptist Writers, edited by G. H. Williams, London, 1957.

R. M. Jones, *A Little Book of Selections from the Children of the Light* – London, no date – early Quakers.

Robert Barclay, *An Apology for the True Christian Divinity*, 9th edition, Dublin, 1800.

Jacob Boehme, *Works*, translated by J. Ellistone and J. Sparrow, 4 vols., 2nd edition, London, 1764–81.

The Threefold Life of Man, London, 1909; *The 40 Questions of the Soul and The Clavis* (1910); *The Three Principles of the Divine Essence* (1911); *The Way to Christ* (1912 and 1953); *Aurora* (1914 and 1961); *Mysterium Magnum* (1924); *The Signature of All Things*, together with *A Dialogue concerning the Supersensual Life*, and *A Discourse between Two Souls* – Everyman, London, 1912. See also *The Confessions of Jacob Boehme*, compiled by W. S. Palmer, London, 1920.

George Fox, *Journal*, 2 vols., 7th edition, London, 1852.

Selected Mystical Writings of William Law, edited by Stephen Hobhouse, London, 1938.

William Penn, *The Peace of Europe, The Fruits of Solitude and Other Writings*, Everyman, London, no date.

John Smith, *Select Discourses*, London, 1821.

Thomas Traherne, *Centuries of Meditations*, London, 1927.

B. Whichcote, *Aphorisms*, London, 1930.

ISLAMIC MYSTICISM

T. Andrae, *Mohammed: the Man and his Faith*, English translation, London, 1936.

A. J. Arberry, *Sufism*, London, 1950.

J. P. Brown, *The Dervishes* (edited by H. A. Rose), London, 1927.

M. Fazil, *Sufism*, in the *History of Philosophy, Eastern and Western*, vol. 2, London, 1953.

H. A. R. Gibb, *Mohammedanism*, London, 1949.

A. Guillaume, *Islam*, Penguin Books, Harmondsworth, 1954.

The Traditions of Islam, London, 1924.

Ikbal Ali Shah, *Islamic Sufism*, London, 1933.

M. Iqbal, *The Development of Metaphysics in Persia*, London, 1908.

The Legacy of Islam, edited by T. Arnold and A. Guillaume, Oxford, 1931.

D. B. Macdonald, *The Religious Life and Attitude in Islam*, Chicago, 1909.

L. Massignon, *La Passion d'al-Hosayn ibn Mansour al-Hallaj*, 2 vols., Paris, 1922.

R. A. Nicholson, *The Mystics of Islam*, London, 1914.

Studies in Islamic Mysticism, Cambridge, 1921.

The Idea of Personality in Sufism, Cambridge, 1923.

Margaret Smith, *Studies in Early Mysticism in the Near and Middle East*, London, 1931.

Al-Ghazzali the Mystic, London, 1944.

Rabi'a the Mystic, Cambridge, 1928.

An Early Mystic of Baghdad (Al-Muhasibi), London, 1935.

J. Wach, *Types of Religious Experience*, London, 1951.

A. J. Wensinck, *La Pensée de Ghazzali*, Paris, 1940.

Texts

J. M. Rodwell, *The Koran*, Everyman, London, 1909.

Margaret Smith, *Readings from the Mystics of Islam*, London, 1950.

Abu Bakr al-Kalabadhi, *The Doctrine of the Sufis*, translated by A. J. Arberry, Cambridge, 1935.

Farid Ud-din Attar, *The Conference of the Birds,* translated by C. S. Nott, London, 1961.

Margaret Smith, *The Persian Mystics: Attar*, Wisdom of the East, London, 1932.

F. H. Davis, *The Persian Mystics: Jami*, Wisdom of the East, London, 1908.

Jalalu'd-Din Rumi, Wisdom of the East, London, 1907.

R. A. Nicholson, *Rumi, Poet and Mystic*, East and West Library, London, 1950.

The Confessions of Al-Ghazzali, translated by C. Field, Wisdom of the East, London, 1909.

Index